The Principal
and
The Autonomous
Elementary School

MERRILL'S SERIES FOR EDUCATIONAL ADMINISTRATION

Under the editorship of

DR. LUVERN L. CUNNINGHAM, Dean

College of Education
The Ohio State University

and

DR. H. THOMAS JAMES, President

The Spencer Foundation
Chicago, Illinois

The Principal and The Autonomous Elementary School

ALBERT H. SHUSTER

Ohio University

and

DON H. STEWART

*Principal, Shiloview Elementary School
Dayton, Ohio*

CHARLES E. MERRILL PUBLISHING COMPANY
A Bell & Howell Company
Columbus, Ohio

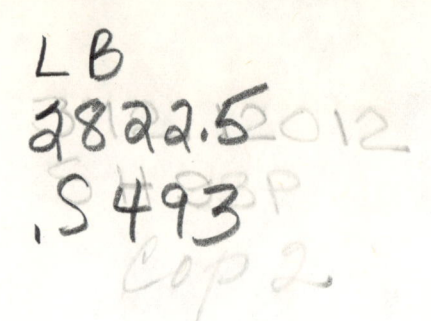

Published by
Charles E. Merrill Publishing Company
A Bell & Howell Company
Columbus, Ohio 43216

Copyright © 1973 by Bell & Howell Company. All rights reserved. No part of this book may be reproduced in any form, electronic or mechanical, including photocopy, recording, or any information storage and retrieval system, without permission in writing from the publisher.

ISBN: 0-675-09011-3

Library of Congress Catalog Card Number: 72-91673

1 2 3 4 5 6 / 78 77 76 75 74 73

Printed in the United States of America

Contents

Preface		vii
1	The Principal's Role Today	1
2	Evolution of the Elementary School Principalship	26
3	Developing Leadership Skills	53
4	Patterns of Elementary School Organization	66
5	Educational Leadership in the Community	100
6	The Changing Role of Supervision	127
7	Curriculum Development	156
8	Leadership Through In-Service Education	181
9	Developing Guidance Services	213
10	Pupil-Personnel Policies	248
11	Administering the School Office	266
12	Administering Auxiliary Services	292
13	Planning and Organizing	333
14	Staff Relations and the Principal	355
15	Evaluation	375
Name Index		405
Subject Index		408

Preface

The purpose of this book is to provide the future principal, the beginning principal and the practicing principal with an understanding of the professional leadership competencies demanded by his position. The authors have not only drawn upon their own experiences, but have sought the latest and most relevant research findings as well as new understandings in the fields of educational administration, management, human psychology, and personnel, and projected them into the role of the elementary school principal. Emphasis is placed on areas of administrative behavior as the basis for developing leadership competencies.

A comprehensive survey of the history of the principalship is presented, to show how this position has emerged into one recognized as a major position requiring great leadership responsibility. The modern elementary school is moving into a period when almost complete autonomy will be granted to its leader. With this autonomy, however, the principal must possess the competencies for a new position in administration and supervision of an elementary school that serves the needs of the immediate community. The principal must develop competencies which will help him become successful in leading his community to the achievement of modern educational objectives.

The book views the principal as a dynamic professional leader who is not hampered by a vast bureaucracy, a leader who is aware of major problems confronting American education, and who is bold enough to do something about them. The authors have emphasized the child-centered school throughout and the principal's role in bringing program change. The changing role of the principal in supervision of instruction is developed, as well as the need for the principal to provide in-service education for staff development. The principal's responsibility for curriculum and instructional decisions is presented in the light of curriculum issues the principal faces and the need for new programs. Guidelines are suggested for interpreting the school's program to the public with the recognition that the principal is accountable for the quality of this program.

The need for a comprehensive guidance program is an essential component to the modern elementary school. Pupil personnel services are interpreted as a means of humanizing the educational environment.

Non-instructional services now consume a large portion of the principal's time. The administration problems of these services are discussed and guidelines suggested to help the principal coordinate these essential functions of the modern school.

The principal's responsibility for fostering staff relations is emphasized in the light of his role in negotiations, teacher appraisal and teacher accountability. Evaluation is considered a realistic means of providing data for determining the success of the educational enterprise.

The authors are indebted to Dr. Wilson F. Wetzler, Dean and Vice President of Manatee Junior College at Bradenton, Florida, who wrote the first edition of this book with Dr. Shuster. We further express appreciation to a large number of professors of elementary administration who have used the first edition and have urged the writing of the second edition. In addition, the large number of graduate students in elementary school administration who have read and discussed much of the manuscript and who made many suggestions for its improvement are acknowledged. The writers are also indebted to the many public school systems and other organizations who have provided us with descriptive and illustrative materials and permitted us to use them, as well as the publishers and authors who have granted us permission to quote from their works. To Mrs. Barbara Williams for her untiring efforts in typing and assisting with clerical details of the manuscript, the authors express gratitude.

Albert H. Shuster
Don H. Stewart

1

The Principal's Role Today

Although the decade of the seventies has brought with it a demand for vigorous leadership on the part of all educational leaders, the elementary administrator in particular is confronted with problems which can no longer be left unresolved. The vast array of problems confronting the elementary principal leaves him no choice but to come to grips with these pressing problems in practical ways. The administrative head of the elementary school who is close to children, teachers, parents, and the citizens of the community must demonstrate his leadership skills to build an imaginative educational program for his community. This need for professional maturity focuses the spotlight on two major aspects of the principal's work: (1) the nature of competent leadership behavior, and (2) his administrative and changing supervisory role.

Today's principal must find his satisfaction in working as a leader of a competent group of teachers and with a broad spectrum of the community in the development of the autonomous school. As he works with them to achieve clearly defined goals, his role becomes one of statesmanship, as he works with faculty and parents in decision making.[1] Unless he finds satisfaction in releasing the talents of his staff and the available resources of the community through working with them, guiding, encouraging, and directing their activities, he will not find the principalship a pleasant career. The principal acquires knowledge about his job, forms habits of working, and devises methods of operation or procedure. Yet, until each of these aspects is incorporated into behavior patterns directed toward educational goals, genuine leadership cannot be said to exist. The principal must understand that his behavior, which can enhance school-community relationships, is a source of power for improving the quality of human existence.

Since we have entered into a new period in education, the principal must not only acquire certain leadership skills, but must also be able to set new educational goals. Although educational literature abounds with descriptions of his tasks and duties, he may begin by re-examining his present administrative and supervisory practices. Until the principal goes beyond the performance of his routine duties, however, he cannot achieve that level of professional greatness characterized by constant thought and attention to everyday work coupled with an ability to move his educational program forward by solving problems in an ever-changing society. Admittedly, the principal must be concerned with doing his job, but he should also seek to understand certain basic considerations of his position in order to set educational goals for an ever-improved school situation.

What are the basic considerations of the principalship which will lead to higher levels of achievement? What should be the principal's philosophy or platform of beliefs? What are his beliefs about the nature of leadership? What are some factors that will influence his thinking and actions? How may he attain the best kind of educational statesmanship possible to him? Even as his role is changing today, he must understand more clearly and positively certain driving purposes present in the principalship before he can develop intelligent, valid, and worthy goals.

The professionalization of principalship will take place as the concepts of leadership are grasped, as the skills are acquired, and as these are implemented into an active, dynamic program. The primary concern in this chapter is to furnish some basic considerations of the principalship that will aid in understanding the nature of the leadership role, the principles of a democratic administration, and certain factors that influence leadership practices.

THE PRINCIPAL'S ROLE AS AN EDUCATIONAL LEADER

The Nature of Leadership

The elementary school principal is faced with the many tasks of administering his school. As an executive or administrator he may function in one way, while as the educational expert he may be called upon to serve in another. His over-all responsibility for the administration of his school may be defined as the art and science of creatively integrating ideas, materials, and persons into an organic, harmonious working unit for the achievement of a desired goal.[2] Since this definition calls for a type of leadership that will demand both executive and educational abilities, the principal should recognize that his most desirable goal is the further development of worthy citizens for his community and for our nation. Leadership behavior operates on continuum from authoritarian to permissive with a strong emphasis today on subordinate involvement.[3] Obviously, this theory challenges the direct or authoritative leadership position.

Principals will vary in their emphases on different phases of school management. Administrative functions common to most schools, however, include leading staff personnel, providing instructional materials, and directing other educational operations. Since the design and purpose of public school organization seem to demand an emphasis on the personnel factor, the principal may consider this the most significant function of his over-all administration. This phase of management of the elementary school focuses attention on the task of securing a competent school staff, assigning them to duty positions within the school, and working cooperatively with them. Even though the students in the classroom are excluded from this definition, the principal still recognizes them as his chief responsibility in his role of educational leader.

The principal ought to be a functional leader, acknowledged and accepted by his staff, school, and community. He does not acquire his leadership simply by virtue of his title; he gains his status by positive achievement. His leadership abilities are recognized through what he has done in the past, what he is doing for his school now, and how he plans and moves forward toward future educational goals.

Additional insight into the meaning of leadership is gained by examining those tasks involving administrative abilities. These tasks are summarized as follows:

1. To understand the theory and practice of elementary school administration.
2. To utilize the staff in selecting prospective teachers.
3. To be competent in helping teachers to analyze their teaching so they can improve on the job.
4. To generate a high level of school morale.
5. To be skillful in using staff members who possess competencies beyond one's own to facilitate school operation.
6. To be skillful in involving staff and citizens in decision making.

The principal gains leadership status by being able to make a contribution to his school in these positive and definite ways, as the goals of the school are being met. The principal is an active member of his staff who works within the group to accomplish educational change. He may understand more than his staff about the mechanics of administering his school, and may have superior training in classroom supervision, so that he can appraise teaching performances for improvement of skills, but unless he knows how to work with his staff and how to keep his educational program moving forward, he is not a true leader. The meaning of the leadership role as it may be played by the modern elementary school principal unfolds in wider and deeper ways if he approaches his job with more understanding as to why the school exists and in what ways he may specifically coordinate efforts toward group goals. Then teachers, students, and parents may know and appreciate better the purposes for which all are striving.

LEADERSHIP APPROACHES

The most common approaches in defining the leadership role have been (1) to describe the personal qualities or traits possessed by the effective leader; and (2) to consider personal qualities in the light of a particular situation. Weber and Weber[4] discuss the personal qualities theory of leadership in terms of research data and conclude that the traits theory as an adequate explanation of leadership is not warranted by the evidence. Hemphill and others point out that where a group has a high degree of control over its members, the leader is expected to dominate, and actually does so, while in groups where members participate to a high degree, these expectations and reports of domination do not occur.[5] Personal qualities or traits of leadership are highly important, but leadership is a function requiring certain personal behavior that has been found consistently successful in given situations. Personal qualities of leadership must be examined within the situation itself.

Gouldner[6] gives further support to the situation theory of leadership, stating that little reliable evidence exists for believing that there are any universal leadership traits. Yet there seems to be evidence that, when several situations have characteristics in common, some similar traits of leaders tend to be effective in each of those groups. In short, some traits or qualities of leadership can prove to be effective in certain similar situations.[7]

Other investigators in the field of leadership have generally concluded that certain minimal abilities may be required of all leaders, but these abilities will also be widely distributed among non-leaders. That is, the principal's faculty probably will possess as a group the sum total of all the desirable leadership traits and his role will be to utilize these effectively in solving school problems. Herein lie the implications for the ways in which principals should be prepared and selected, and for how they should administer the educational program. Effective principals are leaders who are sensitive to human problems and to changing conditions of their groups, and flexible in adapting their behavior to new requirements. An answer, however, is needed to a fundamental question—why do principals fail to implement their learnings about good school administration? Wayson[8] and others believe they are stifled by the bureaucratic malaise. Innovative principals must look at their leadership as a combination of behaviors. Each task requires appropriate administrative behavior. What leadership ought to be or what it should produce is a controversial issue, but to develop the principal by producing in him a readiness to take on or to give up responsibilities in response to changing conditions will produce true leadership.

As the individual principal is faced with his local setting and problems, he cannot use a prescribed course of action, but rather must be in a position to play the role of the imaginative leader. Again, the question of what is meant by leadership is answered by saying that it entails practicing leadership

The Principal's Role Today 5

skills in situations where the principal is confronted by people clamoring for more influence over education. The principal must listen to militant teachers, blacks, irate whites, Chicanos, and other interest groups, and respond to them with positive action for improved conditions.

Certain ways of thinking about educational administration in the elementary school may improve administrative behavior. That is, the principal is better equipped to lead his staff when he can actually draw from these ideas of and suggestions for administrative behavior and translate them into positive, dynamic leadership skills or action. Thelen[9] states that leadership is the set of functions through which the group coordinates the efforts of its individuals. These efforts must result in satisfaction to the participants, as well as in help to the group in meeting its purposes. The demands on leadership are complex. Thelen concludes from his research that there are several approaches to leadership.[10] Of importance here is that the principal know the possible range of alternative behaviors[11] he has to choose from to render effective leadership.

In summary, the meaning of leadership for the principal of the elementary school may be stated as follows: educational leadership focuses attention on the advancement of the group toward more insight, better understandings, and clearer definitions of educational goals, and on initiation of action-activities that promise reasonable achievement of these goals. If personal qualities of leadership take on meaning largely in terms of a given situation, the principal knows the true nature of leadership as he becomes sensitive to and ready for certain techniques and devices for producing results. In addition, he is also sensitive to and ready to develop and use the leadership abilities of other personnel when he realizes that their personal qualities can contribute more than his own in a given situation. Real leadership comes about as the principal is able to recognize when to use other people's skills in response to changing conditions and when to exert personal leadership in the over-all educational program of his school.

Davis[12] summarizes the nature of leadership by asserting that three major factors must be considered: (1) the situation; (2) the people that are involved in the situation; and (3) the characteristics or personal qualities of the leader. To be effective, the principal's leadership depends upon his ability and courage to face the facts in the situation, interpret the facts properly in light of the situation's requirements, and follow the course of action they dictate.

The Need for Dynamic Leadership

Today's principal is confronted with the dual responsibility of serving as an executive and as an educational leader in a world that is in a critical situation. Although historical records reveal many periods of stress that have demanded superior leadership, the present crisis is probably more complex than any other in the history of man.

Demands for educational change are facing the principal from all sides.

The principal must be aware of the major forces that are affecting the world and therefore his school. What happens in the world, the community, and the family, has an influence on how our schools function and establish new goals. Some of the major problems which the principal will surely face during the decade of the seventies are:

1. The development of the autonomous elementary school.
2. Humanizing the elementary school.
3. Seeking solutions to racism in the schools.
4. Making effective use of the community in the educational process.
5. Developing feasibility programs of accountability.
6. Understanding new directions for the principalship.

Development of the Autonomous Elementary School.[13] Defined, an autonomous elementary school is one in which the responsibility and accountability for school improvement is fixed at the building level. New forms of school organization which will make the elementary school an autonomous unit are advocated as a way to meet the demands of citizens who want a greater voice in their children's education. The vast complexity of urban systems, with their central boards of education and large central administrative staffs, have not been able to work effectively with the neighborhood schools. On the one hand, efforts to provide the same curriculum for all children throughout a large city without regard for social, economic and cultural differences and, on the other, the desire to meet the unique needs of the local school, have placed the principal in an untenable position. Numerous illustrations could be cited where these dual efforts have resulted in inherent conflict in the political, social, and economic life of the broader urban community and the neighborhood school.

Some type of decentralization is needed which will incorporate into its organization only those essential checks and balances that will enhance the public education system in its effort to provide the supportive functions of centralization and the program development functions of the local school. It would appear that there are justifiable functions which can be delineated and delegated to both centralization and decentralization organizational structures to enhance and complement each organization in facilitating the total operation.[14]

Of importance here are the new expectations of the principal who works in a local autonomous school. However, it must be recognized from the outset that decentralization will not solve all the ills of a society or social system. Yet the structure for the new organization must allow the fundamental tenets of democracy to be applied to the decision-making process which affects the faculty, parents and children who comprise the local school. This concept is not new to educators—the first edition of this book advocated this same theme, and literature on democracy in education has abounded since the turn of the twentieth century; but not until recently has there been evidence that citizens are demanding more than lip-service to the decision-making processes. Yet many principals face seemingly insurmountable dilemmas in developing skills in this administrative process.

Gross and Herriott[15] pointed out in their study in 1965 that preparation programs for elementary principals have had little or no effect on executive professional leadership. In the relationship between the amount of graduate education preparation and executive professional leadership there was a negative relationship—which is not a comforting thought for those who prepare administrators at the elementary school level. On the other hand, there are probably several reasons why elementary principals haven't initiated some of the practices they have been taught in their preparation programs, among which are (1) failure to grasp from traditional lectures the full impact of the concept concerned, (2) lack of support from their chief school administrators, (3) their own bureaucratic indoctrination from the time of entering the profession, and (4) fear of losing their positions.

Preparation and experience must make a difference if principals are to provide the kind of leadership essential for administering a local educational program. The principal inservice will need to bring to bear all of his knowledge, skills, and understandings of the educational processes if he is to meet the challenge of autonomy. The main thrust of his leadership will be in learning to involve effectively all persons concerned in the decision-making process, and to be able to live with these decisions. When the faculty, the students, and the citizens are all involved in this process, the principal might find it difficult to break out of his bureaucratic "set" to implement something new or untried, perhaps even a decision made by the community to do something that appears to him to be unorthodox. But in this type of school the principal cannot use the central administration as the scapegoat. Obviously, mistakes will be made, but the principal should not only live with his mistakes but learn from them.

Humanizing the Elementary School. It is difficult to believe that in the 1970s it is still necessary for elementary educators to talk about the need to humanize the elementary school. Yet one of the authors recently observed the following incident in a first-grade classroom:

The observer, upon entering the classroom, was given an adult-sized chair at the side of the room. He sat beside the regular teacher, since a student teacher had just gone to the front of the class. The student teacher asked the children to form two lines and select a captain for each line. She held up the arithmetic flash cards of addition combinations, signaling the relay game would be carried out with the flash cards. When the game started the child at the head of each line who first gave the correct answer moved to the rear of the line and the team which returned the captain to the head of the relay line first was declared the winner. Many children had trouble giving the right answers and those who knew the answers became impatient.

When Jane's turn came she couldn't get the answer time after time, but finally, as the excitement grew, she gave the right answer. Tim, who was captain of the losing team, on his way back to his seat, with his arm shoved Jane aside in the aisle and said, "You dummy, you made us lose the game." The teacher remarked that she thought the excitement of the children spoke well for the kind of lesson that was being taught. The observer remarked that he thought the lesson was a poor one and cited the inhumane treatment accorded several of the children who couldn't give the right answer quickly enough. To this the teacher retorted that after all this was a competitive world and children needed to learn to live in it. After pointing out to the teacher that as a college professor, the observer did not compete with the dentist, the plumber or the lawyer, and that she possibly had all of these and more in her room, she understood the objection. The game itself was not wrong, it was the range of competition within the game that created for some children the dislike for the subject, and contributed to their personal feelings of inadequacy.

We have done a great deal toward improving the physical environment in elementary schools across the country. New buildings, with their open spaces, carpeted floors, brightly-colored walls, open courts, controlled temperatures, and the like, have enhanced the physical environment. Even many old buildings have been renovated to make them pleasant places to learn. But our need, regardless of the physical environment, is to provide the kind of wholesome living environment where children experience accepting behavior, both of themselves and of others. The incident cited above fosters rejection, of others as well as of oneself, either consciously or unconsciously on the part of the learner. We need to help children to learn to know their strengths and to build on these in a positive way. Far too much of the school day has been used to reinforce feelings about one's weaknesses, resulting in low self-esteem and aspiration; consequently, many children have developed a poor self image. These children find it difficult, if not impossible, to cope with the pressures of middle-class society.

The principal must examine with his staff their practices in the following areas, which directly effect the life style of elementary children:

a. Evidence of personal acceptance of each child regardless of his social and/or economic status, racial origin, or religious beliefs.
b. Kinds of marking practices in use.
c. Forms and applications of discipline.
d. Number of negative responses given to certain children regardless of cause.
e. Opportunities for each child to interact positively with *all* other children in the classroom.
f. Emphasis given by each teacher to his personal beliefs and values in setting class standards.
g. Source of decision-making power which affects each child.

The Principal's Role Today 9

This list could be easily extended, but let us merely emphasize that we need to examine these practices in terms of their effects on children. As teachers examine their practices and study their effects, it will become readily apparent that much needs to be done to humanize the elementary school.

One illustration of dehumanizing grading procedures is cited here as a case in point. It is not uncommon to find that the child who has learned to spell the most words during the week's spelling lesson fails or gets an F in spelling. For example, one of the authors noted in one fourth-grade classroom that the pretest on Monday showed 18 percent of the children could not spell any of the sixteen words on the test, but 15 percent of the children could spell 80 percent or more of the words. When Friday came and the final test was given, the 15 percent made a 100 on the test and only 4 percent of the 18 percent who couldn't spell any of the words on Monday spelled enough to pass the test, yet all the children spelled at least 45 percent of the words. This analysis revealed that for the 15 percent who made a 100 on the test, they learned only 20 percent of the 16 new words while the least number of words learned by the 14 percent who failed the final test was 45 percent. Obviously in this classroom the teacher failed to take into account the students' individual differences in marking or in teaching procedures.

The principal's role is one of leadership in bringing about the needed changes in attitudes, feelings and relationships. The school must set the pace for good human relationships and community living. Goals should be established for the affective domain just as they are for the cognitive domain. We need to develop ways of evaluating[16] our success in the affective domain to determine whether we are making a difference in the school's environment, and thereby humanizing the school. Suffice it to say that the school must be devoted to practicing the fundamental tenets of democracy and providing the essential experience for building a rich emotional life based on love, respect and understanding.

Seeking Solutions to Racism in Our Schools. There is little doubt that hostility exists between the races in this country and in our schools. Yet there is a strong basis for optimism about what can be accomplished at the institutional level if principals are willing to act. Here the principal must work at all levels of human endeavor—with the individual, the school, the community, and all agencies that can contribute to bringing about change.

In the Detroit study [17] it was pointed out that at the individual level we either openly or unknowingly transmit racism by:

1. Speaking about children "down there" (referring to poor black children in the center of the city).
2. Using test results to label children as inferior.
3. Presuming that black children have less intellectual ability than white children.

4. Thinking that black children are unclean and diseased.
5. Resorting to racial name-calling in emotional situations.
6. Failing to remember black children's names because they "all look alike."[18]

The principal must begin by examining his own values, beliefs, and practices as he relates to minority groups. We tend to deal with stereotypes when forming certain beliefs about minority groups. Certainly the principal cannot lead his staff or anyone else until he understands the great efforts the various ethnic groups have made to enter the mainstream of American life. In these efforts we have failed to empathize with the member of the minority group in his need to be accepted as a person. As Palamores put it, "I know that I am not able to deal effectively with people until I feel that they accept my right to perceive my reasons for feeling the way I do as valid."[19] The principal might also feel that he is not a racist, and well may not be, but he might also examine his beliefs and practices along with his staff, for as mobility continues in this country, all schools will have children from minority groups and the real test of racism will come when practices are examined. Giles, in his book about the tensions and conflict created by America's racial differences, pointed out that "racial difference is not the only, or even the chief cause of difficulty in administering a classroom program so that each feels a part of the whole and is able to benefit from the association."[20] Perhaps too many of our teachers are so culture-oriented that they consciously or unconsciously teach for the monocultural Anglo children. Not only are the black students lost in this cultural maze, but the American Indian, Mexican Americans, and the Puerto Ricans are presently among the highest percentage of illiterates. In addition, they have a high drop-out rate combined with low achievement levels. The youth of all these groups are growing impatient. Leadership within the schools must work to help teachers and children to appreciate each human being not for his race, although this is important to the individual, but because he is another human being with the same needs, desires, and hopes that oneself has.

The principal must seek out persons from races other than his own, whether black or white, who can serve as resource persons to open the doors to understanding. When study groups can be organized in the community and when exchange programs,[21] not only with foreign students, but with students from other sections of our country and of various racial groups can be arranged, the school and community will grow to understand many of the myths concerning different racial groups. We cannot tolerate teachers in classrooms who fail to provide all children with the kind of environment that helps them to feel good about themselves regardless of their racial background. Self-respect, dignity and a feeling of worth all contribute to the child's self-confidence.

Utilizing the Community in the Educational Process. Although a later chapter is devoted to community relations, it is mentioned here as an issue which principals face. The schools belong to the people, and although community involvement has been sought, it has been limited in most cases. That is, we have kept the community from becoming involved in making "real" decisions—decisions that count. No elementary school can be effective if it fails to involve the community in seeking solutions to real problems. The principal should recognize that the community has within it the human resources for ideas as well as the means to facilitate the operation of the educational program. Above all else, perhaps, the principal needs confidence in the democratic process as he seeks to involve the broader school community in solving problems that for years teachers and principals have not been able to solve themselves.

Programs of Accountability. This term has recently entered the vocabulary of education as citizens have begun to ask questions about what return they are receiving for their investment in education. Educators at this time are finding this issue controversial. Accountability is sometimes related to performance contracting—that is, teachers' effectiveness is determined by standardized test results, which are then tied in with salary increments. The principal of the elementary school, whether inner city or suburban, will have to answer to the public on accountability. School faculties, citizens, and pupils must determine what accountability means to them in their particular school. There should be no doubt in the mind of the principal that the school must be accountable, but the type and kind of accountability must be mutually agreed upon through staff-community participation. Chapter 15 discusses this topic, and suggests guidelines to assist the principal in this task.

NEW DIRECTIONS FOR THE PRINCIPALSHIP

Whether the principal of an elementary school is working in an autonomous school or whether he is assigned a building in a centrally controlled school district, his leadership role is equally important. The same tasks must be performed and the same outcomes are relevant. Schools that attempt to make a difference in the lives of their pupils and community have always existed. They have been led by courageous principals who have considered their schools autonomous, either because the chief school officer believed in a concept of the principal leading his school and community, or because of a *laissez faire* administration. Regardless of the basis for his *modus operandi,* the principal of today's elementary school must see that the school serves the pupils and the community through total involvement. "New directions" means that the principal must be an implementor; while the goals for "good" elementary schools haven't changed to any great extent over the years, we have been guilty of rendering lip-service only to these goals. The time has come for the principal to free himself from traditional limitations imposed on him by the central administration or his own "strawmen" for failing to move his education program forward.[22] He is the catalyst for change, and through his dynamic leadership his school makes a difference in the life of the total community. The need for dynamic leadership in a free society may be considered in the light of the call for change in our elementary schools.

The busy elementary school principal may not have the time or the desire to study intensively the needs and changes in our present-day society. Yet he and his school staff should be able to grasp certain societal causes and effects in order to understand the role of the school in our modern world. As an educational leader, the principal must know how to give direction toward the future by being able to look backward, to learn from what has gone before. His education calls for broad training in the areas of sociology, anthropology, economics, and history.

Effective leadership by the modern elementary school principal demands the following:

>1. *Leadership that has vision and courage to use the imagination to solve problems.* An imaginative approach is needed as leadership attempts to develop the individual as a person and to attain improved human relations in accord with our society.
>2. *A diffusion of leadership.* Many persons concerned with school affairs need to participate in educational activities and contribute their kind and share of leadership skills. The successful principal will persuade each person to contribute and share according to his abilities. This is an important tenet of the democratic way of life.
>3. *An acceptance of the concept that education is for all the people.* Active cooperation by school staff and community people, led by the principal, is needed to keep the emphasis on the community school.
>4. *More emphasis upon social education.* The elementary school should provide some reference values leading to a fuller development of a philosophy of life for all children. The principal will emphasize pupil participation in solving problems as the optimum means of developing proper behavior patterns.
>5. *A kind of re-education of people to accept the inevitability of change.* As the principal understands and accepts this obligation, he must help his community to depend less on tradition for going beyond into new areas of challenge. His most difficult leadership task will be to get people to take these steps which are already at the core of our democracy and are the goals of a free society.[23]

The principal should now recognize that the need for leadership is forced upon him by the very nature of our society. He becomes aware of his role when he views the many demands made upon leadership. He must grasp

The Principal's Role Today

the social significance of the problems he faces and understand the complexities of meeting and handling social issues. In addition, as he faces local inhibitory influences, not every principal is cognizant of the fact that dynamic leadership begins and ends with the ability to utilize the techniques of group management and control—to be considered, of course, in the light of our way of life or society.

The principal is an accepted community leader who must help to interpret certain values accepted by group consensus. He moves to implement these values in a positive educational program and constantly examines the effects of such values.

Thus the principal exerts intelligent school leadership when he is well grounded in the demands and expectations of our society. His leadership is definite and positive when he knows how to devise plans of action to carry out these goals. The aim of this book is to show how the democratic values of our society are incorporated into definite techniques and devices that can be applied in furnishing educational leadership to school and community.

Duties and Scope of the Principalship

The duties and tasks confronting the principal range over many administrative and educational activities. These activities contain many variables, precluding any rigid job description of the average principal, even for a given locale. Yet there are common goals for all localities and types of schools which call for some definite duties and tasks in reaching educational objectives. The primary task of the principal is to organize his school in such a way that these objectives can be realized. As an executive, he must provide for his staff the proper facilities for discharging their responsibilities in attaining these ends. Although detailed descriptions of the principal's specific activities are discussed throughout this book, the writers intend to emphasize primarily the leadership roles he plays in carrying out the many educational activities. True, a description of duties and knowledge of them cannot be neglected, but the principal must have an over-all perspective of the scope of his office and must know positively how to apply leadership processes for effective school management. A description of activities in one principal's typical work day will suggest the scope of his administrative responsibilities. In addition to other chores, this principal: (1) held a conference with a teacher involved in a system-wide study of curriculum problems for the elementary schools; (2) conferred with the supervisor of music who was planning a music festival for the school; (3) wrote to the chairman of the Board of Education in response to his request for student and faculty policies regarding use of playground equipment after school hours; (4) met with community representatives concerning plans for multi-age grouping of five-, six-, seven-, and eight-year-olds; (5) had a meeting with the student government concerning policies of conduct on school buses; and (6) met with a committee to plan revision of the school's appraisal form.

It would be impossible to describe here the range of duties and tasks that most principals meet daily. An analysis of this principal's typical day reveals, however, that in addition to certain routine clerical tasks, he deals primarily with problems concerning people. The scope of the principalship extends into the field of human relations, involving feelings, attitudes, prejudices, fears, and the entire range of human emotions.

The broad range of the principal's administrative duties point up his need to utilize the competencies of his faculty and community resources in conducting the educational enterprise. Some of his major leadership responsibilities include:

1. Providing for in-service growth, for himself and his faculty;
2. Fostering community participation in school decisions;
3. Alleviating pressures of conformity on teachers and pupils;
4. Providing auxiliary services for all pupils;
5. Directing programs of continuous evaluation of the educational program;
6. Providing consultants and resource persons for the instructional staff; and
7. Promoting strong ethical relationships among his students, staff, and community.

This brief discussion of the scope and duties of the elementary school principal suggests a framework within which his role as an educational administrator may be more clearly defined. The emphasis in this book is on his specific leadership tasks rather than on his administrative duties in general. The principal can make a list of the duties and tasks required for the effective management of his school; research studies will assist him in understanding what he should expect to do as a principal for efficient control. Until he has acquired effective leadership skills, however, his position may be only that of a highly paid clerical person who demonstrates good organization in conducting certain school tasks. Leadership is the key to successful school administration.

DEMOCRATIC ADMINISTRATION

The principal of the modern elementary school is concerned about his leadership behavior and how he can effectively transform his staff, students, and citizens into a working unit for school improvement. To do this he must practice democratic principles as a vital part of his philosophy. Teachers have been, and will be in the future, the key to pupil growth; consequently, anything which affects teachers will have an effect on children. Thus, the principal's prime responsibility is attention to the problems which affect teachers.

Group thinking and group planning must form the core of this emerging pattern. Some principals may feel, however, that by legal fiat they have status, and thus are to be in complete charge. The legality of the principal's position should not limit his efforts at cooperative administrative behavior. Many principals are either unwilling to share authority or unaware of the opportunities for staff participation in actual operative procedures. Any administrator can manage his affairs in either of two ways: he may order people to get things done, or he may *work with* people in accomplishing certain ends. The principal should adopt those methods of management that are clearly psychological in nature, by considering the needs and feelings of staff members. Such an approach means there is the "we" feeling instead of the "I" kind of management.[24]

One important task of the principal is to motivate his staff to move in a desired direction. To get people to do things, and especially to perform at high levels that bring greater efficiency and personal satisfactions, requires a definite kind of leadership. Yet many principals believe that charting the educational course and directing staff personnel are processes reserved solely for the administrator's office. To the democratic administrator, working with people means motivating and aiding them to determine their goals, and then to assist them in achieving them. The school principal is practicing the democratic approach in his administrative affairs by recognizing his role as an organizer of those natural situations which provide motivation in such a way that all participants do not feel they are being told or ordered what to do and how to do it. Thus all school personnel will be participating in all areas affecting them, particularly in forming decisions.

The psychological or democratic approach to administration may be contrasted with autocratic administration at the following points:

Psychological approach	*Autocratic approach*
1. Staff participation and concurrence on decisions	1. Little or no participation by staff and concurrence practically unknown or disregarded
2. Recognition of staff problems and feelings	2. Feelings and problems of the staff unknown or disregarded
3. Pleasant social climate	3. Social climate of group ignored
4. Stress on cooperative methods in problem solving	4. Orders handed down and understandings disregarded

The principal's leadership role is ultimately determined by the kind of membership he holds in his school's group. If he gains prestige through psychological principles of leadership and is an "expert" in his own right, he may be pictured in figure 1. This principal is oriented towards his teachers. There is no difference in "level," since he is a leader who has gained status by virtue of his abilities. He encourages a free exchange of ideas and participation by his teachers.

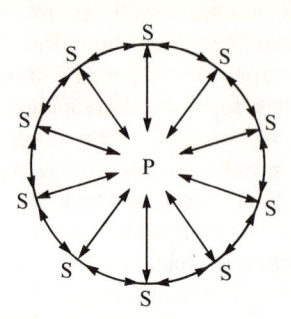

P — Principal
S — Staff Member

Figure 1

The Flow of Communication in the Psychological Form of School Management

In contrast to this kind of leadership, the autocratic principal shows a disregard for having membership in the "in" group or "we" group. In fact, this principal may make special efforts to remain apart from or on the "outside" of his staff. This position is pictured in figure 2.

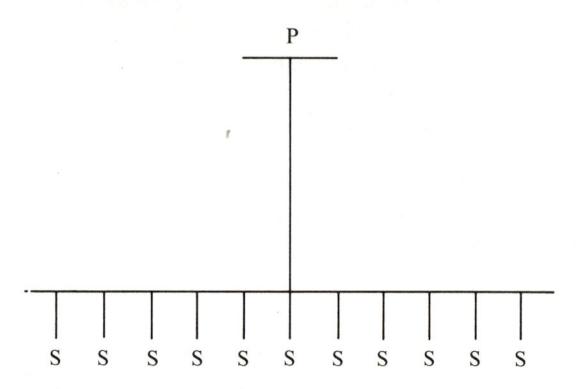

P — Principal
S — Staff Member

Figure 2

The Flow of Communication in the Autocratic Form of School Management

The principal using the autocratic approach will insist upon professional and social distance in this kind of staff relationship. Generally speaking, he maintains his prestige by title and designated authority. He is also more concerned with identifying himself with the higher levels of administration. Frequently he may have goals, desires, and wishes that are entirely different from those of his staff, since communication may be practically nonexistent.

The principal should consider every problem or decision-making task in the light of certain psychological principles if he wishes to demonstrate administrative behavior that will lead to greater staff satisfaction and improved performance. He not only sees a task to be done by school personnel and takes leadership action for accomplishment, but he is also aware of the feelings of his staff. He knows further that a job cannot be undertaken without regard to how people feel about it. Those subtle forces present in the interpersonal relationships of his staff are no longer considered unimportant to an effective performance. In fact, how people feel about a task is as important as getting the job done in itself. In addition, the principal who adopts the psychological approach to his job shows that he is conscious of the climate or atmosphere in his staff relationships. It becomes important to him to establish a favorable, permissive climate, since he knows that people work at higher levels of performance when an executive provides this kind of atmosphere. Finally, the principal brings meaning to a democratic administration by demonstrating his belief in his actual problem-solving methods. His stress is on a cooperative approach to all problems of mutual concern. He refuses to hand down his orders arbitrarily, and by working with his staff he achieves a consensus that is proof of a cooperative attack, as principal and faculty share in leadership areas. When there are mutual feelings of responsibility in administering a program, there will be deepened interest in achieving success on the part of all participants. If the principal is the sole leader, he deprives the staff of sharing in successful projects and removes incentives for increased faculty effort and development of leadership. He accepts the democratic point of view by establishing that kind of school environment most conducive to the mutual benefit of all persons involved in furthering educational objectives.

The Principal's Role in Decision Making

The elementary principalship has been classified as a position of middle management because of its administrative responsibilities to the chief school officer and to the teaching staff. The principal's administrative function, however, requires competence in decision making. The authors believe that the elementary administrator should view his position from a totally integrated vantage point. Although the tasks he performs can be divided into many different categories, he must see his job as a whole and respond to its demands with a consistent pattern of leadership behavior. He cannot respond one way one day and differently the next. His understanding of principles of democratic action in education and of sound leadership practices must direct his behavior in the various spheres of administrative action, since administration exists only because there is an organization—the school—to administer. At the center of the purpose for the organization is the need to make certain decisions.[25] Because a decision was made to establish the organization, some form of administration becomes essential in order to implement the function or functions of the organization. In the case of the elementary school, the principal is responsible for administering the school organization. This places him in a position requiring decision making, since this is the process of administration.[26] Of importance here is that the form of organization established by the principal must insure that the decisions made are the correct ones. This does not necessarily mean that the results of the decision will be the most desirable, but that the best possible process will be used in arriving at the decision. The principal, then, must be cognizant of the organizational principles which he controls in order to insure that correct decisions will be made.

The nature of his administrative position involves him in working with the (1) central office personnel and the board of education, (2) teachers, pupils, and other personnel within the building, and (3) parents and the immediate community. The principal's role in working with each of these groups is overlapping and complementary, depending upon the situation and the task to be accomplished. Central to his role as an administrator is the way he directs and controls the decision-making process. For example, in establishing broad policies which affect working conditions of his teachers and of other teachers in the district, he becomes a participant in the decision-making process, working with representatives from the teachers' association or union and members of the board of education and the central administration in developing broad policies. On the other hand, he will himself be responsible for establishing the organization for studying policies within his school which affect the working conditions of his faculty. Since these are local policies and are largely a part of his management role, he will need to define the limitations within which the faculty-elected committee will work. Here his leadership role changes, but his method of administering is consistent with his basic operational philosophy. As a member of the faculty, he works from within the group to see that adequate information is available, suggest alternatives and facilitate the decision-making process.

In working with the community, he serves as a resource person. Here his talents and skills will be needed to help the community clarify its goals for educating its children. He will refrain from dominating group discussion and seek to help the group in identifying problems. He sees that all members have a chance at problem identification as well as an opportunity to contribute solutions to the problems. He will make available the latest research informa-

The Principal's Role Today

tion and data. Thus his leadership role is to facilitate action by the community in achieving their goals.

Decision making carries with it the need to implement the required action. This becomes one of the paramount functions of the principal who utilizes groups to share in decision making. Groups must feel that the time spent in making a decision is worth the effort. However, if the principal fails to initiate the decisions, he can expect lower group morale and an unwillingness to work toward further decisions. There should be little doubt on the part of the principal that the importance of the decision reached depends upon the action that follows the decision. The action must lead the group to the attainment of its goals.

The Psychological Approach to Administration

The discussion thus far has focused on the principal's need to exert dynamic leadership in a democratic culture. It has been suggested that a principal who is oriented democratically or psychologically toward administrative behavior will be most effective in his leadership role. A question may be asked at this point: Is there evidence that the behavior of the democratic leader reflects upon the behavior of others to produce higher levels of performance and greater satisfaction?

Many studies in business and industrial firms give conclusive evidence of the efficacy of using the psychological approach in administrative areas of behavior. An illustration will be cited of an industrial problem that was solved by decision making through group participation.

Bavelas conducted and reported a study in a case of decision making and group participation among female sewing-machine operators. He was interested in getting the group to establish production goals, even though these operators worked on an incentive pay plan. After selecting a group of high-producing operators, he discussed with them the matter of production. It was made clear to them that they could, if they wished, establish their own production goal. Up to this time the girls had produced between 60 and 75 units per hour. After the group discussed the matter, an agreement was reached by the operators that they would like to establish a new production goal of 84 units per hour. In less than one week they exceeded their established goal and arranged for another group discussion. At this meeting they concluded they would set the goal at 95 units. However, during the next week they fell short of this higher goal. Again they met to decide what to do and decided to establish a more realistic production goal of 90 units per hour. Over a six-month period their work was watched carefully, and it was found that production averaged 87 units per hour.[27]

The beneficial results from this study are obvious, in that production was increased by 10 units per hour. This was the kind of leadership that invoked the involvement of all persons concerned and contributed to changes in group attitude. The point is that these operators could have been ordered to produce more units per hour, but they were already on an incentive pay plan and might not have been willing to comply. Group participation and mutual decision making also brought about a kind of motivation that enabled them actually to exceed their production goal without any increase in fatigue or dissatisfaction.

In another situation, Coch and French sought evidence as to whether the psychological approach by leaders would have beneficial effects upon employee behavior.[28] An experiment was conducted in a manufacturing plant to verify the premise that individuals resist change when frustrated by strong group pressures and forces. Three experimental groups plus a control group were used. Whenever changes were to be made in work methods, the control group went through the usual factory routines. They were told of these changes and their new piece rates by the executives, after all engineering planning and method changes had been worked out at higher levels. Then, before any changes were made, each of the three experimental groups was informed of reasons for changes, plans, and piece rates. Group participation was afforded each experimental group in varied amounts, with some groups establishing more permissive climates and participating more widely. The results were significant in that the control group did not adjust to the new situation as a whole; there was evidence of group dissatisfaction, and 17 per cent even quit their jobs in the first 40 days after the experiment. Among the experimental groups, motivation was evident even for those who showed the least amount of participation. It was clear that the psychological approach was far superior with respect to production, satisfaction, and adjustment. This was evidenced in many ways, even to the extent of no "quits" in any of the experimental groups during the first 40 days after the work changes.

Since much evidence of this kind is available from business and industrial leadership practices, it seems clear that the principal can operate similarly at the executive level to insure greater staff production, improved teaching, and higher satisfactions. The problems may be different, but the elements are identical in that the principal is dealing with people who, in many instances, look upon such matters as decision making as a prerogative of the group, whose feelings should be taken into consideration, and who react unfavorably to pressure from above when group participation is barred.

Some educators distrust comparisons of business practices with those in educational administration,[29] but the modern elementary school principal cannot ignore the research findings of the humanistic approach in business management. More research is needed to prove that the psychological approach to elementary school administration will produce better teaching and improved behavior. Will the principal who accepts this approach actually improve his own school situation? Is it useful in his preparation for educational leadership? These questions still need to be answered, although there seems to be little doubt that, since the early 1950s, social forces appear to be penetrating and modifying not only industrial organizations but virtually all other human institutions as well—in not entirely predictable ways. A similar trend may be noted in school administration, as apparent in such developments as the autonomous school, staff-teacher-parent curriculum planning, and decentralization in city school systems.

The Source of Authority for the Principal

One of the writers has noted among graduate students preparing for positions in elementary administration, as well as among principals in service, a misunderstanding of the meaning of democracy in education. Surely most teachers have had experience with the autocratic principal who operates on the basis of receiving his authority when he signs his contract to serve as principal. In contrast, the "progressive education" era resulted in confusion about the meaning of democracy which led to anarchy in some schools and classrooms. It is true that the principal receives his authority from the board of education, but this should not affect the way he operates his school. Within the limitations established by the board, the principal can foster democratic action for local school policies and programs. This implies that the principal will involve in the decision-making process those who will be affected by the decisions—his staff, pupils, or citizens, separately or together, depending upon the situation.

The school is an organization established by law and it cannot be effective if it functions without regard to regulation and control. The principal's role, once the decisions have been made, is to implement them and to see that the policies are followed until the group affected decides they should be changed. This means that the principal secures additional authority from the group in which he must exercise responsibility. The principal then, although appointed by the board of education, actually receives his authority for action from his staff and the community.

Utilization of Psychological Procedures in Administration

A leader employs many devices and techniques to change the behavior of a group. If the psychological approach to group management is sound, the principal may search further to understand more clearly the specific procedures based on these principles. No precise steps can be stated for every instance requiring leadership skills, since each incident must be evaluated on the basis of its individual merits. However, there are ways of utilizing cooperative procedures in exercising leadership that relate to the elementary school principal. Here we consider three aspects that will help the principal become more adept in the art of leadership based on psychological principles: (1) the principal must develop the human-relations attitude; (2) the principal must follow certain definite practical procedures in the administrative operations of his job; (3) the principal must be able to evaluate his methods and practices in cooperative school administration.

The Human Relations Factor. Preceding discussions have emphasized the meanings and kinds of leadership, with evidence that the human-relations-minded principal has greater promise of administrative success than does the autocratic or dominating administrator. It is important that the principal accept this premise of the human relations factor in his dealings with the staff. He needs to develop an attitude toward his job and his staff which will insure that he approaches his tasks with attention to the personal worth of every individual. To develop this attitude, the principal must be sensitive to the needs of individuals. When the principal practices this human-relations attitude, he can reduce frustration. Apathy, or blocking of group participation, arises when the principal exerts leadership that does not take into consideration the needs and interests of the group. As he learns to be sensitive to people, he becomes in effect aware of their needs and differences. He begins to recognize what potentialities exist and can call upon each staff member to contribute to the educational task at hand.

The principal must lead his staff in such a way that the group members become sensitive to one another and become aware of their responsibilities to one another. He must help the faculty to recognize that it can become an aid or a resource to individual members. Specifically, the group develops a form of leadership by helping a member to develop initiative, express ideas and opinions, and put those opinions into action effectively. The principal fosters the growth of group maturity and encourages group endorsement of individual differences for different contributions.

The principal must allow the individual to share in setting group goals wherever the individual's situation is affected. In addition, the methods for reaching these goals should come from the individual and the group. This practice on the part of the principal will mean more effective group relationships. It has already been stated that as the individual is permitted to participate in setting group goals, these goals will have greater value for him. He becomes involved in the responsibilities that result and desires to follow through on decisions.

The principal must encourage individual expressions of opinion in a permissive, informal atmosphere. He will recognize that this kind of social climate is necessary before any staff member will feel free to speak honestly and frankly. Since differences of opinion must be brought into the open if varying interpretations and perceptions are to be resolved, bringing the common factors within the differences to genuine, accepted solutions will be significant to his leadership. This kind of leadership does not mean that the principal withdraws from the group, but that he submerges himself in it. He must recognize that the consensus method of decision making makes the individual feel important. The individual is never overwhelmed nor overridden, since the group will reach decisions by the consensus method—bringing out different personal contributions, weighing them, and finding the solution agreeable to all. Again, the individual is able to feel his delegated responsibility and is *led* to make his particular contribution. The human-relations attitude on the part of the principal helps him to meet three basic human needs: a sense of belonging, a sense of achievement, and a sense of recognition.

Practical Procedures in the Psychological Approach. The elementary school principal can develop the human-relations attitude toward his position, his staff, and the community, but he must put this attitude into practice. Some suggestions will serve as guides to the many practices available for giving dynamic leadership. This list provides only a framework for administrative operations, and is not to be regarded as complete in itself:

1. The principal must see that communication is open among his office and the faculty and community.
2. The principal must establish rapport with all school personnel and community members with whom he works and comes in contact. He must respect differences of opinion, and must not allow them to cause a breakdown in relationships.
3. The human-relations-minded principal must recognize the value of exchanging ideas and opinions, and provide for interaction of all concerned with school problems to develop cooperation in seeking solutions.
4. The principal must utilize planning and advisory committees to work with him in identifying and seeking solutions to school problems.
5. The principal must recognize and use the services of consultants and resource persons, regardless of their training, if they can contribute to solving problems.
6. The principal must keep the community apprised of the school's progress by keeping them involved in the phases of the school program in which they are most interested.
7. The principal must maintain close contact with the children of his school. They need to know him, his values, attitudes and his feelings about them.

SUMMARY

Professionalization of the principalship depends on the leadership concepts and skills required of and exercised by the administrators of elementary schools. The principal is primarily an educational leader charged with the responsibility of furthering educational objectives, but he must function first as an administrator to initiate action and stimulate staff growth and advancement. His staff will respond to the leadership he furnishes, which will determine to a great degree the effectiveness of the educational program.

The principal requires broad training and deep insights if he is to function as an accepted community leader who directs his fellow citizens away from provincialism and toward the wider concepts of our democratic society. The way in which he practices leadership must reflect this point of view. He may use definite techniques and devices to show the way, but the preferred method is a sound psychological approach consistent with the philosophy of a free society.

The principal must be prepared to (1) work in an autonomous school, (2) humanize the elementary school, (3) seek solutions to racism in the school, (4) use the community effectively in decision making, (5) develop a program of accountability, and (6) understand new directions of principalship.

The principal attacks problems consistently from the viewpoint that he is a leader working *with* people. His administrative acts emerge from the principles that it is important to get staff participation and concurrence, that feelings must be considered, that proper social climate is necessary, and that cooperative methods of problem solving are desirable and necessary. He will gain higher levels of achievement and greater staff satisfaction when he uses such methods of group control.

SUGGESTED READINGS

Bass, Barnard M. *Leadership, Psychology, and Organizational Behavior.* New York; Harper, 1960.

Bennis, Warren G. Kenneth D. Benne, and Robert Chin, eds. *The Planning of Change.* New York: Holt, Rinehart and Winston, 1961.

Dare to Care/Dare to Act: Racism and Education. Addresses and Statements at the 1971 ASCD Annual Conference. Washington: Association for Supervision and Curriculum Development, National Education Association, 1971.

Goldman, Harvey. "Principals for Community Schools," *The Community School and Its Administration.* Flint, Michigan: The Flint Board of Education and the Mott Foundation, 7, no. 1, September 1968.

Griffiths, Daniel E. *Administrative Theory.* New York: Appleton Century, 1959.

Halpin, Andrew W. *Theory and Research in Administration.* New York: Macmillan, 1966.

Heidenreich, Richard H. (comp.) *Current Readings in Urban Education.* Arlington, Virginia: Callys Readings, 1971.

Holmans, George C. *The Human Group.* New York: Harcourt, Brace & World, 1950.

Keynes, Edward and David M. Ricci, eds. *Political Power, Community and Democracy.* Chicago: Rand McNally, 1970.

Parsons, Talcott. *The Social System.* New York: Free Press, 1951.

Wilcox, Preston. "The Meaning of Community Control," *Foresight* 1 (February 1969): 9–14. Detroit: The Black Teachers Workshop.

Notes

1. Arthur J. Lewis, "The Future of the Elementary School Principalship," *The National Elementary Principal,* 48, No. 1 (September 1968): 12.

2. Ervin Eugene Lewis and Oscar H. Williams, *Creative Management for Teachers* (Ann Arbor, Michigan: Edwards Brothers, Inc., 1931), p. 6.

3. See Robert L. Sinclair, "Leadership Concerns," *The National Elementary Principal* 48, No. 1 (September 1968): 16–20.

4. By permission from *Fundamentals of Educational Leadership* by C. A. Weber and Mary E. Weber (New York: McGraw-Hill, 1955), chapter 3. Copyright© 1955.

5. Bernard M. Bass, *Leadership Psychology and Organizational Behavior,* (New York: Harper, 1960), p. 19.

6. Alvin W. Gouldner, ed., *Studies in Leadership* (New York: Harper, 1950), p. 32.

7. Ibid., p. 38.

8. William Wayson, "A New Kind of Principal," *The National Elementary Principal* 50 (February 1971): 11.

9. Herbert A. Thelen, *Dynamics of Groups at Work* (Chicago: University of Chicago Press, 1954), p. 296.

10. Ibid., p. 331.

11. Sinclair, "Leadership Concerns," pp. 16–20.

12. Ralph C. Davis, *The Fundamentals of Top Management* (New York: Harper, 1951), pp. 151–52.

13. See *Priorities for the Seventies: The Detroit Elementary Schools,* The Detroit Study of Priority Elementary School Problems and Concerns, The Board of Education of the School District of the City of Detroit, 1971.

14. See Richard R. Heidenreich, comp., *Current Readings in Urban Education* (Arlington, Va.: College Readings, Inc., 1971), Section III, part 21.

15. Neal Gross and Robert E. Herriott, *Staff Leadership in Public Schools* (New York: John Wiley, 1965), pp. 66–67.

16. See Milton E. Ploghoft and Albert H. Shuster, *Social Science Education for the Elementary School* (Columbus, Ohio: Charles Merrill, 1971), chapter 14.

17. Detroit Study, *Priorities for the Seventies,* pp. 21–22.

18. Ibid.

19. "Dare to Care/Dare to Act—Racism and Education," Address and Statements from the 26th Annual Association for Supervision and Curriculum Development Conference, March 6–10, 1971, St. Louis, Missouri (Washington, D.C.: National Education Association, 1971), p. 16.

20. H. Harry Giles, *The Integrated Classroom* (New York: Basic Books, 1959), p. 4.

21. See Milton E. Ploghoft and Frank Gerhardt, "Human Resources for International Studies," *Childhood Education* 47 (May 1971): 424–26.

22. See Wayson, "A New Kind of Principal."

23. Weber and Weber, *Fundamentals of Educational Leadership,* pp. 19–26.

24. Wilson F. Wetzler, "Administering Schools by Staff Dynamics," *American School Board Journal* 128 (April 1954): 27.

25. See Daniel E. Griffiths, *Administrative Theory* (New York: Appleton-Century-Crofts, 1959).

26. Ibid., p. 75.

27. Norman R. F. Maier, *Psychology in Industry,* 2d ed. (Boston: Houghton Mifflin, 1955), pp. 151–52.

28. Lester Coch and J. R. P. French, "Overcoming Resistance to Change," *Human Relations* 1 (1948): 512–32.

29. Cyril G. Sargent and Eugene L. Belisle, *Educational Administration: Cases and Concepts* (Boston: Houghton Mifflin, 1955), p. 434.

2

Evolution of the Elementary School Principalship

The elementary principal occupies a key position among modern day educators. His leadership role plays a significant part in the kind of an educational program his school projects. The need for dynamic leadership is ever-present in any school situation, with many obstacles and pressures influencing the caliber of administrative behavior. This chapter looks at the evolution of the elementary school principalship (1) from a historical point of view, and (2) in relation to social change, so that those aspiring to be principals, and indeed many who now hold the position, will understand the shift of the principalship from a relatively insignificant position to one of paramount leadership responsibilities. This chapter will also present concepts relative to the professionalization of the principalship. The development of this position has been a slow, difficult road for those who have pioneered it, but the progress made is now self-evident.

DEVELOPMENT OF THE PRINCIPALSHIP

A number of factors influenced the early development of the elementary school principalship, among them (1) the separation of children into grades, (2) rapid growth of cities, (3) consolidation of departments under a single principal, (4) freeing of the principal from teaching duties, (5) recognition of the principal as a supervisory head of a school, and (6) establishment of the Department of Elementary School Principals of the National Education Association.[1] This last-named factor inaugurated the beginning of the professionalization of the position.

About 1830, the population of the cities began to increase, which caused school populations to multiply rapidly. Cities such as Baltimore, Boston,

Philadelphia, New York, St. Louis and others soon reached the point in pupil enrollments that it became necessary for the superintendent of schools to transfer his supervisory responsibility to the principal. Thus the first logical step was to turn local management of the individual school over to the principal. In 1871, *The Seventeenth Annual Report of the Board of Education of St. Louis* pointed out that when pupil enrollments increased from 5000 to 20,000, the duties of the superintendent changed. This report indicated that the superintendent could visit schools frequently when the pupil enrollment did not exceed 5000 pupils. Although size was an impetus for change in responsibility for school management, certain other factors restricted development of the principalship.

Factors which Retarded Development of the Principalship

In the 1850s most school buildings were constructed to facilitate the type of school organization in vogue at the time. One of the factors that retarded the principalship was the monitorial system, also known as the Lancasterian system, of instruction. This system was economical, since the buildings consisted of large rooms of the study-hall type with one or more small rooms attached. The principal's task was to maintain order in the study hall, while monitors or assistant teachers had the pupils recite lessons in the smaller rooms.[2]

A second factor which retarded development of the principalship was the "double-headed school." This was so named because there were two masters —the grammar master and the writing master.[3] The children spent half of their time with one master and the other half with another master, resulting in divided authority. Although this might have retarded the development of the principalship, it could also have led to the decision for change.

When girls were admitted to the public schools, they were taught in separate sections of the building, and thus additional heads or principals were housed within the same building with no one having final authority. This may have caused disunity within the school, and also caused problems in the classification of children.

Factors which Led to the Full-Time Principalship

Pierce points out that although the Quincy School in Boston in 1847 is cited as the first school with all departments under a single head, the records show that this policy existed in Cincinnati in 1838.[4] *The Ninth Annual Report of the Trustees and Visitors of the Common Schools of Cincinnati 1838* pointed out that because of their responsibilities for grading teachers, fixing salaries, and classifying pupils, there should be one controlling head—the principal. Analysis of the duties prescribed by the board of education for the principal shows clearly the behavior skills he would need. Schools throughout the Midwest moved rapidly to a single head for each graded school, but already tradition had set in in the eastern cities, and it was more difficult to break down the "double-headed school."

Perhaps the factor which contributed most to the system of a single head per school was the establishment of grades in schools. Courses of study were developed on a graded basis, which changed the form of school organization. Since it was not practical for a superintendent to classify and grade each pupil, it was logical to place this responsibility upon the local principal. This process also is given credit as the opening wedge toward freeing the principal from full-time teaching. The grading process, if handled effectively, revealed the fallacy of having separate departments with independent heads.

Some Duties of the First Principals. The principal-teacher was the common designation for the controlling head of the school, since teaching was his prime responsibility. This designation led to inevitable conflict, however, as teachers sought clarification of the duties of the principal-teacher. The Common School Teachers' Association of Cincinnati sent an inquiry to the Board of Education in 1839, requesting clarification of the duties of the principal and the assistant teachers. The president of the Board served as chairman of a committee which sent the following reply related to duties of the principal. The principal-teacher was

> (1) to function as the head of the school charged to his care, (2) to regulate the classes and course of instruction of all the pupils, whether they occupied his room or the rooms of other teachers, (3) to discover any defects in the school and apply remedies, (4) to make defects known to the visitor or trustee of the ward or district, if he were unable to remedy conditions, (5) to give necessary instruction to his assistants, (6) to classify pupils, (7) to safeguard school houses and furniture, (8) to keep the school clean, (9) to instruct assistants, (10) to refrain from impairing the standing of assistants, especially in the eyes of their pupils, and (11) to require the cooperation of his assistants. . . .[5]

Assistant teachers were (1) to regard the principal-teacher as the head of the school, (2) to observe his directions, (3) to guard his reputation, and (4) to make themselves thoroughly acquainted with the rules and regulations adapted for the government of the schools.[6]

From the above, it appears obvious that the principal-teacher's position was grounded in authority; such statements as "remedy conditions" and "require cooperation" give support to the status of this early position and the basis for the Association to raise the question of clarification of duties. At times, in some schools, it would appear that we have not moved away from the autocratic mode of administration of yesteryear; while the duties have not changed a great deal over the years, certainly our emphasis on human relations and involvement in decision making has yet to be fully realized.

Early Role of the Principal as a Supervisor

In 1859, it became evident that the principal was to take on a new and important function—that of supervision of instruction. Grading the school and classifying pupils led to time free from teaching for the principal. Superintendent Wells of Chicago mentioned in the Fifth Annual Report of the Board of Education of Chicago, 1859, that the principal was spending a considerable amount of time in helping the other teachers in whatever ways necessary to secure uniformity and efficiency in all the different departments. Wells in 1862 indicated that the principal's duties during classroom units were to examine classes, classify pupils, promote pupils, conduct model lessons and to exercise careful supervision over discipline and instruction of the whole school.[7] Thus the need for more skills on the part of the principal was established. He was no longer just an administrator, but would now need supervisory skills.

It is interesting to note that as early as 1859 in New York, principals were calling for autonomous schools. In a memorandum to the Board of Education they complained of the system of examinations used to evaluate pupils and stated that it was unjust to teachers. The principals pointed out that the examinations did not take into account the different circumstances of each school, and that teachers in unfavorable localities were often compelled to work harder than those in favored communities with no allowance made for differing conditions, thus often causing teachers to emphasize procedures injurious to pupils. It became evident that the principal was destined to become not only the administrative head, but also the pedagogic head of the school, which had occurred by 1900. Annual Reports of Superintendents at the turn of the century are replete with statements that place the principal as the "highest local authority." Such statements developed in relationship to the principal's acceptance of his supervisory role. It was from this acceptance that the supervisory principalship developed. As the number of schools increased, the supervisory principal was given the responsibility for supervising the primary and intermediate grades of several schools. It was pointed out in the St. Louis report in 1869 that "supervision is easily given, and is most efficient in reducing the work of the lower grades to a common standard of excellence, and in the correction of false tendencies on the part of individual teachers."[8]

It is obvious, from the last part of this statement, that principals were expected to be experts in instruction and thus to know whether teachers were using "false tendencies" in pupil instruction. Although the title of supervisory principal has lingered on in many school districts, it seems the position was narrowed again to a single school as subject supervisors emerged from the central office. Of importance here is the fact that the principal was expected to have certain skills and to practice certain behaviors related to the supervisory function of his position. But it would appear that the needed skills were more in line with dictatorial behavior. A study of annual reports from various school systems in the middle and late 1800s tends to depict the principal as an expert in teaching and as a superior to teachers. Principals were selected for being "good" teachers not for being able to lead people. They were expected to see that all teachers taught as nearly alike as possible.

By the turn of the century, several things were happening. Principals who were freed at least part-time for supervision were now finding that clerical duties took up much of their time. In addition, some principals believed that clerical duties should be handled outside of school hours while others believed they should be handled during school hours. This is still the case today in far too many schools. It could be that principals who were finding resistance to supervision from teachers decided on the latter course of action. Or, those principals who did not feel secure in the instructional supervision area found the routine administrative duties more to their liking. Some recognizable distinction's appeared between schools in relation to the principals' behavior. A general supervisor in St. Louis in 1916 stated that principals who did their clerical work outside of the school day realized that their most important duty was to work with teachers and children to give all children the best opportunities for development, to establish unity in the child's training, and to raise the standards of all classwork to the highest level possible by a well-planned program of supervision.[9]

The Elementary Principal Becomes a Professional Leader

Soon after the principal was recognized as a supervisor of instruction in his school and his duties were concerned with quality teaching, a new emphasis emerged. In 1920, under the guidance of the Department of Education at the University of Chicago, and working with elementary principals, a new organization was born. The founding of the elementary principals' organization soon took on national stature when it affiliated with the National Education Association.[10] The organization and its affiliation with the N.E.A., as well as the guidance from the University of Chicago, turned the attention of the principals to scientific study of educational problems. Professional preparatory programs were formalized as colleges and universities began to offer special courses and programs for training principals. Studies were made of homogeneous grouping, age-grade distribution, achievement relationship to mental ability, and the like.[11]

Dissemination of professional information, studies, and recognized school practices of principals was provided by yearbooks published by the Department of Elementary and Secondary School Principals.[12] Thus the professionalization of the principalship was under way. But real progress was to come slowly, for the position still operated largely from a mechanical point of view with strong autocratic tendencies.

Evolution of the Elementary School Principalship 31

THE MODERN PERIOD

In the 1940s and fifties, a number of groups involved in studying educational administration (Cooperative Program in Education Administration) did a great deal to lead the profession in understanding administrative behavior. The C.P.E.A., funded by the W. K. Kellogg Foundation, led to the establishment of university centers across the country, created for the purpose of studying and improving educational administration. A statement from the School-Community Development Study, based at the Ohio State University, points out that through combined research and field service, preparation of educational administrators will be aligned with current needs and in-service administrators' competence will be improved.[13] Such studies contribute to the field of educational administration and lead to further studies more directly related to the elementary administrator.

Today the National Association of Elementary Principals has more than 23,000 members, and has grown into one of the most significant professional groups in the country.[14] Through its support of research investigations, it has made numerous contributions to all facets of the principalship. The official journal of the Association, *The National Elementary Principal,* has served its members well and has made a significant contribution to the professional literature in all phases of elementary education.

In the improvement of the national image of the elementary school principal, the state and local associations must also be recognized. Many of these have not only been strong supporters of the national association, but have made great strides in their own states and regions. State and regional groups have sponsored workshops, conferences, institutes and seminars for the improvement of the elementary principal, and have published important professional journals and newsletters.

Influence of Societal Changes

The above description of the development of the principalship might cause the reader to envision this development as largely a mechanistic process. A look at the broad implications of social change and need, however, provides another approach to understanding this development. Significantly, as the goals of the elementary school have changed, the type of leadership and the demands upon it have also changed. Actually, before the superintendent of schools felt the need of an assistant to help him administer the elementary school, even if by proxy, the purposes of the elementary school were aimed at serving the community. A convenient way to understand the changes in the goals of the school and thus in the principalship is to consider the four periods of community development.[15] In the first period, the common school emphasized religious training. As early as 1647, the General Court of Massachusetts required every township of a certain size to provide some form of elementary education. The schools were not complex or large; there was little need for administrative control and guidance since many boys were apprenticed early to their fathers or to other tradesmen, and the girls were occupied in household tasks.

General literacy was the emphasis in the second period, which saw the American colonies united through newly-won independence. The citizenry quickly realized that, if they were to govern themselves, all voting citizens had to be literate. Massachusetts made the first move in 1837 by requiring compulsory education, and Horace Mann was responsible for its enforcement. Other states soon followed this pattern of compulsory education to insure an informed people. This era marked the beginning of the real growth of the elementary school, based on a realistic goal of universal education. There still remained further development and understanding in education before the head teacher would become acknowledged as a principal.

The third period was marked by the rise of what has been called Jacksonian democracy. The influx of many people from other lands and the migrations into the Middle West and West created the term *social mobility*. The average citizen was not bound by birthright, name, or position to an inflexible and unchanging status. With a good education, he believed, he would be able to improve his station in life, prosper, and rise to a higher status in the eyes of his fellow citizens. The land-grant colleges, state colleges, and universities were created by state and federal governmental actions. This new emphasis on higher education certainly influenced the elementary schools to broaden their curricula.

Two forces had combined to change the administrative role of the principal. Although he still functioned as a head teacher who regulated classes, inspected the plant, passed on instructions to teachers, maintained the school building, and taught classes, one of the first factors to bring about a change in administration was simply that of increased enrollment, causing more complex physical conditions within the school. In short, even as the superintendent of schools had been forced to find administrative help because of the growth factor, so the head teacher unknowingly began to develop the characteristics of an executive, because of the size of the school and of the student body. He had to be released from teaching duties to take over the so-called housekeeping chores of the school.

The second force that influenced the rise in status of the head teacher to that of principal, however, was of a more subtle nature. The common citizen knew there were no limitations, except those of his own making, on his future welfare and prospects for a position in life. The elementary school had to perform its function of preparing the child in a positive and purposeful way. The elementary school had reached the place where it required administrators who could develop the kind of program the community needed and wanted.

Thus, the fourth period in community development took up this new emphasis, which demanded personality, character, and citizenship development. From the middle of the nineteenth century into the early years of the twentieth, the problems that people considered meaningful and significant formed the core approach to learning. The complexities of a changing society were recognized, and children were supposed to prepare to live more successfully, so the learning experiences in the classroom were sprinkled with morals and lessons designed to give the pupil necessary understandings and skills. The American way of life was changing so rapidly during these years that pressing social problems arose which were strangely new and foreign.

It was during this fourth period that the principal achieved a status entailing more prestige and power in educational affairs. He had to grow in stature, since the need for a professionally-minded person was clearly evident. The pattern of administrative behavior changed to that of a sense of responsibility for the organization and management of the pupils and of the total plant. In effect, the principal was attaining the status of the executive who could employ devices and techniques of control that were not merely handed down to him. As society changed, the principalship had to change to keep abreast.

It was imperative that some central authority be invested in a designated executive, especially for the large elementary school, for reasons of economy and efficiency. A professional person was needed to know what the community needed and desired, with the ability to help the whole school staff to reach those objectives.

Perhaps, in viewing these four periods of community development and seeing the rise of the principalship in the light of changes and demands of our society, some question may arise as to how adequately the offices of the principals were staffed, and how well-qualified these school executives were. This question can best be answered by reviewing the known practices of many school administrators responsible for appointing the elementary school principals during the third and part of the fourth periods of community development. The superintendent had little choice in making a selection, since there were actually no persons qualified by training or experience for elevation to the principalship. In many instances the teacher who was considered the best disciplinarian, instructor, and the most physically able member of the staff, would be appointed to the administrative post. Again, an administrative assistant in the central office might be given the responsibility for a certain school. Yet one of the most important educational tasks was often neglected, for a large number of these principals were unqualified to give adequate supervision to the instructional program. At this stage some supervisory leadership came from appointed persons through the central administrative office, leaving to the principals the problems of discipline, clerical duties, and other executive matters, in addition to their own classroom teaching. Because this kind of administrative organization became entrenched, the professionalization of the principalship was slow in coming into its own, even with the demands for leadership evident in the fourth period of community development.[16]

Although steady progress had been made during the past hundred years toward professionalizing the position of the elementary principal, even the need for office space was apparently met only as a new role was played in the internal affairs of the school. Administrative behavior is conditioned by the fact that adequate office space is necessary to carry out the many school objectives. Therefore, as the principal became more an educational administrator, he needed more favorable surroundings in which to perform his office duties. To say it another way, there was a recognized need for more efficiency in administration. Superintendents of schools, members of boards of education, and other individuals soon realized that if the principal and his staff were required to perform their duties under space handicaps, there would be a tendency to yield to the difficulties of their surroundings. There would be an inevitable tendency to adjust to low levels and standards of efficiency.[17] By the same token, adequate space provisions would tend to lead to higher levels of efficiency. Thus schoolhouse planners soon recognized the need for available work space, and the principalship moved another step upward to a position of recognized executive caliber.

Effects of Social, Economic, and Political Factors During the Twentieth Century

The routine duties of the principal which were established as a part of the change from head teacher to principalship during the 1800s carried well into the twentieth century. Even today, in fact, it is not uncommon for some elementary principals to conduct their schools in the tradition of the past. Preparation programs for elementary principals, as well as writings in professional journals, have abandoned the mechanical approach to administration.

During the 1900s schools have endured, but changes have emerged as a result of two world wars and the Great Depression, in addition to a more recent period of social unrest. During the first half of the twentieth century, administrators and teachers were faced with new demands from social, economic, and political factors which developed both at home and abroad. Should educators give direction for improving the human condition, or should they continue their impersonal, mechanistic approach to school administration? The serious threat of the economic depression and the rise of totalitarianism in the world brought this social concern to the forefront. The Progressive Education Association appointed, in 1933, a committee on social-economic problems which formulated a policy under the title, "A Call to the Teachers of the Nation." The Depression and the spread of totalitarian ideologies forced the profession to look at the possibilities of designing an educational system that would lead to the creation of a new society. By 1941, democracy faced the danger of destruction. The essence of a new report by the Progressive Education Association entitled "Progressive Education: Its Philosophy and Challenge" was that the dominant ideals of democracy should provide the direction for education.[18] Administrators were now examining their behavior from the social and psychological approach. Business and industrial research began to have an impact on educators.[19] Administrators were now studying the aspects of administration in which their behavior made a difference. By the middle of the twentieth century, the group dynamics movement was being felt and democracy was the key word in school administration. One yearbook of the Department of Elementary School Principals stated: " . . . under these new concepts the classroom teacher no longer is a person who follows the directions of someone else . . . the classroom teacher rather than the principal or supervisor assumes primary responsibility for education of children."[20]

Elementary principals had to identify a new role as well as new patterns of behavior. Principals have studied and profited from the findings of such groups as the Cooperative Program in Educational Administration and the University Council for Educational Administration. The latter undertook a major study of performance and personality of elementary principals on a national scale. Although much information from the study has contributed to understanding administrative behavior, we are far from being out of the woods in our preparation programs or in-service efforts at improvement. Both from the point of view of research findings[21] and empirical knowledge,[22] there is ample evidence that we have not yet solved the constellation of problems related to administering elementary schools to the point where it makes a difference.

The move toward autonomy for the local school, discussed in the previous chapter, is yet to be realized, but it stands to reason that the population explosion which has engulfed the schools, the urban problem, and the need for coordination of community services with the elementary school are but a few of the circumstances pressuring the elementary school to become truly a community school.

THE CHALLENGE OF PROFESSIONALIZATION

It readily can be seen from the historical examination of the principalship that great strides have been made in the development of the position. As schools and society have changed, the duties and responsibilities have become more demanding and complex. The principalship has attained a high degree of worth and value in the opinion of many citizens. Yet the elementary school principal knows there is still much to be done to bring the position to a level of universal regard and to make it comparable to other professional occupations in terms of trust and responsibility. The purpose of this section is to review the career possibilities, examine the certification requirements, describe preparatory needs of the position, and discuss standards and procedures for selection and appointment to the principalship. As each problem is discussed, a major question should be kept in mind: What can be done to raise the principalship to higher levels of professionalization?

Professional Career Status for the Principalship

The rise in the general professional status of the principalship becomes apparent after tracing its historical development. Furthermore, consideration of the demands of the position indicate that only a skilled, professionally trained person might expect to discharge the many functions efficiently. The specific purpose of this section is to show how the principal may further his professional career status, since an increasing number of personnel and educational responsibilities are being delegated to him. Perhaps the first requirement for career status rests upon the quality of leadership demonstrated. As a person becomes qualified to give leadership, superintendents, boards of education, and community patrons generally will be willing to grant him opportunities for applying his professional knowledge. The challenge of demonstrating personal worth in the elementary schools may reveal the administrator as the truly professional person he is, and there is promise that more school executives will accept this challenge and continue to move ahead professionally.

The principalship will be a more appealing career position when there is freedom from domination by the central office or other agencies that limit the effectiveness of the principal. Of course, this is not meant to suggest that each school should set up its own brand of autonomy, but surely some guidelines for the operation of an autonomous school are in the making. Actually, the administrator needs the opportunity to effect changes in behavior that will be consistent with sound educational objectives. He needs the support of all involved, but he must be free to exert leadership.

The elementary school principalship will earn a professional career status when salary schedules are improved. When school executives of mediocre ability are appointed to the position and demonstrate inadequate leadership, there is little hope that higher salaries will be forthcoming. By the same token, low salaries will attract few capable leaders to the profession. Perhaps greater professional status will be achieved when principals with proven ability insist on salaries commensurate with their preparation, experience, and worth to the schools. This goal will have to be attained through organized leadership, and such leadership seems to be taking form in a number of national professional organizations.

Contribution of Professional Organizations

Professional organizations may be one answer to elevating the status of the principalship. The public relations function can be carried to a high degree through local and national groups. Mere membership in a group cannot in itself be the answer to attaining greater career status, however. The value of these organizations rests in the services they can render for professional growth and for unifying principals in their career and education goals. Through these organizations the principal may identify himself with worthwhile causes, and such association helps to give him the earned status of a professional person.

In connection with the contributions made by the various educational associations in survey reports, conferences, journal articles, etc., it should be pointed out that the individual principal still bears the primary responsibility for his own status. He needs the contributions of the various organizations, but unless he recognizes his own role and assumes responsibility for making a personal contribution of some kind, there is little likelihood of much professional progress for the principalship as a whole.

A principal often lacks interest in and enthusiasm for personal progress leading to a better educational program. National and state organizations have difficulty securing his attention and support. In short, many elementary school principals have not made a maximum personal contribution to their profession. This is not to say that progress has not been achieved. On the contrary, the principalship has been advanced, and many people have been and still are exerting leadership and influence. Of course, not every principal can be expected to produce contributions to the profession of national or even local importance. But the conscientious principal has the responsibility to his profession to make his maximum contribution in his own way. He contributes when he makes systematic efforts to read professional material; when, in spite of a busy schedule, he attends some of the meetings that help him to feel part of the national effort to improve educational opportunities; even when he does something as minor as sending in specialized data when requested.

Since a professional organization or association is only as productive and influential as its membership, its contributions are determined by the quality of the group. The principal must decide for himself how well he has been contributing to his profession, and in what ways he may improve or increase his contribution. Whether or not he makes a large contribution, he is still responsible for performing at a level consistent with his potentialities.

The principal as an individual joins the ranks of those who are known as professional people when he is protected by certification requirements based on sound principles of selection for the job and preparation. With high standards for admission to the principalship and adequate payment for service, there is little doubt that the principal's attitude toward his position will change and that he will be held in a higher regard by other citizens. There is no single method for achieving a professional career status, yet it may be said that the principal will find it difficult to achieve this status until he has demonstrated the leadership skills which are vital to the on-going program of the school. The principal can move more rapidly to a higher status if he accepts this challenge.

Certification and Preparation Problems

It has been suggested that certification requirements and preparation programs for the principalship will contribute to the professionalization of the principal's position. But, since there is no nationwide agreement on either one of these problems, some possible solutions will be presented: a general certification plan with specific implications for leadership; a method by which the principal may utilize present certification requirements for personal evaluation; and suggestions for a preparation program that will develop the necessary leadership skills. These discussions will emphasize the development of certain skills, and they should serve as checkpoints for the principal who views his own certification and preparation problems in terms of improving administrative behavior. It should be noted, however, that under the leadership at the national level of the Department of Elementary School Principals,[23] a series of small regional conferences were held over a period of several years to study ways of improving pre-service programs, recruitment, selection, and in-service programs. The conferences were attended by State Department of Education personnel, university professors, U.S. Office of Education representatives, and elementary school principals. The results of these conferences have fostered improved procedures and programs for elementary principals.

Certification requirements for prospective principals should rest on certain factors that will insure a high level of standardization. Probably no agreement can be reached on the exact nature of these requirements or the agency which should issue the certificate. However, there are some points that should be considered basic for all certification agencies. *First, the certificate should define competencies deemed necessary and important for the prospective principal.* Details of such personal qualities may not be agreed upon completely, but certain desirable characteristics should be clearly and accurately set forth. *Second, certification should rest upon the kind of preparation the individual needs for internal school leadership problems.* It is understood that the certification agencies and the colleges will work closely together in such matters. *Third, teaching abilities should be considered in the certification of the prospective principal.* This is not to say that because a person is a good teacher he may become certified as an administrator. Yet he must demonstrate proficiency in classroom teaching and have some experience in working with children in the elementary school. *Fourth, some evaluative procedures should be set up to appraise all candidates for certification.* Certain tests may be used, advisory committees appointed for appraisal, and other evaluative processes designed to render a decision on the predictable proficiency of the candidate. *Fifth, certification will hinge upon the recommendation of the university or college that has contributed to the preparation of the prospective administrator.* These institutions are in a strategic position for determining a person's acceptability for certification, and the information they can provide should be used. *Sixth, certification should be a cooperative matter, involving local, state, and national professional agencies, including the institutions of higher learning.* Steps can be worked out to insure a careful analysis of certification requirements, and to establish ways and means of appraising the candidate by cooperative endeavors. *Seventh, the program for certification should remain flexible enough to meet the needs of all schools within the state.* There are dangers in this proposal, of course, in that some localities will take advantage of such a certification program. Too often communities permit the minimum requirements to become the maximum ones. However, it is natural that some small, rural elementary schools often will not attract the type of person who seeks a position in the better-paying urban centers. It is clear that the needs are quite different, and these call for appropriate differentiation in certification requirements. Such flexibility should not reduce certification to a meaningless state; instead, schools should be so classified that certified administrators will find certain schools open to them. Both the school and the principal may then progress through various stages of selection according to certain standards. This procedure will provide an incentive for growth. If an inadequate school situation is recognized as such, it will almost inevitably attract a less desirable type of administrator. Of course, the weakness in this proposal is that a poor executive may contribute little to an already unsatisfactory school situation. At least, however, certification will be realistic and meaningful; better supervision may lead both the inferior principal and school to a higher level of certification. These certification problems cannot be solved by organizational schemes alone; they will be solved only when elementary principals themselves demand and work for higher professional standards.

A principal may use the certification requirements of his own state to appraise his particular situation. In studying his state requirements, he may in a sense gauge his personal progress by assessing what he has achieved in the past and what still needs to be done. These certification items may assist him in planning for university course work in the future. In effect, he is able to plan his personal program of development with certification requirements helping him to identify goals for a more successful administration. Generally speaking, most people will give little attention to certification requirements unless the certifying agency has the power to require future and incumbent principals to satisfy the stipulations over a given period of time. Again, the principals themselves should insist that these agencies be given such jurisdiction over the certification policies of the office. Professional growth should be required of every administrator.

Since preparation of the individual for the principalship is an integral part of the entire problem of certification, and since preparation leads to a higher professional status, some attention must be given to this factor. Evidence from studies shows the elementary school principal in a much more favorable light as an educator than he was a decade ago. More persons are receiving higher degrees and securing professional training. Possession of a college degree, however, does not signify that a person is qualified to be an elementary school principal. It is a depressing fact that the professional preparation received by the principal seems to have had little or no effect on his leadership ability.[24] The demands for leadership in the principalship are of such a nature that only through careful study and systematic preparation can any person achieve the status of a professional educator.

The following discussion of general course work is offered to suggest the type of preparation needed for the person planning to become a principal. The fact that colleges have many problems of providing the "right" courses indicates that there is still a need for more widespread agreement on an optimum program. In general, at least four areas of preparation are considered basic. First, a general kind of preparation will provide understanding from the liberal arts point of view. The individual will have an academic major in a field of his interest, with supporting work in other disciplines. Second, he will have the core courses in the field of general administration, as well as specific courses emphasizing the development of administrative leadership. This integrated program will include supervision, curriculum, guidance, tests and measurements, specific administration courses, and so on. Third, attention should be given to the various human-relations courses that will develop in the individual an understanding of his role in society. Fourth, he should be enrolled in a directed internship program. Through this experience he will have the opportunity to practice leadership skills under controlled conditions and to further the development of new skills. Of course, the organization and administration of such a program will be expensive, but there is reason to believe that concerted efforts by the professional organizations and cooperative action by universities will result in a general overhauling of graduate programs. The united efforts of local, state, and national associations of principals working with state departments of education and the universities can result in plans that will lead to better preparation of more leaders for the elementary schools throughout the nation. Some states now require some type of internship or direct field experience as part of the certification requirements. The Ohio Department of Education, with support from the state principals' association, has such a requirement, effective January 1972. But of even more importance is the model program for principal preparation which will be implemented in Ohio beginning in June 1973.[25]

Selection and Appointment to the Principalship
Some school systems have elaborately-organized programs for the selection and appointment of elementary school principals. More frequently, a candidate is hired on the basis of procedures conducted informally by the school superintendent and, occasionally, by some of the board of education members. The principalship will be on a higher plane when there are better-

Evolution of the Elementary School Principalship

organized selection and appointment programs based on realistic standards of training and performance. In spite of the widespread feeling among school executives that low salaries for many of the administrative positions may rule out any formalized hiring program, there should be more systematic procedures for procuring persons to fill these jobs.

Standards for the Principalship. Although state departments of education, the universities, and professional organizations will state the certification and preparation needs for the principalship, there are certain local needs to be considered, especially in cases where it is difficult to attract top personnel. Also, in cases where standards are not well-defined—perhaps because of the absence of local and state requirements—it is highly important that school superintendents and the principals themselves demand that a set of high standards be imposed. There should be at least five minimum requirements for appointment to the principalship. First, as an educator, the prospective principal should give evidence of proficiency and experience. Second, as an administrator, the person may either have experience as a principal or demonstrate that during his teaching career he was engaged in some kind of administrative work. It is expected that preparation and *other* administrative performance be a part of his background—such as chairmanships of responsible committees and positions of trust that call for planning, organization, and leadership skills. Third, the candidate for appointment should demonstrate some knowledge of and experience in personnel management. The prospective principal should be a person who works well with people. Fourth, the requirement that is largely glossed over or forgotten is that of some skill in public relations, or the art of communicating with the citizens of the community. Finally, the person to be selected for the position should have some familiarity with business procedures. He will have to work with many matters that are not directly concerned with educational affairs but which are highly important for directing the total school program.

This brief discussion of five areas suggests some minimum standards for selection and appointment of the elementary school principal. But unless current practices are specifically organized, the standards will become meaningless or unimportant. Some suggestions are now offered which will help improve selection, and may help the prospective principal in seeking employment and preparing to meet certain standards.

The professionalization of the principalship is a challenge that can be met as career-minded administrators demand better certification laws. Then, as standards for selection are set realistically high, prospective candidates will know what preparation is needed and how to go about obtaining it. Systematic plans for selection will further elevate the principalship to a career status, when meaningful appointments are made based on merit as the chief requirement.

THE CHALLENGE OF LEADERSHIP DEVELOPMENT

It is unrealistic to assume that certification requirements, university preparation programs, and local hiring plans will guarantee superior leadership for all elementary schools. Although appointments to the position can be made more wisely if these plans are in effect, there will be many individuals who will be deficient in some areas. Therefore, there will always be a need for growth and skill development for the person already on the job. Even as an in-service program has been emphasized for faculty members, it is equally important that consideration be given to the in-service needs of the principal. He must be provided opportunities for learning new skills and keeping abreast of changing conditions.

Characteristics of a Good Principal

Before in-service plans or skill preparation programs are employed, one must know the desired behavior to teach the prospective principal. As suggested, he must have had various experiences before he is considered for the appointment. We have already pointed out what makes the principal an acceptable administrator. However, further emphasis on this problem may bring into even sharper focus the necessary specific skills, and will also serve to summarize some of their common factors. Although much emphasis has been given to the development of know-how in administrative behavior, there is a point beyond which knowledge does not add measurably to successful leadership.

> The faculty of the Main Street Elementary School were relaxing with coffee during a break of a mid-semester workshop. Their principal was comparatively new, in that he was beginning only his third year with them. Although he had been appointed to this excellent school on the basis of a superior professional preparation program and record, the staff had wondered how he would fit into the situation. They recognized his merits in training and experience, and were gratified to learn as they worked with him that it was important to him that he earn respect from the janitor up to the individual faculty member. He was concerned with everyone's problem, and he seemed to know how to deal with situations. His consideration of the older teachers was marked, while his sensitivity to community factors was just as pronounced as his personal enthusiasm and devotion to his tasks. His faculty members were speaking well of him at this moment, and apparently he had earned the name of a successful leader.

Knowledge of the job at hand must be combined with the ability to associate oneself with other people, to lead discussions, give directions, and to use a personal and professional philosophy of life and education that contribute to overall effectiveness.

To pinpoint more specifically what makes the good principal, a list is given below of behaviors and skills practiced by the effective executive. This list defines the successful principal in terms of what he actually does. The behaviors and functions given here may serve the additional purposes of describing necessary skills and outlining personal objectives for all elementary school principals. This checklist represents the thinking of many administrators who felt a need to define good administration in behavioral terms.[26]

1. The principal is a leader in *curriculum* who:
   —knows and accepts the existing educational philosophy of his total school system.
   —has developed and uses a personal and professional philosophy of life and education that is sound.
   —knows source materials which help in curriculum development.
   —adjust the curriculum to community and pupil needs.
   —utilizes community resources in implementing the curriculum.
   —encourages the experimental approach to teaching and the curriculum among faculty members.
   —is responsible for the total curriculum and gives definite, positive leadership through workshops, subject-matter study groups, etc.

2. The principal is a leader in *personnel* who:
   —has the ability to accept and to respect the individual teacher as a worthwhile member of the faculty based upon each person's personal characteristics, background, etc.
   —capitalizes upon individual strengths, interest, and talents, of each staff member in making classroom assignments and other specified duties.
   —recognizes teacher strengths and weaknesses, and complements and lends aid for improvement through personal counseling.
   —practices the psychological approach in staff management through cooperative planning; individual and group relationships; creating a permissive atmosphere for staff expression; and clarifying specific teacher problems in relation to curriculum, to principles of child development, and to the organization of the school in terms of rules and regulations.
   —knows and employs a variety of techniques in working with staff in solving common problems.
   —evaluates his own behavior objectively and revises future actions, behavior, and growth in light of the results.
   —develops sensitivity to people.
   —fosters, stimulates, and gives direction to professional growth in each teacher, and is also willing to learn.

3. The principal is a leader in *public relations* who:
   —uses the P.T.A. and similar organizations to promote pupil health and welfare.
   —uses these organizations to assist school personnel in developing, defining, or understanding school objectives.

—exercises leadership in promoting parent participation in common problems of the school and of the community.
—encourages parent visits; and facilitates both parent-to-school and staff-to-home visits.
—develops a regular, systematic method of reporting to parents upon particular school developments.
—uses increasingly student participation in the school public relations program.
—studies and practices techniques in training teachers to handle public relations more adequately.
—is alert to good newsworthy stories about the total school program.
—uses parents and community citizens to promote the school public relations affairs.
—watches constantly how to improve on how the school communicates with the community.

4. The principal is a leader in the area of *pupil-teacher relationships* who:
—makes available to the teacher a knowledge of the pupil and the total group.
—encourages teachers to be professional in treating confidential material.
—maintains student records, organizes a reference system, and encourages periodic teacher reports on the pupils.
—encourages teachers in developing respect for the child as a human being.
—helps teachers to distinguish between cause and effect in problem situations and to recognize certain behaviors as symptoms of underlying causes.
—assists the teacher in solving a pupil problem and sees implications of a problem for the total group situation.
—encourages teachers to use teacher-pupil planning in the classroom for the development of pupil leadership and fellowship.
—sets an example for the school in his own relationships with each child by recognizing him as an individual.

5. The principal is a leader for *non-instructional personnel* who:
—employs the pscychological approach to individual and group management by encouraging participation and by making them feel a necessary part of the total school.
—knows the duties to be performed by each person, preferably by a planned job analysis program in cooperation with the central administrative office.
—clarifies duties for mutual understandings.
—sets up definite channels through which requests for services are cleared.
—notifies personnel of special requests in ample, advance time.
—respects work-schedule hours.

6. The principal is a leader in his *relations with the central office* who:
   —understands and tries to accept the policies, situations, and conditions under which the central office works.
   —establishes rapport between his school and the central office.
   —knows and uses the proper, established channels for clearing, requesting, complaining, etc.
   —capitalizes on the special and unique services that are available from the central office to supplement, implement, and enrich his own office.
   —assumes the responsibility for aiding the central office in developing policies and plans.
7. The principal is a leader in *guidance* who:
   —is familiar with and calls upon outside agencies to promote, develop, and protect child health and welfare.
   —understands the total child in relationship to his adjustment.
   —uses as many sources as possible in getting information about the child.
   —is sensitive to the changing needs of each child and is geared to take care of those needs with a flexible organization.
   —is aware of the interest patterns and abilities peculiar to each child; uses these interest patterns and abilities to aid in pupil's total adjustment, as well as to further the learning process.
   —assists teachers in collecting evidence from all possible sources that will help to shed light on adjustment problems.
8. The principal is a leader in *articulation* with the secondary school and other schools who:
   —has an objective, professional attitude toward co-workers.
   —respects honest differences of opinion and judgment.
   —maintains an objective, open mind about himself and the work of others.
   —understands the programs of other schools and sees the relationship between elementary and secondary programs.
   —keeps his staff appraised with other programs and relationships.
   —encourages and arranges for visits of his teachers with total school personnel in the system.
9. The principal is a leader in the areas of *school supplies, plant, and equipment* who:
   —knows what supplies and equipment are available.
   —informs staff of available items and optimum ways of using them.
   —allots items fairly and impartially.
   —furnishes teachers with available items to help them perform satisfactorily and to broaden their concepts of what might be done.
   —encourages continuing exploration of newer and better supplies.
   —uses ingenuity by staff in devising or substituting items that are needed but not available from present stocks.
   —submits request orders properly to central office.

10. The principal is a leader and an *organizer* who:
    —organizes the school in such a way that its purpose and functions may well be accomplished; particularly, so that "growth" of the children in learning and otherwise takes place.
    —works cooperatively in planning and organizing with staff to insure more effective and efficient personnel use.
    —keeps flexibility in the organization.
    —assumes responsibility for making decisions in terms of the over-all situation.
    —maintains as far as possible an organization that promotes mental health and emotional stability of total school personnel.

These ten functions summarize the scope and duties of the principalship. Discharging these functions efficiently and practicably is basic to successful principalship. The principal will need help in attaining the skills necessary for good performance even after his appointment to the position. There are proved programs in which he may develop a higher degree of proficiency; these programs will now be considered.

Programs for Developing Leadership Competencies

Attention is given in this section to those programs of leadership development generally pursued after the usual university course work has been completed. However, the institutions of higher learning may still be actively involved in this phase of development, as will be shown later. There are three programs of leadership development available to the principal or the prospective candidate, in addition to specialized graduate work at a college or university: the apprenticeship program, the internship, and the in-service administrative program.

Apprenticeship or Cadet Training. Since many people aspire to positions of leadership in the elementary school, this brief discussion is designed to stimulate more opportunities for apprenticeship training and to offer some suggestions for its organization and administration. The apprenticeship program generally develops within a school system for the purpose of discovering new leaders and providing on-the-job experiences to promote administrative skills. Many cities find the apprenticeship approach a useful device for supplying principals and assistant principals from within the ranks of the faculty.

The advantages of the apprenticeship training program are numerous. Probably an outstanding feature or strength is the practicing of leadership skills even while teaching. The prospective principal will be given the opportunity to assume certain administrative responsibilities in order to discover how well he can actually handle them, and also to learn whether or not he likes administration. He is learning administration by being a part of an actual school situation, but is still regarded as a member of the faculty. Disadvantages to the program can accrue from poor supervision of the apprentice or failure to give proper guidance and encouragement. There is little need to fear that "inbreeding" will result if the apprentice is required to meet the other standards for appointment.

The details of organizing and administering a good apprenticeship training program will be presented later, but some suggestions should furnish a perspective of what may be expected of this program. First, the objectives of the apprenticeship should be stated. This step will be taken by the administrative officers of the school system, the principals' organizations, and certain faculty personnel. Second, policies and details for the type of apprenticeship will be worked out on the basis of experiences needed, allotments of time, selection of apprentices, and other factors included in the program. Third, understandings as to performance, evaluations, and future outcomes should be defined.

The pattern for selection, appointment, and the actual experiences during training will be very similar to that described for internship. Whatever applies to the internship is generally applicable to the apprenticeship. The apprentice is in reality a full-time, bona fide faculty member who is serving in much the same capacity as the intern. This factor might well be the only point of differentiation between these two preparational leadership programs. Therefore, the following detailed account of the internship should also suggest how the apprenticeship may be organized and administered.

Internship. Business and industrial executives have become increasingly aware of the importance of their supervisory development programs.[27] Many of our future foremen, superintendents, and executives will be developed through training programs of various kinds. The nature and purpose of the internship is to improve the quality of school leadership, to provide field experiences leading to skill development, and to improve the overall school program. Attention is given here to the ways in which leadership skills may be developed; some broad plans for organizing and administering the internship will be suggested. A prospective candidate will be able to gain a better perspective of the role of the elementary school principal if he serves as an intern in some school. At least nine objectives are evident in a good internship program:[28]

1. To develop a broader, more comprehensive view of educational administration,
2. To provide actual experiences in carrying out real administrative responsibilities,
3. To develop needed skills and techniques in leadership found useful in the elementary school,
4. To help the prospective administrator to translate good educational and administrative theory into practice,

5. To help to recognize and to determine the personal qualities that make a successful principal,
6. To stimulate professional growth on the part of those persons who sponsor the internship,
7. To make available to the administration consultant services of staff members of the universities,
8. To help the cooperating administration to identify executive talents and abilities within their own ranks,
9. To help the cooperating administration to select administrative personnel from outside their own staff.

These purposes emphasize value not only for the intern, but also to the cooperating school system. There is usually a flow of qualified people to that system which has a good internship program. In addition, turnover of school personnel will be considerably reduced as faculty and administrators feel the influence of the internship. There seems to be little doubt of the incentives for better leadership and more advanced study as a stimulating internship influences a school system. Of course, no intern should be exploited by being relegated to the status of a highly-paid clerk. Also, it should be pointed out that whenever a good teacher enters such a program, there is inevitably a loss to the teaching ranks.

In organizing the internship program, the university will follow generally the three-point pattern stated in the section on the apprenticeship. Although the different aspects of each program call for some variations in organization, many suggestions apply to both the apprenticeship and the internship. Faculty personnel should be involved in organizing these programs and should understand the purposes. When they have been prepared for these apprentices and interns to work within their school, the faculty are in a better position to cooperate and contribute effectively.

When the prospective candidate has been selected according to procedures similar to those for selecting the regular principal, he will follow a supervised, charted course within the school. According to the policy of the university as to the number of semesters involved and how the time will be divided, the intern will generally need certain experiences. There will be emphasis, of course, on those methods designed to foster his leadership development while he is performing in a school situation. He will take designated field trips for definite purposes, analyze the experiences, and evaluate them in the light of personal considerations. He will be given opportunities for dealing with group situations and problems. The theories of group dynamics will be brought into play as he solves actual problems with people. The curriculum problems at various grade levels will occupy some of his time, when teachers bring significant questions to him for an answer. The case approach will be emphasized, with real boys and girls as problem cases needing his help. Assignments made from community experiences will bring home to him the realization that working in the community takes planning and skill. Additional work with special-child problems, supervision, discipline cases, and so on, will constitute much of what he will do as an intern and, at times, as an acting assistant principal.

Evaluation of performance will be made continuously. University and school personnel will assist him as he makes his own self-evaluations. Thus, with a variety of experiences enabling him to practice his leadership skills, and with opportunities provided for development of additional ones, the intern receives careful guidance and helpful encouragement in his program of growth.

In-service Plans. There is probably no disagreement among educators that the average incumbent principal can and must improve professionally. His selection and appointment to the principalship should have been made on the basis of merit. However, in spite of many wise appointments, there is still need for all administrators to grow on the job, and there is a decided need for further training for those persons who are less qualified but who have received appointment. Although superintendents should not impose an in-service plan for school administrators, they must provide some kind of leadership to bring principals to the point where they will want to grow professionally. Since there are many techniques and devices for encouraging this advancement, the specific purpose here is to suggest how such techniques may be used so that the principal will feel impelled to take advantage of in-service plans. Development of this self-initiative or willingness to improve one's status seems to be the core of a successful in-service program for the elementary school principal.

Leadership for an aggressive in-service program must also come from the state association of elementary principals. At the local level the principals should form themselves into an organization that will in turn elect good, aggressive leaders. Finally, the local superintendent and officials of the state department of education can be useful in furthering in-service plans.

To insure more initiative on the part of the individual principal, several plans of action are now suggested. First, the state association of elementary principals will accept the responsibility and take the initiative for supporting in-service activities. It will continuously encourage them and furnish ideas, suggestions, materials, and even personnel for fostering a receptive attitude among the administrators. Second, the local association will take steps to promote in-service work. Committees should constantly study ways to develop professional growth and report to the membership. Plans of action that will involve each person in active in-service work should be worked out and adopted by the members. Each principal will, of course, be free to find and to work out the plan best suited to his particular needs and interests, but he will be involved in worthwhile, recognized activity. The local organization should devise some controls for initiating and following through on the in-service activities of the membership. Third, funds will be obtained (from the local school system) to bring in regular consultants from the universities. The state department of education may also furnish consultants. Fourth, the local superintendent of schools will be requested to set up performance checks and ratings if they have not already been established. These evaluations will uncover administrative needs and stimulate the principal to profit from the findings by embarking upon some in-service activity. Fifth, the central administrative school staff will be requested to make annual suggestions, in the light of evaluations, regarding their opinions of in-service activities by the association or by the individual principal. Sixth, self-evaluation forms will be worked out cooperatively by the group. These evaluative activities will be encouraged by the association and help will be offered by colleagues or by the central office staff to group members who request it.

Clearly, motivation should arise at the local level. Usually the leadership will come from within this group. However, when the group is willing to delegate the supervision and evaluative activities to the central office, and actually requests such help, there will be an extended use of the many devices and tools of in-service training. Motivation for the use of these techniques should arise from local and state associations, as well as from the superintendent's office, the state department of education, and so on. Some important aspects of in-service education for principals are attendance and participation at professional meetings, reading journals and research materials, participation in community organizations, formal and informal study groups, workshops, communication bulletins, evaluation committees, field trips, surveys, case studies, and participation in action-research projects.

SUMMARY

The rich history of the elementary school principalship was a slow evolutionary process. Some of the factors which hastened its development to a professional position were (1) the development of the graded school, (2) the rapid growth of cities, (3) recognition of the principal as the supervisory head of the school, (4) the relinquishing of teaching responsibilities, and (5) the establishment of the Department of Elementary School Principals of the National Education Association.

The school administrator is faced with many challenges that can be met only as he is prepared and able to give positive leadership. To raise the status of the principalship, which in turn will encourage better-prepared leaders, certification requirements of the states need to be studied. The principals themselves should insist on higher standards, better preparation, and definite policies for selection and appointment.

Leadership development should begin with a knowledge of what makes a good principal. In addition to formal course work in a college or university, leadership can be improved through programs of apprenticeship, internship, and in-service plans. Each approach to skill development and preparation is designed to give meaning and depth to the principalship. The in-service plan probably needs more direction in that it is, for the most part, a voluntary matter after the administrator is appointed to his position. Motivation for personal growth should come from local levels, although the national organizations may furnish leadership in many ways.

SUGGESTED READINGS

Better Principals for Our Schools: A Cooperative Approach to Competence. Washington, D.C.: Department of Elementary School Principals, National Education Association, 1961.

Campbell, Roald F. and Russell T. Gregg. *Administrative Behavior in Education.* New York: Harper and Row, 1957, Chapters 6, 8, and 12.

Culbertson, Jack A. and Stephen P. Hencley, eds. *Preparing Administrators: New Perspectives.* Columbus, Ohio: University Council for Educational Administration, 1962, Chapters 1, 5, and 7.

Cunningham, Luvern L. "Continuing Professional Education for Elementary Principals." *The National Elementary Principal* 44, No. 5 (April 1965): 60–68.

Forester, J. J. "Selecting and Training Elementary School Principals." *The National Elementary Principal* 24 (October 1954): 32–35.

"Forty Years of D.E.S.P." *The National Elementary Principal,* February 1961, p. 30.

"In Big Cities, the Principals Say . . . ." *The National Elementary Principal* 32 (February 1953): 31–34.

Jenson, T. J., James B. Burr, William H. Coffield, and Ross Neagley. *Elementary School Administration.* 2d ed. Boston: Allyn and Bacon, 1967, Chapter 13.

McIntyre, Kenneth E. "The Selection of Elementary School Principals." *The National Elementary Principal* 44, No. 5 (April 1955): 42–46.

Newell, C. A. "Interns Practice Administration." *The School Executive* 74 (March 1955): 86–87.

Norton, J. K. "Preparation Programs for Administrators." *The School Executive* 75 (January 1956): 84–85.

Pharis, William L. *In-Service Education of Elementary School Principals.* Washington, D.C.: Department of Elementary School Principals, National Education Association, 1966.

Pierce, Paul R. *The Origin and Development of the Public School Principalship.* Chicago: University of Chicago Press, 1935.

Shuster, Albert H. "Principals for Nongraded Schools: Pre-service and In-service Education." *The National Elementary Principal* 47 (January 1968): 10–14.

Notes

1. Paul Revere Pierce, *The Origin and Development of the Public School Principalship* (Chicago: University of Chicago Press, 1935), p. 7.
2. Ibid., p. 8.
3. Ibid.
4. Ibid., p. 9.
5. Ibid., p. 12.
6. Ibid.
7. Ibid., p. 16.
8. *Fifteenth Annual Report of the Board of Education of St. Louis,* 1869, p. 133.
9. Pierce, *Origin and Development,* p. 22.
10. J. C. Morrison, "The Principalship Develops Supervision Status," *Tenth Yearbook, Bulletin of the Department of Elementary School Principals* (Washington, D.C.: National Education Association, 1931), p. 160.
11. Pierce, *Origin and Development,* pp. 23, 24.
12. See the yearbooks published in the 1920s by the National Education Association.
13. *Factors Affecting Educational Administration: Guideposts for Research and Action,* No. 2 of the College of Education Monograph Series on the School-Community Development Study (Columbus, Ohio: The Ohio State University, 1955), foreword.
14. *Annual Report* 1970–71 (Washington, D.C.: National Association of Elementary School Principals), p. 8.
15. Adapted by permission from *Administering the Elementary School,* William C. Reavis, Paul R. Pierce, Edward H. Stulken, and Bertrand L. Smith, pp. 3–5. Copyright,© 1953, by Prentice-Hall, Inc., Englewood Cliffs, N. J.
16. Henry J. Otto, *Elementary School Organization and Administration,* 3d ed. (New York: Appleton-Century-Crofts, 1954), p. 653.
17. Paul B. Jacobson, William C. Reavis, and James D. Logsdon, *The Effective School Principal* (Englewood Cliffs, N. J.: Prentice-Hall, 1954), p. 429.
18. Elmer H. Wilds, *The Foundations of Modern Education* (New York: Rinehart, 1942), p. 601.
19. See Chapter 1 for some of these studies.
20. *The Elementary School Principalship —Today and Tomorrow,* Twenty-Seventh Yearbook of the Department of Elementary School Principals (Washington, D. C.: National Education Association, 1948), pp. 263–75.
21. See Neal Gross and Robert E. Hericott, *Staff Leadership in Public Schools: A Sociological Inquiry* (New York: John Wiley, 1965), chapters 6, 7, 8.
22. See William Wayson, "A New Kind of Principal," *The National Elementary Principal* 50, No. 4 (February 1971): 9–19.
23. *Better Principals for Our Schools: A Cooperative Approach to Competence* (Washington, D.C.: Department of Elementary School Principals, National Education Association, 1961).
24. Gross and Hericott, *Staff Leadership.*
25. This is a cooperative endeavor developed by the Professional Growth Committee of the Ohio Department of Elementary School Principals, the State Department of Education, and most of the state universities in Ohio.
26. James B. Enochs, "Elementary School Administrators Evaluate Themselves," *Elementary School Journal* 51: 17–20. Quoted by permission of the University of Chicago Press, publisher. Copyright 1950 by the University of Chicago.
27. *Supervisor Training* (New York: Esso Standard Oil Company, 1949).
28. Fritz C. Borgeson, "Preparing the Principal for Leadership," *The National Elementary Principal* 34 (April 1955): 15.

3

Developing Leadership Skills

The elementary school principal can and must acquire leadership skills to achieve an effective educational administration. The discussion of leadership in the previous chapter was intended to give a philosophical and psychological basis to serve as a springboard to continued progress in development of the leadership function. In this chapter we present a specific approach to help the principal develop, through practice, educational leadership skills.

The principal should examine the quality of his behavior and observe the relationships that exist between tasks being performed. This way of thinking about problems is a kind of leadership skill, for the principal is stimulated and challenged in his approaches to the total job. He may then translate the results of his analysis into more effective, positive action. The degree to which he accepts and uses such analysis will reflect his grasp of educational leadership skills.

THE PRINCIPAL'S ADMINISTRATIVE BEHAVIOR

Areas of Administrative Behavior

The organization and discharge of the principal's duties depend upon his understanding of the job, his administrative preparation and experience, and the demands on his time from all levels. An unfavorable combination of these factors may cause him to spend his school day in a dull routine. As an office manager he may receive high commendation, while his educational efforts and leadership may leave much to be desired. Therefore, understanding the vital areas of administrative behavior will help the principal take stock of his functions so that he can set up guides for broadening his professional vision.

The elementary school principal who accepts the role of the leader suggested throughout this book is not to be considered a mere technician. A glance at research material concerning school administration reveals the importance of analyzing tasks and defining areas of responsibility.[1] Commendable as this approach to leadership may be, some attention must be given to the *quality* of administrative behavior:

> Whether a task is satisfactorily accomplished or not depends as much upon the quality of performance as upon the knowledge of what must be done and the inclination to do it. In this respect administration is something like swimming. One may know the theory of swimming, may in fact be able to go through the correct motions; but when placed in water, he may not be able to keep himself afloat. Adjusting his bodily position, his breathing, and his motions to the water is still to be learned. Adjusting to the new medium is a necessity. . . . Any behavioral act is a complex of many behaviors, none of which can be said to exist alone; nor is total behavior a mere summation of them. Improving the quality of one aspect of behavior may likewise enhance the quality of another. . . . We therefore submit *nine areas of critical behavior* for consideration, in the belief that evidence will support the fact that the quality of administration is, in large measure, dependent upon behavior in each and all of them. These areas of behavior are applicable to many walks of life. We found them in administration, and we postulate their significance in the leadership position administrators hold.[2]

Eight of the areas of administrative behavior[3] mentioned above are discused in this section, together with checklists for action and illustrations from school experiences, to help the principal define even more sharply his leadership role and to furnish him definite guidelines for charting his course.

Setting Goals

Whether he realizes it or not, the principal is responsible for the objectives of the school's educational program. Even when a particular task calls clearly for goal-seeking behavior, the results will reflect the actual understanding of goals held by those responsible for discharging such tasks. In addition, there must be agreement on these goals by the faculty and the community if people are to work together effectively toward common ends.

In his leadership role, the principal leads both staff and community in educational programming. Just what is the best type of educational program for the community? Does this school meet the needs of the community? Should the elementary school attempt to meet the special needs and abilities of each boy and girl? These questions, along with many others, point up the leadership role expected of the principal. This kind of leadership brings unity out of the great variation of meanings for elementary education in the minds of staff and citizens. A checklist suggesting positive action within

Developing Leadership Skills

the school and community, furnishing guideposts for educational leadership by the principal, is as follows:

1. Determine the role of the elementary school in the community and social order.
2. Involve principal, staff, pupils, other school administrators, board of education, parents, and total community in determination of the school's educational objectives.
3. Emphasize the democratic approach to goal setting.
4. Assemble evidence of goals agreed upon cooperatively.
5. Establish long-range goals with intermediate goals selected as means to the end.
6. Continuously re-examine goals in light of current, changing conditions.

The principal's role as an educational planner will center around this checklist, since he is concerned with goal-seeking behavior. He recognizes the fact that a particular goal may be obscured or overshadowed by the multiplicity of other goals. By giving thought to the problems of school objectives and utilizing the leadership skills involved in setting, defining, accepting, and clarifying goals, and choosing between alternatives, the principal exerts a positive influence. The following illustration shows the wide applicability of this phase of leadership:

In one school, a parent made it clear to the principal and to several teachers that he believed there was only one kind of program for all elementary schools. His description was a narrow concept of what the school should do for the child. Another parent came up with a modification of this idea and went on to say that the child should learn "or else." "There was little point in trying to worry along with those youngsters who couldn't do the work." Other parents took an opposite view, and the principal recognized a pressing need for joint meetings of staff and community citizens to get more united thinking. The principal led the way, with the result of bringing needs and understandings out in the open. Under his leadership, school and community patrons took positive steps for improvements, and certain problem-solving experiences clarified school objectives and procedures.

Still another illustration reveals that mutual acceptance of a goal is necessary if the principal is to expect achievement. This kind of acceptance will often help the principal to focus attention on a particular problem that might otherwise be unapparent to others:

A principal who was deeply interested in the prospects for a special fund-raising project about to be launched in his school armed himself with facts and statistics to support his personal enthusiasm. In his eagerness to make a good showing, he quickly assembled his staff and announced what he wanted to accomplish. He set up a goal for each teacher and room, and gave sound, logical reasons for his statements. In doing so, he assumed the spokesmanship for the group. The staff felt some sympathy for his project and his enthusiasm, but rejected his leadership because they wondered about his personal motives.

It becomes clear that, while people may accept goals, there is often distinct disapproval of the methods employed to achieve them. The principal is faced, therefore, with two basic tasks: to lead in defining the goals, and to persuade his staff to take part in setting and accepting the goals.

Policy Making

School personnel expect to follow the administrator and work within a framework of established policy. They are aware that final authority rests with the administration. Nevertheless, the effective principal tries to bring school policies before his staff. He becomes a more efficient executive when he knows how to secure staff cooperation in establishing and recognizing any particular policy. His philosophy must be one of not only exercising authority in administering policies but involving the staff in revising and/or modifying policies which directly affect them. As he moves forward with the educational program, the principal insists on making every vital decision on the basis of clearly defined policy.

The following checklist will help the principal give leadership in this area of administrative behavior:

1. Identify school policy clearly.
2. Involve all interested persons in the policy-making process.
3. Clarify the democratic processes employed in policy making.
4. Record policy decisions and make them available.
5. Provide opportunities for changing policies and clarify procedures to be used.

As the principal participates positively in management of the autonomous school, he may consider at least eight areas in policy making from the personnel point of view. These areas of direct concern to him are:

1. Hiring personnel (their recruitment, selection, and their work assignments).
2. Induction of staff members and the in-service education program.
3. Evaluation of personnel for rating, promotion, transfer, demotion, and discharge.
4. Salary program and payment schedules.
5. Evaluative practices of the total school program.
6. Job requirements and work days (dates and length of work day).
7. Services and benefits for personnel, and certain health and safety measures.
8. Use of personnel in management of the school.

Developing Leadership Skills 57

These broad functions will best be administered if the principal proceeds according to established policy. Specific policy-making activities by teachers and community representatives include:

1. An *advisory council*, consisting of committee chairmen of all regularly established committees including a community representative. Its function is to assist the principal in making the concept of democracy a reality in the lives of all people connected with the school and to give direction to adminstrative action in solving school problems. The committee also assists in making the school budget.
2. A *faculty meetings committee*, elected by the faculty. Its function is to plan the agenda and accept the responsibility for professional meetings.
3. A *curriculum development committee*, to keep abreast of curriculum trends and research. It studies possible modifications in present programs before recommending changes. It gives attention to the system-wide curriculum problems, but emphasizes the particular needs of the local school. Parents can serve as resource persons on this committee.
4. A *faculty grievance committee*, to provide the faculty with a means of dealing with professional or personal problems between the principal and any staff member. This committee works closely with the principal to reconcile differences.

The principal uses these committees to assist him in defining, interpreting, evaluating, and recommending policies. New ideas and suggestions will emerge from these committees, to help shape future policies or call for dynamic rethinking. Basic to the leadership function of policy making is the execution of the policies developed. The principal is the chief administrative officer of his school, and as such he is expected to design administrative practices that will inaugurate group-developed policies smoothly.

Determining Roles. The roles of the principal, staff members, and even community citizens should be clearly defined and understood in the educational program. These roles will undergo continuous change and will vary in certain localities.

Many teachers are not aware of their roles or responsibilities, either in the operation of the school or in the discharge of classroom affairs. The principal advances the overall learning effectiveness by helping his staff to see how their roles fit into a functional pattern in the administrative structure, and how each person's assignment affects the total organization. As he furnishes this type of leadership, the following checklist may serve as a guide:

1. Specify all roles involved in the operation of the educational program.
2. Establish a purposeful basis for determining roles.

3. Consider the full potential of each person in determining his role.
4. Minimize friction and conflict resulting from misunderstandings of roles or responsibilities.
5. Make evidence available which will indicate that parents, citizens, board of education members, school personnel and other administrators have a working knowledge of what is expected of them and that there is consistency in their expectations concerning others.

The use of job-analysis procedures will assist the principal in determining roles. An illustration is given to indicate the importance of having roles clearly specified:

> A superintendent of schools instructed the various principals to submit to him their thinking concerning the organization and use of a faculty advisory committee in each school. Mr. Green, the elementary school principal, was not sure just what would be his relationship to this future committee. He called several of his colleagues to get an answer and was surprised to learn they were just as much in the dark as he. No one seemed to understand what part he would play, nor the role of the committee. To settle the issue once and for all, Mr. Green agreed to ask the superintendent to clarify the relationships involved. To the embarrassment of both administrators, the evident confusion was not materially helped. They decided that in the absence of past experience, perhaps the best approach would be to get the committees operating in each school and let the thing work itself out in time.

This situation illustrates the results of giving too little thought to the place of a committee organization in the total strcture, despite insistence on democratic procedures. Any changes in structure and organization will call for corresponding changes and descriptions of the roles people are to play in carrying out educational objectives.

Another case is described to show how positive, beneficial results may be obtained by carefully describing roles and working relationships:

> Mr. Wright, principal, cleared with the superintendent a project he had in mind for examining the grading system in his school. He felt that a study could materially aid his reporting procedures to parents. He suggested a study committee composed of certain teachers, parents, a consultant from a local college, and local supervisors. The committee would bring its report in the form of a recommendation to the staff and parents' council. All working relationships were carefully explained, with each person's role clearly defined. The committee became interested and enthusiastic, and when they completed the study, a report was made. Their concern was contagious, and each person helped to sell the total findings to school and community.

Coordination and Consultation. No elementary school principal can state categorically that his school program operates in such a way that every educational activity is planned and organized to achieve definite objectives. Some principals are more successful than others in accomplishing this ideal—the ideal being a coordination of educational activities in terms of administrative leadership based on skill, preparation, and know-how. Frustration and confusion will be minimized when the charting and steering of the course are put in proper perspective, and especially when each activity is recognized as leading to the realization of certain school objectives.

The elementary school principal faces the responsibility of getting his staff to see the need for pulling together as a team. Many teachers are unaware of the total job and cannot see the school as a whole. Thus the principal becomes the responsible leader in providing the structure that will lead to coordination of effort. He may find himself so engrossed in administrative details that he either has no time or loses sight of the objectives of his school and his office. In much the same way, his staff members may be so preoccupied with details or have so little understanding of accepted aims and policies that team play is unknown. To develop unity or to eliminate working at cross purposes, school personnel can take steps to improve coordination. The principal has the responsibility for taking the initiative in leading his staff toward better coordination of educational efforts. A checklist of five points is suggested for developing this leadership skill:

1. Establish a school-wide policy concerning the need for team work.
2. Work out definite coordination plans for all operating duties.
3. Produce evidence periodically of both good coordination and lack of it.
4. Emphasize how effective coordination is producing good results.
5. Take constructive steps toward constantly improved coordination of educational efforts.

As the principal charts his course of action and tries to see all the educational tasks in their proper perspective, it is again apparent that the coordinating responsibilities are largely his. The challenges to the principal are illustrated in the following cases:

> In the Main Street Elementary School, the first-grade teachers were constantly asking for opportunities to confer with their principal concerning certain problems. Time and effort spent in these conferences were considerable, but it was not these factors which gave cause for concern to the principal. It soon became evident that many common problems were arising, plus the additional worry of friction and misunderstandings, coupled with some teacher competition. He invited his first-grade teachers, together with the second-grade staff who were involved to some extent, to an informal meet-

ing to define more sharply these common problems and to map strategy for action. It was not long before this group asked for more opportunities to work out some answers. In time they gave evidence of being a more efficient team of workers engaged in a common enterprise. Improvements were noted in certain areas as a result of this working together.

Appraising Staff Performance. The problems of evaluation are not confined to any particular person or group or to certain processes. Evaluation is a continuous process involving all pupils and most staff members. Although other chapters will deal with various problems in evaluation, this section will describe briefly a phase of educational leadership that will assist the principal in improving his overall appraisal procedures. Increased emphasis on this leadership role should take into account three areas: (1) the effectiveness of classroom teaching; (2) the overall effectiveness of the administration; and (3) the state and community efforts toward providing significant opportunities for the pupil. When the principal assumes leadership in getting facts about the effectiveness of his school program and can be objective and decisive in leading toward improvement, the educational program can be interpreted more intelligently to the community.

The principal can improve his appraisal procedures by using the following checklist:

1. Establish purposes for all appraisal activities.
2. Define clearly the role of the principal in the appraisal program.
3. Establish and agree upon cooperatively-derived criteria for the appraisal program.
4. Involve as many concerned persons as possible in the appraisal process.
5. Make findings, interpretations, and recommendations for action clear and available.

Implications of administrative behavior in the area of appraising educational effort and effectiveness are far-reaching and complex. An illustration will suggest some of the numerous benefits that result when the principal utilizes this type of leadership.

> Mr. Smith had read with dismay some of the "poison pen" letters in the newspapers, which were critical of the public school system. While he knew of some discontent he did not feel alarmed until the letters became a weekly news issue. He felt concern over the reaction to his school's educational program by the majority of patrons. He also wondered to what extent the school's purposes and objectives were in harmony with what he and many others felt to be valid. After discussion with many key people, it was agreed that a properly conducted survey might yield valuable information. Mr. Smith set things in motion, and an extensive survey was soon under way. This organized effort was supported by some educational experts

Developing Leadership Skills 61

as well as lay citizens called in to assist in the task. When the results were brought in, tabulated, analyzed, and studied, the school leaders were able to see what kind of program the public believed in. Mr. Smith was in a position to map the educational program more intelligently, because this appraisal gave him the facts he needed.

Thus the elementary school principal, in long-range planning or even in achieving intermediate goals, is able to use appraisal procedures to produce a more effective school. As the school's chief executive, he will seek constantly to be the leader who emphasizes the cooperative appraisal of the program or an individual's effectiveness. Appraisal will give him answers to many questions, and he will be in a more strategic position to do something about his problems.

Working with Community Personnel and Resources. The principal is concerned with two other areas of administrative behavior: working with community leaders to promote educational improvements, and utilizing the educational resources of the community as widely as possible in his school program. Since these two areas of behavior are discussed at length in Chapter 5, they are mentioned only briefly here.

One of the principal's most difficult tasks is that of translating his educational program to the community through identifying, explaining, or interpreting the issues and facts pertaining to his school. This leadership skill is necessary for good public relations. In addition, the alert principal is aware of values that will accrue to the educational program when intelligent leadership is demonstrated in these two areas of administrative behavior.

Involving People. Examination of the eight areas of administrative behavior reveals that the principal is concerned with effective use of group procedures in solving school problems. On most occasions he will work with several individuals, but in certain situations he will work with only one other person in searching for a solution. Since, usually, his administrative behavior involves many people, this fact points up the need for his leadership skill in the application of group procedures. Principals are probably, along with other administrators, less skillful in this function than in any other administrative activity.

Even though all areas of administrative behavior call for application of skill in group procedures, two aspects of the problem merit special consideration. How shall the principal use effective group procedures, first, for improving teaching, and second, for improving the quality of thinking about the educational program of his school? His task is to turn apathy into active interest and support. He knows that there will then be greater understanding of and stronger belief in what is being accomplished. Equally important, he will learn what else can be done to improve present practices. He must furnish the leadership to point out and to devise ways for getting involvement-support for the educational enterprise.

The problem of involving people in educational matters requires carefully planned devices or techniques of group control. The checklist below will guide the principal in involving people more effectively in school affairs:

1. Recognize the necessity for community involvement and participation in school affairs.
2. Establish a policy or pattern for involving people.
3. Develop an active pattern of involvement.
4. Provide opportunities and experiences for school involvement in the community.
5. Devise broad and varied principal-directed patterns of involvement for greater participation.

The principal has, then, the responsibility of interesting many people in the work of the school. The more skillful he is in maintaining working contacts with all groups, the more effective he will be in clarifying educational goals, planning for their achievement, and making important decisions affecting school affairs. With positive and sustained effort toward developing staff and lay participation, the principal actually practices leadership skills by getting group consensus in solving problems and by placing responsibility for action upon the proper persons.

> The principal appointed a curriculum-planning committee that was charged with the responsibility of assisting him with curriculum problems in preparing for the monthly meeting. Until that time there had been little or no participation by the faculty in this important activity. When it was evident that the principal meant what he said and gave a certain amount of honor and prestige to serving on this committee, there was a greater degree of success in the work of this group. More important than anything else, other faculty persons were less reluctant to accept a responsibility suggested by the curriculum committee, since it was felt that joint planning meant respect both for staff members and the administration.

Communication. Many principals may believe that communication is simply projecting ideas through the channels of speaking, writing, hearing, and reading. These tools are basic to communication, of course, but the feelings and concerns of involved persons must also be considered. Since people have ideas they wish to convey to others, the process of communication means three things: the wish to express an idea, the awareness of feelings and concerns incorporated within the idea, and the desire to discover what thinking or reactions have resulted from the communication.

The principal must be aware of these aspects of the process of communica-

Developing Leadership Skills

tion in leading his staff and other people. He may be the person who can improve the quality and effectiveness of their workmanship through adequate techniques of communication. He has at his disposal many formal processes and techniques to improve communication with school personnel. Some of these devices may be beyond his means in terms of time, finances, or ability, but he can master many of the varied media of communication and use them to good advantage.

As with all other aspects of leadership, the principal is advised to approach the problem of communication through the psychological principles of group dynamics. Communication, whether formal or informal, becomes most effective when the principal shows genuine concern for conveying his ideas and for how well they are received. If a particular communication device will bring out his ideas and achieve the desired end, the administrator uses it. If, during the process of communication, however, he discerns an unhealthy climate, or that individuals are working at cross purposes, he re-examines his way of communicating. Communication gains optimum results when he who communicates and those who receive feel there is freedom for exchanging ideas, criticizing, suggesting, or offering alternatives. Communication as a process must be based on psychological principles of behavior, as shown in the following checklist. The principal must:

1. Have a clear purpose for communicating.
2. Consider the nature of the communication structure, to insure a flow of ideas.
3. Provide various means for communicating.
4. Realize the effectiveness of communication.
5. Constantly consider more effective means of communication.

The principal views the structure of communication from many vantage points. One of his responsibilities is to emphasize the common values and benefits derived from sound communication processes. He follows through by practicing good communication procedures, thus setting the pattern for his staff.

The following case demonstrates that, although frequently the principal assumes what is clear to him, it may not be equally meaningful to other individuals involved:

> . . . there was lack of understanding among faculty members as to what was being done by the coordinating committee and other subcommittees which they had authorized. After some examination of the situation it was obvious that misunderstandings were the result of poor communication. After some discussion it was agreed that a house organ would be developed to report activities of committees at regular intervals. When it was agreed that everyone would be adequately informed, then fears and suspicions that were evident at the beginning of the discussion seemed to disappear.[4]

Examination of the literature in the area of communications reveals that this is a highly specialized field. It would take years of training and experience for any principal to develop this art fully. We do not intend to minimize this training period, nor attempt to give short cuts leading to improved communications. Realistically, the principal may adopt the attitude of many personnel directors in business and industry, who accept certain principles of effective communication for thinking through and planning what to do in an important communication problem.[5] There is no one way to tackle a communication problem, since the use of several different approaches is more likely to insure success.

From the personnel viewpoint, six principles can help the school administrator attack his communication problems:

1. Lack of agreement may not be due to lack of understanding on both sides. *Knowledge* of the other man's point of view is no guarantee of *agreement*.
2. Many times, the important step in a communication problem is merely to keep the lines of communication open, thus avoiding a rigid impasse.
3. We expect people will react to logic—but frequently they don't. At least, they may not react the same way we do because they see the issue from a different viewpoint.
4. We tend to rely on facts to be convincing. But frequently we aren't really presenting facts—we are putting forth a conclusion we have reached.
5. People react to facts based on their attitude toward the facts and toward the source of the facts.
6. The important principle of communication to work for is the "principle of trust." People tend to believe those whom they trust. You can help build this trust by demonstrating consistent interest in the individual, his welfare, and his view point.

SUMMARY

Leadership skills for effective educational administration can be acquired. Examination of the eight areas of administrative behavior provide the principal with a framework for analyzing the quality of behavior, the methods for performing administrative tasks, and working relationships. The leadership roles involved in working with community personnel and in utilizing community resources are discussed briefly.

SUGGESTED READINGS

Association for Supervision and Curriculum Development. *To Nurture Humaneness: Commitment for the 70's.* The ASCD 1970 Yearbook. Washington: The Association, National Education Association, 1970.

Bass, Bernard M. *Leadership, Psychology and Organizational Behavior*. New York: Harper, 1960, Parts I, V, VI.

Campbell, Roald F. and Russell T. Gregg. *Administrative Behavior in Education*. New York: Harper, 1957, Parts 2, 3.

Griffiths, Daniel E. *Human Relations in School Administration*. New York: Appleton-Century-Crofts, 1956.

Griffiths, Daniel E., et al. *Organizing Schools for Effective Education*. Danville, Illinois: Interstate Press, 1962.

Hemphill, John K. "Relation Between Task Relevant Information and Attempts to Lead." *Psychological Monograph* 70, No. 7 (1956).

Sinclair, Robert L. "Leadership Concerns." *The National Elementary Principal* 48, No. 1 (September 1968): 8–15.

Notes

1. *Factors Affecting Educational Administration: Guideposts for Research and Action*, No. 2 of the College of Education Monograph Series on The School-Community Development Study (Columbus, Ohio: Ohio State University, 1955), p. 20.

2. Ibid., pp. 18–19.

3. The eight areas of administrative behavior, including the guidelines discussed in this section, have been adapted by permission from the monograph cited.

4. *Factors Affecting Educational Administration*, p. 53.

5. See "When You Have a Communication Problem" (New York: Employee Communication Division of the Esso Standard Oil Company, 1955).

4

Patterns of Elementary School Organization

This chapter will stress the role of the elementary principal in planning, implementing, and evaluating organizational change. We will not present detailed working models of each organizational pattern, but rather a variety of ideas to stimulate the principal to search for more information about a particular design or pattern of organization he might consider adaptable to his own school situation.

Whenever two or more individuals work together, patterns of interaction develop quickly. All human endeavor falls into patterns, a combination of mental and physical efforts to control environment and establish comfortable life rhythms. A feeling of personal security usually results in some form of organization. Schools are an enlarged version of these human patterns. School organizational patterns are extensions of the thinking of an individual or a group, and as such, they fall heir to the same basic danger, that of becoming so entrenched, so routine and comfortable that the style and pattern becomes outmoded and outdated and no longer serves a changed society.

We do not attempt to predict the future, nor to make a complete assessment of the many organizational patterns for elementary and middle schools now in use, being tried as pilot projects, or postulated in theory. Rather, we wish to make the principal aware that in all probability, if a better organization for instruction is to come about, *he is the determining factor,* the catalyst for the action/reaction activities and confrontations which comprise the necessary prelude to change. The continued success of a program after it is in operation also depends upon the principal's ability and skill in the use of in-service activities. A large order? Indeed it is, and the principal who contemplates organizational changes must keep an open mind, must expect to call upon all the professional knowledge and skill at his command, and must know where to turn and who to call upon for assistance in every phase of the change pattern.

BASES FOR ORGANIZATIONAL CHANGES

There have always been forward-looking individuals who questioned the advisability of the graded school organization, which tended to force all youngsters over hurdles and into a mold from which they were to emerge as conforming individuals. The question was, and still is, conforming to what? It has been evident to some educators and laymen that conformity in many areas of the schools, including teaching styles, punitive types of discipline, rigidity of methods and expectations, uniformity of materials, gradedness, and all the rest, was contributing little to the development of the uniqueness and potential of each individual. Yes, our children read more and better than they did a generation ago. Yes, they have more knowledge at any particular age than their counterparts of a generation ago. However, the schools have been and are being accused of squelching individuality and smothering creativity, most often by demanding that routine and undifferentiated assignments be done in prescribed ways. To some extent we have recognized our guilt and have made some positive strides in restructuring programs and reorganizing instruction to meet the real needs of children. Although some progress has been made, we are just on the threshold of some significant changes, especially in the elementary and middle schools.

But, although the principal is the agent for change, Goodlad, after observations in more than 350 classrooms in more 100 schools, has found

> The principals to be, on the whole, rather unaware of the instruction going on in their schools, generally satisfied, with it, and possessing no clear plans as to what they intended to change, improve, or accomplish in and with their schools. Their attention was focused on the immediate—the daily maintenance and operation of the schools. Like the teachers, they expressed much interest in modern educational developments and wanted to talk about them.[1]

These observations sound like an indictment of this group of elementary principals and their reluctance to leave the comfortable status quo. But the last sentence gives us hope that they want to make changes. At least they are talking about them! At least they are listening! After listening and discussing, the next step is conceptualization. The alert principal who can visualize the benefits of a program designed more completely to meet children's needs, and to reduce tensions, conflicts, failure, and frustrations, has a wealth of information, models, surveys, reports, books, schools, professional assistance, and more to assist him in turning his vision into reality. Involving himself in the necessary search for an organizational pattern that fits his school, clearly defining long-range goals and behavioral objectives, implementing the necessary in-service activities, and organizing and supervising all the necessary details, can be a deeply satisfying experience in professional growth.

Organizational changes are prompted by two very different reasons. The first is voluntary planning by administrators and teachers for new instructional patterns. These educators are deeply concerned about finding better instructional materials, methods, and techniques that can be formulated into organizational and instructional patterns more clearly and completely suited to the educational and human needs of children. Second, some educational changes are being brought about by force or decree. Often it is a temptation to do the expedient thing, to construct a temporary solution to meet the demands of a vocal and possibly militant group. Special or militant groups with their particular needs, problems, or vested interests are not the only groups forcing schools to change patterns. The courts are also forcing schools to take a look at organizational structure that goes far beyond expedience and demands new educational patterns that will eliminate educational inequalities based on ethnic background or geographical location. In theory, equality of opportunity is right, a basic belief of our democratic society. In the coming years, educators are going to face more demands and mandates for change, some new and frightening in their implications. For some, the experiences will be traumatic, for others, an inspiring challenge. The challenge will be to set up educational opportunities, many times by a change in organization for instruction, to match the legal requirements. Schools should, however, be anxious to go far beyond the legal aspects, and institute programs because they *want* to meet the intellectual, social, physical, and emotional needs of all children.

As this is written, evidence is mounting that many schools will be forced by court decisions to reorganize in ways that will theoretically eliminate racial imbalance and other inequities, both in staff and student population. In 1971, a California Supreme Court decision declared unconstitutional school support based on property evaluation because of the wide inequities in the ability of local communities to support local schools. If this landmark decision is upheld in the United States Supreme Court, the entire tax structure for the support of schools may well be changed from support based on property values at the local level to some more equitable method that will assure the same amount of money for the education of every child, regardless of his geographical location in each state, and possibly in the entire United States. As educators, we may have to make strenuous efforts at every political level to assure that this is not interpreted to mean the *same* education for each child, but the *same opportunity for education,* with the door left open to differentiate the program according to the needs of the child. Let us insist that if financial inequities are eliminated in each state, and perhaps the nation, schools shall retain local autonomy for planning and implementing instructional programs for the particular needs of the local school community.

There are, and will continue to be, wide variations in the educational needs of individual schools and school systems. What will happen when every school in a state has the same amount of money *per child* to spend for education? Will it then be more logical, more feasible, to compare programs for their effectiveness in meeting the goals of the organization and the needs of children? If all school monies come from the state level, possibly the national level for complete equity, will there be more state and federal mandates, more demands for conformity, rather than more assistance? These and many related questions concerning school organization and its related problems may well have to be answered in the near future. Perhaps the threat of state or federal control will be the stimulus for motivating some educators toward voluntary planning for change. If educators are to do more than merely meet the mandates of the law, they must voluntarily join the growing group in the teaching profession which feels we must enhance our image as professionals by making relevant and realistic changes because we want to, not because we are forced to.

A school organizational pattern can follow any number of routes to a destination, but there should be many guideposts along the way to keep the principal and his staff moving with direction. Heathers says that "The three I's of the new education are Ideas, Inquiry, and Individualization." These are the themes of the current reform movement. It is imperative that teachers and administrators develop a conceptual understanding of these themes. The reform movement has floundered because the key people have lacked a conceptual grasp of the themes. Inquiries can and should be conducted by students of all ages, at all levels of ability, and in all areas of the curriculum.[2] As educational leader of his school, the principal must recognize that the three "I's" apply to his relationship and work with his staff as well as to the teachers' interaction with students. Most writers who concern themselves with the mechanics of educational change express the common feeling that *success of any efforts to change human patterns of action depends upon motivation*. This means that schools, working with the community to institute change, must motivate parents to become involved. It means that the principal, working with his staff, must motivate teachers to build positive attitudes and techniques for change. It means that staff members, working with children, must motivate these learners to build new patterns of self-direction and self-reliance, thus helping to build a sound self-image for every child. Coopersmith says:

> Self-esteem is a better predictor of a child's future success in school than intelligence. Just as we cannot expect a starving child to perform calisthenics, we cannot expect a child lacking in self-esteem to strive for academic competence. He must first have the conviction that it is possible for him to succeed and that his efforts will be rewarded with some degree of success.[3]

The authors believe that the elementary and middle-school principal must realize that teachers have the same need for recognition, success, and reward. We will suggest a number of ways for the principal to enhance the self-esteem of each person on his staff.

A school organizational pattern is a framework within which planned activities serve the needs of children. A desire to change the organizational structure implies that we can find more effective motivational devices and situations to facilitate all phases of learning. Let us be wise enough to realize, however, that motivation with too much pressure may be devastating to an individual or a group. Concerning the motivation of children, Frymier says:

> Motivation consists of many factors, and anxiety is one. Stress and pressure induce anxiety, thereby increasing motivation. But there is a point where the organism is adversely affected and achievement level falls off. "Bearing down" with "hard homework" and "raised standards" are the kinds of stress that parents and teachers typically employ. The dangers of "going too far" are very, very real. Knowing where to draw the line and "ease up" rather than "bear down" demands concepts and instruments and techniques far more sensitive than exist in education.[4]

Let us believe, however, that we *have* concepts, instruments, and techniques, at least in the embryo stage, that sensitize us to the needs of children, that can be developed and inculcated into our educational systems. Perhaps the application of these concepts does develop slowly, for we must acknowledge individuals do not change their attitudes easily.

These statements, combined with those of many educational writers on the educator's need to learn techniques of human relations if we are to exist and progress in a crowded and nervous world, again emphasize recognition of human values and the uniqueness of the individual—child, youth, and adult—when planning for organization change. If the principal, his school, or his school system, are planning to make an organizational change, more guidance will be needed than that found in one chapter in a book. The authors believe the activity required to search out an organizational pattern, define it, implement change, and constantly appraise progress and evaluate results, can be a highly satisfying professional challenge for the principal and his staff.

A SCHOOL ORGANIZATIONAL PATTERN

In general terms, a school organizational pattern is a framework for planning and sequencing instruction and learning experiences for the benefit of the whole child. Recognizing that our democracy has required and sponsored public school education because of a continuing belief that an educated citizenry is necessary for intelligent self-government, but realizing also that we live in a world significantly different than the world of even one generation ago, a brief review of various educational organizational patterns may serve to emphasize four points. First, although hampered by many pressures, lack of support, and the inertia of tradition, schools have made a number of successful attempts to revamp existing organizational patterns or to devise new ones in attempts to improve instruction to meet more adequately the needs of children. Second, the principal contemplating organizational change for his school needs information about organizational patterns now in operation, from which he may select ideas and operational techniques adaptable to his school's needs. Third, most recent suggestions for developing organizational patterns to meet childrens' instructional needs and to develop human values stress the need for behavioral and attitudinal changes on the part of participating adults. And four, not a single pattern has been universally accepted, and therefore not a single one offers a panacea for educational ills. Many different patterns are advocated within the vertical dimension of school organization. The horizontal dimension is of far greater magnitude, offering in-depth opportunities to improve instruction. In the past, much thought and effort has been given to planning and instituting programs that gave promise of improving instruction, often in the face of great resistance, because the educators advocating change were fighting the status quo. Now, as more and more successful instruction programs are publicized, a more accepting climate for change is being created in the minds of educators and laymen, enabling today's educators to plan and institute change, both in physical building structure and the organizational pattern, and in the programs which give the organizational pattern life and meaning.

    Historically, we have had ungraded schools, since all the children in small schools with first through eighth grades were taught by one teacher in all subjects. When schools became too large for one teacher, the logical sequence was to add an additional teacher and divide the grade levels, making a first-through-fourth and fifth-through-eighth combination, each with its own area or room. As enrollments increased, it still seemed logical to divide children into grades by ages, using chronological age and "one year's achievement" as stepping stones for placement and advancement. Concerned educators knew this pattern did not fit all children, yet it became (and still is) strongly entrenched. Even today some of the blame for resistance to and lack of change can be laid at the feet of educators who received their schooling in such a graded structure, were fortunate enough to survive or even excel in such a learning situation, and now not only condone it but perpetuate it. They show little willingness to analyze its weaknesses, particularly in relation to the problems it creates for those children who lack the personal adequacies to achieve continuous success.

Today, few school districts are so small that the entire school population is housed in one structure. Small school districts are consolidating with neighboring districts, on the theory that size will reduce cost, to offer a more comprehensive and higher-quality educational program to all students. As inadequacies and inequalities in education become more noticeable to greater numbers of people, educators must look at possibilities for revising organizational structure to eliminate inadequacies and provide greater equality of opportunity. The process of change has been slow but continuous, as different schools have tried to solve the increasingly complex problem of more students needing more relevant instruction. From the one-room, one-teacher school housing eight grades, more complex patterns of organization have become the life-styles of education. As schools increased in size, staff, and complexity, various patterns began to emerge. After the traditional eight grade-four grade pattern was established, kindergarten was added to the more progressive systems, and from this came such patterns as K-8-4, K-6-6, and after the advent of the junior high school in 1910, the K-6-3-3 pattern or some variant, which divided almost all school systems into elementary, junior high, and senior high schools. Most of these patterns retained the self-contained classroom concept in the lower grades and added departmentalization at the senior high level, and in some areas of the junior high, to provide for the needed specialization on the part of the teaching staff.

Organizational Patterns that Have Been Tried

Three basic patterns have emerged: schools strictly graded, schools graded but regrouped in various ways for instruction, and ungraded schools. The first sent children through a vertical pattern rigidly structured and divided according to increasing difficulty of subject matter, and each child was expected to ascend the ladder in steps corresponding to his chronological age. The second philosophy, that of regrouping within a graded structure, came about because educators recognized the instructional problems resulting from inter- and intra-individual differences. The ungraded concept evolved from the second philosophy, minimized or eliminated gradedness, and proposed to allow and encourage students to progress through subject matter at their own best pace. The graded concept of vertical movement through a series of annual steps is still with us. Often criticized because it ignored individual differences and expected all children to move at the same speed through "graded" material, there nevertheless were differences in the graded structure, as follows:

1. *Strictly graded*—Children of the same age studied the same materials and were expected to make the same progress.
2. *Graded heterogeneous*—Thirty or more children were grouped with one teacher regardless of achievement or ability.

3. *Graded-homogeneous*—Attempts were made to group according to appraised ability and achievement in relation to classmates of the same age.

4. *Graded-with specialist assistants*—Special areas of music, art, physical education, special education, etc., were taught by subject specialists.

5. *Semester plan*—Sometimes called the "vestibule" plan because it was conceived as a readiness structure to prepare children to enter a "regular" classroom, this was simply a way of providing smaller segments of gradedness by allowing more time for successful progress. For example, a child could take two and one-half to three years for first and second grades.

6. *Alphabet grouping*—Using alphabet letters to designate groupings, such as $A,B,C,$ or $X,Y,Z,$ this was a further breakdown of homogeneous grouping in attempts to group more closely for instruction according to supposed potential.

7. *Cooperative group plan*—This was unusual, especially when proposed by James F. Hosic in the 1920s, since it involved cooperative planning and teaching by a group of teachers under a group chairman.

The second basic pattern, that of the graded school which recognizes the differences in quantity and quality of pupil achievement, has brought into focus a number of organizational variations:

1. *Multiple-track*—In this plan, students completed units of work (all of the same nature) in varying amounts at varying rates of speed, usually in three ability groupings (tracks). This made it possible for faster students to complete eight years of elementary school in seven, while slower students could take nine years to complete the same work.

2. *Gary plan*—The platoon idea of scheduling was used, which scheduled one-half of the total group studying fundamental subjects into classroom areas while the other half was involved with special activities in other areas. The two halves reversed positions in a block of time. This plan attempted to strike a balance between social/creative activities and academic activities, as well as to make full use of all areas in the building.

3. *Social maturity grouping*—This plan used assessment data and professional judgments to assign students to groups balanced on the basis of friendship patterns and social development.

4. *Teacher personality-student maturity grouping*—Recognizing that *both* teachers and students vary as individuals, efforts were made to match a particular type of teacher with a group of students supposedly possessing some common social characteristics. Attempts to group in this way recognized that some teachers accepted and worked with less mature or more advanced children than did other teachers.

5. *Departmentalization*—This plan assigned children to areas by subject, such as math or reading, and the greater the number of students and teachers the more likely it became that there would also be some form of ability

grouping within the departmentalization. It is antithesis of self-contained, since the emphasis on division of subjects tends to push teachers to become "subject matter specialists" rather than generalists or teachers primarily concerned with child growth and development. Seldom used below the fourth grade, this plan has been traditionally grade-level oriented.

6. *Subject grouping with a block of time*—Inter-grade grouping used the block of time for a subject, such as reading, but limited the movement of children to a grade level for regrouping. Inter-classroom grouping broadened the concept by including a wider range of grade levels and ability in the block of time, allowing more levels of instruction within a particular subject.

7. *Activity grouping*—Within this broad category, many attempts were made to provide for individual differences, with such grouping arrangements as "gifted class," opportunity group, extra-curricular group, self-selection group, subject interest groups, special project groups, and others.

Individual Progress Plans. Organizational structures which include plans for individualized instruction have existed for many years. Some work under the graded plan, but most operate on the premise that individualized instruction by its very nature negates a graded structure, and therefore advocate a complete restructuring of the organization from graded concept to ungraded concept. Removing grade-level designations accomplishes nothing, however, and neither will reorganization, unless teachers can take advantage of the opportunities to individualize instruction. The following list of ungraded organizational structures or individualized progress programs is far from inclusive, and is given only as an indication of the varieties of plans that have been promulgated by various schools over the years.

1. *Combined grades*—This is an administrative device used when there are too many children in two consecutive grades and lack of funds dictates that additional staff must be kept to a minimum. For example, the principal with a fourth grade of 43 and a fifth grade of 44 regroups these pupils into a fourth grade of 30, a fifth grade of 30, and a "combined" group of 27. Although this is not really ungraded, it does break the traditional pattern of strict grade-level grouping.

2. *Ungraded primary*—This organizational pattern is a structured learning environment designed to maximize opportunities for development of each child as an individual and as a member of a group. Continuous progress is the goal, rather than the usual expectation of each child's meeting norms or precise grade-level standards because of his chronological age.

3. *Ungraded elementary*—This is an extension of the ungraded primary to include all children in the elementary school, whether kindergarten through sixth, kindergarten through eighth, or some other combination. This pattern eliminates also the traditional primary-intermediate designations.

4. *Ungraded preschool*—Some schools enrolling four- and five-year-olds place them in heterogeneous groups and allow the child to spend from one to three years in this ungraded situation. Observation and testing of his social and intellectual maturity determines the time for placement on the next step of the vertical instructional ladder of the school.

5. *The Winnetka plan*—In this plan, self-instructional materials were used extensively and individual progress was stressed and personalized by the use of cards listing goals and showing academic progress.

6. *The Dalton plan*—Although still graded, individual progress was encouraged by the use of "contracts" with each student which outlined that student's responsibility for a definite amount of work to be done within a specified block of time. In the first part of the plan, most of the thrust for individual achievement was scheduled to be accomplished through individualized instruction, while the second part, physical/social development, was planned for whole-class instruction.

The principal planning a change in organizational pattern will necessarily have to assess the present grouping practices in his school. Research into the various methods of grouping may lead him to believe that there are more questions than there are answers. He and his staff must recognize that as long as the pupil-teacher ratio remains at 30 or more to 1, continuous grouping and regrouping of children for instructional purposes must occur. They must recognize that the individual and corporate needs of children and teachers determine instructional grouping. These needs range from a child's need for individual attention to the staff's need to plan some large group instruction to conserve time and energy and to eliminate repetition. It has been previously stated that the principal will encounter much resistance to change. In a 1960 article, Shane[5] listed thirty-two "Historically Interesting and Educationally Promising Plans" that have been tried in American schools during the last century. Our intention here is only to show that there is a wealth of information available which describes the various strengths and weaknesses of grouping procedures. The most important question that must be answered is, "What procedures does *this* staff, in *this* building, feel can be adopted to individualize instruction with the resources and personnel available?" Few elementary principals have the time to work through the maze of research regarding grouping; therefore, it is strongly urged that the principal fix his professional eye on the goal of individualized instruction, then, with his staff, select the grouping policies that will lead to this goal. Keeping grouping patterns flexible will allow the staff to meet the needs of the organizational structure. More recognition of the variations in child growth and development, leading to differences in expectations and instruction, will serve as a continuing reminder that groupings should be kept flexible.

Any descriptions of groupings, gradedness, or nongradedness, confront difficulties of precision because of overlapping terminology and differing interpretations. To this problem must be added sparsity of research funds and skill for experimentation at the local level, lack of ability on the part of the principal to include special personnel in planning and implementing organizational change, wide gaps between theory and practice, and lack of supportive research data. Those principals who contemplate establishing nongraded programs should take some advice from Anderson:

> The success of the nongraded arrangement depends ultimately on the improvement of curriculum. What is especially difficult about running a nongraded school or a nongraded classroom is *not* how to organize the program, or how to group the pupils, or how to report pupil progress to parents, or how to set up recordkeeping systems, or how to help teachers solve the numerous other administrative problems that arise. What *is* difficult is how to solve the *curriculum* problems that the organizational scheme raises.
>
> For example, which skill experiences are best arranged through individualized programs in which pupils can proceed at their own rate of speed, and which experiences are best reserved for groups? What topics, presented under what conditions, are appropriate for classes composed of youngsters whose academic potential and achievements range over a wide spectrum? What kinds of experiences can be shared by youngsters in multiage classes in which a great range of responses and contributions is possible? Just how does a spiral curriculum work? How can we better teach for the process goals? These and other questions bedevil the teachers in nongraded schools. Until our curriculum experts begin to attack these problems and produce specific recommendations that teachers can understand, progress will be at a snail's pace.[6]

In an article discussing the various methods of grouping, Shane concludes:

> It seems reasonable to conclude that the "best" grouping procedures are likely to differ from one school to another, the most desirable practice often being dependent upon such factors as: (1) the competence and maturity of the local staff; (2) the nature of the physical plant; (3) school size; (4) class size; (5) the local curriculum or design of instruction; and (6) a highly intangible quality—the intensity of the desire of a teacher or a group of teachers to make a particular plan work effectively.
>
> The philosophy and ability of the able teacher are undoubtedly more important than any grouping plan, however ingenious it may be, with respect to creating a good environment for teaching and learning.[7]

Terminology in relation to precise definitions of organizational patterns can also be confusing. We speak of the "nongraded school," the "flexibly scheduled school" and the "middle school" but the terms can and do overlap. In an article written about school organization, Kopp states that,

> In an unpublished doctoral study Stanley C. Carlson[8] identifies eight basic organizational patterns, namely:
> Age Grade Grouping
> Interage Grade Grouping
> Social Personality Grouping
> "Homogeneous" (ability) Grouping
> Platoon Grouping
> Departmental Grouping
> Individual (contract)
> Large Group (team teaching)
>
> Neither the "nongraded school," the "middle school," nor the "flexibly scheduled school" is considered to be a basic organizational pattern in this particular study. Yet, nongradedness can be implemented within any one of the eight organizational patterns listed. For example, schools that are "graded," organizationally speaking, can indeed work toward the goal of nongradedness within that traditional, graded organization.[9]

Kopp also says, "Too much emphasis may have been placed upon changing the school organizational pattern rather than upon changing *teacher attitudes* about individualized instruction."[10]

Recent Developments in Organizational Patterns

Other plans have been advocated to challenge the major features of the self-contained classroom. One of these was the *dual progress plan*, which, although not a radical departure from the conventional pattern, was not well accepted by elementary educators. This plan advocated the use of full-time specialists who taught one or two areas only, in rooms equipped as laboratories for those subjects, rather than in general purpose (self-contained) classrooms. Heather's words concerning the bases upon which the plan was built give a brief insight into its philosophy:

> The dual progress plan derives its name from the fact that the plan provides two bases for a student's advancement in the curriculum. It calls for grade-level grouping and advancement in the English/social studies segment of the curriculum and in physical education, while employing nongrade-level grouping and advancement in mathematics, science, art, and music.
> To facilitate nongraded advancement in these curricular areas, the plan calls for cross-graded grouping, subject by subject, on the bases of students' actual advancement levels and their learning rates. In short, the plan provides that a student may progress in the different curricular areas at different rates in accordance with his relative capabilities in those areas. His grade

placement simply indicates his level of progress in the imperative learnings of the English and social studies areas.

This provision of two bases for progress has important similarities to typical nongraded programs except that it places different subjects on the nongraded side of the curriculum. In the great majority of elementary nongraded programs, reading and mathematics are the only nongraded subjects. In the dual progress plan, reading is designated as a grade-level subject while science, art, and music are placed alongside mathematics as nongraded subjects.

A second major feature of the dual progress plan is that it replaces the self-contained classroom and its general elementary teacher with a departmental organization employing only specialist teachers. The plan provides that the school's instructional staff contains six categories of full-time specialists within the major curricular areas. One category is the core specialist who teaches English and social studies. The others are specialists in mathematics, science, art, music, and physical education. In addition, the plan allows for specialists in such areas as remedial reading and speech, library, and foreign language.[11]

Open space, team-teaching elementary and middle schools, organized in various ways so far as team structure is concerned, offer many models of effective direction for the professional staff's thinking and planning for individualized instruction and psychologically sound methods for working with children's growth and development problems. Those mentioned here are examples of organizational patterns already in operation and under evaluation by schools in many different localities. For example, there are more than 1,000 middle schools in operation, with many more added each year. Again, these brief explanations of recent organizational patterns present only a skeletonized version of the philosophy and planning. If the principal chooses to adopt one of these plans for his school, he will of course make an in-depth study of the pattern, its requirements, and implications. Most elementary principals operate programs in conventional buildings, and again we emphasize that it is his responsibility to assess the possibilities for change, both physical and educational, within the confines of his building. Many recent organizational patterns have been adapted for use in conventional buildings.

Two plans which utilize college-level personnel in the process of organizational change, from its conceptualization to its evaluation, show how cooperation can directly benefit two separate entities—the local school and the teacher-training institution. The local school that wants to change its organizational pattern may, through cooperative endeavors with one or more teacher-training institutions, enlist the assistance and skills of highly-trained personnel. In turn, the training institution greatly increases the effectiveness of its staff members' talents and skills because working in a real situation puts to practical use the philosophy and theory of instructional processes. The two plans discussed here are the Individually Guided Education concept and the Multiunit School concept.

INDIVIDUALLY GUIDED EDUCATION—MULTIUNIT SCHOOL ORGANIZATION[12]

The multiunit elementary school[12] organization was developed to allow continuous educational improvement by the staff. This form of organization for an elementary school has grown out of the work of Klausmeier and others at the Wisconsin Research and Development Center for Cognitive Learning, which was started in 1964. Although the original concept called for Instructional and Research Units at the building level, the teams have been changed to Individually Guided Education (IGE). This multiunit organization incorporated the best practices in the vertical and horizontal organization for instruction. Role differentiation and group decision making are also key factors in this organization.

The multiunit provides for arranging instructional programs to fit the students, rather than making children fit the organization. Basically, the purpose of any form of school organization should be to provide the best possible plan for meeting the needs of *all* pupils. The multiunit plan is illustrated in Figure 3. It can be seen from the illustration that there are three interrelated groups at three levels of operation which make up the organizational hierarchy.

Figure 3 also shows that each unit has a team leader, three teachers, teacher aide, an instructional secretary and a teacher intern. This unit serves approximately 150 pupils. As is true in most team or cooperative teaching units, the teacher in the unit is responsible for planning, carrying out, and evaluating the unit's instructional program. The unit is also responsible for its own inservice education. A unique function of some units is involvement in planning and conducting research and development, or preservice teacher education.

The units meet at least weekly, for as little as half an hour or up to half a day if necessary. Klausmeier feels that at least two-hour meetings per week appears to be necessary during the first year. The instructional secretary and teacher aide carry out the routine tasks related to their functions. They work directly with the teachers and children. The unit leader, however, is responsible for inservice education of the paraprofessionals.

Of importance to the multiunit's operation and success are the three committees which function at the level of the classroom, the building, and the system. These committees are (1) the Instruction and Research Committee,

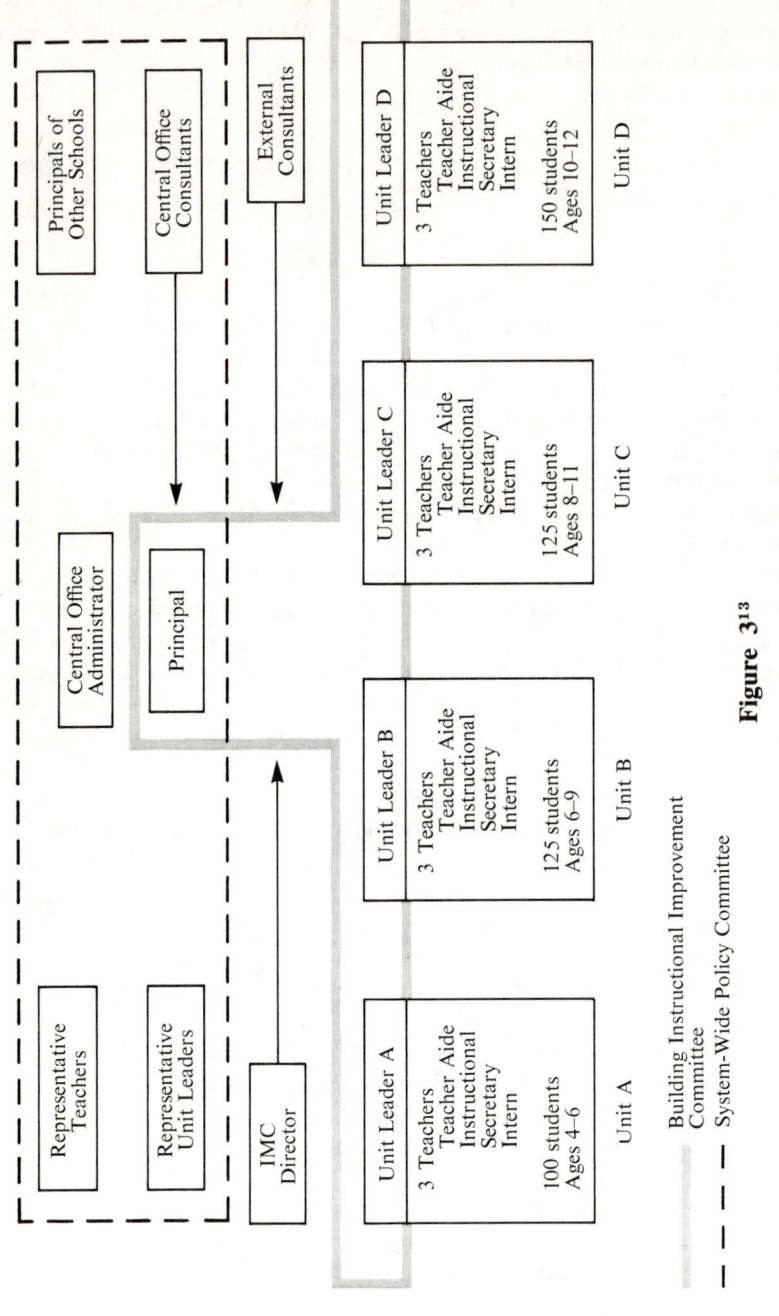

Figure 3[13]   *Organizational Chart of a Multiunit School of 600 Students*

(2) the Instructional Improvement Committee, and (3) the System-Wide Policy Committee.

Presently, the Individually Guided Education Unit provides for a self-renewing system of elementary education. The system thus allows for differences in rate of learning, style of learning, and in the substance of what is learned.

Some advantages of the Multiunit quickly become evident: (1) decisions are made at the appropriate level in the organization by individuals and groups; (2) leadership is provided at all levels of the organization; (3) roles are clearly defined, producing excellent performance of specialized tasks; (4) communication between teachers, administrators, central office, parents, and others in the community is facilitated; and (5) the self-renewing function is enhanced by immediate feedback from evaluative activities.

The Middle School Concept

Middle schools are proliferating rapidly on the American educational scene, based on the rationale that ten- to fourteen-year-olds should be offered a different kind of instructional program than has previously been offered in the upper elementary grades or in junior high school. The middle school, the school between, usually covers a three-year age span. This segment is taken from the school's vertical structure somewhere between the fifth and ninth years, inclusive. The most common pattern is 5-3-4, but there are variations, such as 4-4-4 and 5-4-3. There is a great deal of fluidity in the middle school concept since local school communities structure these "schools in between" to meet the needs of their local school community. One researcher says "the value of the new pattern may be in helping to solve problems that are primarily social or economic or administrative rather than purely educational. Big cities across the land trying to cope with the pressures of *de facto* segregation, decrepit slum schools, Negro boycotts, intransigent white parent groups, and deficient budgets see more than a glimmer of hope in the 4-4-4 or 5-3-4 system."[14]

The direction of the middle school concept is clear—that of doing a better job of matching institution, staff, and instruction to the needs, interests, and potential of children within the chosen age range. Much variation exists, as it does within every organizational pattern. In some instances innovative and interesting programs are housed within old buildings, while in other instances conventional classroom patterns and techniques carry over even into a new building built specifically as a middle school. The great hope of the middle-school proponents is that it will exist as a free unit to serve as an educational laboratory for the peculiar and particular needs of children in the selected age range. By "free unit," we mean that it is not a super-elementary or a watered-down junior high school, but a carefully planned, separate educational entity embodying imaginative uses of space, time, and talent. Among the needs and characteristics of ten-to-fourteen-year-olds, these proponents list:

1. Increasingly early maturity of students;
2. Greater need for technology than elementary schools can provide;
3. The student's need to share more completely in directing his own learning;
4. A high level spirit of inquiry and experimentation;
5. Need to explore as many areas of interest as possible; and
6. Need of many opportunities for decision making.

If the middle school merely takes away another elementary grade or two, only to emulate the traditional junior high school, it has no justification for its existence. But when it offers an educational program geared to the special needs of the students' ages within its organizational pattern, it justifies itself. Grooms states:

> The middle school may be identified as the administrative unit following the elementary school. The middle school is a system of education developed for the 10- to 14-year-old age group. Emphasis is placed upon support of the student in the learning situation as he ascertains his capabilities for learning and for orientation to his environment in light of his developing physical, social, intellectual, and psychological attributes.[15]

Because of the stress on self-direction and increased opportunities for exploratory activities, one resultant hypothesis is that middle-school students will develop more adequate self-concepts than students of like age in conventional schools. This could be a positive factor, because evidence is accumulating to prove that how a person feels about himself and his situation may be as indicative of academic success as an aptitude score.

The philosophy and ideals of the middle school could have great impact in helping elementary principals change their organizational patterns. Working toward compatible goals would certainly benefit both units, and many elementary schools advocating team teaching and open-space concepts have certainly influenced patterns for the middle-school concept. Teacher preparation for change is vital, and the changed attitudes toward individualized instruction, positive human relations, and cooperative planning are the factors most likely to bring success to the middle school organization.

The Stress on Team Teaching

All of the recently developed organizational plans have one common characteristic—the instructional patterns are planned and carried out by a team of adults. Team teaching is not an organizational pattern, but an educational device which seeks out and develops the strengths of all involved adults. The term "team teaching" has become associated with many different kinds of adult groupings for cooperative teaching, so the term actually has many meanings. Goodlad and Rehage say

> Communication would be enhanced if the term were used only in referring to ventures embracing all three of the following characteristics: (1) a hierarchy of personnel—team leader, master teacher, auxiliary teacher, teacher aide, intern teacher, clerk, and so forth; (2) a delineation of staff function based on differences in preparation, personal interests, and so on, or on the kinds of learning activities planned; (3) flexibility in grouping, embracing all the students under supervision of a team.[16]

The term "cooperative teaching" might be more accurate, but "team teaching" has a verbal charisma that makes it easily acceptable to many principals and teachers. Can there not be a team structure without the hierarchy? Evidently there can be, for there are numerous teams composed of peer teachers, primarily due to lack of money to differentiate the staffing, or lack of planning for upward mobility within the team. Often these teams of peer teachers elect one of the group to serve as team leader for a specified period of time, and to serve as liaison to the principal and the other teams in the building. This method does have the advantage of offering leadership experience to every teacher on the team. No matter what descriptive term is used—team teaching, cooperative teaching, associated teaching—the concept enhances the possibility for each teacher's professional growth, increasing the knowledge and competence of the whole staff to the benefit of all students through the implicit agreement of the team members to attempt to solve instructional problems together.

Another advantage of teaming is the increased opportunity for the individual teacher to specialize in an area of her choosing. It is a moot question as to whether training and experience as a generalist teacher should precede specialization within the team. Certainly one expectation of a team teacher is that she can make a contribution to the team. This can be an academic strength in a teaching area as well as a skill in a particular performance. We must look toward more specialization in staffing the team-teaching school in order to recognize and develop the strengths and skills of individual teachers.

Team teaching has been called everything from a throwback to the days of the one-room schools to the most promising venture schools have ever attempted. In the introduction to a book about team teaching, Spears states:

> A firm tie joins the past and the present of American education, and this accounts for the continuous progress that we make. In our search for the emerging school, we come to realize that we will never find it. Perhaps

we never should. It is rather the spirit and the key to the great success of American education that we find. The greatness of our nation exists not so much in possessing as in striving and searching for. There isn't the one best school or the one right idea. Team or cooperative teaching, for instance, will not be exactly the same thing in any two schools.[17]

In the same book, Singer offers his definition of team teaching: "Team teaching may be defined as an arrangement whereby two or more teachers, with or without teacher aides, cooperatively plan, instruct, and evaluate one or more class groups in an appropriate instructional space and given length of time, so as to take advantage of the special competencies of the team members."[18] Singer's definition and Goodlad's and Rehage's definition of a team hierarchy, although noticeably different in concept, have some common points. They provide for cooperative planning for instruction, grouping, and evaluation, flexibility is built-in, staff functions are differentiated, students are grouped for special purposes, aides are used wherever possible, and teacher specialization is encouraged.

Without exception, those writing about team teaching consider lack of preparation to meet the challenge and accept the opportunities inherent in the team structure the greatest threat to the team venture. There is not enough preparation to meet the human problems of team interactions and associations. Moving from the teacher of an autonomous, self-contained classroom to a fully cooperative and involved team member is a large step. Each teacher's cultivation of her own strengths in efforts to improve her own teaching personality and competence depends upon her ability to cultivate self-criticism and to absorb and profit from criticisms of others. Sharing success is fun, but sharing the problem of improving teacher competence and the instructional program is not an easy task.

Team teaching is a device to enlist the aid of professional teachers in planning their own future and the future of the school, taking them out of relative isolation and placing them in an atmosphere of sharing, cooperative planning, and decision making. Only when teachers can relate to each other freely and openly can the promises inherent in new organizational patterns be brought to life.

Role of the Principal in Organizational Change

Organization is a means to an end, the end being that of improvement of the teaching/learning situation. We can safely assume that the organizational pattern, the activities within the pattern, and the results of the activities will differ for every school because of the many variants involved. As has been said, if the principal does not exercise his prerogative and assume his professional responsibility for leadership dedicated to achieving relevant change in his school, change may be forced upon him. Voluntary change which keeps the controls, processes, and procedures in the hands of the principal and his planning group is a much happier way to solve educational problems.

There is much in the literature to assist the principal in establishing patterns for making changes. For example, Mager's excellent book, *Preparing Instructional Objectives*,[19] is written in an understandable and meaningful style. Educators have been remiss, often because of lack of know-how, in establishing behavioral objectives for instructional programs that can be simply stated, understood by students and teachers alike, and structured in such a way that they can be easily and quickly evaluated. The principal should write out concise behavioral objectives incorporating three characteristics: (1) conditions under which the learning will take place; (2) observable learner behavior; and (3) definition of minimum level of achievement. When working to establish organizational change, the principal should try to spell out *all* goals in terms of behavioral objectives. A little reflection on education's intimate concern with all problems of human growth and development, the requirements of systems and society, and the difficulty of changing attitudes, reveals that some aspects of educational change must necessarily be defined only in general terms.

The principal works with his staff to insure that, regardless of the organizational pattern chosen, certain fundamental considerations will be incorporated in the long-range planning to establish the change firmly and insure its continued success. Consideration must be given to:

1. Growth and development factors.
2. Developing success motivation.
3. Importance of human rights.
4. Equalization of educational opportunities.
5. Detailed conceptualization of the proposed program.
6. Built-in evaluative techniques.
7. Flexibility to include new ideas.
8. Recognition of individual differences.
9. Stating objectives which can be measured, as often as possible, by observable behavior.
10. Knowledge of a learning hierarchy (Bloom's taxonomy).
11. Sensible limits on pressure.
12. Understanding that we are educating for a society that may be markedly different tomorrow.

Although we have said that we would not attempt to predict the future of school organization, a point must be made here. The alert principal keeps himself informed of new educational ideas that give promise for improving and enriching his school's organizational pattern and activities, and also keeps himself informed of new educational software and hardware that can be incorporated into the ongoing instructional program, or into a revised or new organizational pattern. He also constantly endeavors to make necessary changes in programs and guides and urges teachers to make instructional changes.

From a 1960 report listing problems of most concern to elementary principals, two stood out. The report said,

> From these national analyses it becomes apparent that the leading problem for public elementary school principals, at least as viewed by the respondents, is supervision of instruction. It is of similar interest to note that provision for the exceptional child was a consistent second. . . . it becomes apparent that the type of responsibility which is causing the greatest difficulty lies in the field of instructional activity. The general improvement of instruction, programs of education for meeting the needs of children, and programs of special education, all cause concern, with emphasis on the qualitative aspects of the educational offerings of the school. That the educational administrators are expressing and reflecting this type of sensitivity is most reassuring. Second, these findings suggest a drive and dedication toward encouraging the principals of elementary schools to apply their efforts to the instructional phases of the administration of an elementary school.[20]

So the voices crying from the wilderness have been heard time and again! The challenge is becoming more sharply pointed each year—change or be changed.

The question then becomes, "Change to what?" As educational leader, the principal must first determine which direction, into which organizational pattern, he wants to lead his staff. As Mager puts it, "If you don't know where you're going you're liable to end up someplace else."[21] Breaking with tradition involves overcoming mass inertia. Moving into a new organizational pattern takes time, planning, professional assistance, and community, staff, and administrative support. But it is done more frequently than ever before, and the enthusiasm of those who have broken ranks and marched to a different drum is catching, making it easier for those who want to change to do so. College personnel are advocating change, supporting it, in some instances initiating it, not from the standpoint of theory, but through working with elementary schools in every phase from planning to evaluation. This involvement at the local school level enhances the image of the local staff and imbues the change process with professionalism, which can have great positive impact with the board of education, administrators, and the community.

Any curriculum change must recognize that the wide range of individual differences mandates a variety of teaching/learning styles and situations, regardless of the name of the organizational pattern. Sinclair, speaking about making curriculum responsive to human differences, says "Future schooling will be characterized by four semi-autonomous curriculum phases that interrelate and at the same time make unique contributions to the total educational environment."[22] Since, as the educational leader, the principal is supposed to be somewhat visionary, searching for means and methods to improve instruction and enhance positive teacher and student self-image, it is well to take a brief look at each of the four phases mentioned by Sinclair:

Independent Skills Phase

The independent skills phase is characterized by automated instruction and pre-planned curriculum packages, including programmed materials. Individuals and small groups pursue skill objectives, such as reading skills, by means of self-instructional procedures. Substance lends itself to pacing, and sequencing is also characteristic of this type of learning environment. In this phase learners would develop techniques for judging their own progress.

Individual Inquiry Phase

. . . the individual inquiry phase is designed to encourage the uniqueness of each student by concentrating on personal values, interests, and skills. This phase is interdisciplinary oriented. Students learn to solve real problems and evaluate possible solutions by assembling and analyzing information and concepts from a variety of academic disciplines. A learning consultant serves as tutor, counselor, and diagnostician. A large portion of the entire time devoted to the curriculum in the individual inquiry segment is spent outside of the school and classroom setting.

Group Awareness Phase

This phase is characterized by group inquiry into various knowledge areas that lend themselves to understanding human relations. The curriculum stresses an awareness that individuals behave in different ways in groups and that the causes for human behavior are multidimensional.

Personalized Continuum Phase

In the personalized continuum phase students make decisions about what they learn, how they will organize their learning, and what the timing of the pursuits will be. Master teachers, psychologists, and subject matter specialists will work in instructional teams and will be available to the students upon request. Furthermore, specialists in utilizing resources and knowledge will work closely with each student so that he learns to create and use an abundant educational environment that is appropriate for his needs. This segment, then, conjures up a humane setting in which the student learns how to learn so that he can better cope with whatever future society demands.[23]

Obviously no student would profit equally from all four phases. The opportunity is provided for directed (either teacher or automated) learning as well as exploratory learning, always with the support of highly-trained and concerned adults and the entire school organizational program. Sinclair concludes:

> There is an urgent need for administrators and teachers to more clearly understand the influence environment in different curriculum phases has on the growth and development of children. Only by altering climates which discourage learning and by building and maintaining compelling environments that foster learning will it be possible for elementary schools to better connect with the personal and academic needs of elementary youth.[24]

Hierarchy for Instituting Change

Recognition of the need for change is the base from which all else builds. A hierarchy for change, then, would start with this base and add to it those concepts which the elementary or middle-school principal would use in structuring the entire change process. A hierarchy for change might look like this:

1. Recognition of need for change.
2. Assessment of present program.
3. Principal's selection of an organizational pattern.
4. Principal's commitment.
5. Principal's written philosophy and goals.
6. Selection and organization of the planning group.
7. Explanation of all previous steps to the planning group.
8. Securing commitment of the planning group.
9. Research, visitation, fact finding, continuous pre-service and in-service activities.
10. Seeking all help available (finances and personnel) to support the change process.
11. Defining long-range goals and behavioral objectives.
12. Dissemination of information and promotion of chosen organizational pattern.
13. Selecting or devising procedures and instruments for continual assessment and evaluation, with the recognition that these must be much more sophisticated than those found in the traditional teaching organization.

Recognition of need for change must always come first, but the further one goes, the more likely that juxtaposition of steps in the hierarchy can occur without significant loss of effectiveness. Some steps may not be as important as others, but there is no *un*important area. Each makes a significant contribution to the overall planning. The important point is that the principal must realize that change must be organized and consistent, yet flexible enough to include new insights that offer improvement to the ongoing program, to obtain the most effective results.

The hierarchy puts the burden of selection of the organizational pattern on the principal, which is the best procedure in terms of conserving the principal's time and energy and avoiding repetition. This phase could be accomplished with a group of selected parents and teachers, if this is the principal's choice. The group requires a great deal of background information before it can make a selection, and some of the information is not easy to acquire. The principal's responsibility increases, since he must channel all information through his office, and guide the group through the process of selecting an organizational pattern most appropriate for his school.

A PATTERN FOR INSTITUTING CHANGE

Many patterns are available as guides for change, but none of them is a panacea for all educational problems. Neither is there a basic pattern incorporating all the possibilities for constructive growth, since each school is unique in its growth potential. Rather, after the principal or his planning group selects an organizational pattern, it should be recognized that the selected plan is a guide, a broad base upon which is built an individualized organizational plan for the school, recognizing that school's strengths, weaknesses, and unique potential. The change pattern suggested here emphasizes the role of the principal and lists the major areas of concern to him.

The question as to what pattern the principal and his planning group can use as a guide for implementing change can be answered in part by a broad-based pattern that includes three essentials—ascertaining the present situation, opening communication channels, and bridging the gap between theory and practice. These can be categorized as (1) assessment, (2) information dissemination, and (3) building bridges.

The organizational pattern may be changed by one individual school using only local personnel and/or consultant help, or changed within a system by cooperative efforts of all schools and personnel. It may also be changed by cooperative efforts on the part of local staff and one or more teacher-training institutions working as a consortium to achieve organizational change through a specific plan sponsored by the teacher-training institution. What guide, then, incorporates the three essentials?

Assessment

Both formal and informal assessment contribute facts with which the principal and his planning group will work. The formal assessment would be some form of survey or opinion poll. Many models of these are available in the literature, and the principal and his planning group will save time and probably accomplish more by using a survey instrument already formulated and researched. The informal assessment is continuous, and consists of listing as objectively as possible the opinions, attitudes, and feelings brought about through the day-to-day school activities and school/community interactions.

Numerous surveys have shown that the American public understands the need for educational change, and believes that schools should change educational instructional patterns to include such things as team teaching, non-gradedness, teaching structured work-study skills, and orientation to the world of work. Today's school patrons are aware that this is a fast-changing world, and want their children to be prepared to live with change. They not only expect schools to improve, but also expect them to be accountable. They want quality education, which includes programs for gifted and special education, instruction to meet the needs of *all* children, and programs that help children become self-starters, self-directed, and self-evaluative.

The principal and his planning group should assess the credibility gap between what the school patrons want and how much they are willing to support what they say they want. In considering the more recent organizational patterns, the planning group will recognize that in almost every instance more adult help is recommended for instruction and supervision. The planning group should attempt to assess (1) whether the board of education will agree to and be able to afford more assistance for the teaching staff, such as teaching aides and clerical aides, (2) whether volunteers are available to take over some of these responsibilities if the school cannot afford paid aides, (3) whether federal funds are available for a pilot project, and (4) if training programs can be made available to any and all aides, paraprofessionals, volunteers, and regular staff.

The principal and his planning group will need to ask many questions about the staff, the school's philosophy, the possibilities of changing physical features within the school building, the readiness of the community to cooperate, and the approval and support of the board of education. A representative list of assessment questions might include:

1. What organizational plan has been inherited?
2. What is the philosophy (gradedness, grading, promotion, etc.)?
3. Can staff leadership be identified?
4. Is there a climate for change within the school itself? Have individuals and groups been experimenting with new techniques, methods, materials?
5. Are staff members involved in all initial phases—visitations, discussions, exploratory reading, workshops, other inservice training devices?
6. Can the proposed new organizational pattern operate in the present physical school plant, or would changes have to be made with approval of the board of education?
7. What professional help is available?

8. Has a target date for the major change been made?
9. Are there plans in writing and in sequence to meet the target date?

Many more questions could be added and volumes could be written about assessment, yet questions that lead only to the accumulation of facts achieve nothing unless they are used to disseminate information about the need for change and the possibilities for positive change within the local school.

Information Dissemination

Dissemination involves conveying to all involved personnel the findings of the assessment section and the related needs for program change proposed by the principal and the planning group. The first step is dissemination of information about the current school program—the curriculum, regular and special personnel, cost per pupil, condition of buildings, areas of specialization now in progress, methods of evaluating pupil progress. The second step is informing the school community of growth potential in the proposed program. This information is geared to show citizens what the school program can become, to show that the school wants to incorporate into its instructional patterns the best available procedures and methods. It should also show that teacher specialization and cooperative teaching are ingredients in a new approach designed to facilitate evaluation of new tools for learning and new technologies for education. The third step offers as much objective proof as possible, drawing from the literature and from visitations and consultants, that the end product of the new organization can be happy, satisfied learners, enlightened parents, more professional cooperative teaching, a high level of teacher/principal/student cooperation, a more open climate for experimenting and learning, and better parent-teacher relationships.

Dissemination of information should take advantage of and use all the multimedia materials and know-how available to the school—video tape, filmstrips, color, graphics, artwork, charts and graphs, and teacher-made materials, plus the usual communication channels of discussion and question-and-answer groups. Again, the schools that affiliate with a teacher-training institute will receive high-level assistance in the mechanics of assembling, editing, and disseminating information.

Building Bridges

The unknown is often frightening. One of the main objectives of the principal and his planning group is to allay the fears that accompany the inherent threats to the psychological security of each individual involved in any change process. In every step of the process, every possible communicative and psychological tool should be used to help each involved individual build the attitude that "I will attempt the new, not just because I am encouraged to do so, but primarily because I am *supported and feel secure in doing so."* With the possible exception of the college-level personnel working with the school, the principal cannot assume that any person or group understands fully the implications of the organizational changes being structured. The board of education, the school officials, the staff, the parents and community, all need to have bridges built to them, and the best bridge of all is "Come and help, we need your ideas and support for planning better instructional programs for all our kids." If their interest is aroused by the dissemination of provocative information, each of these individuals and groups will find it easier to cross the bridge to active involvement in the program. The principal must build numerous bridges from traditional to modern educational concepts, and from generalities to specifics, among them:

From the self-contained concept of a classroom with an all-knowing teacher to the concept of a group of professionals sharing ideas and talents for improving instruction;

From school to community;

From principal to school officials, board of education, staff, parents, professional assistants;

From teaching techniques with questionable results to those techniques proven most effective;

From research to use; and

From pre-service activities for teachers which carefully prepare them for the new program to continuous in-service activities which increase their knowledge and skills and support their efforts to improve.

None of these activities guarantee that a new program will be understood and accepted by all teachers. In spite of the best efforts, some teachers will not be able to cope with leaving the security of the traditional. These teachers must be permitted to leave the district or be given an "honorable transfer" to another school if possible. Sometimes neither plan is feasible, and the principal will have to live with the situation and hope that peer-group pressure will bring a change in the recalcitrant teacher's attitude.

In thinking about the role of the staff (including the principal) as a change agent for adopting a new organizational pattern, Kopp lists three steps, and states:

> The competent elementary principal will assume the leadership in areas one and two and look for overt evidence in the third. The three steps are:
> I. RESEARCH
>   A. *Carry on a local status study.*
>   What are our specific educational objectives?
>   What do we wish to achieve via an organizational pattern?

B. *Assess developments and trends found in the literature.*
      Compare these developments and trends with what is being done at the local level.
II. INTERNALIZATION
   A. *Teachers and principals should become "sold" on the program they are developing.*
   B. *The proposed program should be truly understood. It ought to be thought of as "our program."*
   C. *The proposed program should be implemented as a pilot program.*
III. SATISFACTION IN ATTAINMENT.
   A. *Is there overt evidence that the program is working?*
   B. *Does the program meet the acid test of evaluation against previously established objectives to measure the various factors of child growth?*

The principal who institutes a new organizational pattern usually has a deep feeling of personal involvement in the development and ongoing supervision of the program; almost without exception he feels that the new organizational pattern is "his baby," that he is personally responsible for its success. When the goal is individualization of instruction on a mass scale, in an effort to achieve educational excellence, this is indeed a serious and long-range professional challenge to any principal and his staff. We state unequivocally that it will be nearly impossible for a principal to change his school organizational pattern *without changing teacher attitudes about individualized instruction and the urgent need for better human relations.* Without exception, all the newer organizational patterns consider imperative the need to individualize instruction at every level and the need for improved human relations, the improvement of the self-image of every individual involved in the total educational endeavor.

Imperatives for the Principal Who Wants to Set New Goals. Although our list is by no means comprehensive, it reiterates the fact that the principal is the vital personality in any pattern for change within the school. As chief administrator in his school, the principal exerts enormous influence both overtly and subtly. His commitment to improve educational organization and instruction is the master key which turns on all other energies available to assist him. Heavy pressures bear on the principal, many of them negative pressures which tend to resist change. Goodlad says:

> The "systems" of which the school and its principal are a part exercise enormous constraints—constraints which are essentially conservative and which serve to discourage change and innovation. The systems are not only the formal, political ones of state and local organization for education,

they are also informal, exerting subtle pressure by way of implicit and explicit expectations for schooling and for the behavior of teachers and administrators.[26]

Upward mobility toward educational excellence must take into account the realities of these pressures and constraints, but the principal must not let them put a lock on his thoughts, hopes, dreams, and plans for improvement. This list, then, mentions some of the imperatives for the principal who wishes to enhance his professional growth.

1. He must be a lifelong learner, with an innate desire for constant professional involvement in every area related to improvement of instruction for all children.

2. He must not be just an explorer who finds interesting new areas, promotes their efficacy, and then moves on. The brave principal is he who stays to see the team efforts bear fruit, to see the ideas, concepts, and words become reality in a vital, humanistic, positive, forward-looking program.

3. He is capable of visualizing beyond the everyday clerical tasks, frustrations, and human frailities, willing to accept the multitude of details necessary for the planning and operation of the program.

4. He is accountable, willing to accept personal responsibility for success or failure.

5. He is willing to learn how to handle the complex problem of communication with many persons and groups, without which there is no possibility of meaningful or successful change.

6. He must learn to be a human relations specialist more than a content specialist. In the areas of content knowledge in the instructional program, the teachers may well be more knowledgeable than he, and he must accept this.

7. He must be able to recognize forces that resist change and use every technique at his command to cope with and circumvent them.

8. He must be able to verbalize his vision. His should be the most objective outlook in his school, since teachers are necessarily concerned with a narrow segment of the program, while he attempts to envision the entire concept and chart the goals which will bring this concept to life.

9. He must be able to make decisions regardless of pressures.

10. He must be able to analyze his own style of leadership, and change his style if it is not conducive to cooperative efforts for improvement at all levels and in all areas.

There is no attempt to put the above list in order of importance. Item 10, leadership style, is probably the determining factor insofar as growth in all or most of the other areas is concerned. The principal who can change his style of leadership to the cooperative style, if his present style is found wanting, will find that he has a deeper personal belief that teachers can change *their* attitudes and instructional styles. He presents a convincing argument for change in that he shows his staff that cooperative planning and working produces more and better results in making needed changes to meet the needs of children. Seeing teachers move toward professionalism, seeing them become committed to improvement of instruction, watching a program move from the planning stage to implementation, are all delightful experiences. The sense of accomplishment and fulfillment that accompanies successful change, the relaxed and accepting atmosphere that almost always results when human needs are taken into consideration, makes the whole experience most gratifying to the principal.

Learning activities and all the planned teacher/learner interactions come directly from goals. The principal has the major responsibility for goal setting, and if the task seems overwhelming, he is reminded that many schools have made organizational changes successfully and that assistance is available from many sources. The literature is replete with information and examples, and resource persons from many areas of the educational scene are available, most willing to share their knowledge and experiences. This sense of sharing is one of the best features of the movement toward reorganization of teaching in efforts to improve instruction.

Adding Preschool Education to the Organizational Pattern. Studies and reports proliferate to state the case for and list the advantages of early childhood education. Whether or not the organizational pattern of the school should include preschool at the lower end of the instructional ladder, and possibly junior college at the upper end, cannot conceivably rest on the decision of the individual principal. Regardless of the advantages, only authority and support from the total school system, both financial and philosophical, can add such a significant responsibility to the school. For example, as this is written, many schools are overcrowded, understaffed, physically outmoded, and in serious financial trouble because of lack of support at every governmental level. It is illogical to believe that elementary principals, many of them struggling to improve instruction in antiquated and overcrowded buildings, without adequate support for present programs, will be anxious to add preschool instruction to their organizational patterns and responsibilities. Yet the elementary principal must accept the responsibility for moving his community in this direction. The Headstart controversy continues largely because Headstart was not originally placed with the public schools, but educators in many places rejected the idea without trying to make this a dynamic beginning school experience for young children. Principals need to provide parents with data sufficient for them to see the need for extending educational opportunities downward.

SUMMARY

As stated at the beginning of this chapter, we have intended to emphasize the principal's role in planning for, implementing, maintaining, evaluating and improving the school's organizational pattern. Since the principal is the educational leader to whom the staff and community looks for guidance, it is obvious that few changes will be made unless the principal himself can visualize a new and better organizational pattern for instruction to augment or substitute for the present pattern. If he cannot visualize the possibilities, if he does not make a personal commitment to strive for implementation of the new pattern, it simply will not get done. No educational position offers greater opportunity for personal professional growth or opportunity to change educational patterns significantly than does the elementary principalship. For the forward-looking principal who wants to see his staff grow professionally, a new organizational pattern which involves teachers in decision making may be just the impetus needed to start the process of school/staff/community involvement in inaugurating change. No matter what the principal inherited when he moved into his present building, from that point on he is responsible for instituting improved instructional practices and processes within his building, and supervising efforts toward continual improvement. He will usually find that once a choice has been made, once his commitment is firm, once goals and direction have been established, once outside professional help has been obtained, the momentum will carry him and his staff into new, exciting, challenging realms of professional endeavor. This is the real thrill of cooperative planning: the discovery that combining the many personal and professional skills and talents of individuals can make his school an exciting and fulfilling place for staff and adult helpers and a place where children love to be.

There are two dimensions to the educational pattern. One is the outward dimension (pupil/teacher/facilities interaction) planned for a particular age, level of instruction, need, or ability. Second is the upward dimension correlated with a time line for sequence in the experiential and instructional patterns. Every organizational pattern was originally designed as an instrument for improving instruction. Many wide-ranging variables affect the planning, implementation, and ongoing evaluation of the selected pattern. Every modern program stresses humaneness in every facet of administrator/teacher, teacher/learner, and school/parent relationships and situations, and the fact that individualization of instruction must be a built-in factor. However, teachers do not have one student, or five, or even ten. Most have twenty-five or more, and "individualization" of instruction is a term that frightens many teachers *if* they believe it will be at the expense of classroom control and efficiency. The principal's task is to bring to his staff, with all the skills and tools at his command, the necessary techniques for humane teaching and individualization of instruction. He must express through words and actions the solid assurance that such teaching *enhances* control and efficiency because it minimizes the traditional "confrontation" situation which often led to a power struggle between students and teacher.

An organizational pattern has the inherent probability of improving the learning environment if: (1) it embraces a philosophy and an action program for change in which the teacher is not only encouraged but expected to serve the individual needs of children; (2) the teacher sees the organizational pattern as a device for achieving individualized instruction; and (3) the organizational pattern is clearly defined, with specific objectives within a comprehensive framework.

SUGGESTED READINGS

Anderson, Robert H. *Teaching in a World of Change*. New York: Harcourt, Brace and World, 1966.

Dean, Stuart E. *Elementary School Administration and Organization*. Washington, D.C.: Office of Education, Department of Health, Education and Welfare, 1960.

Frymier, Jack R. "The Need for an Optimal View of Pressures." *Theory Into Practice*. Columbus, Ohio: The Ohio State University, College of Education Publications, 1968.

Goodlad, John I. "Educational Change: A Strategy for Study and Action." *The National Elementary Principal* 43, (January 1969).

Heathers, Glen. *Organizing Schools Through the Dual Progress Plan*. Danville, Ill.: Interstate Printers and Publishers, 1967.

Hillson, Maurie, ed. *Change and Innovation in Elementary School Organization*. New York: Holt, Rinehart and Winston, 1965.

Howard, Alvin W. *Teaching in Middle Schools*. Scranton, Pennsylvania: International Textbook Company, 1968.

Klausmeier, Herbert J. and G. T. O'Hearn, eds. *Research and Development Toward the Improvement of Education*. Madison, Wisc.: Dembar Educational Research Services, 1968.

Klausmeier, Herbert J., R. Morrow and J. E. Walter. *Individually Guided Education in the Multiunit School: Guidelines for Implementation*. Madison, Wisc.: Research and Development Center for Cognitive Learning, 1968.

Kopp, O. W. "The School Organization vis-à-vis Improved Learning." *The National Elementary Principal* 47, February 1969.

National School Public Relations Association. *Differentiated Staffing in Schools*. Washington, D.C.: U.S.A. Education, Special Report, 1970.

University of Toledo. *The Ohio Model and the Multi-Unit School*. Toledo, Ohio: College of Education, 1971.

University of Wisconsin. *Making Teaching and Learning Better*. The Wisconsin Improvement Program 1959–61. Madison, Wisc.: Teacher Education and Local School Systems, School of Education, University of Wisconsin, 1962.

Notes

1. John I. Goodlad, "Educational Change: A Strategy for Study and Action," *National Elementary Principal* 43, No. 3 (January 1969): 8.
2. Glen Heathers, "Highlights of Address on Inquiry," Holliston's Project Model Middle. Title III ESEA 67-2988, Bulletin No. 3, April 1967 (Holliston, Mass.: Holliston Public Schools), p. 17.
3. Stanley Coopersmith, "How to Enhance Pupil Self-Esteem," Today's Education, *NEA Journal,* April 1969, p. 28.
4. Jack R. Frymier, "The Need for an Optimal View of Pressures," *Theory Into Practice* (Columbus, Ohio: The Ohio State University, College of Education Publications, 1968), p. 5.
5. Harold G. Shane, "Grouping in the Elementary School," in *Change and Innovation in Elementary School Organization,* ed. Maurie Hillson (New York: Holt, Rinehart & Winston, 1965), p. 13.
6. Robert H. Anderson, *Teaching in a World of Change* (New York: Harcourt, Brace, and World, 1966) pp. 50–51.
8. Stanley C. Carlson, "A Study to Determine Relationships Between Elementary School Organizational Plans and Desirable Educational Characteristics of the Classroom" (Doctoral dissertation, The University of Nebraska, 1967), p. 94.
9. O. W. Kopp, "The School Organization vis-à-vis Improved Learning," *The National Elementary Principal* 48, No. 4 (February 1969): 44.
10. Ibid.
11. Glen Heathers, *Organizing Schools Through the Dual Progress Plan* (Danville, Ill.: Interstate Printers and Publishers, 1967), pp. 2–3.
12. The ideas expressed here were adapted from a speech by Herbert J. Klausmeier, "Individually Guided Education in the Multiunit Elementary School," given at the Instructional Leadership Conference sponsored by the Department of Elementary Education, Ohio University, Athens, Ohio, June 1970.
13. Ibid., p. 4.
14. Judith Murphy, *Middle Schools,* Educational Facilities Laboratories, New York, New York, pp. 6, 7.
15. Ann Grooms, "The Middle School and Other Educational Innovations" (Speech delivered at the National Association of Secondary School Principals National Convention, February 25, 1967, Dallas, Texas), p. 7. Printed and distributed by Institute for Development of Educational Activities, Dayton, Ohio.
16. John I. Goodlad and Kenneth Rehage, "Unscrambling the Vocabulary of School Organization," *Change and Innovation in Elementary School Organization* (New York: Holt, Rinehart and Winston, 1965), p. 10.
17. David W. Beggs, III, ed., *Team Teaching, Bold New Venture* (Bloomington, Indiana: Indiana University Press, 1964), pp. 9–10.
18. Ibid., p. 16.
19. Robert F. Mager, *Preparing Instructional Objectives* (Palo Alto, California: Fearon, 1962), p. 12.
20. Stuart E. Dean, *Elementary School Administration and Organization,* Bulletin No. 11, OE-23006 (Washington, D.C.: U.S. Department of Health, Education, and Welfare, Office of Education, 1960), pp. 99–100.
21. Mager, *Preparing Objectives,* preface, p. vii.
22. Robert L. Sinclair, "Curriculum Phases: Toward Making Curriculum Responsive to Human Differences" (Paper presented to the Twelfth Annual Instructional Leadership Conference sponsored by the Department of Elementary Education, College of Education, Ohio University, Athens, Ohio, June 1971).
23. Ibid.

24. Ibid.
25. Kopp, "School Organization Syndrome," p. 45.
26. Goodlad, "Educational Change," pp. 9–10.

5

Educational Leadership in the Community

Educational leadership by the elementary school principal does not function apart from the people and the community served by the school. By the very nature of our society, the schools express the beliefs and values of that society. The principal is in a unique position as a community leader, and his prime responsibilities consist of the following: (1) he must examine and understand the belief and value structures both as a professional educator and as a well-informed participant in the community; (2) he must give direction to the educational program that will be truly representative of the will of the people, including minority groups, and dedicated to their highest aspirations and ideals; and (3) he must be able to turn inward to examine critically his own administrative behavior in terms of its effect on educational processes and outcomes, always evaluating the results in the light of accepted goals.

This threefold responsibility places the principal of the elementary school in the forefront in community-school relations. The importance of the community-school concept or the autonomous school cannot be overestimated as a matter for administrative concern. The principal is a professional educator who should be able to carry on school affairs according to his own convictions. Yet he must recognize the importance of complete staff and community involvement in developing the educational program.

This role as community leader suggests five guideposts for administrative behavior. The first of these is dedication to the task of *improving the quality of learning experiences*. Second, the principal assumes the modern role of a leader willing to lend his personal energies and skills in *raising community goals and improving standards of living*. His talents and abilities are no longer confined to just his school building. By virtue of his broader education and experiences, the principal moves in ever-widening circles to embrace the problems of the community at large. He studies and learns to understand

and to work with the power structure of the community. He serves as an active participant in community matters. He also uses a powerful instrument — his school — to bring about desirable changes for advancing his community. Third, the principal should *develop the techniques of communication* and get across the basic understandings of public education in his community. The complex job of understanding the people, improving processes of group thought, and developing personal convictions must culminate in translating the products to the community in a manner and form which will be understood by composite community groups. He will find that available communication media require his skilled use for effective and beneficial results. Fourth, the administrator needs to be aware of a dual responsibility in assisting other social agencies in the community to advance the general welfare and in working with them to *promote educational goals for his school*. The principal cannot work apart from other community agencies, either by withholding his personal support, by failing to cooperate, or by refusing to call upon them to supplement the educational program. Each community agency may contribute to the on-going educational program. In some ways the principal must *remain in the background, yet still exert leadership*. The art of being able to listen, to reason instead of argue, and to call upon and bring out new leadership suggests a community-minded principal who is emotionally mature. This ability also requires discerning the thinking of the people to discover their hopes, fears, and wishes for their school.

Two specific factors stand out in viewing the principal of the elementary school as a community leader and participant. The first is a consideration of the basic community understandings necessary to effective leadership by the principal. The principal will be a more constructive citizen only when he knows and understands his particular community as a part of our American society. His basic understandings should include knowledge of both material and human resources within the community. He especially is concerned with the implications of such resources for the educational activities of the elementary school. He must be vitally interested in discovering the real needs of his community, and he must seek to understand different points of view on community matters. He can give intelligent leadership only as he becomes well-grounded in facts, community beliefs and values, and in strong personal convictions.

The second factor is the leadership responsibilities of the community-minded principal. Certain clear-cut responsibilities for educational leadership emerge from basic understandings of the community. Near the top of the list of these responsibilities, if not first, is that of securing the community's support of public schools. There must be community participation in solving school problems as well as sharing in the development of the school program. From his understandings of the whole community, the principal will also be charged with defining or establishing basic problems and issues, particularly for that segment of education which is his responsibility. He may well be involved in other problem- and issue-defining activities within the community.

UNDERSTANDING THE COMMUNITY

Educators know that children learn particular patterns of behavior from interaction with other people. Parents, teachers, and peer groups act as socializing agents to help the child become the kind of person he will eventually be. The wider community setting involves other forces which act as socializing agents. The elementary principal is interested in the nature of the community because of its influences that are conducive to growth and development of the child.

Nature of the Community

The technical and psychological aspects of the community should be well understood by the modern principal. For all practical purposes he is the representative of the people in the community, and he must know what kind of education they want and are willing to support for their children. Since these desires and wants may be inadequately expressed or vaguely identified, the principal is faced with the task of getting at such beliefs and values. Community concepts become guides to his thinking only if he is able to capture the true nature of the community.

At the risk of over-simplifying the matter of discerning the nature of the community, two approaches will be suggested. These approaches do not supplant the broader knowledge which should form the core of the principal's intellectual background and academic preparation. The specific purpose here is to bring together some common elements to give a picture of a community. The two approaches may be stated in the form of questions: What components of community life are always present? and What makes up the good community?

Components of Community Life. The community can be complex or relatively simple in organization, industrialized or farm-centered, reactionary or progressive, or varied in many other ways. The people who live in the community give it personality and ultimately determine to a large degree the behavior of its children. In addition to the people and other elements of community life, there are five components[1] always present which condition and give direction to an educational program:

1. The natural endowments of the community, or the presence or lack of certain resources, set the stage for community life. Equally important are the uses made of natural wealth for a given area. The ingenuity, energies,

and creative actions of the people may combine to raise the community to higher levels of existence. Perhaps ignorance, selfishness, or short-sightedness may hinder the use and development of natural resources to the detriment of community life. The principal may first come to know his community as he views, surveys, and explores the availability of resources and sees the quality of community decisions, learns how well these are being used, and for what purposes. Those persons who are instrumental in formulating the decision-making methods and the decisions themselves will also constitute part of his survey.

2. The structure and organization of the community for carrying out its functions and services are present at both formal and informal levels. The legal basis of these fixed arrangements determines much of the structure and guides the organization of personnel in serving the community. The principal needs to understand these channels through which the life of the community flows. He is able to evaluate for himself how well the community makes decisions, and he becomes aware of his own role and effectiveness as he deals with the structural and organizational features of the community. He needs to know the extent to which citizens use their voting power and whether minority groups are a part of this power. In short, he needs to be acquainted with the legal factors or plans through which community services can be rendered, as well as the various interest groups seeking to achieve particular goals.

3. The structure of community life becomes important only as processes and methods are put into operation. There are various ways of accomplishing goals. Structure is the form, while process is the flexible way of putting vitality and activity into the structure. Wide variations may exist between a more or less legal structure and the ways in which community ideals and attitudes are developed and expressed. The principal must be able to identify and discuss intelligently the processes used in community matters in order to insure his own acceptance. He also faces the difficult task of contributing leadership when existing processes may be stifling community growth. Such a task requires deep insight into human behavior, as well as careful analysis of statutes and customs at the local level.

4. The principal must see the community as a corporate body with a personality. The ideals and attitudes of the people may be thought of as a state of mind, perhaps an *esprit de corps*. It is difficult to pin down the exact reasons why some communities are possessed with a confident and aggressive spirit, while apparently similar areas are actually depressed or submissive in attitude. But the principal knows that the morale of a community can be raised when people are actively involved in decision making. He encourages *all* members of the community to assist in giving direction to the school and to share in setting goals. The school belongs to the people, but he must help them clarify their desires for a relevant educational program that will enhance community living. Although the task of administering a

school is easier, in some respects, in a satisfied, progressive community, the principal finds his role as an educational leader merging into that of the community leader as he understands more clearly the ways he may help more people meet their basic needs.

5. Probably most people understand interdependence in community life. Economic life is no longer affected merely by local or state conditions, but by national and international affairs as well. Yet there still remains a kind of interdependence at the community level that is exceedingly complex. The members of the community are motivated by powerful drives for social action, whether or not they are aware of the reasons. The principal can grasp this concept of dependence upon others for welfare and progress. As a professional educator, he meets responsibility and challenge by serving others. His understanding of the threads of interdependence, however complex, gives him perspective in viewing the community as an entity working for common goals.

Understanding these five factors will lead to further understandings. The community will be subject to constant change. Even as his school can never stand still, neither will his community remain static. The principal will need firm convictions as to the kind of community he considers most suitable for children's development and growth.

The Good Community. The principal may need to extend his study of the real nature of the community by knowing what are considered favorable conditions or aspects of the good community. It is not enough to say that there needs to be abundant wealth, the presence of democratic processes, and the like. These matters are important in providing a physical setting for the child, but the principal must study other interrelations within the community. In addition to the physical setting of the community, two essential points contribute to the understandings of the community-minded principal.[2]

1. The good community provides a laboratory of human relations for the growing child. His social and intellectual development take place as he meets problems, wrestles with them, and solves conflicts for himself. The community should encourage these interactions, and should see that the child is permitted to share in the varied life of the total community. In fact, all citizens ought to be encouraged to participate in the affairs of the community. The good community may be judged in terms its citizens' freedom from restriction in the matter of creative expression.

2. The good community functions in another way in the lives of its children and citizens. For the child, the activities are child-centered. People realize that the transmission of culture is important, but there is also concern for how it is done. The good community makes the child feel he is a definite

Educational Leadership in the Community

part of its affairs, and takes an active interest in preparing him to adjust to the American way of life. Children study the community from a personal, first-hand basis. For all citizens, the good community follows the same pattern in making community business everybody's business.

The principal needs to understand the community because he must recognize the public attitudes and pressures that will ultimately determine elementary school practices. The child should learn about his community because many pupils will spend the major portions of their lives in their community; the school has had to take over many functions of the home; the trend in education has been to draw heavily upon the community for curricular and teaching materials; the schools are accepting the challenge of educating for better communities; and finally, because there are distinct educational advantages to the child growing out of the processes used in gaining understandings of his community. Since influences in the community do affect the future behavior of the child, the principal must examine the question of *who* makes up the community, for what the people believe and value determines the "personality" of the community and thus the eventual development of its children.

Understanding the Citizens of the Community

The nature of the community is the first basic understanding required of the principal if he is to give intelligent direction to the elementary school. The second understanding is concerned with the citizens who compose the community. This foundation for educational leadership may be considered in the light of (1) the concepts held by the people, and (2) the importance of the principal's working with the leaders in the community.

Concepts Held by Citizens. As has been pointed out, the thinking of the citizens will largely determine the educational program for the community and the school. People form certain concepts of education in the community or in a particular school through existing lines of communication. What ideas they hear and how they hear them makes a difference in their final conception of the school and its personnel. Whenever judgments and decisions are made by the citizens of the community, their acceptance will depend in large part on how well the people have been informed.

What people actually want for their children also influences the educational program. All parents have in mind certain aims for their children, and there is rarely unanimity as to what is most desirable, either for the present or the future. But it becomes exceedingly important to get these wants defined or verbalized in order to consolidate community action.

Citizens believe that the schools are responsible for meeting their needs and providing what they want for their children, and they will evaluate performance in terms of these concepts. Therefore, they will expect certain teacher-principal performance in the belief that their children will get the most benefit from particular methods of meeting these needs.

The principal may use these three concept determinants of educational programs in arriving at an understanding of the influence of the citizen in the community. He will want to know how effective are the existing lines of communication which, effective or misleading, are shaping educational judgments and decisions. What the citizens want for their children becomes important to him as a means of functioning more effectively in his school and in community-school relations. He will also be provided clues to bring about needed changes in communication and to establish future leadership on a community-wide basis. His understandings of citizens' concepts in terms of evaluative statements will further assist him in looking at his educational program. Citizens' conceptions of educational needs and methods may not be generally accepted by educators, or of the highest caliber; yet, since they do represent the thinking of the people who support the schools, the principal should be fully cognizant of them. He should not and cannot immediately change the community personality if its values and beliefs differ from his. Yet if educational leadership must first be grounded in basic understanding of community thinking or values, leadership moves forward from that position by helping people to re-think, re-define, and re-design older ideas, to be supplanted by their newly-discovered ones. The principal learns to work with people on the level at which he finds them.

COMMUNITY POWER STRUCTURE

We stress throughout this book that the school does not operate outside the community, and that the "good" school is a community school. It meets the needs of the pupils and serves the purposes of the community. To insure the school's goals and the community's goals, the principal must have certain fundamental understandings of the power structure of the community and know how to work within it. His leadership in bringing about school improvement will be tested in terms of how he goes about this. Surely the principal cannot accept the premise of isolation in today's schools; traditionally, until the early part of the twentieth century, schools and their operations were left to the discretion of the board of education and the administration. However, there has been an increasing desire among citizens to be more actively involved in school decision making. Educators have wanted citizen involvement, but perhaps many educators wanted this involvement only in areas which they did not consider their "sacred" territory.

Role of the Principal in the Community Power Structure

First, the principal needs to recognize the role of groups in the democratic processes. During the past fifty years, we have learned a great deal from research conducted on groups. One must recognize that groups consist of a collection of individuals, all of whom have a mutual goal. But although the goal might be the same for all individuals in the group, each individual's motive for working toward the goal might be different.

Group politics was first analyzed by a group of English scholars "who rejected the idea that communities consist mainly of individuals on the one hand and government on the other. . . . This group pictured the political process as functioning mainly through groups—churches, trade unions, consumer cooperatives, families, social clubs, etc."[3] However, they noted the influences of property and of groups which seek to protect economic interests, and thus recommended creating additional groups to promote non-property interests such as health, education, safety, security and the like.[4]

Our communities appear to have everything but stability. Yet, according to Berelson, Dahl, Kornhauser and others, this is the goal of a desirable political process. The democratic process is acclaimed for moderating dissension and promoting compromise in providing for the human welfare or the "good life." In the past, however, the masses have had little influence in redirecting their leaders. But the theorists believe that in the twentieth century, the basic purpose of the political system is stability.[5]

On the other hand, critics of the stability theory point out that such an emphasis can degenerate into acceptance of the status quo, resulting in a community that does not meet the real needs of the people. Bay further points out that the aim of a political system should be to produce an environment that enhances man's quest for the "good life" for all.[6] Perhaps there is a beginning, as small as it might be, at least to modify the stability aim of our political system as the non-elite gain sufficient power and influence to attract attention and cause man to see the true picture of society, its poverty and the accompanying problems. We must find ways to alleviate these conditions for the betterment of humanity. To do this, the composition of groups must include all segments of society dedicated to eroding the status quo.

A second group consisting of John Dewey, Walter Lippmann, E. E. Schattschneider, and others, sought to be more objective in studying groups, and concluded that political events occur largely as a result of pressure groups. A disturbing conclusion was reached: "The great public which liberals envisioned—the public of rational individuals or rational, open-minded groups of such individuals is a myth."[7] Walter Lippmann[8] indicated the public is merely a "phantom," while Dewey[9] pointed out that there are many publics, each with its own desires, programs, and inner contradictions.

Of importance to the principal is that he recognize that groups are the only power structures that do produce results. Groups, however, are often dominated by the elite of the community. Whether the community be small or large, there are those people who enjoy prestige, and who exert great influence on others. Although the real source of power in a democracy is yet to be truly identified, some authorities point out that real democracy recognizes the impossibility of direct influence by most members of political groups. Yet it is also pointed out that hierarchy and leadership from the top is inevitable.[10] Schumpter further points out that democracy is competition of the elites; non-elites have little or no opportunity to participate in decision making. Yet the demands by non-elites to share in the decision-making process, assuming an open system that permits their participation, seems to be all that can be required of any political system. That is, if the political system is open and provides for choices of policy by placing low-income citizens, minority groups and the elite in direct competition for power and decision making, then the system has met its basic need.[11]

Great strides have been made in recent years toward having all citizens share in the decision-making process. We do have evidence that people are breaking down the elite power structure and providing for participation by racial and low-income groups in the decision-making process for public school operation.[12] The principal need not be a social scientist to distinguish between an open and a closed community. Citizens attempt to maintain the status quo for their schools, but not all do so for the same reason. The power structure in one community might be tied to the economic life of the community, thus any additional expenditure for schools would disturb the economic elite. In another community, new ideas might be considered dangerous because they disturb the minds of the power structure and because the ideas are foreign to the community, thus it becomes essential to maintain equilibrium. One of the authors knows of school administrators who must call a certain community businessman before making commitments. It becomes important for the principal to recognize that community power structures differ as much as do communities. It will take time to study and determine where the power rests in each community; the larger the community, the more difficult this might be. The principal, whether preservice or inservice, will find it wise to become knowledgeable about community power structure.

American society is now attempting to bring all segments of society into the mainstream of its life. Racial groups have forced passage of civil rights legislation, and volunteer groups have helped them to register to vote. Black leaders hold major offices throughout the land. Yet these individuals have little individual influence. When new groups form and use their power to achieve their goals, they enter into competition for power with the established groups, and thus broaden the base for decision making. The elementary principal must recognize that involvement in school decision making should extend beyond the elite group. The principal must develop an awareness of the power structure in his community, and at the same time work to extend this power to more segments of society. Keynes has identified some broad judgments about American politics and community power which could serve as guides to the principal in studying his particular community, among them:

1. Community politics is largely a matter of power conflicts between groups.
2. The rich, who are often businessmen, constitute a particularly powerful group in most communities.
3. Studies of public decisions usually reveal influence by diverse political actors—both groups and individual.
4. To a degree that cannot be precisely ascertained, political groups are dominated by powerful elites.
5. In America, regardless of whether groups or elites rule, in combination or alone, most citizens are rarely active in politics, and fewer than half of them vote.
6. Among those who do not participate, there is widespread apathy to political matters.[13]

Identifying the Community Power Structure

The principal can seek information on his own for analyzing his community's power structure by keeping careful records of who is actively involved in certain community projects and public issues. Radio and television reports and newspaper articles are sources of information. However, certain persons in the community might also provide valuable information. University research teams from political science departments or public relations departments could be employed as consultants. In addition, College of Education teams will learn a great deal of information when they are used to study the school's curriculum or the system's plans for reorganization. They can also be used as consultants on bond issues or levy increases. (Public school people have not been too successful in this area. In Ohio during the two recent years, only 29 percent of local requests for additional school funds have been approved by the people.[14])

Using Information about Power Structures. School improvement on a broad front is not easy to accomplish. Yet most of today's schools need vast changes in philosophy, curriculum, organization, pupil personnel practices, instructional procedures, etc. While community involvement is important in bringing about change in the schools, the principal's success in implementing change depends upon his effectiveness in bringing together those forces which can accomplish the tasks. If the change involves new priorities for funds, then the principal will need to seek the support not only of parents, but also of the power structure. This might require an occasional afternoon of golf with the "right" people, or other activities which will help the principal secure a sympathetic ear. If this is the way the power structure works, then the principal must be adept at the game.

EDUCATORS AND POLITICS

The local school becomes increasingly important with decentralization and the principal's new role in the new political structure. Educators have had a traditionally weak position in political organization. Administrators and teachers refrained from entering politics, sometimes by board-of-education edict, and often for fear of losing their jobs. In fact, it was believed that the schools themselves should be isolated from politics. The procedure established in the Commonwealth of Virginia for securing a school board was believed to be free of political manipulation. This procedure provided for the circuit court judge to appoint three school trustees from each magisterial district, which constituted a separate school district within each county. These trustees, in turn, appointed a board of education member from each school district in the county.[15] The only problem with this procedure was that the judge was appointed by the governor. Yet this sophisticated procedure was thought to have kept the schools free of politics.

Working with Minority Groups

Educational Differences between Rural and Urban Communities. Since World War II, changes have come about rapidly in both urban and rural areas. Rural education has been concerned with school reorganization and consolidation. This change, however, has almost been mandated by state departments of education. Parents in the rural communities, although interested in education, have not sought educational change. In fact, they have fought and resisted consolidations. Suburbia has attempted to keep up with the latest innovations in teaching, team teaching, language labs, and technology in general, and the problems of financing education. In the cities, the schools have shared the blame with other urban agencies for all the social ills of the ghetto—poor housing, unsanitary conditions, and lack of supportive services. Ghetto parents have been caught in the middle with their children. At school the children are required to live and think with a different set of values than used at home. Thus the child has to make a decision between his teacher's way or his parents' judgment. This conflict often resulted in behavior problems at school or in the child actually rejecting himself.

Dissatisfaction with children's progress in the inner city schools contributed to the problems in these urban communities. While educators were attempting to provide *equal* education for all children, classrooms were homogeneous. That is, the curriculum for all third grades across the city was the same. Radio and television instruction, textbooks, and other materials were the same for all children. Consequently, the needs of the ghetto children were not being met. A combination of all these problems and growing dissatisfaction with the efforts to reach solutions have led to militancy on the part of parents, children, and the immediate community.

Today's schools are changing and classrooms in more and more urban areas are becoming more heterogeneous. Large sums of money spent in the cities have resulted in diversity in the classrooms. New methods of teaching low-income children are being tried; new materials for reading programs in the inner city have been developed. Programs of behavior modification, team teaching, use of paraprofessionals, open-classroom and intensive teaching techniques are helping to meet these children's needs. But even with the expenditure of these vast sums of money, educators did not get at the root of the problem. Only with the second great wave of spending by the federal government has real progress been made in solving some of the problems of low-income children. To fund most of these new programs, the government insisted that advisory boards consist of at least fifty per cent parents. For the first time, parents who had been lost in the maze of educational bureaucracy in large cities have become involved in the mainstream of their children's education.

Working with Large Minority Groups. Urban communities and their schools have been dominated and controlled by whites, even when they are predominately Black, Indian, Mexican American, or Puerto Rican. Often the minority group was not consulted or involved in the decision making. Such situations lead to racism, for the minority group feels it is being told by whites what is best for its members. The reverse situation would produce the same results.

The ideal situation would, of course, be one where race differences do not exist and all groups work together harmoniously, sharing equally in making decisions for improving school and community living. But even in a pluralistic society, no racial group should have the power to dominate another group. It appears that the next step in furthering group needs is to see that decisions affecting the local school and community are determined by the local community. That is, decentralization of power is needed to permit the community to determine the direction of its school. A neighborhood school which is predominately black should be guided by the parents of the children of this school. If the values, expectations and desires are determined by the community and if these objectives are to be realized, then the principal, whether white or black, must work closely with his staff and the community to realize the attainment of the objectives. A persistent theme of this book is that those who are directly affected by decisions must be permitted to help make these decisions and to assist in their implementation

Creating and Working with Local School Advisory Councils. The principal of a neighborhood school, regardless of his race or the constituency of the community, must encourage community participation in school matters. For years, parents have wanted a voice in what is being taught. They have sought a voice in hiring or firing teachers and principals and a host of other concerns, but they have not gotten effective action on their demands. This is not to say that a central school board should act on all parent demands. Our point is the necessity for some local control of the neighborhood school. We suggest that guidelines be established at the state level for operation of local school controlling boards, be they councils, advisory committees, or local boards. If guidelines are developed at the state level by professionals and lay citizens, these local controlling boards will know their relationship to the central board of education. Some of the concerns the guidelines might deal with are:

1. Minimum educational requirements for all teaching and non-teaching personnel.
2. Elements of collective bargaining.
3. Parents' grievance procedures.
4. Philosophy of humanizing the school.
5. Procedures for major changes in the educational program.

Whatever direction the guidelines take, they must not interfere with the powers of the central board, yet they must provide for local control. As an illustration, School A has had a principal who, for five years, has dominated the teaching staff, pupils, and parents. He has not understood the community and used his authority to put only what he considered "good" educational practices into operation. Under the guidelines, a local advisory committee could recommend that this principal be dismissed, transferred to another district as principal, retained as a teacher, or transferred to another district as a teacher. The local committee would then interview applicants for the position and recommend the one they feel would give the desired kind of direction to their school. The candidates would have to meet the professional requirements established by the state and the central boards of education, and all procedures would have to be negotiated with the association or union representing the principal. But the point is, the school program would operate on policies made at the local school level providing for an autonomous elementary school.

The local school advisory council should be an elected council which serves the immediate school. This council operates under the guidelines of the central board of education, as previously discussed. If such a council is not now functioning, the elementary school principal might initiate the idea in his community. In some schools the principal has used the P.T.A. officers as his advisory council. However, this should be broadened to include the entire attendance district. Procedures should be established for running for a position on the advisory committee, eligibility regulations drawn up, and an election held. The school could serve as the center for this activity, since this must remain a non-partisan election.

The school could provide various educational programs to serve all those interested in running for the advisory committee. Programs presenting hints for speech writing, developing posters and brochures, and calling news conferences would be important educational activities for the candidates. The school auditorium could serve as the meeting place where candidates could air their views. This school function could be extended to all persons from the attendance district interested in running for public office. The school then becomes the center for forums of all types, and candidates have an opportunity to learn how to improve their communications.

Once the council is elected, it must abide by the guidelines for local advisory councils. The principal will serve as an ex officio member of the council without voting rights. His leadership will be needed in many different ways. He will need to see that council members do not use the council to espouse their own selfish causes. He will need to keep before the council the goal of improving the educational program. The council members should be concerned primarily with establishing policies for the local school. They must not however, conflict with the legally established central board of education.

The local advisory council will work closely with all community agencies. The school thus takes on new meanings in the life of the community, as everyone works together to improve services for education, health, housing, etc.

Role of the Principal in the Changing Community

The principal might find himself in a school which is 90 percent white and 10 percent black, but which has started a transition. Within five years the school might become 90 percent black. This transition requires creative leadership. The principal will let his staff know the changes that will be expected of them. He may suggest that if teachers feel they cannot adjust to the new racial balance, they might want to transfer to another school. For the good of the community, he needs the best-prepared staff possible, whether white or from minority groups. Paraprofessionals who understand and relate to the children's problems should be employed to aid in the total educational process. A school that is shifting from a white to a black population will have to change its program to accomplish the things which are important to blacks.

The principal will need to measure constantly the tempo of the community to see that the school is moving in the desired direction. The local council can bring in help from other agencies, some of which may not have been deeply involved in the community prior to the transition. The principal will need to coordinate these efforts. The school staff will have to include liaison workers —visiting teachers, social workers, health and housing coordinators, etc.

Needs of the Community. The principal does catch a glimpse of community needs when he studies the nature of the community and its human and material resources, but he must look closer to discover the real needs.

Since people of different communities hold somewhat different beliefs and values, what they believe must be determined by the elementary school administrators. Despite variations in beliefs between communities, the principal may find a common denominator in community personalities. After studying a community by the three methods mentioned in this chapter, the principal may use a fourth psychological approach. He will find, in general, that people acting as a community corporate body have four important needs. They must have a feeling of physical and economic security; know feelings of unity as a group; experience feelings of community achievement; and know and be guaranteed a feeling of status.

Physical and Economic Security. A community needs assurance that its economy is reasonably sound. Problems of adequate housing, good government, established business enterprises, and the like must not be overwhelming to the point of creating widespread frustration. But it is important that all agencies work together to provide each family with an improved environment. In carrying out daily activities, a spirit of well-being must be prevalent and apparent to the citizens. The struggle for survival absorbs much of the energy of a community. These needs must be met.

Unity. When the people of a community are satisfying many needs as a group, there are times when a need may be intense enough or sufficiently threatening to produce an emotional reaction. Emotional security evolves when people feel contented and safe. Even as the child needs wise leadership, the institutions of the community provide the emotional overtones that make it a good place to live, and which weld the citizens together in common bonds.

Achievement. The community has a need for achievement other than financial. Goals must be achieved by the community, and new obtainable goals must be set. Repeated failure to master situations can lead to a community neurosis, since feelings of frustration cannot be tolerated very long. Con-

Educational Leadership in the Community   115

tinued satisfactions of achievement feed the community need for mastery and lead to achievement of even higher goals.

Status. Closely related to the need for achievement is the role of the community in obtaining recognition and acceptance as an entity in itself. Many civic committees strive to do the correct and proper things in order to be like more successful cities or towns. People learn very early in life that it is well to gain approval and avoid censure. Even the community works for its proper place in the sun. Customs and codes of behavior are either adhered to or changed if it seems that the community will gain higher status in the eyes of its own people or its neighbors as a result.

The elementary school principal may capitalize upon these inner drives of the people of the community. In his final analysis and interpretation of all data concerning the community, he rounds out his personal understandings when he becomes aware of these deeper psychological forces that give meaning to community action.

RESPONSIBILITIES OF THE COMMUNITY-MINDED PRINCIPAL

Clearly, the principal must use his understanding of the community to exercise his leadership responsibilities in school-community situations. He is in a unique position to render the kind of leadership that will benefit both school and community. Public support for the school and the amount of community enthusiasm depend largely on the leadership skills and characteristics of an individual principal. He may fail to recognize his responsibilities or wish to sidestep them, but he cannot deny failure, in some part, when his leadership produces poor community relations and thus impedes educational progress. Shane places the full responsibility for leadership on the professional educator and the schools ". . . because obviously it is to help each community to develop basically enlightening opportunities for all children and youth. . . . This responsibility of the educational profession to establish and maintain good education obviously cannot be met by educators working apart from their communities or in high-handed fashion."[16]

Four areas of responsibility suggest the kind of person the principal should be in the community setting:

1. The principal is responsible for securing community support for his school.
2. The principal is responsible for defining and establishing certain basic problems and issues in school and community.
3. The principal is responsible for using the total resources of the community for educational purposes.
4. The principal is responsible for meeting the needs of the community and changing its behavior in certain respects.

Securing Community Support

Emphasis has already been placed on the importance of securing public support of community projects. Although the elementary school will reflect the kind of leadership exemplified by its principal and staff, the administrator is faced with a leadership responsibility in securing and maintaining the cooperative support of the educational program by interested, dynamic community citizens. His responsibility for good school-community relations goes beyond a good-will campaign or selling-the-school approach. The complex task of leadership involves at least three factors which underline this important responsibility for any school administrator.

First, the principal may view his task as that of organizing the citizens for definite purposes. He will want to encourage liberal use of representative citizen committees. A cross section of people will better insure wider participation and diffusion of understanding, as well as broader feelings of personal interest and concern. Basing his approaches on sound psychological procedures and his understanding of inner drives and needs, he will recognize which problems have emotionally charged issues or blocked communication routes.

It is the responsibility of the elementary school principal to recognize hindrances to full public support of the school and its program. These may be summarized as follows:

1. The channels of communication are clogged, cumbersome, or otherwise not free or fully clear. The air seems charged with emotional issues because of inadequate avenues of communication.

2. The school does not have friendly, free communication with the children. No attempts have been made to develop these channels through the years, and the children thus do not carry pleasant school feelings to their homes.

3. The system of reporting pupil progress to the home has been inadequate. Confused and frustrated parents have talked with teaching personnel and discovered some ragged thinking.

4. Children do not receive enough useful personal guidance. Parents feel that the individual child may have been buried in the mass of numbers and treated with indifference.

5. Other agencies in the community have not been called upon by the school. Their services and relations to the school are ineffective or practically nonexistent because avenues of information are neglected.

6. The needs of the community have scarcely entered the picture as the educational program has developed. No one seems to remember how, why, or when a particular school objective came into being.

7. No one seems outwardly concerned about doing anything to alleviate prejudices, fears, and other community antagonisms. The schools seem just as aloof and conservative as any other institution.

8. An inspection of the total school organization does not reveal the kinds of activities likely to produce citizens who will adjust adequately to community life.

The second step in securing community support consists of the principal's attempts to help people recognize their educational tasks. The citizens need to be brought into the picture by deciding together what the schools can do better. Even apparently successful programs can be scrutinized to find different and improved methods or techniques. Vigilance in keeping the community interested and alert for newer and better ways of getting things done will do much to earn public support. The most effective procedure for securing community support of the school may well be the attempt of principal and citizens to appreciate the actual contributions the school makes to community living.

The third step toward insuring full community support depends on the principal's ability to sustain his role as a community leader. To give effective leadership by initiating and developing activities as have just been mentioned is important. However, constant attention and concern are needed, and this responsibility must rest ultimately upon the principal. The emphasis here is on his recognizing and accepting the role of maintaining community enthusiasm.

Better Community Perspective

A further responsibility for educational leadership is the principal's ability to define and establish certain problems and issues for and with the citizens of the community. The preceding discussion is linked closely with this responsibility, in that the principal must first define problems and issues when he works for community support. This responsibility may be explained by listing some general problems and issues. Communities differ as to the problems and issues which are important to them at a given time. With changing conditions in population, value systems, patterns of community organization, and the like, it is impossible to state or prescribe this leadership responsibility in rigid terms. However, seven suggestions will give the principal a perspective of his responsibility for helping the community to better understanding of problems and issues concerning education.[17]

1. *Understand the importance of the family as a basic institution in American society.* People are generally concerned about their children's growth and development. Their interest in child welfare includes concern for the education of the child. The principal strengthens and clarifies the family role.

2. *Make clear that the school is only one of many agencies that affect the lives of the children and all citizens in the community.* The school as an instrument in serving people has an important but single role to play in connection with other service agencies.

3. *Define clearly the purposes of the school for the community.* This point has been mentioned in connection with other problems, but the principal always faces the responsibility of getting the school's purposes clearly defined and established in the minds of the people.

4. *Show what ideas and values are acquired by the child in the classroom.* Much discussion may center on these ideas and values, especially if they conflict with popular notions. The principal can face real problems when conflicts in values result in behavior inimical to desired beliefs and patterns. He must demonstrate real leadership in defining these value systems to the satisfaction of the community.

5. *Develop common values for the common good.* In a real sense, the community becomes unified when leadership brings a common set of values acceptable to the people.

6. *Describe the importance of utilizing all available professional help in the education of the child.* The principal and his teachers are responsible for the learning experiences, but to show the added values of other resources is a responsibility of the principal if some citizens cannot accept this viewpoint.

7. *Clarify the controversial issues and attacks on education.* There are those who will criticize educational practices, methods, or philosophy and win over the public, whether or not there is justification. The responsibility of the principal cannot be avoided if he desires intelligent public conclusions based on facts.

Thus, the responsibility of the principal in defining educational problems and issues to gain community support and understanding is serious and vital to good school-community relations. There will be times when he will discover new evidence and different outlooks which will demand a change in his own philosophy and patterns of behavior. By the same token, the citizens of the community may have to modify their views on the basis of clearly defined and understandable facts. The principal's leadership responsibility may turn from defining issues to helping people see new ways of doing and acting through effective compromises. In every instance the principal should stand solidly on an issue only after the public has been well informed and misunderstandings have been resolved. He is moving forward to a higher phase of leadership activity by setting the stage for changing and improving community behavior.

DISCIPLINE IS A COMMUNITY PROBLEM

The community-minded principal readily recognizes the attitudes of the community toward discipline. Discipline is not a problem of the school alone, and any effort to improve pupil behavior must be a cooperative endeavor with the community. Communities across the nation face the problem of juvenile delinquency, and school personnel are blamed for laxity. Criticism aimed at the school's and teacher's unwillingness to face the real issue requires dynamic leadership on the part of the principal. He must summon community groups and social agencies to examine environmental weaknesses which may lead to antisocial behavior in and out of school. Only when parents work cooperatively with teachers to solve adjustment problems will pupils emerge with self-discipline and a sense of responsibility.

Discipline in the elementary school should be based on clear-cut policy arrived at cooperatively by the administration, faculty, and community members. That is not to say the rules and regulations for individual classrooms must be spelled out in rigid, specific terms, although certain school mandates must be distinctly described in writing. The principal should be in a position to furnish leadership in the following areas to insure a properly disciplined educational situation:

1. Establishment of a philosophy of discipline;
2. Working with and helping the beginning teacher (or even the more experienced person who needs assistance) with classroom control problems; and
3. Defining the roles of teachers and parents in school disciplinary situations.

A Philosophy of Discipline

By cooperative efforts the staff of the elementary school should arrive at a definition and understanding of discipline. The principal can help the faculty find a common basis in this important area by resolving his own thinking in a way consistent with the modern approach. He should accept the philosophy that disciplinary action has two purposes: (1) to help children become more mature persons as they progress from the dependent role toward a more independent one; and (2) to prevent discipline problems and maintain the order necessary for efficient teaching-learning conditions.[18]

Teachers may have to be led to understand that control in the classroom means more than exercising power and domination to maintain perfect order. The educational contribution of the administrator in formulating a philosophy of discipline can mean broader insight into the role of the school by staff members who may have previously concentrated only on the second purpose stated above. Perhaps another look at the meaning of discipline may lend support to this philosophical viewpoint:

> Your teaching task in discipline is the same as your teaching task in every other field. Children do learn some things by listening, but you know that they are more apt to remember and to act on their own words, their own ideas. . . . The weight of their experiences in your classroom must be on what they do to share their problems: *their* analysis, *their* proposals, *their* examination of the results.[19]

A philosophy of discipline for the modern elementary school must be predicated upon the staff's willingness to help children become more independent persons, to help them recognize the need for optimum working conditions, and to help them achieve a degree of self-discipline that comes about through their achievement of meaningful personal goals. The principal can use this framework as a guide for leading his staff in developing certain policies, analyzing present behaviors, and devising newer, more effective ways of working with children.

Help for the Beginning Teacher or One Who Needs Assistance. Research studies support the thesis that beginning teachers have more discipline problems than do the experienced personnel. This section furnishes practical help to all new teachers. The principal's early consideration of the new or beginning teacher, with reference specifically to discipline, may fall into a framework of the following ten activities, depending upon the amount of time available. However, guidance, not dominance, during the first six weeks of school may be crucial!

1. *Give time for either an individual or group conference to orient and induct the new teacher into the school.* Devote time to the problems of classroom control and to setting up certain principles for action. If no time is available before teaching begins, an early scheduling of this conference is in order.

2. *Enable the new instructor to plan and prepare for the first few days of school.* Where pre-teaching workdays are provided, the principal may request from the beginning teacher a written outline of plans for initiating the learning program with purposeful activities. The principal may point out helpful things to be done with special equipment. The main point is to give the teacher a sense of security by having a definite plan of action. Teachers will thus be led to seek goals even during the first day of school, and will follow the philosophy that such motivated behavior is constructive in nature.

3. *Assemble all pertinent data available about the child for study by the teacher.* If the teacher is able to get acquainted with the child before seeing him in class, as well as to secure supplementary data in many other ways during the school term, there is little doubt that more effective teaching can be done. The principal who helps the new teacher study records[20] lays the groundwork for future guidance approaches in the classroom, and helps the teacher understand each child in terms of his response to his group. Thus the teacher is better prepared to know how to relate himself to the child.

4. *Suggest practical ways of working with children to prevent disciplinary problems from arising.* The new teacher may have learned from college courses many devices conducive to good control, but he needs at this point

Educational Leadership in the Community 121

an opportunity to come into contact with ideas to refresh his thinking or supplement his body of knowledge. For example, it may be nothing new to the teacher to hear the principal discuss how the physiological needs of children dictate the use of the larger muscles in certain activities. Yet, as the new teacher is offered opportunities for hearing and talking about these needs, classroom theory is translated into practical ways of working with pupils.

The principal can render a valuable service to the new teacher in helping her prevent some discipline problems; a research study by Shuster points up the need for the beginning teacher to receive aid in securing control of the class.[21] Thus the beginning teacher should be encouraged to think through the many practical procedures which can be brought into play in controlling the classroom, particularly in the areas of methods of work, social control, physical aspects, and emotional control.

5. *Discuss causes of behavior problems.* Again, when teachers are more aware of definite causes of poor behavior, many negative experiences can be avoided. The principal is not expected to conduct a course in human growth and development or in principles of mental health, but he may help the new teacher see that some behavior problems arise from deficiencies in physical needs, unhappy home situations, personality flaws, and so on. A child often acts in a way that may offer his only hope of finding satisfaction. When the principal helps the teacher to see how behavior is caused, she begins teaching with the kind of understanding that may be "felt" by the children.

6. *Suggest specific school policies relating to specific behavior situations.* Usually the elementary school faculty is guided by certain rules or patterns of conduct expected of the children. For example, teachers may be expected to maintain order in the hallways, on the playground, and in the cafeteria. Familiarity with what is expected of all children in the school gives the teacher a guide for following prescribed ways of behavior. Equally valuable to the new teacher should be the concept of getting children to discuss standards of behavior, according to maturity level and expectations. The principal should help the teacher understand that self-discipline is achieved when teacher and students work together in facing problems and share in making wise, intelligent agreements about behavior that are then tried out in real situations. Even when rules are prescribed (such as "no running in the halls"), the teacher is encouraged to use the modern, creative approach of permitting group analysis of existing rules for clarification, and group setting of standards of good behavior.

7. *Help the teacher to express what may be the best discipline approach to use the first day of school.* The new teacher may wonder whether it would be wiser to be harsh and severe, or to radiate friendliness. Of course, the principal knows that the expressions and manifestations of the teacher's

personality will determine to a great degree the overall atmosphere of the classroom. He can help the new teacher see that every teacher must play the role that harmonizes with her own personality. It is well to begin the first day with an attitude that is businesslike, firm, and positive. The beginning teacher should expect the principal to support this approach although it does not mean an absence of friendliness, humor, respect, willingness, and consistency. The school administrator may contribute much by affirming his faith in the teacher who is relaxed but firm, and who is thoughtful of the welfare of each class but tolerates no noisy, undesirable classroom situation. At the same time, the principal needs to assure the teacher of his support for a classroom which is active and which radiates a busy noise.

8. *Point out the importance of teacher personality and creation of a desirable emotional climate.* Beginning teachers should be encouraged to recognize the value of such things as personal magnetism in establishing good rapport with children. Although discipline problems are not prevented simply by a display of the teacher's personality, such impressions and personal influences are certainly important. The creation of a free, permissive climate in the classroom should be considered a major factor in developing the kind of behavior desired in the modern school. The principal may discuss and illustrate ways in which this type of classroom can be organized and show the teacher some existing situations in the school.

9. *Acquaint the new teacher with certain physical conditions in the school.* Explore all aspects of the physical plant that could lead to possible disciplinary situations. The beginning teacher should be able to recognize those conditions that are conducive to tension or disruption. For example, congestion in hallways might arise from improper use of lockers or crowded conditions during a recess period; these are situations which may not always be anticipated by the inexperienced teacher. The principal is aware of these physical aspects and must point them out to the staff, since this kind of leadership can minimize internal strain. Cooperative efforts in discovering these aspects and seeking their solutions should be a continuous process.

10. *Show how parents are to be involved in disciplinary cases.* Although the next section is concerned with this subject, it should be noted here that the beginning teacher may derive much help from the principal if sufficient time is given to this important aspect of classroom mangement. Early understanding of these working relationships gives a greater sense of security and direction to every faculty member.

These ten administrative activities are designed to assist the inexperienced or insecure teacher in approaching the problem of classroom control. The principal must vary procedures according to the time available for working together and according to the needs of the moment. In every instance he should be interested in helping staff members arrive at the concept of self-

Educational Leadership in the Community 123

discipline as the primary goal for all children. The principal can concentrate on definite processes that will insure a self-disciplined child by encouraging teachers and pupils to analyze their experiences together in activities of identifying, exploring, and analyzing day-to-day behavior problems; to set up and agree upon standards of behavior; to work together in achieving agreed-upon goals under student leadership according to maturity level and past experiences with other teachers in democratic settings; to evaluate behavior in such ways that children can discern for themselves how well they are behaving in the light of agreed-upon standards; and to decide what new steps, if any, are to be taken if evaluation reveals weaknesses.

Working with Parents

Since parents are to be involved as much as possible in every aspect of the school program the principal is highly concerned with enlisting their aid in preventing unwholesome conditions and practices, as well as in solving disciplinary problems as they arise. Either he or a staff member may be called upon to perform these functions, but in every case at least two approaches can be employed that will help school personnel become more effective in such relationships.

First, attention must be given to planning ways of solving a behavior problem. In order to prevent problems or to solve them, the staff member is in a stronger position to take action if he plans in terms of identifying or isolating the factors involved; discovering the *why* of the situation; agreeing upon *how* (at least tentatively) a course of action may go; defining the school's role (principal, teacher, or pupil) in the situation; and defining the parent's role.

When the staff member plans a course of action that follows this five-point guide, he is in effect giving time and study to the behavior problem, or to the prevention of one. Actually, his planning may be considered the preliminary exploratory and analytical activities necessary for insuring intelligent decisions and action.

The second approach concerns the conference with the parent. A well-planned conference that follows sound techniques should prove beneficial. Thus, a checklist[22] for both principal and teacher in working with parents may include the following things to do, either as an individual or as a group:

1. Make early contact with the parent concerning a present or foreseeable problem;
2. Develop friendly relations;
3. Recognize the partnership bond between school and parent;
4. Be ready with tentative suggestions;
5. Know your own limitations as well as those of others involved;
6. Watch for scapegoating from any direction;

7. Consider the feelings of parents;
8. Watch for defense mechanisms;
9. Try to come up with at least a tentative solution by the end of the conference; and
10. Bring pupils into the conference.

These ways of working with teachers, pupils, and parents can lead to improved behavior. If the goal is greater self-discipline for all children, the principal accepts the thesis that he can aid his staff and the parent group by his leadership. He should help teachers see the value of the following general guides to teacher behavior in maintaining the proper classroom atmosphere:

1. Learn to know each child.
2. Respect the individuality of each child.
3. Give children security.
4. Organize interesting and meaningful activities.
5. Set reasonable standards for achievement and conduct.
6. Evaluate on the basis of many growth factors.
7. Handle discipline stituations as they arise.
8. Keep yourself and the classroom cheerful.

SUMMARY

The principal of the elementary school has a dual role in community life: he is responsible for providing the educational experiences wanted and needed by the community; and he can and should demonstrate leadership in changing certain behavior patterns and thinking of its citizens. In order to fulfill these obligations the principal may approach his educational and community tasks by (1) gaining basic understandings of the total life of his community; (2) spelling out clearly his particular responsibilities in light of these understandings; and (3) employing techniques and devices that have been found useful.

Since community influences affect school practices as well as child behavior, the principal first studies the nature of the community in terms of its resources and people, as well as the community power structure. His understanding of its needs is grounded in the community's system of beliefs and values. His ability to see meaning in community action may depend upon how well he understands the four fundamental needs of any community. These needs include the natural desires for physical and economic security, for unity, for achievement, and for status. Although the principal may have little or no control in satisfying such community needs directly, he is better able to appreciate the thinking of the citizens and the reasons for their behavior. He may lend his personal support as a citizen in helping the community to greater satisfaction of one or more of these needs.

The principal must secure community support for his school, define and establish certain basic problems and issues in school and community, and use the total resources in the community for educational purposes. Specific leadership skills can assist him in playing a more effective role as a school-community leader.

There is no single, prescribed way to give leadership in school-community matters. Each principal must analyze his own situation and decide upon a course of action in the light of his own understanding. Yet there are common problems in every community, and the principal may utilize the approaches and skills set forth here for discovering where to start, how to plan, and where and how to take definite steps to demonstrate the competencies and abilities needed in his school and community.

Discipline is considered a major problem by many principals. The modern principal must lead his school staff by giving them practical suggestions, planning specific courses of action with teachers in solving disciplinary problems, and by helping them understand the need for pupil involvement in developing self-discipline. However, the success of any effort to improve pupil behavior depends on the principal's awareness and ability to relate the problem to the community. Thus discipline is not a problem of the school alone, but one which requires continuous community study.

SUGGESTED READINGS

Austin, Ernest H., Jr. "Cultural Deprivation—A Few Questions." *Phi Delta Kappan,* October 1965.

Bernard, Jesse. *Marriage and Family Life Among Negroes.* Englewood Cliffs, N.J.: Prentice-Hall, 1966.

Bunzel, John H. "Pressure Groups in Politics and Education." *The National Elementary Principal* 43 (January 1964).

Clear, Delbert K. "Decentralization: Issues and Comments." *The Closing House,* January 1970.

Fantini, Mario and Marilyn Gittell. "The Ocean Hill—Brownsville Experiment." *Phi Delta Kappan,* April 1969.

Filbin, Robert. "Do Superintendents Spend Enough Time on PR?" *Phi Delta Kappan,* November 1971, p. 192.

Hunter, Madeline C. "Home-School Communication." *The National Elementary Principal* 47 (November 1967): 24–30.

Levine, Daniel U. "Urban Education, Segregation, and Children in the Inner-City School." *School and Society,* February 1970.

Nisbet, Robert. *Community and Power.* New York: Oxford, 1962.

Olsen, Edward G., ed. *The School and Community Reader.* New York: Macmillan, 1963, Chapters 4, 9, 11.

Ostrom, Vincent. "The Interrelationships of Politics and Education." *The National Elementary Principal* 43 (January 1964).

Sheehan, Pete. "Why the Money Ran Out in Youngstown." *Phi Delta Kappan* 51 (November 1969): 118–21.

Young, Whitney M., Jr. "Community Communication." *The National Elementary Principal* 48, May 1969.

Notes

1. Adapted by permission from *Community Leadership for Public Education,* Truman M. Pierce, E. C. Merrill, Jr., Craig Wilson, and R. B. Kimbrough, pp. 233–41. Copyright © 1955, by Prentice-Hall, Inc., Englewood Cliffs, N. J.
2. William E. Martin and Celia Burns Stendler, *Child Development: The Process of Growing Up in Society* (New York: Harcourt, Brace, 1953), pp. 480–90.
3. Edward Keynes and David M. Ricci, eds., *Political Power, Community and Democracy* (Chicago: Rand McNally, 1970), p. 11.
4. Ibid., p. 11.
5. Keynes, *Political Power,* p. 206.
6. Christian Bay, "Politics and Pseudo Politics: A Critical Evaluation of Some Behavioral Literature," *American Political Science Review,* March 1965, p. 40.
7. Ibid., p. 11.
8. Walter Lippmann, *The Phantom Public* (New York: Macmillan, 1925).
9. John Dewey, *The Public and Its Problems* (New York: Henry Holt, 1927).
10. Joseph Schumpter, *Capitalism, Socialism, and Democracy,* 3d ed. rev. (New York: Harper and Row, 1962), pp. 270–71.
11. Ibid., pp. 290–96.
12. *Reconnection for Learning: A Community School System for New York City,* Mayor's Advisory Panel on Decentralization of the New York City Schools, 1967.
13. Keynes and Ricci, *Political Power,* pp. 207–13.
14. John R. Hoyle and Eldon L. Wiley, "What Are the People Telling Us?" *Phi Delta Kappan* 53 (September 1971): 49.
15. *Virginia School Laws.* Bulletin, State Board of Education 27, no. 2 (August 1944): p. 18.
16. Harold G. Shane, ed., *The American Elementary School,* Thirteenth Yearbook of the John Dewey Society (New York: Harper, 1953), p. 95.
17. Roma Gans, "Issues in School-Community Relations," *Educational Leadership* 11 (February 1954): 297–99.
18. Marcella H. Nerborig and Herbert J. Klausmeier, *Teaching in the Elementary School,* 3d ed. (New York: Harper, 1969), p. 537.
19. James L. Hymes, Jr., *Behavior and Misbehavior* (Englewood Cliffs, N. J.: Prentice Hall, 1955), p. 26.
20. See Chapter 9 for a complete discussion of studying records which lead to better understanding of children.
21. A. H. Shuster, Jr., "Supervision and Non-Professionally Prepared Teachers," *Educational Administration and Supervision* 42 (May 1956): 283.
22. Acknowledgment is made to Miss Marilyn Southard, student teacher at Madison College, Virginia, for her suggestions in a research paper, "Working With Parents on Behavior Problems."

6

The Changing Role of Supervision

As the pattern of school organization changes and elementary schools become more autonomous, a new pattern of supervision will emerge. Although the principal's time will be concerned with instructional leadership, he will not be able to devote time to traditional classroom supervision. Nor would such use of his time prove useful. Research studies do not generally support the premise that instruction improves through classroom observation by the principal. The principal must show leadership that inspires interaction among teachers, community, and pupils to produce a relevant curriculum based upon the best instructional practices known.

The modern concept of supervision implies a dynamic process for releasing the creative ability of children, teachers, and the community. The philosophy of educational administration and supervision that recognizes the elementary school principal as the best person to coordinate the activities of the community and the school for developing an educational program which will in turn enhance community living, is based on sound judgment. Probably no other community worker has such broad associations with its citizens as does the principal. He is a welcome visitor to families of all social and economic levels. Neither race nor religion should be a barrier to his relations with school patrons. Through his intimate relationship with the community and his close association with the children and teachers, the elementary school principal is potentially the greatest force on the educational scene today for promoting school-community leadership and providing instructional supervision.

A primary function of supervision is to free teachers from traditional controls which have inhibited teaching-learning situations. The principal must understand how to provide favorable conditions in order that teachers may work and feel free to express their ideas and opinions. This permissive type of environment results in increased productivity which improves the instructional program. Thus, competencies in this leadership area are of major importance to the principal, who is the key person in building staff morale and group confidence. His ability to stimulate interest and to generate enthusiasm in his staff for developing a sound, forward-looking educational program depends on his application of the basic tenets of democracy and of the principles of leadership.

HISTORY OF SUPERVISION

Supervision Defined

Supervision is defined in many ways, from what is known as "snooper-vision" to that process which leads to an improved teaching/learning situation for children. And if supervision is seen by some as "snooper-vision," the term might equally well mean "super-vision," the ability to see further, and more clearly. Supervision is currently thought of as an activity that promotes and encourages growth on the part of teachers, administrators, supervisors, pupils, and the whole community when it contributes to solving problems or accomplishing important goals. Wiles observes:

> Supervision has many different meanings. Each person who reads or hears the word interprets it in terms of his past experiences, his needs, and his purposes. A supervisor may consider it a positive force for program improvement; a teacher may see it as a threat to his individuality; another teacher may think of it as a source of assistance and support.

And Good defines supervision as:

> All efforts of designated school officials directed toward providing leadership to teachers and other educational workers in the improvement of instruction; involves the stimulation of professional growth and development of teachers, the selection and revision of educational objectives, materials of instruction, and methods of teaching, and the evaluation of instruction.[2]

Supervision must be cooperative in character, that is, it must be based on purposes consistent with the aims of democratic living. Thus the methods and procedures employed by the supervisor must take into consideration the worth and dignity of each teacher. Supervision must also be creative in nature rather than prescriptive, as it was in the early 1900s. The supervisory program must develop in an environment that provides release of the individual's talents and abilities. The supervisor encourages creative self-expression in order that teachers and pupils may be released from fears and anxieties in the process of developing critical thinking.

The Changing Role of Supervision

Guiding Principles of Supervision

Although educators do not agree unanimously on the guiding principles of supervision, certain principles are becoming acceptable to a large number of educators. There is general consensus that the following characteristics of supervision, adapted from a number of studies, are most effective in providing better learning situations for pupils:

1. When it is creative.
2. When it offers professional administrative leadership.
3. When it is oriented to human needs.
4. When it provides an atmosphere of acceptance, support, and understanding.
5. When it functions in a cooperative and democratic framework.
6. When it is adaptable to expressed and defined needs.
7. When it deals with essential changes for improvement of instruction rather than expedient change brought about by outside forces.
8. When it provides leadership in defining the organization's objectives.
9. When it involves all persons concerned with the school's objectives in a process to attain them.
10. When it is rigid enough to require professional conduct and accountability but flexible enough to encourage the professional and personal growth of each person.
11. When the entire process is perceived by adults as being geared to the needs of children.
12. When the principal understands that there is a growth process involved in understanding the tasks, skills, and processes of school supervision.

Differences of opinion quite naturally arise when a service such as supervision is rendered. Such differences have many causes, some of which are: (1) the different skills and competencies of supervisors; (2) the individual differences of the people with whom supervisors work; (3) the wide differences in supervisor's working environments; and (4) the needs of the situations.[3] It is worth remembering, however, that constructive differences of opinion are wholesome and can lead to group or individual growth.

EMERGING SUPERVISORY ROLE OF THE PRINCIPAL

In the modern and forward-looking school systems of this country, the elementary school principal has attained a high degree of professional status. The principalship has changed from a position of jack-of-all-trades to one of a highly-qualified specialist in the art of administration and supervision. One of the writers recalls the variety of duties of his first principalship in a consolidated twelve-grade school. Among the many tasks involved, in addition to teaching the sixth grade, were those of custodian, bus driver, maintenance man, basketball coach, truant officer, and projector operator for the Saturday night movies. Administration and supervision of the school were almost incidental responsibilities. Today, the principal is saddled with so many administrative and clerical details that his supervision of the instructional program can easily suffer. In one study, 75 percent of 2300 principals surveyed stated that they had primary responsibility for instructional supervision, but 74 percent of 2194 respondents indicated they spent less than 20 percent of their total work week in supervision, ranging from 1 percent to 19 percent.[4] Any supervising principal can readily explain the discrepancy between theoretical responsibility to supervise and actual practice—lack of clerical help, lack of administrative assistance, and too many office demands.

Increased teacher militancy and insistence on a voice in the instructional program also force the principal to look at the supervisory aspect of his role. How much shall teachers be involved in planning and implementing the instructional program? What happens if a teacher or team of teachers becomes completely autonomous and makes no effort to correlate instruction either vertically or horizontally with the work of other teachers? Does the autonomy of an individual teacher or group cause fragmentation of the instructional program? Or can such autonomy, under the skillful direction of the principal, increase the skills and extend the effectiveness of all involved? The principal who supervises democratically and enlists the aid of all personnel in finding solutions to problems probably has little to fear from such pressures. Rubin says, "It is one thing to invest personal creativity in accomplishing a designated end and quite another to create one's own ends. Thus the task of school leadership is to ensure that the organization's objectives, collectively determined, are pursued by the entire staff."[5] Teachers must be free to achieve both the school's objectives and their own in the way that best utilizes their capabilities and skills. The task of the principal, then, is to release the creativity of each teacher so she can focus on the best possible way to achieve her personal objectives.

Many consider the elementary principal the most important person in the middle-management group of the school system. It can no longer be said that elementary principals are ill-prepared for such a responsible position. In a 1968 survey, 71 percent of 2,295 respondents came to their positions from a classroom teaching situation or from an elementary assistant principalship, while 15 percent came from secondary classroom teaching, compared to 22 percent in 1958. Ninety percent of supervising principals held M.A. degrees or higher in 1968, compared to 15 percent in 1928.[6] Despite this increased professional training and experience, despite this desire to perform the supervisory role efficiently and competently, the realities of the elementary school situation lock the elementary principal into the middle-managerial role.

Although much has been written about the instructional leadership and the supervisory functions of the position, it appears that the managerial role will not be abdicated.[7] Apparently principals believe their legal responsibility to the board of education is more managerial than instructional. While no research suggests that a "tightly-run ship" is a criterion of a board of education for a good school, there is reason to assume that such is the case, since this is the part of the operation to which principals devote most of their time.[8] It can further be generalized that individuals tend to spend their time doing what they feel most comfortable doing. Thus many principals feel they are better equipped to manage than to work with teachers on improved instructional procedures.

Perhaps the new supervisory role of the principal places him in a decision-making role related to instructional procedures. He should be fully aware of the competencies, skills, and understandings of the supervisory staff. Various community agencies are also at his disposal which can render a variety of contributions toward improving and enriching educational experiences. The role of the principal calls for more skill in group dynamics. In the face of mounting pressures from all sides, including teacher demands for more autonomy and greater power, the relationship between teachers and principal must change. The principal must be ever on the offensive, striving for school improvement through his own style and methods, striving for professional growth for all personnel through group dynamics and instructional leadership, striving to create incentive for improving personal and school performances. He must recognize that application of democratic principles enhances the climate for professional growth. Although he is a decision maker, he allows his staff to share in this process.

During the growth years of the elementary principalship, the principal's major responsibility was classroom supervision. In the years since 1948, studies indicate there has been little change from the conclusion of a nation-wide study which said, "Clearly, if supervising principals had a free hand, they would really become supervising principals. They would trim their administrative and clerical duties . . . and give more time to the improvement of instruction and community leadership."[9] However, the changing nature of the elementary school and of the principal's functions in the emerging educational enterprise will surely bring changed concepts of the principal's supervisory role.

The elementary principalship is really a person, not a role, and the old adage that "What you are speaks louder than what you say," is an apt description of the difference between the successful and the unsuccessful principal. Since the principal is so important to the overall success of the public school system, boards of education can and should use newer methods of selection to find the right principal for the right school. Since personality, or "charisma," seems so extremely important, why can't boards of education and superintendents use, as one evaluative tool for selecting a new principal, the "personality inventory" now used successfully by industry for placing management personnel? Why shouldn't boards and administrators set up selection teams composed of representatives from all facets of the community who will have contact with the principal? The inclination of teacher-training institutions to rate student teachers, intern principals, and others training for the principalship according to their effectiveness in working with *people* rather than *things* is all for the best. A community has the right to try to ascertain in advance whether a prospective principal has the qualifications that will match the needs of the local school. If, as many educators say, school changes can come about only with the help of new kinds of administrative behavior, then one of two things must happen: either a new breed of principals must be found with the courage to break through traditional educational barriers to promote needed change, or, we need to look to sources other than our schools for educational administrators who are not steeped in practices of the past and who will apply new principles of administration to solving educational problems.

Speaking of the changing role of supervision, Young says that supervisors must be "teachers of teachers who serve as consultants on teaching and learning."[10] He also states:

> Teachers have rejected the traditional concept of supervision. To many teachers it has been an encroachment upon their professional status. Many supervisors claim they are agents for the improvement of instruction while the teacher perceives them as evaluators who pose a threat to his security. Rather than observing a teacher's global teaching act (artistry) and making apriori judgments of its merit, a consultant on teaching (teacher of teachers) guides a teacher in the systematic analysis and modification of his teaching performance.
>
> In order to serve this function, a new model is needed which facilitates *teaching*. The following procedure is suggested.
>
> 1. Observe and code the teaching performance.
> 2. Provide feedback to the teacher.
> 3. Analyze the teaching behavior, patterns, and strategies.
> 4. Conduct training.
> 5. Provide for practice of new behavior.
> 6. Make follow-up observation-coding.
> 7. Analyze the new behaviors.
> 8. Repeat the cycle as necessary.

Supervision as a Legal Responsibility

Many states have made legal provisions for defining the supervisory responsibility of the elementary school principal. These provisions reflect the importance attached to adequate supervision by state school boards. An example of such a provision is found in a publication of the State Department of Education in Ohio, which sets forth the standards for the elementary schools: "In a school or combined schools having fifteen approved classroom units or more, the services of a principal responsible for supervision of instruction, administration, curriculum, evaluation and community relations shall be provided."[12]

This statement places the responsibility for supervision squarely on the principal. The elementary principal who is an able leader of his staff, children, and community may also be a capable supervisor. His leadership embraces a larger proportion of the parent population than any other school position. The children attending his school have parents who are generally young and vitally interested in their children's well-being. This condition affords an unusual opportunity for working toward total school improvement. Thus this all-important position requires knowledge of elementary curriculum, sincere conviction of the need for a democratic environment for learning, and the necessary skills to provide an atmosphere conducive to faculty growth. The question may now be asked: What changing concepts in supervision must the principal recognize in order to enhance the educational program through his leadership?

PLANNING CONSTRUCTIVE, DEMOCRATIC SUPERVISION

Improvement of pupil learning is the only justifiable cause for the existence of a supervisory program in the public schools. Although desirable concomitant benefits result from a good supervisory program, the essential purpose is to achieve improved and enriched living for all individuals. A growing trend places the responsibility directly upon the shoulders of the elementary school principal for providing constructive supervisory assistance to his staff. Even though he finds himself in a constantly changing role (that is, at times he is a member of a group, a counselor, a status leader, a community leader, and an educator), his success in developing the school's staff depends upon his understanding of democratic, creative supervision.

Whether the principal is just beginning his first year or has been principal for many years, he cannot have an effective supervisory program if it is not democratically conceived. As discussed in chapter 1, the basic structure of democracy must furnish the framework in which the supervisory program is planned. Thus the first criterion for planning a supervisory program is that it involve the cooperative efforts of the entire staff. Teachers must feel free from restraints if their full power is to be brought to bear on the problem of instructional improvement. The principal as a status leader must create a free, permissive atmosphere in which teachers can speak their minds. Teachers will not trust the principal's motives if he is constantly exerting authority. Consequently, a principal-directed program may not reflect the true feelings of all teachers. The successful principal works within the group rather than from without, since teachers have confidence in the principal who can help them. As a group member, he should feel free to voice his opinion as would any other member of the group.

If he intends to survive as an elementary principal, and to supervise his school successfully, he must develop his power of "super-vision," the ability to see further and more clearly. Goodlad states:

> To go beyond survival as an elementary school principal—to be a self-renewing person and to build a self-renewing school—requires at least three things. First, to go beyond survival requires an awareness of the major forces and ideas influencing the school setting. Second, it requires an understanding of the major ideas and recommendations in education being made for coping with these forces. And, third, it requires an educational environment in which both new and old ideas are continually appraised and tested—an environment in which there is rational consideration and implementation of change.[13]

Staff Agreement on Goals

The second criterion for planning the supervisory program is that it be organized around problems that are real to the teacher. Only problems which teachers face regularly as they work with children in the school environment will stimulate them to work for solutions. Principals sometimes inject or invent an idea that they personally wish to initiate as a regular part of the school's program. Such ideas are not usually welcomed by teachers who may already feel overwhelmed with unsolved problems. Individuals work best when they are free to identify and work out their own problems as recognized members of a group. The fundamental concerns of teachers will probably be the best and most logical starting point for initiating a program for improving instruction. The principal must establish the need for changes, using his skills in group dynamics to help the staff establish challenging behavioral and instructional objectives. Too many pressures are on the principal, too many needs of children are unmet, too many human needs are unsolved for him to "stand by" and wait for action. He is the catalyst who precipitates action, then structures activities to analyze problems and find solutions. There will never be complete agreement on goals or on methods of reaching those goals. As professionals, however, the staff should recognize that once consensus is reached, it should be followed until further information changes the decision.

Shared Responsibility

The third criterion for planning the supervisory program is shared responsibility. A human relations theory states that leadership grows from a group's consent to grant authority. Teachers say this theory means that teachers as well as administrators deserve authority because they are part of the group with power to grant authority. Principals with sufficient personal integrity and security to work with their staffs democratically usually have the pleasure of seeing the staff revitalize itself and make rapid progress in improving the instructional program. We do not imply that the principal should not accept his legal responsibilities for efficient operation of the school. To say it another way, for the administrator to realize his maximum contribution to the instructional program requires recognition of shared authority as an effective administrative procedure. When the principal has capitalized on the collective intelligence of his staff to formulate supervisory and educational policies, it then becomes his responsibility to execute these policies. A faculty which has shared in decision making will lose faith in its leader if he fails to fulfill this duty. Principals who adhere to these practices in administration earn the right to be called leaders, and they do more than merely exercise authority that is given to the office itself.

Modern techniques of supervision are based on the concept that the number of areas of specialization and the complexity of the instructional program are too great for the principal to be held solely responsible for making all decisions affecting the entire program. As teachers begin to accept responsibility for the school's program, the unique leadership qualities demanded of the principal become more evident. He is the instructional leader, but not the instructional specialist; he identifies more with his faculty than with the central office; he finds that the need for "control" over teachers is a poor concept; he recognizes that promoting the growth of all school personnel serves the larger purpose of improving the entire instructional program. Militant teachers, demanding more autonomy, more decision-making power, more voice, should not threaten the principal who promotes such a philosophy of supervision. Meade states:

> As the militant teacher reaches for greater power over the affairs of the school, he would do well to remember that leadership cannot avoid the onus of accountability. Whoever makes the decisions about what to include or exclude in the curriculum, about whether to impose restrictions on student dress, or whether to use team teaching, must expect to account to the public for the consequences of these decisions. But as teachers we are likely to be in a poor position if an accounting is demanded of us. Many of our decisions about schooling are based on custom, assumption, or mystique.[14]

Sharing the decision-making process means that everyone involved, including the principal, may depend on the support of the total group when an accounting is called for. Thus, when teachers work with principals skilled in the art of leadership, they come to identify the success or failure of the school with their own success or failure.

Psychological Principles of Good Supervision

The fourth criterion in planning a supervisory program is that the principal be adept in the best-known procedures for working cooperatively with his staff. The principal skilled in group dynamics understands that certain basic psychological principles help teachers develop positive, confident self-image, promote psychological well-being, and facilitate personal and professional growth. Four major areas will encompass most of these psychological principles, although the list could be endless if it included every supportive measure. The principal knows *how* he is working *with* the staff when he understands and uses these psychological principles:

1. *Recognition and promotion of individual interests.* Does the principal know each teacher's special interests, talents, and strengths? Does he provide opportunities for each teacher to utilize these special interests, talents, and strengths? Does he know what voluntary contributions of time and talent the teacher has made? Has he observed which teachers will accept the opportunity to work with new A-V equipment and materials? Does he know what efforts the teacher has made to experiment and innovate, to change her teaching style or the classroom learning environment? Which teachers are eager to work on new instructional materials to produce transparencies and tapes, to try new methods? Does he know with what kinds of groups this teacher prefers to work? The teacher who is at liberty to pursue some of her own interests will have a better understanding of what such freedom can mean to her own students, and will attempt to adapt her teaching strategies to the needs and differences of individual learners.

2. *Providing positive motivation.* There is no question that people react positively to honest praise. Does the principal use every opportunity to recognize achievement, no matter how small? Does he provide opportunity for each teacher to be a leader in the areas in which he feels competent? Does the principal recognize individual teacher's efforts to better themselves professionally through college courses, workshops, and visitations? Does he help a teacher celebrate when a new degree is achieved? Are teachers' attempts to innovate recognized and rewarded, at least verbally? Are attempts made to encourage and reward, at least verbally? Are attempts made to encourage and reward creativeness? It is true that most schools cannot offer financial rewards as motivation. It is also true that most teachers, recognizing the financial limitations, respond glowingly to a note from the principal, a word of commendation, and recognition in a staff meeting for work well done, for a creative idea, and for time and talent given above and beyond the call of duty.

3. *Provide opportunities for problem solving.* Are the problems the principal proposes for study a reflection of only his own interests, or are they problems that reflect the concerns of teachers and community? Is he following

logical steps to identify and solve problems? Can he identify the types of problems individual teachers prefer to work with—which like to do research, which are best at synthesizing the work of a committee or the entire staff, which are best at preparing reports for visual or oral presentation, which are good at long-range planning? Every teacher should be given the opportunity to work in as many areas of problem solving as possible, but differentiation of grouping for problem solving can be a positive factor since it encourages teachers to experiment and work within their own areas of interest.

4. *Recognition and support of individuality*. It is a psychological truism that there are leaders and followers in every group. One danger in teaming teachers is that one may unofficially dominate, and attempt to assume the decision-making role for the group. One promising way to eliminate this problem is to have the team elect a chairman or leader for a specified length of time. Rotating the leadership gives each teacher an opportunity to perform the leadership role. Every principal concerned with staff improvement feels the need for more skill in "reading" personalities, for there is so much to learn and many questions to ask. How well does he recognize individuality? In what ways? Can he accept individual teaching styles based on the personality of the teacher? Can he be diplomatic enough to encourage the growth of all without letting the strong ones dominate or the timid ones get smothered? Does he have enough knowledge of children and learning to merit the respect of the staff for his own individuality? Wiles, many years ago, identified and divided into five areas the skills a supervisor needs: skill in leadership, skill in human relations, skill in group process, skill in personnel administration, and skill in evaluation.[15] Success in planning the school's program depends on the principal's ability to identify his weaknesses in these areas and to work toward a higher level of proficiency.

GIVING IMMEDIATE ASSISTANCE

This second basic problem of the elementary principal as supervisor remains a continuing need demanding leadership expertise. Many authors characterize the elementary principal as a "man of action," and this is indeed a necessary quality for his day-to-day responsibilities. Not too many years ago he was faced with helping unqualified teachers face teaching problems, and often had to take immediate action in areas of instruction, discipline, and classroom management to help these persons acquire teaching proficiency. Today, the teacher supply has outstripped the demand, and the problem of orienting, training, and sustaining teachers without certification qualifications and student teaching is a minor one. Still, the principal must be aware that beginning teachers have some immediate needs, even when they have had student teaching and are fully certified.

The principal must be prepared to give immediate assistance to anyone in any area of his school, since the essence of supervision is assistance in solving problems. Even when he disagrees that a situation requires an immediate solution, he should still be able to suggest a temporary solution and then work with the teacher to understand the problem and make necessary changes. This is especially true in a highly emotional situation, such as when a teacher is extremely angry, or upset to the point of tears. He must make immediate arrangements for her class to be covered until the teacher regains her control or a substitute can be obtained. Later, when emotions return to normal, the situation can be viewed objectively and alternative behavior suggested to the teacher. The principal has a responsibility to aid all teachers, new or experienced, when immediate help is needed. If he cannot provide it himself, he must use every resource to obtain it. All teachers need to feel that they have a resource in their principal and can rely on him for assistance.

Need for Knowledge of Curriculum and Instruction

Teachers respect the leader who can help them with their immediate classroom problems. This help may come in the form of assisting in identification of procedural weaknesses, problems of organizing the room for learning, or weaknesses in the environment. The principal may also be called upon to work side-by-side with the teacher and children in unit development, or to help evaluate certain aspects of the teaching-learning situation and suggest teaching strategies.

Moreover, the principal who does not understand the growth and development characteristics of the children for whom he is responsible cannot effectively help his staff with instructional problems. Fundamentally, then, the question is whether or not the principal must be an expert in the skills of instruction. Until principals and teachers achieve a high level of professionalism in the analysis and synthesis of all aspects of the teaching/supervising/decision-making processes, the principal will remain a man of two worlds—the instructional leader who is the catalyst for essential change, and the instructional specialist. Most principals, however, find it difficult to play these two roles. It is important that the principal have a knowledge of and experience in curriculum development in the modern school, but he must also be able to use his leadership skills to help the staff identify and institute essential change. As a competent leader the principal must be able to identify factors which lead to effective teaching, and as the instructional leader he must know how to use the human relation skills to change the identified factors to result in more effective teaching.

The two concepts concerning the principal's position in the area of supervision of curriculum and instruction may be summarized as follows:

The Changing Role of Supervision

1. The "master teacher" concept, held at the beginning of the development of the principalship. This concept evolved from the principal's being a teaching principal, on the assumption that the best qualified, most competent teacher would make the best principal. Many schools still believe the principal's role in supervision is that of the "master" teacher, who is able to demonstrate to any teacher, in any area of instruction, the best and most successful teaching techniques. In this age of specialization, this expectation is hardly realistic.

2. The "instructional leader" concept. The principal, aware that many competencies are available to him through staff members, must be the instructional leader but not the instructional specialist. Because of the increased emphasis in teacher training toward subject specialization, even for elementary teachers, and the team approach to teaching where teachers are well-prepared in teaching strategies and in subject specialization, the principal cannot maintain competencies in all fields. It would be capricious on his part to attempt autocratic supervision; his role is rather to bring together the right combination of ingredients to solve the recognized problem.

There is another significant trend in the way teachers seek help. Teachers are turning to other professionals, specialists, other staff members, and college consultants for solutions to instructional problems. This seems to be especially true in team-teaching schools or in schools where the principal has created an atmosphere of inquiry and exploration, a sense of openness and a sharing in the problems of education.

The elementary principal's supervisory role includes many aspects, and one of the most important is the ability to offer logical, sound advice toward solving instructional problems. This may be done in many ways, including the use of consultants from outside the school system, but in many instances the assistance from the principal takes place in a face-to-face consultation with an individual teacher. A teacher tells how her principal helped with her fifth-grade class:

> I sought help in identifying why my classroom seemed to end up in confusion in my efforts to use group work in a unit. I pondered the problem for several days before going to my principal, as I knew he was very busy, and I didn't want to burden him. However, I decided to talk the problem over with him one day after school and get whatever suggestions I could.
>
> During the course of our discussion I indicated that I wished he could see the situation so he would know exactly what I was seeking. He immediately said he would be glad to visit my room the next day. I then discussed my plans with him for the next day's activities.
>
> Following the observation, the principal discussed with me what he had

observed. As our discussion progressed, he pointed out the need for visiting each interest group to determine whether each member of the group knew exactly his responsibility to the group. Our discussion continued around the pitfalls of group work. The principal pointed out the need for teacher guidance (not manipulation) in helping each child in the group to make a written plan for achieving his purposes, then to indicate in his plans how and what he was going to do to achieve his plans. Such help gives the child a secure feeling rather than leaving him in a state of confusion, we both agreed. My principal further indicated that this was only one possible solution to the problem and that I might be able to identify other solutions with the class. When I mentioned to him I would like to read further about using groups in unit work, he suggested several books.

I can report that within the week I had already noticed improvement in the organization for learning as well as improved morale toward group work.

The principal earns respect from his staff by his proven ability to assist teachers with the classroom or human relations problems that concern them. Regardless of the teacher's preparation or previous experience, the principal must be prepared to give direction when the need is evident. Such help not only improves teaching-learning interactions, but also builds stronger bonds for further participation in problem-solving situations, a necessary corollary to staff involvement in the decision-making process. As schools grow larger and programs more complex, there is increasing differentiation of staff and greater need for and utilization of specialists. The principal's role shifts even further from that of "master teacher" to that of strategist or coordinator, who gets the right help to the right person at the right time. The supervisory role has enlarged to include professional assistance beyond the principal's immediate capabilities.

Need for Action by the Principal

The incident cited above demonstrates how a principal can give immediate help to a teacher who cannot wait for long-range in-service education programs to unfold. The principal must recognize the importance of each staff member's individual problems. Plans of action are initiated only after mutual agreement by principal and staff, and then the principal should follow his role in the plan to completion. The teacher is primarily interested in a solution, and if the principal fails in this part of the plan he is gambling on losing the respect and confidence of the teachers.

One of the writers recalls a teacher who labeled her principal a good listener but a "do-nothing." Yet many principals pride themselves on being good listeners to their teachers. Such pride is unfounded if cooperative efforts to solve problems do not evolve from the listening. Supervision involves interaction between two minds, the principal's and the teacher's, in discussing and evaluating professional competencies and job requirements in an effort to create new insights and to improve the teaching/learning situation. Not infrequently, a principal's lack of action results from a feeling of incompetence in dealing with basic curriculum problems in the teaching of reading, arithmetic, language arts, music, and other areas. Even this feeling, however, does not justify lack of effort to help the teacher. More specifically, the principal's success in supervision depends upon his ability to render the right kind of leadership in helping teachers seek solutions to problems.

Other specific areas in which the principal may be called upon to render assistance are:

A. Help for beginning teachers in:
    1. Adjusting to the community and the school —its philosophy, staff competencies, teaching expectations, and program requirements.
    2. Applying "theory" to real-life teaching.
    3. Bridging the gap from the college atmosphere to the professional teaching situation. Although the closer relationship being developed between teacher-training institutions and the public schools is helping to alleviate this problem, four years of college does not complete teacher education.
    4. Diagnosis and treatment of learning difficulties, with particular recognition that beginning teachers may have difficulty accepting the idea that some children are unable to work with materials designed to meet the needs of the "average" group. Here the need might be practical suggestions for individualizing instruction.

B. Help for all teachers in:
    1. Securing instructional aids and teaching them how to use them.
    2. Understanding the concept of the IMC and the multi-media philosophy of instruction.
    3. Understanding the techniques of staff involvement in decision-making techniques, evaluation procedures, procedures for reporting to parents, etc.
    4. Understanding the many pressures on children and the problems that affect their daily lives and personal achievement.
    5. Developing techniques and utilizing materials to better meet the individual differences of pupils.
    6. Helping teachers gather and interpret information about children, such as test results, anecdotal records, health records, psychological reports, perceptual-motor skill needs, etc.
    7. Securing special help for children with special needs. (For example, arranging for a tutor or a special class for the neurologically handicapped child.)

This outline is merely suggestive of the areas in which the principal may be called upon to give assistance. Actually, this entire book is based on the assumption that the gamut of the elementary principal's knowledge and skills is aimed at giving every possible assistance to the instructional staff. Indeed, lack of professional competencies in certain areas should not prevent the principal's assisting the teacher in seeking a solution to her problem.

UTILIZING RESOURCE PERSONS

Need for Clearly Defined Responsibilities

Not infrequently, a principal feels challenged to defend his delegated responsibility for the operation of his school. Continued misunderstandings between principal and central supervisor are inexcusable. Such misunderstandings cause teachers to take sides; if not openly involved, they should reserve judgment on any unpleasant incident. Misunderstandings among the staff may be the fate of a school system whose staff members have no clearly defined responsibilities. It is the superintendent's responsibility to see that each staff member is apprised of his duties and his relationship to all other staff members, and the principal has a similar responsibility for his particular school.

In recent years, specialists of all kinds have been added to the staff of the central office. Invaluable services can be rendered by a competent staff of specialized supervisory personnel. The effectiveness of the supervisory program, however, depends on the quality of the relationship between the supervisory staff and the principals with whom they work. Ample opportunity for the staff to discuss their relationships with each other in improving the overall instructional program must be provided.

One of the writers is acquainted with a large school system that held monthly staff meetings for over seven years before the elementary and special supervisors were ever invited to attend. Neither the principals nor the supervisors understood their relationship to each other. The supervisors did not have a feeling of belongingness. Their work was not coordinated, and consequently they were working with little purpose or true perspective.

Both principal and supervisor are instructional leaders, and both are on the same team trying to achieve the same ends. To be a member of the team, one must participate with the team. Therefore, it is important that the principal use the supervisor *as a member of his team*. Real leadership by the principal will make the supervisor feel that he is a valued resource person who can contribute to cooperative group action.

The supervisor should be invited to faculty meetings and committee meetings in which groups are searching for solutions to challenging problems.

He should know the purpose of the meeting beforehand and the part he may have in the meeting. The good principal provides such information for the supervisor. The principal should refrain from simply issuing him an open invitation to attend faculty meetings. Rather, he advises the supervisor of his faculty's desire for the supervisor's assistance in attacking a specific problem.

THE SUPERVISORY HELP TEACHERS WANT

Teachers' needs vary from those of the inexperienced teacher to those of the teacher with many years of service. They also vary with the differences of personalities, amount of preparation, and differences in the level of professional growth. The principal must be alert to these differences just as the teacher is aware of the differences among her pupils.

Orientation Needs

The beginning teacher wants some form of orientation to his new position. Programs of orientation should be designed to assist the new or beginning teacher in making the maximum adjustment to teaching. Some school systems attempt to meet this problem through various teacher committees. This desirable practice does not relieve the principal of his role in the orientation of the new teacher.

A 1969 North Central Association study involving 259 principals and 1197 teachers pointed to the following basic needs of teachers in orientation programs:

> 1. New teachers should be assured in every way possible of the interest of the administration and teaching staff in their success and welfare.
> 2. A period of orientation and training for new teachers should be provided prior to the opening of school.
> 3. New teachers should be made acquainted with the philosophy under which the school operates.
> 4. New teachers should be informed of books, materials, and supplies which are available in order that they may become acquainted with them, with their use, and with the methods by which they can be secured within the system.
> 5. Handbooks containing rules, regulations, and procedures should be given to new teachers prior to the first day of teaching.
> 6. Administrators and supervisors should set up a plan for regular consultation with new teachers concerning their problems.
> 7. The principal and supervisors should work to put the new teachers at ease in their positions.
> 8. Constructive assistance toward solving classroom problems should be given the new teachers.

9. The faculty should make a conscious effort to assist the new teachers and to make them feel that they are an integral part of the school staff.
10. Teachers, supervisors, and principals should work together in planning and carrying out the various phases of the orientation program.[16]

The principal can show leadership here by delegating responsibility to staff members for helping new or beginning teachers, but he must not refrain from assisting the new teacher himself in the areas listed above, since he must develop a close working relationship with new staff members.

The supportive role is diverted somewhat from principal to teaching peers in a school where team teachers, or at least multi-grade or grade level groups, plan together. There is more possibility of immediate help and assistance from teaching peers than from the principal, because of the usual heavy administrative responsibilities. Consciously planned by the principal and his staff, a situation in which new teachers are supported and assisted by fellow teachers is not an abdication by the principal of his role as supervisor, but rather an indication of his ability to delegate authority.

However, the principal *must be available,* for immediate assistance when needed by an individual teacher. One writer recalls an incident which, if it had not been handled promptly, could have developed into a very sticky situation.

> A new teacher brought her fifth grade class to the office area where all children who had brought permission slips were being given the tuberculin test. Without realizing it she had allowed her students to become quite emotionally upset because of the teasing and joking going on about how much it hurt, how many students had fainted the year before, etc. Her class went through the line, and a very few moments after the class returned to the room the intercom brought the frantic message in a very frightened voice, "Please come quick. I'm desperate. My children are fainting all over the room." The principal reached the room in record time, and indeed found that mass hysteria had taken over, five children were slumped across their desks in a faint, the teacher herself was very pale and shaking, and the rest of the children were doing their best to make the situation even more exciting. The principal sent the teacher and one of the ringleaders for water and towels, quickly gave orders for the windows to be opened wide (it was cold outside) and made every child get up on his feet and start moving. He put one student in front to direct some exercises, then attended to the five who had fainted, three of whom had quickly come out of it. Within moments the room was under control, the teacher was breathing normally, and things got back to normal. To give the teacher more time to recover he asked her to take the five outside for a few minutes. When all was peaceful again he took time to discuss with the class what had happened, what they thought had caused it, and what could have been

done to avoid it. There was no condemnation of the teacher or any student; just a calm discussion of how rumors and misinformation can cause unfortunate and unwanted things to happen. Back in the office, the principal took time to call the homes of the five students who had fainted, report the incident briefly to each child's mother, and ask their cooperation in seeing that the incident was played down.

Because of the principal's immediate help to the teacher, his added authority, and his deft handling of the parents, there were no repercussions from the incident.

The Principal's Classroom Visitation

Most teachers want the principal to visit their classrooms, and the traditional supervisory technique of classroom visitation should not be ignored. However, as a result of its traditional connotation, this technique has had maleficent influences on many teachers. The classroom visit formerly focused on the teacher and her behavior in the classroom. Suggestions for improvement were usually imposed upon the teacher. But the classroom visitation technique, properly used, can be a valuable asset for meeting teacher needs. More than 20 years ago, a study of attitudes toward professional improvement found that all teachers surveyed felt a well-planned visit from the principal, followed by a conference, was beneficial to their improvement. This same study further reported that 70 percent of the teachers were enthusiastic about classroom visits by the principal. Today, it is doubtful that a similar survey would show such high percentages. As teachers gain more autonomy, more authority and professional stature, more power and prestige in the decision-making process, the trend is toward less need for a classroom visit by the principal. Teachers now turn more to professional peers and college-level personnel for advice and instruction. In a series of studies done through the Center for Educational Research and Service at Ohio University dealing with curriculum and instruction in widely diverse sections of the state of Ohio, teachers consistently report that they get the most help from fellow teachers for improving classroom practices. The principal ranks second and the supervisor third as sources of help for classroom improvement. This trend, however, does not eliminate the need for the principal to continue classroom visitation. He must use the classroom visitation technique for firsthand observation of the ongoing instructional program, so that teachers will know he is basing his suggestions on concrete facts.

Planning is essential to the success of the classroom visit. The visit must be made with a purpose mutually agreed upon by the teacher and the principal. Unannounced visits only arouse the teacher's suspicions and cause feelings of distrust; planned visits allow the principal to see the teacher at her best. The visits can take on new meaning when the principal teams with the teacher for certain learning activities, thus permitting him to see the teacher's functioning philosophy. All classroom visits should be followed by an individual conference.

THE CONFERENCE METHOD

The conference is another device for stimulating professional growth. We believe that skill in the conference method is vital to the principal's success.

The conference method is one of the principal's supervisory techniques. As a conference leader, he may find himself, in his day-to-day work, exerting leadership with individuals, small groups, or large groups. The conference device can assist him in making decisions, contributing his knowledge and experience, learning from the ideas of others, and so on. The principal will never know what combination of factors, influences, or skills are to be brought into play at a given moment unless he has had time to organize. The principal's role as leader is probably most accentuated as he works with people in daily tasks and long-range planning activities. His success as an administrator is coupled not only with his breadth of knowledge and experience, but with his ability to work with people, lead them, stimulate them, and in every way prove his leadership abilities in the *ways* he gets things done.

The principal may be considered "in conference" whenever he is in consultation or discussion, or participating in an interchange of views. He may have called a meeting of the first-grade teachers, an administrative council, or some key people to figure out the scheduling of a series of reading-readiness tests. He may have planned a meeting of the maintenance staff to discuss ways and means of effecting savings. He might meet with a group of parents to work out answers to a problem concerning the use of school facilities and equipment, or he might have a routine conference following a planned observation with a teacher. Several distinctive features of the conference approach are present in every instance, whether the principal is solving a problem, discussing policy, or dealing with in-service educational affairs. In contrast to a situation dominated by one man, as in the case of "lecturing" or "telling," or in contrast even to a disorganized talk-fest, the principal knows that:

1. There should be mutual agreement on the purposes of the conference;
2. He should furnish leadership in helping conferees analyze the problem at hand;
3. All parties should share equally in making decisions; and
4. Conclusions must be reached and plans for action agreed upon.

If the principal is the conference leader, he may also have to act the role of moderator. Yet the keystone of the conference method is the skillfully-led discussion aimed at giving an individual or members of a group an opportunity to think through questions, to state and defend views, and to arrive at answers to the problem.

The following list points up definite advantages in the use of the conference approach as a device for improving teachers' professional growth:

1. Group or individual participation in a conference provides opportunities for all to learn the extent of mutual problems.
2. Mutual sharing may result in the conferees' and the principal's learning of sound ideas and new experiences.
3. The individual, the principal, or the group is given an opportunity to test and evaluate new ideas.
4. Strong opposition to his ideas may result in the principal's reexamination of his position.
5. The sum of everyone's backgrounds, experience, and training is invaluable when pooled to solve a common problem.
6. The principal as well as the conferees may be stimulated by the interest and enthusiasm of the group.
7. The conference enables the principal to keep alive important considerations which are often discussed only on an individual basis.
8. Opportunity is provided for uncovering problems that may otherwise go unnoticed.
9. Adamant feelings and jealousy may be transformed into good will through free discussion, mutual interest, and cooperation of conferees.
10. Each participant becomes conscious of his dependence on others.
11. Opportunity is provided for demonstrating mature thinking based upon sound judgment.

Developing Skills for Effective Conference Leadership

The critical question at this point is how the principal should proceed so that he will be an effective leader in the conference method. When the principal functions in this role, he is more than just a chairman, moderator, or parliamentarian. It is his primary responsibility to stimulate the group's thinking, to get each member of the group to contribute to or take part in the evaluation of group thinking, and to guide the group toward an eventual result or conclusion.

The principal as a leader is also a thinker; he will elicit discussion as he guides the group's thinking along some organized channel. He will make his contribution by talking, but more so by getting others to talk; and he will avoid sermonizing or lecturing, as indicated in figure 4. His leadership role is accentuated as he brings out other people's viewpoints in the manner depicted in figure 5.

In the *Lecture* the Talk is *at* the Audience

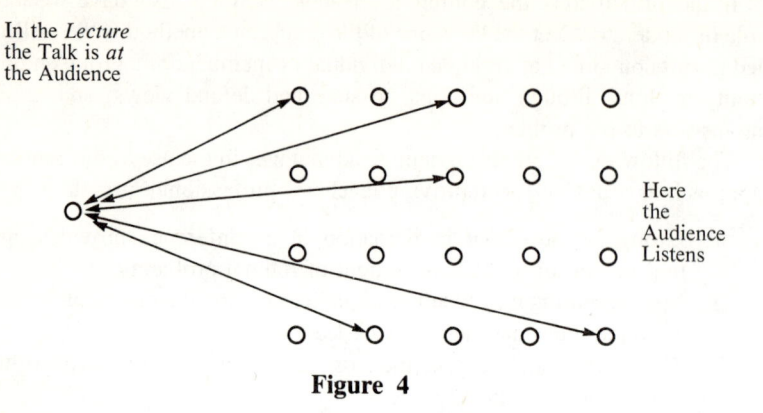

Here the Audience Listens

Figure 4

The Principal Leads by Telling

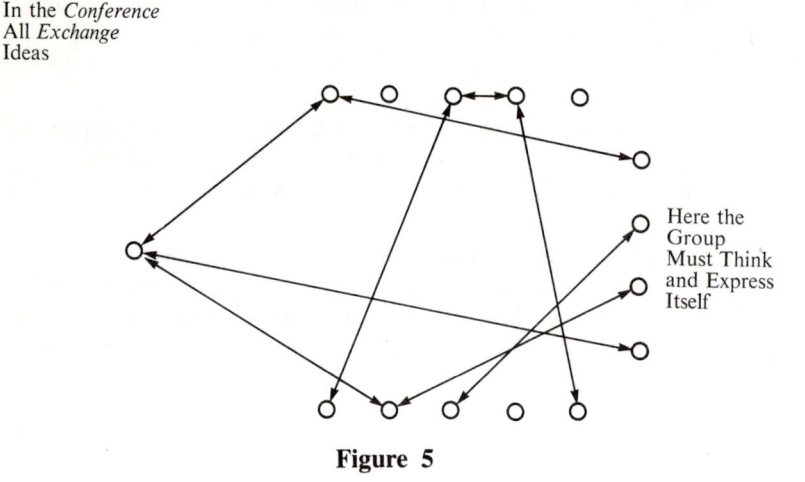

In the *Conference* All *Exchange* Ideas

Here the Group Must Think and Express Itself

Figure 5

The Principal Leads by Sharing

Duties of the Conference Leader

Since the principal requires leadership in many kinds of conferences, it is important for him to recognize his various conference-leader duties. He must also keep in mind that it is his responsibility to develop leadership skills and abilities in others. A list of the conference leader's duties will serve as a practical aid to the principal seeking to improve his conference techniques:

The Changing Role of Supervision

1. Pre-plan for the conference, taking into account its purpose or objective and the discussion.
2. Open the conference on time.
3. Present important data which is not familiar to conferees.
4. Get the discussion under way.
5. Encourage each conferee to participate in the discussion.
6. Keep the discussion channeled toward the objective.
7. Provide occasional clarification and interpretation.
8. Mediate differences in order to reach agreements.
9. Diagram conclusions where appropriate.
10. Close the conference at the scheduled time.

The most frequent objection to conferences is that time is wasted and nothing is accomplished. Therefore, it is extremely important that the leader accept responsibility for guiding the group thinking to some kind of conclusion; otherwise, no particular purpose will be served by the conference.

Although the leader may sense the spirit of the discussion and realize that more time is needed, he should close the conference on time, as scheduled. A stimulated group or individual will arrange later conference dates, but lengthy and exhausting conferences may crush continued interest or defeat future action. Proper exploitation of the conference method will help move the staff forward in a given direction. In addition, staff leadership is to be encouraged; wider use of the conference technique may result, especially if the administrator improves his leadership role by demonstrated abilities in this area.

In brief, there are five stages of instruction which have implications for the principal's leadership role in the conference. These are: (1) Leadership begins with careful preparation in uncovering facts, making plans, formulating questions, or in other ways being prepared to solve problems. (2) The principal thinks through his method of presenting the plan and gets other persons to participate in planning. (3) He needs the ability to apply findings arising from concerted efforts in problem-solving, which will bring about positive action. (4) Leadership in problem-solving requires skill in evaluative techniques. (5) As a result of directed leadership, certain desired results will come into being, or real learning will take place. Changes in thinking, attitudes, and behavior grow out of leadership by the principal.

PROVIDING FOR CONTINUOUS PROFESSIONAL GROWTH

No school is better or worse than the quality of its teachers and its educational leader. The need to understand and adjust to one's environment in today's rapidly changing technological age is even more pronounced in view of the turmoil of social crisis and international problems. Teachers can no longer be complacent. The personal goals that the principal holds for his staff must be similar to the ones the teacher holds for his pupils. That is to say, education for the staff must be a continuous process; it must go beyond the formal stage if teachers are to keep abreast of the times. Research in education suggests the need for improvement in many areas. Teachers, like doctors, engineers, and other professionals, must recognize the need for growing professionally in service if they are to help children cope with the complexities of modern life. The principal must furnish leadership to help the staff advance professionally.

Setting the Stage for Growth

The principal must set the stage to insure continuous professional growth of his staff. He must be aware of the factors that motivate people to work toward self-improvement. For some members of his staff, intrinsic motivation is of utmost importance, while for others, extrinsic motivation contributes to growth. A report compiled for the North Central Association of Colleges and Secondary Schools makes the following comments and lists extrinsic and intrinsic devices which can be used to promote professional growth:

> Extrinsic motivation is that type which is provided by means which are external or outside of the person's inner emotional reactions. Intrinsic motivation, on the other hand, comes from the application of those incentives which appeal to the innate and inherent inner desires of a person. These include, among others, the natural desire to attain recognition, to be successful, and to participate in decisions affecting one's own welfare. In many cases the application of an incentive for extrinsic motivation may carry with it many elements of inner satisfaction to the individual. Both individual urges should be appealed to as far as the total school staff is concerned. Some teachers will respond more quickly from one type of motivation, and other teachers will respond more quickly from entirely different types of motivation. Certainly the appeal to the extrinsic and intrinsic desires of the individual furnishes two entirely different incentive approaches to the motivation problem.[17]

The following groups of extrinsic and intrinsic incentives should be of great value to those who wish to use this approach in improving in-service professional growth:

    A. *Extrinsic*
        1. The salary schedule provides extra salary for additional training and experience.
        2. Teachers are required to attend summer school at regular intervals.
        3. Teachers are assigned to committees to study problems of the school.
        4. Teachers and teacher groups are commended upon work well done.

5. Teachers are given a visiting day and required to make a report on the visit when they return.
6. Teachers are sent to conferences and workshops with expenses paid.
7. School workshops are conducted for the staff. Outside speakers are provided for group meetings.
8. Articles calling attention to professional recognition attained by teachers appear in the local press.
9. Capable and experienced staff members are assigned to work with new teachers.
10. Supervisors are assigned to work with members of the staff who need help.
11. Teachers who do good work are given promotions and responsibilities.
12. Individual teachers are asked to report at teachers' meetings on courses they have taken, speakers they have heard, or articles on education they have read.

B. *Intrinsic*
1. Teachers who seek to improve the curriculum and other areas of school work appreciate being given an opportunity to do so.
2. There is a natural desire to attain status which is satisfied by an additional degree or training. This desire can be stimulated by calling attention to the increase of the status of the school and pointing out that it also increases with the attainment of individual status.
3. Teachers by nature desire to do the best possible work they can.
4. Teachers desire to receive more salary in comparison with other professions and thereby to increase the status of the profession.
5. Teachers desire to attain recognition for effective work which they have accomplished.
6. Teachers receive satisfaction from participation in decisions which affect their own work.
7. Teachers like to feel that they are part of a team working together for the common good and sharing both successes and failures.
8. Teachers like to feel that contributions and suggestions are appreciated.
9. Teachers appreciate being given opportunities to develop their own qualities of responsibility and leadership.
10. Teachers enjoy being told, at regular intervals, that their work is appreciated.[18]

For those teachers who thrive on intrinsic motivation, as many people do, provision must be made for developing a personalized feeling toward the school's program. It is clearly the principal's responsibility to provide opportunities for his staff to identify school problems and work toward their solution. Teachers receive satisfaction from participating in decisions which affect their own work. This approach has only recently been utilized to help teachers grow professionally.

The elementary principal who can develop a climate of inquiry and sharing will do much to help teachers achieve the professional status they desire. Using the team approach of determining goals and freeing all participants to work toward those goals will help, more than anything else, to avert destructive teacher militancy. Too often in the past, some person in the central office developed the courses of study, and teachers were expected to follow the guides slavishly, with great regard for content and subject matter, and little regard for the learner or learning skills. The supervisor took the blame for a bad program, or the credit for a good one, and the teachers received neither blame nor praise for the job accomplished. Their role was simply to do as directed by the supervisor. This kind of "directed activity" persists, but the teaching profession is forcing changes where schools are not forward-looking. Without the responsibility of planning the programs, teachers felt little sense of accountability, and it was understandable that all too often teachers took credit for childrens' achievements, but no one took the blame for childrens' failures.

In order to develop a personalized feeling on the part of the staff, the principal must be alert to the need for recognition of his staff members. Self-satisfaction derives from a feeling of individual or group achievement. Progress is achieved when the principal is aware of the power which may be released from within his staff when they are intrinsically motivated and given skillful leadership.

Provision for Individual Activities

The professional leader must be alert to activities which can result in professional growth, whether they require the use of intrinsic or extrinsic forms of motivations. Programs aimed at providing for teachers' continuous professional growth should allow for individual as well as group activities. The principal's recognition of individual differences among teachers is comparable to the educational principle by which the teacher recognizes pupil differences. Some individuals learn more efficiently through experiment; others learn through study and reading alone. The principal should endeavor to provide conditions under which meaningful activities can be undertaken by individual teachers, for major self-improvement is accomplished through the efforts of the individual.

Intervisitation

Intervisitation is a useful device for stimulating teacher growth. It enables the teacher to compare other teaching-learning situations with the experiences she is providing for her own class. Some results of intervisitation by teachers are summarized by Hathaway, who states that teachers obtain:

1. A feeling of satisfaction with our own system and teaching situation.
2. New ideas to enrich our own teaching and give zest to our lives.
3. A better perspective on teaching.
4. A feeling of satisfaction from the fact that we could actually use many of the techniques we have observed.
5. A view of ourselves as others see us.
6. A feeling of friendship with teachers outside our own community.
7. A better concept of democracy through our own group experiences and leadership.

If classroom observation is an activity which can lead a teacher to grow professionally in service, then provisions should be made for teachers to be free to visit and observe other classrooms, both in the buildings where they teach and in other schools. The principal may compile a list of the names of teachers in his building, as well as in the overall school system, who are considered master teachers and who are willing to be observed. Obviously, it is desirable for the observing teacher to view superior, modern educational practices. Careful selection and planning for observation are necessary to the success of this device, which is an in-service aid to teacher growth.

The teachers who are to be observed must be selected particularly for their ability to use the best-known teaching practices. However, since some teachers are better than others at certain kinds of teaching, the principal should plan the observation in light of what the observing teacher needs and wants to see. It is equally important to inform the teacher who is to be observed of the purpose of the visit. A follow-up conference for evaluation should be arranged after the observation. The observed, the observer, and the principal should be present at the conference.

The principal demonstrates leadership by developing a plan to enable teachers to observe. In small schools, he may arrange to substitute for the teacher, which has the added advantage of keeping the principal in touch with the classroom, or he may arrange for a supervisor to substitute. Although these efforts are a means of getting the intervisitation program started, it is desirable that substitutes be provided at school-board expense, which is perhaps the only feasible plan for large schools. Many school systems have achieved this goal by keeping school boards informed of teacher needs. Such a plan will facilitate intervisitation as a device for teacher growth.

SUMMARY

The function of the elementary school principal has grown from the management of menial administrative duties to a position of great importance in leadership for improving community living. The principal's role in supervision is changing as a result of the greater number of well-prepared teachers.

In addition to his other unique qualifications, the elementary principal in many states has legal sanction for his supervisory responsibilities.

Principals are faced with five basic supervisory problems: (1) how to plan constructive, democratic supervision; (2) how to help the teacher who needs immediate classroom assistance; (3) how to utilize effectively general and special supervisors; (4) how to know what supervisory help teachers want and appreciate; and (5) how to provide for his staff's continuous professional growth. Skill in these areas will lead to successful cooperative projects for improving the environment for pupil-teacher learning and for improving the quality of living in the community.

SUGGESTED READINGS

Adams, John B. "What Makes a Good Teacher Great?" *The National Elementary Principal* 49, no. 2 (November 1969): 38–40.

Amidon, Edmund J., Kathleen M. Kies, and Anthony T. Palisi. "Group Supervision: A Technique for Improving Teaching Behavior." *The National Elementary Principal* 45, no. 5 (April 1966): 54–58.

Anderson, Robert H. *Teaching in a World of Change*. New York: Harcourt, Brace & World, 1966, Chapter 6.

Curtin, James. *Supervision in Today's Elementary School*. New York: Macmillan, 1964, Chapter 10.

Goodlad, John L. "Beyond Survival for the Elementary Principal." *National Elementary Principal* 46, no. 1, September 1966.

Lucio, William H. and John D. McNeil, *Supervision: A Synthesis of Thought and Actions*. New York: McGraw-Hill, 1962, Chapter 1, 2, 5.

McNally, Harold J. "The American Principal Tomorrow." *The National Elementary Principal* 50, no. 4 (February 1971): 8–19.

St. Mary, Maurice E. "The Administrative Team in Supervision." *The National Elementary Principal* 45, no. 5 (April 1966): 59–61.

Stoops, Emery and James R. Marks. *Elementary School Supervision*. Boston: Allyn and Bacon, 1965, Chapter 10.

The Elementary School Principalship in 1968 . . . A Research Study. Washington, D.C.: Department of Elementary School Principals, National Education Association, 1968.

Trask, Anne E. "Principals and Supervision: Dilemmas and Solutions." *Administrators Notebook*: Chicago: Midwest Administration Center, The University of Chicago, December 1964.

Wayson, William W. "A New Kind of Principal," *The National Elementary Principal* 50, no. 4 (February 1971): 8–19.

Young, David B. "Effective Supervisory Conference: Strategies for Modifying Teacher Behavior." Paper Presented to an annual conference of the Association for Supervision and Curriculum Development, Chicago, 1969. (E.R.I.C. #ED 041 840.)

Notes

1. Kimball Wiles, *Supervision For Better Schools* (Englewood Cliffs, N.J.: Prentice-Hall, 1967), p. 3.
2. Carter N. Good, *Dictionary of Education* (New York: McGraw-Hill, 1955), as quoted in Ben M. Harris, *Supervisory Behavior in Education* (Englewood Cliffs, N.J.: Prentice-Hall, 1963), p. 335.
3. Adapted from Jane Franseth, "Supervision in Rural Schools, A Report on Beliefs and Practices," U.S. Office of Education Bulletin 1955, no. 11 (Washington, D.C.: U.S. Government Printing Office, 1955), p. 3.
4. *The Elementary School Principalship in 1968 . . . A Research Study* (Washington, D.C.: Department of Elementary School Principals, National Education Association, 1968).
5. Louis J. Rubin, "The Principal and the Teacher: The Risks of Autonomy," from "Frontiers in School Leadership: A Synthesized Report of a Seminar." California University, Santa Barbara, Center for Coordinated Education. Sponsoring Agency—Ford Foundation, New York, January 1968 (E.R.I.C. #ED 022 261).
6. Ibid., pp. 13, 24.
7. See Egon G. Guba, "Missing Roles in School Leadership: Matters Tended and Untended," from "Frontiers in School Leadership: A Synthesized Report of a Seminar." California University, Santa Barbara, Center for Coordinated Education. Sponsoring Agency—Ford Foundation, New York, January 1968 (E.R.I.C. - ED 022 261).
8. *Principalship in 1968 . . . Research Study.*
9. "The Elementary School Principalship—Today and Tomorrow," National Education Association, Department of Elementary School Principals, Twenty-Seventh Yearbook (Washington, D.C.: DESP, 1948), p. 90.
10. David B. Young, "Effective Supervisory Conferences: Strategies for Modifying Teacher Behavior" (Paper presented to annual conference of the Association for Supervision and Curriculum Development [ASCD], Chicago, 1969). E.R.I.C. # ED 041 840.
11. Ibid.
12. *Minimum Standards for Ohio Elementary Schools* (Columbus, Ohio: State Department of Education, 1970), p. 13.
13. John I. Goodlad, "Beyond Survival for the Elementary Principal," *National Elementary Principal* 46, no. 1 (September 1966).
14. Edward J. Meade, Jr., "The Cost of Leadership," from "Frontiers in School Leadership: A Synthesized Report of a Seminar." California University, Santa Barbara, Center for Coordinated Education. Sponsoring Agency—Ford Foundation, New York, January 1968 (E.R.I.C. #ED 022 261).
15. Wiles, *Supervision,* p. 18.
16. N. Durward Cory, "Incentives Used in Promoting Professional Growth of Teachers," North Central Association of Colleges and Secondary Schools, Chicago, Ill. Sub-Committee on In-service Education of Teachers. (E.R.I.C. # ED 027 254).
17. Cory, *Incentives.*
18. Ibid.
19. Genevieve E. Hathaway, "We're Enthusiastic about Visiting Day," *Educational Leadership* 7 (April 1950): 42.

7

Curriculum Development

The processes of administration have long been recognized as procedures for facilitating instructional progress and curriculum development. It is not uncommon, however, to find that certain administrative practices actually impede instructional advancement. Since change is inevitable in a society built on technological developments, reluctance to accept newer techniques in preparing children to live effectively must inevitably give way. Although this statement may seem controversial, some authorities suggest the time lag between discovery and application of research findings on educational processes is at least fifty years. Dynamic and vigorous leadership is needed to close the gap between the kind of curriculum experiences now provided for many boys and girls and the kind needed for wholesome, enriched, democratic living.

Programs for instructional improvement can and do meet with success when they are carefully planned and skillfully developed by teachers, administrators, supervisors, and laymen. Where change is needed, the alert principal recognizes the obligation to involve in decision making those people who will be affected by proposed changes.

Even today, most school systems are content to let the textbook or program writers dictate the curriculum for each grade. Although these writers are to be commended for the improvements in their products during the past decade, few books or programs accommodate the particular needs of all children in our nation's diverse environments. In general, textbook writers do not intend that their books should become the core or center of a given curriculum. What is to be taught and how it is to be taught are paramount questions in considering the improvement of instruction.

The "what" and the "how" are matters involving local decisions if the schools are to be considered community institutions. This chapter will suggest many guides for the educational leader to use for improving instruction and for advancing the quality of curriculum experiences. No principal can be an educational leader without a thorough understanding of curriculum designs.

Meaning of Curriculum

The most prevalent concept of curriculum is defined simply as *all* experiences the child has while under the influence of the school. The writers prefer to use what they consider a more useful definition of curriculum, adopted from Benne and Muntyan: "The curriculum is a selection of experiences which the school as a social system influences significantly and which learners enact and undergo in the process of their deliberate induction into the culture."[1]

It is not only the experiences which the children have under the direction of the school that are important; their reactions to and interactions with these experiences are of equal importance. Consequently, one must consider many factors in developing a curriculum. Upon careful examination of the above definition, these factors become evident: the school is a social system; there are people involved; and there are interactions with the culture. Thus, the way students are affected by the curriculum will depend upon the aims and philosophy of the school and community, the political, social, and economic structure of the community, and on other similar factors. Undoubtedly, the factors which affect the way children react to or interact with curriculum experiences reflect the nature of the individual school and the community. Analysis of these factors results in only one conclusion: the leaders of each school must accept their responsibility for contributing to curriculum progress.

FACING CURRICULUM ISSUES

The administrative approach to curriculum development initiated during the 1920s served a unique function in American public education. This approach usually began with the superintendent's deciding upon the curriculum change. Although some improvement resulted from this approach,[2] this early development was chiefly valuable in that it brought an awareness of the need for further curriculum development. The failure of the administrative approach to bring about educational changes commensurate with expectations[3] has been due to lack of educational leadership. Actually, the most common failure has been lack of administrative foresight in recognizing the need to involve those people who will be affected by the anticipated change. Since the administrative approach to curriculum change was usually initiated by the superintendent and passed down the line to a few teachers, it was seldom completely successful. Even when tried on a system-wide basis, there was little chance that all teachers could be involved or would feel the need for the initiated change.

Today the emphasis is on program development at the level of the individual school. Although this approach shows promise of success, school administrators are still reluctant to let principals and their staffs deviate too far from the community norm. This approach makes the principal responsible for improved learning experiences. Specifically, he leads his staff and community in the following activities:

1. Analysis of pupil successes and failures;
2. Study of the characteristics and resources of the immediate community or neighborhood;
3. Study of marking practices and retention rates;
4. Study of methods and materials;
5. Study of the continuity of the total school program—kindergarten through grade 12, with emphasis on individual sequencing; and
6. Study of research findings.

This approach to curriculum procedures and processes permits teachers and parents alike to work on problems which are close to them. Under this plan, the principal needs to know the scope of the curriculum which will best serve the needs of his school.

Scope of the Curriculum

The elementary school generally serves children ranging in age from five to twelve, from kindergarten through grade 6. The scope of the curriculum cannot be determined effectively unless the school adopts some statement of purposes. As the principal leads his staff and community in determining the school's purposes, he is at the same time defining the scope of the school's curriculum. The scope of the curriculum may be determined by what the staff and community believe the school should accomplish and contribute toward successful community living. The educational experiences or scope of the curriculum must be broad enough to insure each child the opportunity of achieving these aims. Thus the principal gives leadership in determining the scope of the school's curriculum by:

1. Cooperatively analyzing the essentials for successful democratic living.
2. Cooperatively determining the school's philosophy.
3. Identifying the aims inherent within the philosophy.
4. Working toward the initiation of these aims.
5. Continuous, cooperative evaluation to determine whether the aims are being achieved.
6. Cooperatively re-appraising the purposes of the school, which will lead to further modification of the curriculum in view of a changing social structure.

No school can afford to neglect its responsibility for re-examining its purposes in an emerging, changing society. *These changes mean, among other things, new patterns of living, different interpretations of human rights, and a need for more precise use of fundamental tools, as required for competent democratic citizenship and personal success.*

Many descriptions of the essential elements for successful democratic living have already been written. Among some of the early attempts to identify these elements as specific objectives[4] are the "Cardinal Aims of Education," adapted from the work of Herbert Spencer. These are: (1) Health; (2) Command of Fundamentals; (3) Citizenship; (4) Worthy Use of Leisure; (5) Vocations; (6) Worthy Home Membership; and (7) Ethical Character. Continual efforts have been made to redefine the aims of education. The aims more commonly accepted today are the four major concerns of education as stated by the Educational Policies Commission: (1) Self-Realization; (2) Human Relationship; (3) Economic Efficiency; and (4) Civic Responsibility.[5]

Dangers in Analysis of Educational Aims. Inherent in the analysis of any educational process are the dangers involved in arriving at "specifics." The curriculum-minded principal guards against such an analysis if it emphasizes the externals of learning in such a way that the facts, skills, etc., become ends in themselves.[6] Caswell warns against the opposite extreme, that of centering attention on the inner urges of the child and his immediate problems in order to determine his educational experiences.[7] But Berman points out that individuals have to make so many adjustments in life for which they have not been adequately prepared that the intent and substance of the curriculum should be geared to (1) the ongoingness of life, and (2) to human processes such as perceiving, knowing, and organizing.[8] The educational leader must channel the thinking of his staff and community toward an examination of these differences, in order to arrive at a workable definition of the behavior to be sought.

Sequence in the Curriculum

Sequence is, traditionally, the order in which learning experiences in the curriculum are organized. For example, children in the past were led into learning, guided by preconceived abstract objectives.[9] These objectives had little in common with either the interests or maturity level of the child. Children were thought of as little adults, so what was good for the parents was also good for the child.

At least three valid approaches are used in determining grade or sequence of learning experiences. These are to:

1. Adjust the learning experiences to the level of development of the child while holding the instructional goals constant.
2. Assume the curriculum experiences to be located at a given grade level and provide learnings to adjust the child to these experiences.

3. Solve problems of grade placement by altering the instructional goals.

When the principal understands the concepts of sequence, he will be in a better position to lead his staff in seeing individuals in terms of their differences rather than forcing all children into the same pattern. For example, he needs to understand that logical order or sequence does not necessarily mean the way a given subject is presented in the textbook. True, science may be a subject which has traditionally been presented in a given logical order, but children's interests cannot be ignored in teaching. Children do not always learn according to some adult plan. A study of energy, for example, might begin with its nature and importance to man. However, seeing a crane lift steel to the top of a building at a construction site near school may spark the children's interest, and provide a logical starting point for teaching. This may lead to identifying other simpler machines which do work for us, with consideration given to simple machines used in daily living. Then attention can be given to the nature of energy and how it is obtained and conserved. Some children might, because of their maturity, pursue further experiences about energy while other children move to another area of science. This procedure permits the sequence of experiences involved in learning to be developed according to the circumstances surrounding the learning situation. Concepts are then learned according to the learners' comprehension and maturity.[11]

Sequence of learning experiences concerns the order in which these experiences are to be met by the child. The educational administrator must lead his staff and community in gaining knowledge of the total development of children, *so that teachers may select appropriate learning experiences related to problems of social living based on developmental need*. The principal may use two important questions as a guide for developing curriculum sequence:

1. What constitutes readiness for a novel learning experience?
2. At what grade level can most children accomplish a particular skill?

ADMINISTERING THE CURRICULUM

Most authorities writing in the forties and fifties agreed that the principal is the key to curriculum building. Burton and his co-author state that "curriculum can be developed only in individual schools and classrooms."[12] This has been the point stressed throughout this book: the individual school must be free to meet the needs of the immediate community. Otto reminds us, "It is within the power of the principal to control the kind of curriculum which it will be possible for teachers to provide."[13] Reavis and his collaborators state, "The leadership in improving the curriculum rests chiefly with the principal."[14] The leaders of modern elementary educational programs must accept this responsibility.

School autonomy is rapidly being recognized in matters of curriculum improvement. Although many advantages will accrue from recognizing the local school unit as the source for initiating instructional growth, the basic advantage appears to be that it is easier to achieve full *participation and move toward group consensus in a smaller organization rather than in a large one.*

Control of the Curriculum through Administration

As the school's educational leader, the principal is responsible for many administrative tasks. These tasks eventually become policy in one form or another. The personnel-oriented leader will initiate the desirable practice of sharing these administrative tasks with his staff for enactment into policy. However, regardless of his pattern of administrative behavior, he must be aware that he controls the structure of the curriculum by the way in which he organizes and administers the school. For example, time schedules, the instructional program, use of resources, classification of pupils, development and selection of materials, marking, and promotional policies are positive influences on the curriculum.

The Daily Schedule. The daily schedule is frequently the control factor in the teacher's use of time. The opening of school, the physical exercise period, the recess period, the lunch hour—all affect the working periods of the school day. The time for opening and closing the school is ordinarily set by the board of education to comply with state standards, but within this framework the principal must be cognizant of the need for a flexible school program. Although the principal is responsible for developing the school's curriculum, the curriculum is still actually built by the teachers and their pupils, under the influence of many outside factors. The so-called traditional schools are known for their rigid and arbitrary schedules. Teachers are required to teach a given subject at a certain time, and no flexibility is tolerated. Such practices obviously shape the experiences of school children and inhibit changes in educational programs. Team teaching, non-gradedness, and the like, require flexibility in scheduling, which should be left to the teachers involved. The principal's role then is to coordinate the scheduling of teachers' plans to facilitate the instructional program.

The daily schedule must be arranged so that teachers are free to plan with their pupils for the learning experiences. Recess schedules in primary and intermediate grades should not be rigidly prescribed for all teachers. The modern teacher who plans with the pupils for their learning activities knows that children are active and that they need to move about in their learning-unit work, so it may not be necessary for all to leave the room at the same time. In a modern classroom environment, children are encouraged to accept responsibility for going to the toilet and getting a drink of water as needed.

Primary children should be free to engage in short periods of playground activity under their teacher's direction as the situation demands; this may be deemed necessary one or more times during the day. Intermediate and upper elementary grades may have to follow a regular schedule, where regular physical education programs are not available, because of crowded conditions on the playground. The point here is that the principal should be conscious of teacher needs and desires concerning the school's schedule. He should not make inflexible rules concerning times for various activities. The modern classroom makes varied demands upon the teacher and pupils; the school administrator either facilitates or hampers a curriculum program by administrative action. The principal must consider certain characteristics of a modern classroom in planning the school schedule:

1. The instructional program is flexible—there is no set time for each subject.
2. Time is usually organized in large blocks and scheduled by the teaching team.
3. A variety of resources are used: films, film strips, pamphlets, I.P.I., T.V., etc.
4. Field trips, excursions, and the like, are important aids to learning.
5. The community is a laboratory for learning.
6. Problems important to the children are the basis of learning experiences.
7. Provisions are made for teacher-pupil planning.

The principal actually controls the curriculum. He may fail to give good leadership if he does not make the necessary provisions for flexibility in the school's schedule. Such provisions, if they are cooperatively derived, should enhance curriculum experiences. One teacher recently sought guidance concerning his teaching plans from one of the writers. His principal had presented him with a schedule which he was to follow in teaching each subject, including spelling and handwriting. Some teachers would use this situation as an excuse to provide only limited experiences for children. Therefore, a desirable goal would be the removal of the "straw men" which are sometimes used as barriers to protect teachers who are not interested in improving learning activities for children by utilizing the staff in schedule planning.

Instructional Factors. Instruction is the vehicle by which the subject matter is learned, regardless of the curriculum pattern followed by the teacher. When "What is to be taught?" is clearly in mind, then "How is it to be taught?'' looms as most important. The principal aspiring to become an instructional leader must consider many factors when determining strategies for instruction. Psychological principles of learning, effective motivation, interests, needs, abilities, and past experiences of the pupils are among the factors that determine the use of certain instructional strategies, including indentification of the need for puposeful use of subject matter. The instructor should choose strategies in the light of their effectiveness under similar conditions and for certain children. Thus, selection of teaching strategy should be determined by the particular goal to be accomplished, with consideration to (1) the differences of the pupils, (2) their socio-economic backgrounds, (3) the content to be learned, (4) available teaching aids, and (5) competencies of the teacher.

Inherent in the instructional process is at least one additional major factor which should help determine the choice of instructional strategies. The teacher, in most cases, recognizes her own personality weaknesses and may shy away from procedures which will cause her confusion and frustration. *Only when teachers feel secure in changing or varying their methods of instruction, or when their ego remains unthreatened during the process, will they make positive attempts toward instructional improvement through new strategies.* Good administrative leadership helps the staff in creating favorable conditions for experimentation.

Instructional materials have an effect on curriculum change. Each new resource for teaching and learning must be assessed for its unique contribution to achieving instructional objectives. Again, the principal is in a strategic position to make available through his leadership learning resources which will encourage improved teaching procedures. Needless to say, good teachers usually find new materials to facilitate learning. However, the principal who accepts the responsibility for securing needed funds for educational media from the school board, and who works with his staff in developing appropriate materials, will gain staff approval as a curriculum leader. The proper screening and selection of resources for use in the elementary schools may become a major in-service educational activity.

A limiting factor in a good developmental program is the scarcity of equipment and materials in the average classroom. Every classroom needs a wealth of materials, for at the heart of individualized instruction is the need for material organized in a logical manner. Although computers will facilitate individualized learning, the expense is still too great for most schools. If gifted children, slow learners, and so-called "normal" children are to make adequate progress, each classroom must have materials suitable for all levels of ability. The developmental concept discussed above implies that in a modern classroom, children learn to select the materials that will best serve their immediate purposes. For example, a child interested in the motor on his dad's power mower may seek information about the combustion engine. He may pursue this interest until he has gained all the information to satisfy his desire. Thus the child, under the teacher's guidance, plans a systematic attack on his problem in relation to his level of development and the physical environment. The traditional organization of subject matter often forestalls such an interest, possibly until the child reaches a general science class in secondary school.

Field Trips and Excursions. Modern programs involve extensive use of the community for first-hand learning experiences. Carefully planned field trips or excursions contribute meaningful instruction to practically every subject in the curriculum. The principal should exhibit leadership by helping to facilitate use of field trips as a means to improve curriculum experiences. It is not uncommon for teachers to remark that their principal is afraid the children will be out of the building too often. Statements like this are evidence of poor leadership and lack of foresight on the part of the principal. An unrealistic and naive attitude is present when the administrator is unaware that misuse of the field trip need not be a common practice. There should be a recognized effort to improve its effectiveness rather than to remove it from the curriculum. The principal can strengthen the use of field trips or excursions by leading his staff in a discussion to formulate policy and by using the following guide for planning the field trip:

1. Evaluate the advantages in taking the field trip so that as many contacts as possible may be utilized.
2. Determine the purpose or possible combination of purposes for conducting field trips.
3. Examine survey data for:
    (*a*) materials that will develop useful concepts;
    (*b*) situations around which activities may be organized that will assist pupils in developing desirable attitudes, skills, and understanding.
4. Make necessary arrangements in advance with:
    (*a*) school authorities;
    (*b*) owners or representatives of places to be visited;
    (*c*) parents;
    (*d*) transportation officials.
5. Pupils should be adequately prepared for the trip as to:
    (*a*) purpose;
    (*b*) need for special clothing and equipment (notebooks, field glasses, etc.);
    (*c*) individual or group responsibilities.
6. Final evaluation and follow-up:
    (*a*) teaching values; enriching, vitalizing, motivating, socializing, etc.);

Curriculum Development 165

    (*b*) constructive influence on pupils' appreciation, attitudes, understandings and skills;
    (*c*) application to over-all learning experience.[16]

As the principal helps his teachers understand the value of field trips in the curriculum, he also provides improved learning experiences for children. His encouragement of this learning activity results in teachers' wider use of enriching experiences.

Classification of Pupils. The way pupils are grouped has an effect on the kinds of experience provided in the curriculum. The principal to a very large extent controls the procedures used in the grouping process. Although no one would deny the need for grouping under mass-education conditions, the failure of educators to give more authoritative direction to a plan of school organization that would better meet pupil needs has caused principals to think in terms of adjusting the child to the curriculum. The lock-step type of organization in the public schools has outlived its usefulness, and courageous leaders must work with parents and teachers to develop a plan of organization superior to the grade-level approach. In spite of the emphasis on nongraded schools, team teaching, and individualized instruction, one major research investigation reported that "with the exception of a small cluster of special classes, the classrooms in our sample were overwhelmingly self-contained and had little or no instructional association with each other."[17]

Our purpose here is not to discuss the pros and cons of homogeneous or heterogeneous grouping or any of the other variables in the situation. Research is ample on this subject. However, an understanding of better practices for classifying pupils is needed to aid the elementary principal when he seeks to involve his community and staff in studying the problem. Since it is obvious that some method of grouping children is necessary to continued mass education, the functions of grouping are quite clear and generally acceptable. Otto states the functions of classification:

    1. To allocate pupils in conveniently sized groups to rooms, classes, and teachers so the work of the school may proceed in an orderly, systematic fashion.
    2. To facilitate the execution of educational policy (by differentiating the curriculum according to pupil ability).
    3. To place each child in a school environment which will provide the best stimulation and opportunities for growth.

One can see that these functions of classification tend to serve the purposes of administration. Although sincere efforts are made to "fit" the child to the school, the task of adjusting the curriculum to the child is hampered by the structure of the organization. The principal will find the following points helpful in stimulating group thinking on the problem of grouping:

1. Identify the objectives of the school and of public education.
2. Study child development.
3. Identify relationships between (a) chronological age groups, (b) social groups, and (c) physical growth.
4. Group according to findings of identified relationships.
5. Organize groups in accordance with the best means of achieving the school's objectives and the basic principles of child development.

Present methods of classifying children for group assignments operate largely on the assumption that grade level indicates a certain intellectual competence in subject-matter achievement.[19] Caswell, in a review of many investigations concerning the variability of instructional groups, concludes that ". . . wide variations among pupils in given instruction groups is the rule . . . the notion that nonpromotion, even if used widely, operates to reduce the range of achievement in a class to the spread of one or two grades simply is not true."[20] Cook, in a summary of similar investigations, found variables at ". . . the first grade level, between three and four years; at the fourth grade level, five and six years; and at the sixth grade, seven and eight years. Language, science, geography and history and . . . in arithmetic . . . between six and seven years at the sixth grade."[21]

There appears to be ample evidence to support the claim that the present grade-level approach to pupil classification has little to offer the curriculum-minded teacher who endeavors to meet individual needs of children.

Ungraded Grouping. As early as sixty years ago, a plan was devised to facilitate individualized instruction by organizing the school day in two parts—(1) the tool subjects, and (2) the other subjects, such as art, physical education, etc. The Winnetka and Dalton plans were of this type. Children contracted with the teacher to do certain problems independently, permitting each child to progress at his own rate of learning. The real problem with this type of learning was the over-emphasis on subject matter and inadequate emphasis on child growth and development.

The nongraded school must not be just another form of school organization based on additional levels within a given grade. The diversity within human beings is so great that any form of grouping must be flexible, and must seek to fulfill the needs of each individual. For example, a group of one hundred pupils may have three or four teachers, and the pupils may have a wide range of I.Q.'s, achievement scores, and even chronological age differences. The grouping might be by daily demand—large group, small group, or individuals working alone—but the grouping will depend on the purpose the teacher or pupils have for being together. That is, it will depend on the need of each individual. That need might be cognitive or affective. The children might be of the same age or different ages, depending again upon needs.

When grade labels are discarded, the emphasis can then be upon the child and his particular need at any given time. In a nongraded organization, the team might decide that Johnny's need is to be in the first reading group, since he has always been in the last group. Through group adjustment this can be accomplished. On the other hand, there might be children who need to be with friends while others need to expand their life space to include some new acquaintances. Some children, for a time, might need to be with a warm, friendly, sensitive teacher, while other children might need a firmly structured experience. These are but a few of the factors upon which to base decisions in developing the basic grouping patterns within the elementary school.

The principal must accept the major responsibility for the way his school is organized. He must struggle against those who want to maintain the status quo. His task is constantly that of seeking alternative school models which will enhance the total development of each child as a human being.

Marking and Reporting Pupil Progress. Teachers are presently handicapped by marking methods and traditional reporting procedures. A modern curriculum program cannot progress when there are inconsistencies in the school policies. The principal must work to free teachers to utilize their creative talents in improving the teaching-learning process. Although much progress has been made toward improving marking systems, considerable advancement is still to be desired. A teacher who was beginning to show signs of professional growth related the following illustration to one of the writers:

> I have just completed my first unit of teaching. For eight years I had been reading and hearing about how to teach a unit. I finally gained sufficient confidence to try to organize and teach a unit combining my social studies and science, entitled, "What Made Our Community Grow?" After carefully keeping records of the growth of my pupils, I came to what was a block to unit teaching as far as I was concerned. Our report card used five marks, and a mark was required for each subject. Although I had used an essay type of test at the end of the unit, I could not honestly give a mark for science. My pupils had grown, but I was unable to determine specifically to what extent. Some I knew would get A's, as they always did; for others should it be D, C, or B? Although I reconciled the matter in the only way I knew, I never felt that I had done the right thing.

The inconsistency is obvious. Traditional methods of measuring pupil progress must give way to more appropriate evaluation procedures. Of course, parents want to know what progress their children are making, and they have the right to know. However, an essential point in the total evaluative process is that the method employed to mark and report progress must convey to the parent as well as to the child the same concepts or understandings of measuring which the teacher held in determining the mark in the first place.

Many investigations report the inconsistencies between teachers' marks and the actual achievements indicated by standardized tests. One research finding revealed that those boys who dressed less attractively and in general were not especially liked by their teachers received considerably lower grades than girls.[22] Those children for whom the teachers had neither a liking nor a dislike stood a 50/50 chance of getting either a high grade or a low grade. Some of our present marking systems have little value either as a means of motivation or as a method for reporting to parents. In addition, they are inconsistent with modern philosophies of education and discourage teachers from trying sound psychological methods of teaching. What, then, is the role of the modern educator who faces this problem in his school?

As with all other aspects of the school program which need modernizing in order to provide children with better instruction, leadership is needed. The principal is in the key position to furnish this leadership. Many parents are quite content with some marking systems based on letter grades, and in many cases the more letters, the more pleased they are. One of the authors recently sat in on a system-wide report card revision. The card being revised used O, S, and U as symbols to report progress. The parents initially insisted on using either numbers or at least six letters, A, B, C, D, E, and F. It was evident that these parents were basing their opinions on understandings derived from their own school experiences. Unless good leadership is practiced, parents will have a sound basis for criticising any marking plan which is not clear and acceptable to them. In the school system just mentioned, the O, S, and U plan had been in use for some fifteen years without any periodic efforts made to keep parents informed of its meaning. If adequate leadership had been exhibited in this school system, the faculty and administration might have been in a more favorable position to eliminate an inadequate marking program and move into pupil-parent-teacher conferences as an improved means of reporting pupil progress. The point here again is that the principal controls the curriculum through the school's policy of marking and reporting. The following check list should serve as a guide to the principal in freeing teachers from traditional marking and reporting procedures where such a step is necessary to further curriculum improvement:

1. Prepare teachers for change in the marking system through in-service activities.
2. Invite parents to attend in-service meetings.
3. Present parent groups with research evidence pointing up pros and cons of marking.
4. Work toward modification—not discarding everything.
5. Help parents to see some of the inequities in marks by presenting real marking situations to them.

6. Make literature available on the subject.
7. Have parents, teachers, and pupils plan for revision of the present marking system.
8. Use questionnaires to obtain information on marking and reporting from all parents of school children periodically. Parents can thus be kept informed concerning their needs.
9. Provide orientation for parents of preschool children, fourth-grade children, and children in the first year of junior high school concerning marking and reporting practices in use.

The principal's perspective must be broad enough to include the overall school program and the many aspects which he controls. Restrictive administrative controls must be relinquished to allow teachers to do creative, constructive teaching.

Departmentalization. Provisions for departmentalizing instruction seem to be an outgrowth of the "reading and writing" schools in the New England states.[23] Otto[24] points out that the "single-teacher-per-class" plan was initiated in Boston's Quincy Grammar School in 1848. This practice rapidly spread throughout the country. The original concept of departmentalization is based on the assumption that a teacher can be most effective teaching within his specialized field. Although recent research is somewhat limited in this area, there does not appear to be any clear-cut advantage, in terms of achievement, for elementary school pupils who experience departmentalization. A study in 1923 reported that pupils under the single-teacher plan made higher achievement scores in grades five through eight than did those pupils who were departmentalized.[25] Another study in 1930 indicated that the departmentalized program was just as effective as the single-teacher plan for grades four, five, and six, but that other advantages accrued from the single-teacher plan.[26]

The use of departmentalization as a plan for organizing the elementary school has won and lost adherents. In the early 1900s, New York used extensive departmentalizing in the upper elementary grades. The plan continued to grow in use even into the 1940s, but some reduction in use is taking place in the first six grades. Prince reported on a survey made in 1941 of 154 cities in which he found evidence favoring the reduction of departmentalization in the elementary grades.[27] In 1945, he again found evidence of a reduction in departmentalization.[28] He reported a survey of two hundred school systems in which 68 percent had either discontinued or had plans for decreasing the amount of departmentalization.[29] Apparently little good can be found in any plan or organization of elementary schools which subjects children to constant readjustment to subject-matter specialists. Many factors essential to meeting individual needs are lost by departmental teachers who teach 150 or more children every day. Secondary school teachers (where departmentalization is practiced extensively) use this argument as a means of avoiding individual instruction, feeling that no teacher can become intimate with 150 pupils or understand intelligently their physical, social, emotional, and mental needs. However, one writer points out that teachers in departmentalization are in most respects similar to those in self-contained rooms.[30] That is, they are autonomous. Teachers do not plan together for their instruction, and consequently, weaknesses of any given teacher are experienced by all the children she teaches. Elementary school pupils' close association with their teachers has been one of the strong factors in support of the school's organization around the self-contained classroom. Principals are frequently forced into departmentalizing by thrift-minded superintendents and school boards. Principals sometimes consider departmentalization satisfactory simply because the secondary school is organized in that fashion, but such generalizations are hardly justifiable in the case of elementary school leaders.

The Self-Contained Classroom. The trend away from the self-contained classroom does not appear to be as rapid as some educators would like to believe. Although numerous schools report a move toward some other form of school organization, some studies show that little more than new labels have been applied to various kinds of classrooms.[31] This plan provides one teacher for a specified number of children in a classroom unit. In discussing the self-contained classroom, Caswell and Foshay state:

> This basic group should be formed so as to assume commonness of interest and concern in order that large group enterprises may be developed most readily as the central part of the curriculum . . . differences in abilities and in attitudes are desirable . . . the group should live and work together according to all the best precepts of democratic action, developing a sense of having a home and personal counselor within the large school situation.[32]

Proponents of the self-contained classroom argue that it recognizes the importance of meeting varying individual needs, and permits grouping within the class on the basis of needs, abilities, interests, and social relations, as demanded by situations which arise. They point out that the pupil profits from a warm, intimate relationship with the teacher, and this is essential to pupil adjustment.

On the other hand, Anderson indicates that much of what is acclaimed for the self-contained classroom is still myth, and difficult to prove.[33] Certainly many of the things teachers believed about the self-contained classroom have been refuted in the past decade. One of the authors interviewed 116 six-year-olds who had self-contained kindergarten teachers but who had been teamed with four first-grade teachers, and only one child indicated she preferred school as it was with one teacher in the kindergarten room. From this and other emperical evidence, it seems the "mother image" is not as deeply desired as we once thought. Regardless of the form of organization there is need for those who are members of a team to have certain specialized skills or to have available consultants and supervisors to assist as needed. The principal should be the key person in deciding when and how to use available resource personnel in situations where self-contained classrooms are desired by the staff, community, and principal.

IMPROVING THE CURRICULUM

This section will clarify the role of the principal as he works with his staff and the community to improve the curriculum. The authors believe that successful curriculum development takes place in the classroom with the teacher and pupils; however, the principal's leadership, based on his understanding of how to improve the curriculum program, is essential for promoting unity among the staff and community. This section will discuss how the principal can demonstrate sound leadership in developing the curriculum.

The principal of the modern elementary school must accept responsibility for the total instructional program, which helps the social, physical, mental, and emotional needs of all educable children in the community. All these areas are closely related, and growth in one area depends on growth in another. Growth, then, depends upon the quality of each related factor and its constituents. Creative ability, aesthetic appreciation, and moral and spiritual values all contribute to the makeup of the individual. The extent of growth in these areas, as well as the degree of quality, however, will further depend upon the proper balance of experiences which the school provides.

Maintaining Balance in the Curriculum

One basic need of principal and staff, as well as of the community, is an intelligent perspective of the total school program from kindergarten through grade twelve. The present piecemeal approach held by many administrators and teachers accepts at least three distinctly different phases of public education—elementary, middle school or junior high, and senior high school. If educators view and appraise the total program in the light of anticipated outcomes, the schools can expect to produce educated children who will become useful citizens. In the past, educators have spent too much time debating the issues of curriculum development and placing importance on the "either-or" of curriculum issues; they should unite in their thinking to clarify and project values that are soundly based and properly balanced.[34] Elementary school leaders should determine the extent to which their school program reflects adequate balance between each of the conflicting values in the following list:[35]

1. Process values and outcomes,
2. Skills and content,
3. Initiative and compliance,
4. Spontaneity of expression and restraint,
5. Creative and trained responses, and
6. Freedom and responsibility.

For purposes of illustration, we may analyze the fifth point: One of the objectives of the language arts program of all elementary schools is to teach children to use the English language effectively as an instrument of expression and communication.[36] On the other hand, the nature of the elementary school, as well as the organization of society, demands that children learn to restrain certain desires. Learning to think and analyze before speaking is a desired goal. The staff and community need to be led by the principal in ascertaining to what extent a balance in such a value can be maintained.

The principal must accept the responsibility if his school curriculum is out of balance, perhaps, for example, heavily weighted on the competitive side or extremely limited in its use of the cooperative approach. When children are being taught arithmetic, for example, it would be out of balance to have heavy concentration on drill with little effort to relate the content to actual life, so balance should be restored to obtain the optimum results. Obviously, balance is also needed between the school's more formal offerings and the informal offerings where each of the previously listed values is applicable. Whether the school is using a formal approach to teaching subjects or a modern individualized approach, balance in the curriculum is an important goal to be achieved.

New Curriculum Programs

The elementary principal is responsible for initiating new curriculum programs in his school. This means not only up-dating the social sience, mathematics and other curriculum areas, but also studying the need for completely new programs to serve the community.

Early Childhood Education. A massive attempt to provide educational opportunities for pre-primary-age children was recently made through federal funding. In 1965, project Head Start provided preschool education for millions of children considered economically disadvantaged. Although the full

Curriculum Development

impact of the Federal Government's effort to stimulate preschool education has not yet been ascertained, there were only 33 states in 1968 providing financial aid of some sort to local school districts for kindergarten education.[37] Efforts, however, are continually supported by both state and federal funds to gain public support for providing educational opportunities for preschool education programs. Both professional educators and the public need to understand goals and the nature of preschool education. Doubtless, some of the cause for public disinterest may be found in the misunderstanding of the nature of the nursery and kindergarten programs. While it is not the purpose here to detail a curriculum for preschool education, it should be clear that the elementary principal has a major leadership role in his community in furthering the development of preschool education.

Some of the values attributed to nursery and kindergarten education are:

1. Developing individuality and independence of the child;
2. Providing a setting for growing adjustment to the stress and strain of living with other children;
3. Aiding the child in development of confidence in adults outside the home;
4. Providing opportunities for physical development;
5. Widening the child's interest in the world about him; guiding him into habits of observation and investigation; and
6. Contributing to the general educational development of the child.

Obviously these values differ with age level and specific needs of individual children, but they are also values which continue throughout the elementary school.

Bilingual Education. For too long now, the school has spent most of its time educating only those children who have fit the curriculum pattern. We are long overdue in recognizing the need to change the program to provide for all children. Often children who used a language other than English have been subjected to programs for the mentally retarded or have been placed in remedial and nonacademic classes.[39] It does not take a major research student to know that minority students drop out of school because of low aspiration and low morale. When Spanish-speaking students, for example, must spend vast amounts of time studying English, they are obviously getting behind their English-speaking counterparts. It has been found that such programs result in the Spanish-speaking student's being three to six years behind in his academic work by the time he is a teenager.[40]

Bilingual education provides the opportunity for the hundreds of thousands of children whose native tongue is not English to learn and study in their own languages while at the same time studying English. This obviously requires teachers who can use the native tongue of the students involved.

The principal who finds himself in such a school must provide leadership for developing a bilingual educational program for these children. He can find some financial support for his program if the children are from low-income families. The enactment of the Bilingual Education Act, Title VII of the Elementary and Secondary Education Act (ESEA) should be just the impetus the principal needs to get his community behind such a program.

Sex Education. Although in some communities sex education is still a controversial issue, interest in sex education for elementary school children is growing. Many parents are confused and frustrated and feel threatened by the so-called sexual revolution. They are alarmed, as are community health authorities and social agencies, at the tremendous increase in venereal disease and illegitimate pregnancies. Today's young people are not much different when it comes to learning about sex than previous generations. Parents are not well enough informed, for the most part, to render the assistance their children need. In addition, youth are "turned off" by their parents when it comes to learning about sex. Children and youth are still getting sex information from a variety of sources—commercial sources, as well as from the proverbial "grapevine" of one ill-informed child to another.[41]

Today's principal must accept responsibility for initiating a study of sex education problems in his community. He has a rich opportunity to provide leadership in the development of desirable social relationships between boys and girls. During these early years of their childrens' education, parents are in constant contact with the school, and the elementary school principal is in an excellent position to involve them in studying programs of sex education. Some of the early programs which have met with success and which large numbers of parents have found acceptable were developed in Oregon and Delaware.[42] Newer programs which have achieved success can be found in Washington, D. C. and New Haven, Connecticut.[43]

Although certain groups have objected to sex education in the schools, great strides have been made in recent years. Many of the Catholic schools now accept and have developed excellent courses in sex education. Many teachers and parents have come to realize that sex education encompasses far more than learning to define terms and processes. It involves, also knowledge of bodily functions and attitudes of social, personal and moral responsibility.[44] Yet the task of establishing sex education programs is one in which the principal must move slowly, since sex education deals with social values and values vary from one segment of society to another.[45]

With new emphasis on health education in the schools and in teacher preparation, one may hope that teachers will be better prepared to teach sex education in the elementary schools. Teachers must not only be knowledgeable about the subject, but must also feel comfortable in helping school children acquire understanding and attitudes that lead to intelligent behavior.

It should be noted that the U. S. Office of Education takes the position that each community must determine the role it should play in family life and sex education. This must be the guiding factor for the principal in working with the community. The community and its agencies are the ones to decide what is desirable as well as what is possible to attempt, but the principal provides the leadership to help the community determine the school's role in sex education.

Paramount for the principal who wants to provide a sound program of sex education is that he work closely with all segments of the community to find those common elements which can be agreed upon before initiating the program. The principal might find that the best procedure for getting started is to provide a program for the parents; that is, set up a program with a series of meetings for parents by their children's grade level, have outstanding consultants available to show how such a program would function with children, then have each grade-level parent group elect a parent to serve on a school-wide committee to work with teachers in developing the sex education curriculum. It is important that the emphasis be placed on developing desirable attitudes toward life and the factual acceptance of the procreative processes.

CURRICULUM PLANNING

The keystone of a successful program of curriculum development emphasized in this chapter is the quality of leadership provided by the principal. In the final analysis, however, it is the teacher who determines the kinds and quality of experiences boys and girls have during the school day. Alice Meil made this clear when she said that teachers in the individual school receive the most fundamental type of help when the local school is made responsible for curriculum planning.[46]

It has been pointed out that how the principal controls the curriculum to a large degree determines its effectiveness. The purpose here is to suggest an operational plan for the principal, his staff, and community to use in working together in curriculum planning.

Beginning Curriculum Revision

It has been stated many times in professional literature that the principal is the controlling force in the school, whether for good or bad. That is, if he is an alert leader with respect, faith, and confidence in his staff and is cognizant of the need for community participation in decision making, curriculum revision will be a continuous process. Frequently, the problem of how to start such a program is an obstacle to the new principal or to the leader who is growing on the job. Research indicates that the following practices encourage a program of curriculum reorganization:

1. An experimental approach to teaching.
2. Good group relationships of principal, supervisor and teachers.
3. Evidence of group leadership; leaders keep things going, avoid complacency.
4. Rethinking of each problem to identify cause, seek preventive action.
5. Studying needs of children: how they learn, grow and develop.
6. Concern for community and social needs.
7. Implementation of decisions.

As the educational leader becomes more conscious of his role, he works to discover ways of encouraging and giving impetus to curriculum development.

Principal's Role in Curriculum Planning

The principal who is charged with the responsibility of local curriculum planning must clarify his personnel responsibilities in the situation. That is, he should define his relationship to the various supervisors and members of the administrative staff concerning curriculum planning. The principal needs to know what concepts are held by the resource people as well as the extent of their understanding of the problem at hand. The principal cannot embark upon a program of curriculum planning leading to major changes if the central administrative and supervisory staffs are satisfied with the present program or will not support the local effort. Too often, the central office holds to the bureaucratic, traditional point of view that all schools must do the same thing in the school district. The principal must exert strong leadership in getting the differences in his school community recognized. Thus it seems advisable that the administrator keep the following principles in mind as he leads in planning the curriculum:

1. The central administration, the supervision staff, and representative teacher and community groups should determine the approach to be made.
2. The approach decided upon should recognize the autonomy of the local school, its social, economic, and cultural environment, and other characteristics peculiar to the school.
3. The approach decided upon should be consistent with the school's democratic purposes.
4. The approach should be flexible enough to allow for experimentation without jeopardizing the welfare of the pupils.
5. The teachers in the individual school should be agreeable to the approach and reassured of their individual security in the changed situation.

Curriculum Development

With the approach clearly stated and agreed upon, the principal, if he has school-board sanction, is ready to embark upon a broad program of curriculum revision. Although piecemeal approaches to curriculum revision have sometimes grown into broader studies, the principal must guard against hasty decisions which seem to offer the solution to a problem. It is not uncommon for staff or parents to believe that dissatisfaction with the curriculum can be remedied simply by changing textbooks. Obviously, a change of textbooks may be one of the needs, but the principal must help the staff in making a thorough evaluation and giving an adequate interpretation of the results. The principal's role is that of expediter for initiating the new or modified curriculum plan. Of course the new plan will require continuous evaluation and modification to meet changing needs as time goes on.

Outcomes of Curriculum Revision

As indicated, a good curriculum should reflect the combined thinking of the teachers in the individual school, representative community members, the principal, and resource personnel from the central office staff. A thorough study, which is essential to the revision program, should result in profound professional growth for all those who share in the process. A deeper understanding of the objectives of education, pupil purposes, teaching methods and procedures, and principles of learning as they relate to the psychological drives of the human organism can be gained, as well as the concomitant benefits of learning to work together and gaining respect for the ideas of others. The principal should be aware that basic to the functions of all committee work are the sharing and exchanging of ideas, the new challenges and insights gained, and the realization that "ultimately the plans are carried out by the teachers."[47] The basic outcome which all personnel strive for, and to which the good leader is devoted, is the advancement of civilization through improved learning and living experiences for children.

Interpreting the School's Program to the Community

The modern school must adopt modern means to convey and interpret its program to the public. Rural schools in most cases are still serving as community centers for many activities. Agricultural, homemaking, and other organizations are in close touch with school leaders, and school activities thus draw large numbers of parents. For example, one of the writers delivered a commencement address to thirty-seven graduates of a rural high school, and to his surprise, over a thousand people were present for the occasion. However, in modern America people are generally becoming more involved and interested in their schools. Thus the alert and resourceful principal is constantly seeking ways of interpreting the school's program to the community. The following list may suggest ideas for furthering this endeavor:

1. Radio and television programs.
2. Newspaper publicity.
3. Various school publications and special school bulletins.
4. School forums dealing with current topics.
5. School night or open house.
6. Parents' bi-monthly meetings with homeroom teachers to discuss objectives of the grade, pupil needs, teacher needs, etc.
7. P.T.A. meetings.
8. Community members serving on various school committees such as faculty, advisory, curriculum, etc.
9. School activities such as band concerts, glee club, exhibits, etc.

The pupils must be recognized as the basic means for interpreting the school's program. Happy school children are the best evidence of a good school. Obviously, innumerable other opportunities to interpret the school to the community need to be capitalized on by the principal and his staff.

SUMMARY

The principal must be a leader in instructional improvement and curriculum development if educational progress is to be achieved. The school staff and the community must be brought into the planning process. It behooves the principal to give direction to his staff's thinking in order to provide a curriculum that will insure each child the opportunity of achieving maximum success from his school experience. The principal is often unaware of the factors that he controls which affect the curriculum. Some of these are: (1) the daily schedule, (2) the use of resources and field trips, (3) the classification of pupils, etc.

The principal must respond to community needs in initiating new curriculum programs when needed. He works closely with the community in developing such programs as bilingual education, early childhood education, and sex and drug education. As the school becomes more autonomous in its relationship to the central office, the responsibility increases for broadening the base of local curriculum development. All segments of the community must be brought into the process, including decision making.

SUGGESTED READINGS

Battle, J. A. and Robert L. Shannon. *The New Idea in Education.* New York: Harper & Row, 1968, Unit III.

Berman, Louise M. *New Priorities in the Curriculum.* Columbus, Ohio: Charles E. Merrill, 1968, Parts 1, 2, 7.

Bruner, Jerome S. *The Process of Education.* Cambridge, Mass.: Harvard University Press, 1961, Chapter 3.

Dewey, John, *Experience and Education*. New York: Macmillan, 1938.

Frazier, Alexander, ed. *A Curriculum for Children*. Washington, D. C.: Association for Supervision and Curriculum Development, National Education Association, 1969.

Fossett, Barbara, "Health Education in the Elementary School: A Humanistic Curriculum." *The National Elementary Principal* 48 (November 1968): 61–69.

Hartwell, Alfred S. "A Curriculum Design for Social Change," *Educational Leadership* 25 (February 1968): 405–7.

Overly, Norman V. *The Unstudied Curriculum: Its Impact on Children*. Washington, D. C.: Association for Supervision and Curriculum Development, National Education Association, 1970.

Shuster, Albert H. and Milton E. Ploghoft. *The Emerging Elementary Curriculum*. 2d ed. Columbus, Ohio: Charles E. Merrill, 1970, Chapters 4, 16.

Smith, B. Othanel, William O. Stanley, and J. Harlan Shores. *Fundamentals of Curriculum Development*. Rev. ed. New York: World, 1957, Part V.

Taba, Hilda. *Curriculum Development; Theory and Practice*. New York: Harcourt, Brace & World, 1962.

Wright, Betty Atwell, et al. *Elementary School Curriculum: Better Teaching Now*. New York: Macmillan, 1971, Chapter 5.

Notes

1. Kenneth D. Benne and Bozidar Muntyan, *Human Relations in Curriculum Change* (New York: Dryden, 1951), p. 5.

2. B. O. Smith, W. O. Stanley, and J. H. Shores, *Fundamentals of Curriculum Development* (Yonkers-on-Hudson, N. Y.: World, 1950), p. 623.

3. Ibid.

4. Elmer H. Wilds, *The Foundations of Modern Education* (New York: Rinehart, 1950), p. 557.

5. The Educational Policies Commission, *The Purposes of Education in American Democracy* (Washington, D. C.: National Education Association, 1938), p. 50.

6. Ibid.

7. Hollis L. Caswell and A. W. Foshay, *Education in the Elementary School* (New York: American Book Co., 1950), p. 78.

8. Louise M. Berman, *New Priorities in the Curriculum* (Columbus, Ohio: Charles E. Merrill, 1968), p. v.

9. Caswell, *Education*, p. 174.

10. Smith, Stanley, and Shores, *Fundamentals*, p. 318.

11. Albert H. Shuster and Milton E. Ploghoft, *The Emerging Elementary Curriculum*, 2d ed. (Columbus, Ohio: Charles E. Merrill, 1970), pp. 328–29.

12. William H. Burton and Leo J. Brueckner, *Supervision: A Social Process* (New York: Appleton-Century-Crofts, 1955), p. 369.

13. Henry J. Otto, *Elementary School Organization and Administration*, 3d ed. (New York: Appleton-Century-Crofts, 1954), p. 124.

14. William C. Reavis, et al., *Administering the Elementary School* (Englewood Cliffs, N. J.: Prentice-Hall, 1953), p. 127.

15. Alexander Frazier, ed., *A Curriculum for Children* (Washington, D.C.: Association for Supervision and Curriculum Development, National Education Association, 1969)', p. 40.

16. Adapted from Ellsworth C. Dent, *The Audio-Visual Handbook* (Chicago: Society for Visual Education, 1946), pp. 31-32.

17. John L. Goodlad, M. Francis Klein, and associates, *Behind the Classroom Door* (Worthington, Ohio: Charles A. Jones, 1970), p. 54.

18. Otto, *Elementary School Organization,* p. 167.

19. Robert Beck, Walter W. Cook, and Nolan C. Kearney, *Curriculum in the Modern Elementary School* (Englewood Cliffs, N. J.: Prentice Hall, 1953), p. 363.

20. Caswell and Foshay, *Education,* p. 362.

21. J. E. Lindquist, ed., *Educational Measurements* (Washington, D. C.: American Council on Education, 1951), p. 11.

22. W. D. Monroe, ed., *Encyclopedia of Educational Research* (New York: Macmillan, 1950), p. 379.

23. Monroe, *Encyclopedia,* p. 1114.

24. Otto, *Elementary School Organization,* p. 25.

25. Monroe, *Encyclopedia,* p. 1114.

26. Ibid.

27. T. C. Prince, "Trends in Types of Elementary School Organization," *American School Board Journal* 106 (June 1943): 37-38.

28. T. C. Prince, "Less Departmentalization in the Elementary School," *American School Board Journal* 111 (September 1945): 25.

29. Ibid.

30. Robert H. Anderson, *Teaching in a World of Change* (New York: Harcourt, Brace & World, 1966), p. 32.

31. See *Behind the Classroom Door,* 1970.

32. Caswell and Foshay, *Education,* pp. 323-24.

33. Anderson, *Teaching,* p. 82.

34. Laura Zirbes, "Concern for Balance in the Curriculum," *The National Elementary Principal* 33 (May 1954): 32.

35. Ibid., pp. 32-33.

36. The Commission on the English Curriculum of the National Council of Teachers of English, *The English Language Arts* (New York: Appleton-Century-Crofts, 1952), p. 8.

37. See Minnie P. Berson, "Early Childhood Education," *American Education* 4 (October 1968): 7-13.

38. Shuster and Ploghoft, *Emerging Elementary Curriculum,* p. 177.

39. David Ballesteros, "Toward an Advantaged Society," *The National Elementary Principal* 50, no. 2 (November 1970): 26.

40. Ibid., p. 27.

41. Marian V. Hambert, "Sex Education in the Elementary Schools," *The National Elementary Principal* 43 (November 1958): 53, 54.

42. Information about these programs can be secured by writing to the appropriate state departments of education.

43. Betty A. Wright, et al., *Elementary School Curriculum: Better Teaching Now* (New York: Macmillan, 1971), p. 286.

44. Shuster and Ploghoft, *Emerging Elementary Curriculum,* pp. 308, 309.

45. Hambert, "Sex Education," p. 54.

46. Alice Meil, "Planning for Continuity in the Curriculum," *Teachers College Record* 43 (November 1952): 135.

47. Alice Meil, *Changing the Curriculum* (New York: D. Appleton-Century, 1942), p. 179.

8

Leadership Through In-Service Education

There is an increasing emphasis on the use of in-service educational programs to provide staff members with the opportunity for continuous growth. The principal is considered the key person responsible for educational progress and staff growth through his direction of these programs. It will be noted here that a unique connotation is given to the meaning of in-service education programs by the omission of the word *training*. Webster defines *training* as "systematic drill, or exercise under supervision." The term *education* is much broader and encompasses all those learnings which better equip the individual for living more effectively as well as for teaching.

Modern in-service education programs serve the personal and professional improvement of all school personnel when administrators and supervisors share with teachers in the opportunity for growth. This concept is different from that held during the early development of in-service "training" programs. Supervisors were generally considered to be better prepared than the teachers. Therefore, they conducted training programs for teachers in order to improve teaching techniques.

One of the misconceptions of some teachers and administrators is the view that in-service education is an administrative "gimmick"[1] to keep teachers busy. However, it is aptly stated by Wilborn that in-service education should be thought of as an integral part of the professional experience: a quest for professional perfection.[2]

At least three forms of in-service education programs are widespread in the nation's schools: (1) the earning of required college credits; (2) a program of travel or community work; and (3) an organized effort planned around local, state, and national problems. The last-named form of in-service education is dealt with extensively throughout this chapter, since this aspect of in-service activities basically concerns the leadership function of the principal and the supervisor. We also include a brief consideration of the first two forms.

This chapter seeks to answer certain questions concerning in-service education. Some of these questions are: (1) What contributions can the principal make to in-service education? (2) Why do teachers need to improve themselves? (3) Should in-service education be the same for all teachers? (4) To what extent is the principal responsible for setting directions and guidelines?

THE PRINCIPAL'S CONTRIBUTION TO IN-SERVICE EDUCATION

The principal, as leader, administrator, and supervisor of his school, is charged with the responsibility for improving the quality of instruction within his building. He must have an abiding faith in his staff; he must firmly believe that they can grow. The good principal recognizes the value and meaning of intrinsic motivation, and in so doing indicates to his staff his belief in them. Thus the principal's role in in-service education is that of a dynamic leader. His status as a dynamic leader is immeasurably enhanced if his staff sees continuous effort on his part to improve his own professional competencies.

The alert administrator is cognizant of the need for a meaningful in-service program. He refrains from using this time to cover routine matters that could be brought to the attention of the staff in writing, for example, by memo or the use of a weekly bulletin. He also refrains from setting up projects or activities unrelated to the important problems teachers actually face.

Basically, then, the principal's responsibility is specifically (1) to establish an environment favorable to staff identification of problems; (2) to assist his staff in developing plans for attacking these problems; (3) to assist the staff in implementing its plans so that solutions can be found; and (4) to provide assistance in evaluating the results. Hence, the principal provides the leadership essential to professional staff growth.

Working with Other Members of the School System

There are at least three specific groups with whom the principal must establish a favorable working relationship: (1) the central office staff, (2) his own staff, and (3) the state department of education at the state office or as represented by the county office or regional center. The second of these has been elaborated upon throughout the book; the first and third relationships are discussed here.

The way the principal works with other members of the school system depends to a large extent upon the value he attaches to the services they render in his institution; yet, as leader of his school, he is responsible for coordinating the system-wide in-service educational activities with those of his own school. Some of the ways he may do this are by serving on a system-wide committee, by appointing a faculty member to serve on such a committee, or by having a faculty member represent the school on a system-wide *instructional council* established for the purpose of improving instruction.

Conferences, Workshops, and the Instructional Council

The Educational Conference. The educational conference at the state and national levels is a motivating device which may stimulate greater local school activity toward teacher growth. Although its basic purpose may be recognized as a means of providing some degree of uniformity to the state's schools, other values can also accrue. Teachers and principals should be provided the opportunity to attend state conferences. Hearing new ideas helps to keep local school personnel from becoming too provincial and complacent. Frequently, the awareness that others are working to solve similar problems may arouse a feeling of participation in a vital project and generate pride in one's profession. The principal, then, must work toward relating his staff and school to the state and nation.

The Educational Workshop. The educational workshop connotes more active involvement by the participants, and is popular at every level of educational endeavor.

Many teachers, because of their personal interest in their own professional development or the development of school curriculum projects, pay their own way to many workshops. Some workshops, seminars, and conferences at both state and national levels are being underwritten by the federal government, state departments of education, and foundations and groups sponsored by industry. The principal often receives information about these meetings, and, if possible, should help a qualified teacher find the information, then assist her in filling in the necessary information when asking for financial assistance. It is a great boost in morale for any school when a teacher is chosen to attend a state- or national-level conference for which her expenses are paid by an outside group. She, in turn, has an obligation (usually a happy one) to share her experiences with as many in her local school district as possible. The principal should make every effort to influence the board of education to provide funds to enable teachers and principals to attend educational meetings.

A good example of quality workshops sponsored by the educational community are those of School Management Institute. SMI is a nonprofit organization started by the Ohio School Boards Association. Its purpose is to provide stimulating inservice seminars for all school personnel. Seminars are scheduled for three days nearly every week, in a central location, on topics pertinent for superintendents, principals, business managers, teachers, transportation supervisors, curriculum workers, and the like.

The Instructional Council. This council has at least two purposes: (1) to permit system-wide participation in curriculum modification and instructional improvement, and (2) to coordinate in-service growth of all members of the school system.

The council should be organized so that each school has a certain number of representatives on the council, depending upon enrollment, but it is important that teachers maintain the majority block on the council. That is, the council should not be "loaded" with principals. All supervisors, and of course the school superintendent, who is an ex-officio member of all committees, should be members of the council. Representatives from the central council of the P.T.A. or other civic groups should also be invited to serve as official members of the council. Figure 6 illustrates the organizational pattern of an instructional council. The council's design for a given school system will vary according to the number of schools.

The council's function is to study carefully all problems affecting curriculum and instruction submitted from any source. The elected representatives are expected to take these problems back to their individual schools for careful study. At some designated date, the problem is brought before the council for further study and action. In this way the council knows the feelings of teachers in the entire school system as presented through their elected representatives. Suggestions and plans for action can then be made, based upon the thinking of all. After careful consideration and acceptance, the plan is presented to the board of education for legal approval before the new plan or policy is initiated. However, the council must act with caution and careful consideration in presenting any plan to the board. If P.T.A. or local school council representatives have also studied and approved the plan, there need not be fear of moving ahead of community thinking. This democratic way of administering such an instructional program may seem fairly slow in achieving its objectives, but decisions made in this manner are likely to be more secure and acceptable over the years.

If no instructional council has been functioning in the school system, the principal may demonstrate educational statesmanship by initiating action for establishing a council. He may prepare data and briefs for presentation at a routine administrative meeting and give evidence of the values to be derived from such a council in terms of better classroom teaching and improved working conditions.

The school executive should be certain that the individual school is not

Leadership Through In-Service Education 185

```
                    ┌──────────────────┐
                    │ Board of Education│
                    └──────────────────┘
                             │
┌──────────┐        ┌──────────────┐        ┌──────────────┐
│Supervisory│       │ Superintendent│       │Administrative│
│   Staff   │       └──────────────┘        │    Staff     │
└──────────┘                │                └──────────────┘
      ╎         ┌──────────────────────┐            ╎
      └ ─ ─ ─ ─ │ INSTRUCTIONAL COUNCIL │─ ─ ─ ─ ─ ─ ┘
                │ (18 Teachers, not more│        ┌────────┐
                │   than 3 Principals)  │────────│ P.T.A. │
                └──────────────────────┘        │ Council│
                                                 └────────┘
```

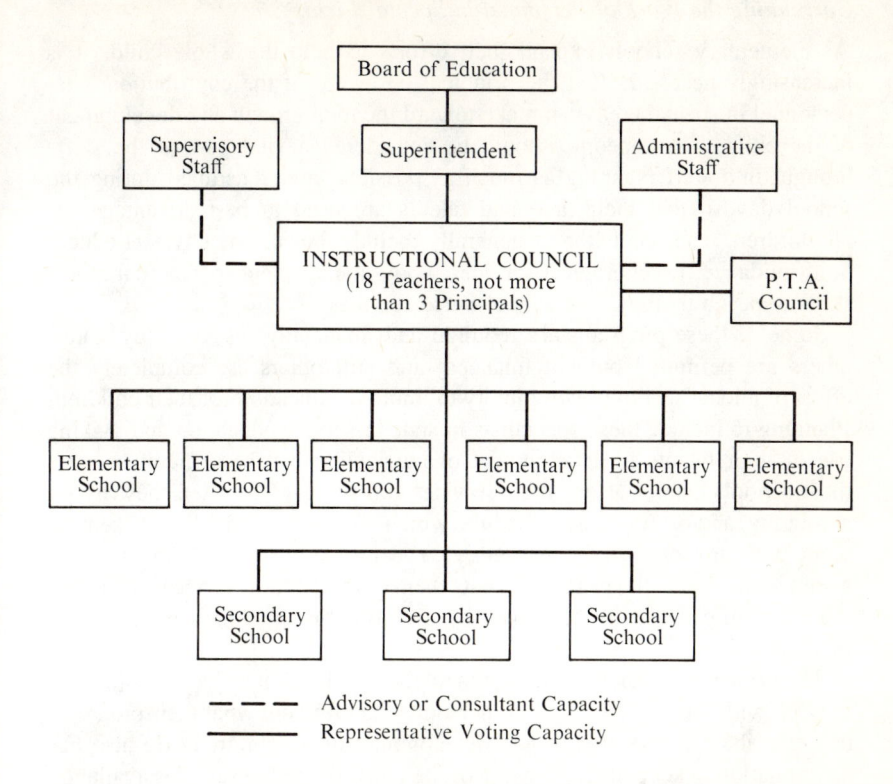

```
Elementary  Elementary  Elementary  Elementary  Elementary  Elementary
  School      School      School      School      School      School

          Secondary      Secondary      Secondary
           School         School         School
```

― ― ― Advisory or Consultant Capacity
───── Representative Voting Capacity

Figure 6

Organizational Pattern for System-Wide Instructional Council

working at cross purposes with system-wide in-service educational activities. A dispute may result if the staff of the school is required to follow an edict handed down from either the central office or the instructional council, for such an edict may be foreign to the needs and desires of the school's staff. However, the school need not lose its identity with the division-wide program. Certain school personnel may be called upon because of their interest and competence in teaching a given subject. They might conduct an experiment in this area, which in turn may result in a modification of the division-wide in-service program. Maximum participation in a division-wide organization may jeopardize real efforts on the part of the local staff to improve, due to other problems thought to be more important at the time by the city or total staff. On the other hand, inadequate participation in division-wide planning may stagnate local efforts. The principal must give leadership to his staff members by helping them find the optimum program relating to their needs.

Correlating the Work of Personnel in Special Fields

As elementary schools expand their efforts to help the whole child, it is increasingly necessary that the principal be aware of the contributions that personnel in special areas can make toward the total growth and development of the child. These people should be considered a vital part of the staff, brought into staff planning as much as possible, and scheduled during the school day so that their time and talents are used to best advantage for all children. The special areas generally include music, art, physical education, guidance, psychological services, body management (perceptual motor skills), speech therapy, and school nurse services.

Some of these programs are required and financially supported by states; others are permitted but not financed; and still others are completely the effort of a local school or community to improve education for their children. Planning to include these specialists in staff in-service education and making use of their talents in development of curriculum can be difficult because most schools cannot afford their services full-time. Most often they are on a rotating and/or traveling schedule which makes it difficult for them to work with any one staff consistently. The problem of scheduling is often a sticky one, but if the principal wants them involved in in-service education, the problem can usually be solved by giving notice of time schedules well in advance.

The principal cannot be an expert in all these fields, but he has an obligation to work with each of these special personnel and find out what their programs can contribute to the growth and development of all children. He also has an obligation to keep his staff aware of the range of special services available, their limitations, and the routines necessary to schedule these services, such as referrals on a particular form for requesting psychological services, grade-level or total staff involvement in working out music and art schedules, etc.

It is advisable that the principals and the curriculum director meet with all rotating personnel in the spring and plan schedules for the following school year. Only in this way can the school year begin with all services scheduled, thus eliminating conflicts in schedules and the many hours that might be necessary to remedy the situation on a crash basis. Planning in this way, deciding which special person will be in what building and at what time, gives staff all the information necessary to arrange their daily schedules for the following year to include the special services of these people and their programs.

TEACHERS SEE A NEED FOR IMPROVEMENT

The principal of a modern elementary school recognizes his profound responsibility for helping his staff to grow professionally. A complacent faculty may cease to improve; thus the principal must play his role well if educational progress is to be made in his school. There are at least four possible arguments that emphasize the need for teacher improvement: (1) modern society poses complex problems; (2) scientific research in the fields of education and child growth and development are contributing to our understanding of curriculum and child needs; (3) stimulation of action research within the school is important; and (4) audio-visual techniques pose a fascinating challenge in their use as tools to help teachers see themselves.

Modern Society Reflected in the Classroom

Good schools during all ages have sought to help children grow into responsible citizens. As needs of individuals have changed, curricula and teaching procedures have also changed. Slow as they have been, these changes were inevitable.

For example, the automobile age brought with it a host of changes in social living, the jet age stepped up the pace of change, and now one can hardly visualize the many possible ramifications of the space age. New learning activities in the form of electronic devices are bidding for time and attention, not only commercial television, but educational television, computerized learning systems, and others. The problem of the school is to evaluate and use judiciously these techniques and materials for the improvement of education.

As primary changes are brought about by material advances in science, so also are they brought about by evolving social attitudes and patterns. For example, the Supreme Court decision of 1954, forbidding school segregation by races, created a certain amount of social confusion and profound change in some parts of the nation. Today the social attitudes and patterns assault the school in mounting numbers—permissiveness, drugs, black power, change by violence, pollution control, population explosion, ecological problems—the list seems endless. Too, schools across the nation are confused by court decisions that seem to be eroding certain values and standards traditionally set by the school. Erosion of moral values causes added problems for school personnel. As examples, witness the current frightening trend toward stealing as a "thrill" with the added fillip of "you are not guilty of anything wrong unless you get caught," and the "new morality" of personal freedom without responsibility so long as you hurt no other person. These and many other problems affect the home and community life of our children, and pose problems of control and guidance of children which almost evade solution. For many persons, including teachers, this has brought about a reexamination of personal, school, and social values.

Communicating the Need for Improvement

Shannon[3] says that "One cannot have any preconceptions as to where somebody ought to be and the kinds of things he should have experienced before getting under way with in-service education."

The alert principal is cognizant of the many differences found within his staff. He accepts these individual differences just as the modern teacher understands pupil differences. He must plan to meet the many professional growth needs of his teachers by personally identifying some of them and by helping the teachers appraise their own needs. The personnel-minded administrator reviews the personal data form of the teacher's application, as well as other confidential information in the teacher's personnel file, for clues which will help him to understand teacher needs.

Most of all he uses his day-to-day associations with the teacher and his observations of her teaching to evaluate her strengths and weaknesses. He accentuates the positive by discussing with her the strengths and talents he has observed, making every effort to keep the discussion on a casual and informal basis. The formal conference required by a school board or a system is another matter and is discussed in the chapter on evaluation. At every opportunity he reminds her that he is eager to help her in any way he can toward improving her teaching strengths and talents.

MEETING TEACHER NEEDS

Needs of the Beginning Teacher

The new teacher's needs are many and varied. As discussed in chapter 6, these needs can be considered and met through an adequate induction program. We are concerned here, however, with helping the beginning teacher become successful in his initial year of teaching. The beginning teacher in most cases has just completed a teacher-education program which culminated in a student-teaching experience. Student-teaching programs across the nation are as different as the teachers themselves. The beginning teacher's student teaching may have ranged from a full-time off-campus experience to a one-hour-a-day approach. Although we may assume the full-time experience is the more desirable, even this experience varies. There are full-time off-campus programs where some student teachers experience only one or two full weeks out of a quarter or a semester in actual responsibility for directing the learning experiences of children. Suffice it to say that much is being done by the Association of Student Teaching, the National Association for Colleges of Teacher Education, and other agencies, to improve teacher-education programs.

In Shuster's[4] study of beginning teachers, 68 percent favored some type of required in-service education program during their initial year of teaching. Although such a requirement would no doubt be helpful, it may be difficult to administer in some smaller schools. However, city- or county-wide programs of in-service education for beginning teachers should be explored. These programs, to be successful, must be developed around areas of teacher-need which beginning teachers have recognized and identified as important to them.

Two other ideas sponsored by some colleges appear valuable in giving additional experience in actual school situations: (1) requiring a pre-student teacher to observe and participate in the routine of opening school in the fall, then discuss with the principal and staff the pre-planning and scheduling necessary to make this opening of school routine smooth and successful; and (2) the move toward the exploratory participation program in which the pre-student teacher is assigned to a school on a one-half day for five days-a-week basis and expected to assist in the actual instruction of children.

Many beginning teachers seem to lack the organizational skills necessary to make the classroom run smoothly. There seems to be a wide gap between training and teaching, a gap that swallows the beginning teacher when she discovers that classroom management must be planned before instruction or learning can take place. Her only actual contact with the problem of classroom management probably took place during her student teaching, and even here she had an experienced teacher to back her up and the responsibility was not completely her own. Suddenly she discovers that the methods courses did not mention all the nitty-gritty details that must be taken care of in order to guide thirty or more active children into and through the learning process. An example will illustrate the point:

> The principal's impression of Bonnie D. as a new teacher coming into his school was good. She was alert and eager to get started "right," as evidenced by the fact that she had been in the building many times before opening day, had decorated her room, talked to the other teachers, and worked out some plans with them; in fact, she had done many things to prepare herself. Excitement carried her through the first week, but by the end of the second week she was in tears. Why? What had happened? As they discussed the problem the principal soon discovered that her management of details was poor. A number of casual observations of her class had told him this, but now Bonnie was ready to discuss the problem and try to solve it. She had not discussed it with other teachers because she was ashamed of her lack of ability. The principal made sure that the attack was against the problem and not against the teacher. Together they worked out some procedures that would help solve the problem. Using experience-chart paper which could be stored or posted as needed, they put down the following ideas:
>
> 1. Activity chart for the day, or for the week.
> 2. Helper's chart for the week. Every child was given responsibility for a room detail.
> 3. Chart for opening exercises on which were listed routine activities and suggestions for activities that individuals or small groups might want to work on for presentation.
> 4. Assignment chart for the day.
>
> In addition to these, the principal suggested that the teacher plan with

the children some simple rules or guidelines that would help make it pleasant for everyone in the room to live and work together. These, too, were to be put on chart paper and posted. Bonnie's ability to handle details did not change overnight, but her classroom management improved steadily through the year. During a spring conference she stated that using the chart idea for control and direction was "the best idea she had ever had!" The principal felt gratified that the successful use of such a simple device had led her to a feeling of accomplishment.

A Written Philosophy for Schools

Many studies have pointed out the need and desire of new teachers to learn something of the school's philosophy and objectives. Most states require as a standard for state approval that each school have a written philosophy and objectives. However, all too often, the teacher just beginning or new to the district is not introduced to this "guide for action," when in fact she should be invited to review it and suggest changes for staff consideration.

In a large city elementary school which was visited by one of the authors, it was noted that the faculty had just completed setting down some statements which gave direction to their thinking. Few, if any, of the teachers in this school had had this kind of experience previously, and the principal indicated this was a most valuable experience for him. He pointed out that as a result of it he had a much better understanding of his teachers as well as an appreciation of why they used certain teaching procedures. The following statements represent their combined thinking in developing a school philosophy. It is not used here particularly to serve as a model, but to indicate how a principal may lead staff thinking during the year's in-service education program.

A PHILOSOPHY OF EDUCATION FOR THE TIFFIN ELEMENTARY SCHOOL

The statements listed below are concepts that we hold to be true and worthy of being a foundation for activities in the school. These concepts were developed through a series of meetings with all teachers and the principal participating.

WE BELIEVE:
  (about the child)
  That each child is a unique personality.
  That children vary greatly in abilities, habits, attitudes, interests, and past experiences.
  That children have certain needs which must be recognized if growth is to be continuous. Among these needs are the need for success, confidence, security, love, and recognition by classmates and teacher.
  That the physical well-being of the child is necessary for maximum achievement.

Leadership Through In-Service Education

That children require structure to their daily living, and that any philosophy which would permit children to do whatever they please regardless of the effect upon themselves or others, is not conducive to good mental health and is contrary to reality.

That all children cannot be expected to accomplish the same goals in achievement within a given time.

(about learning)

That motivation is the heart of the learning process.

That real learning results in some change or modification of behavior in children. This is not necessarily reflected in overt action, but may be concerned with habits, attitudes, and ideals.

That the rate of learning for all children is not the same.

That the child responds to a total learning situation; his personality cannot be detached as specific skills are learned.

That children will respond more favorably to praise and encouragement than to condemnation and criticism.

That each child should be placed in a situation where the goals established are attainable for that child.

That meaningful explanations and experiences should precede drill and practice for retention.

That the tool skills are not an end in themselves, but are a means of accomplishing desirable goals.

(about areas of learning)

That the elementary school must assume the responsibility for teaching the tool skills.

That the elementary school should contribute toward greater understanding by the child of his community, nation and world.

That the elementary school must continually strive to develop in children an understanding of the responsibilities as well as the rights of citizenship in a democracy.

That the elementary school must foster the concept of the peaceful solution of controversial issues and problems.

That the teaching of moral values and Christian concepts should be an integral part of the classroom experience. That these values and concepts can best be taught by daily application in situations that are real to children.

That the elementary school should assist the child to develop creatively in his ability to express himself through art, music, dramatics, and literature.

That the elementary school should help the child to better understand himself and his relations with others.[5]

New or beginning teachers would profit from such a joint experience, but when personnel are added to the staff after the philosophy has been developed, the principal has several alternatives. Some procedures which he might initiate are: (1) put a copy of the philosophy in the hands of each new teacher; (2) call a general meeting to consider any statement which the staff might care to modify or which the new teachers might care to discuss; (3) have personal interviews with new teachers concerning the statement of philosophy; or (4) ask each interested teacher to submit any statement she wishes concerning the philosophy. It would be valuable to have some annual activity to encourage staff thinking about modification of the philosophy.

Helping Teachers Write Objectives. A recent idea for getting teachers to put into writing some of the methods and expected behaviors for achieving school objectives is called "Agreements To Teach." This method should be used only if the staff is prepared for it and if the staff agrees that it will serve the teachers' and school's purposes. It is mentioned here because it promises to be a valuable way of acquainting the new teacher with the directions in which the staff is moving. The "Agreements To Teach" would have to be updated from year to year as the program moves on and new ideas, materials, or methods change the pattern. These agreements should be simple and to the point. They are not designed to give definitive answers as to exactly what should be taught or even to describe a suggested method. They are written only to give a broad overview of what the team members or a group of grade-level teachers feel should be the responsibility of every teacher within the group. The following list is one under consideration by the teachers in the Alpha Team (six- and seven-year-old children) in one of the author's school, and is only suggestive, since no two school situations or team situations can ever be alike.

AGREEMENTS TO TEACH—ALPHA TEAM

1. I agree to move the children under my direction from basal reading to individualized reading as soon as they attain skills necessary to work on their own.
2. I agree to use the phonics materials chosen by the team as supplementary helps to enhance and broaden the reading experience.
3. I agree to use all A-V equipment and materials available to me in the most creative manner possible for the improvement of instruction.
4. I agree to use the adopted math book and workbook as tools for teaching concepts, thus laying the groundwork for the individualized math program in the next two teams.
5. I agree to teach writing with overhead projection, making it as dramatic as possible by using color for giving directions and presenting letter forms.
6. I agree to teach the S.H.E.S. health program as approved by the board of education, following the guide furnished by the school and using every supplementary means possible to expand the concepts.

7. I agree to teach science with the A.A.A.S. materials as outlined in the teachers' guide furnished by the company.
8. I agree to teach social studies with the unit method, using the units as outlined for the year by the team, and working with the team to work out details.

Helping the Older Teacher See a Need for Change

To the young, beginning principal, or the alert, experienced principal, the older teacher sometimes presents a problem. Principals face the common problem of whether to use special methods to help older teachers recognize the need for improvement. Perhaps this group of teachers has certain common characteristics, such as the facts that their own children are grown and gone, their health may be becoming a problem, and they may be looking toward retirement rather than striving for continuous improvement. If research in the subject is indicative, no particular special methods of encouragement are really necessary, but the principal should be alert to problems connected with health, such as possible limitations on physical activities.

If approached from the humanistic standpoint, the older teacher is in the same position so far as in-service needs are concerned as is the younger or beginning teacher—she has needs that are peculiar to her alone, and needs related to the group with which she works. Her personal attitude is the key to the problem, as it is when anyone is asked to change or adapt, and in this respect age does not seem to be a criterion. Some older teachers are more alert and alive when nearing retirement years than at any other time in their life, while a younger teacher may become stagnated early in her teaching career. The older teacher usually has seen principals come and go. Thus the vigorous young principal who attempts to overpower or who underestimates the potential of the older teacher has lost sight of a valuable source of guidance.

Perhaps the fact that older teachers are as much or more agreeable to change relates to the fact that they feel secure, because of tenure or confidence in their experience, and therefore do not feel threatened when change is desired. The older teacher has many resources for useful contributions. The principal could use her special talents by assigning her leadership in special projects, group discussions, the local school or district instructional council, or as a grade-level leader or team chairman for a particular project in which she is interested.

The principal who looks to older teachers for guidance and assistance gains their respect. Most of these teachers have spent many years in one school and may have relatively low professional qualifications or may not have had recent training to stay up-to-date. Thus they are dependent upon some kind of in-service education and need a good educational leader—their principal. Frequently, all that is necessary to ignite the spark is to place the older teacher in a leadership position, with the responsibility of accomplishing a group-set goal. Such responsibility, however, must be within the teacher's range of ability. Again, the key to satisfactory relationships lies in a psychological question, "Do the principal and teacher see each other as threats or allies?"

Problems for Married Women Teachers

Married women can and do make good teachers. Frequently they are also mothers, and thus may possess better insights into child growth patterns. Married as well as single teachers have in-service education needs, and meeting their needs sometimes presents problems to the elementary school principal. The married teacher has chores to accomplish at home after school, and often prefers to return to school in the evening for a meeting. On the other hand, the single teacher may prefer to stay at school and complete her work in the afternoon. Thus the principal must plan with his staff if he is to adapt an in-service program to their personal needs. Obviously, some give and take must be accepted by both single and married teachers if a program is to have continuity. That is to say, the principal as a supervisor must be creative and endeavor to build a program around the personal needs of teachers insofar as possible, but not to the detriment of the program. If the program has been cooperatively agreed upon, teachers can also help to make the decisions necessary to implement it effectively.

A faculty consisting wholly of married teachers is in itself no cause for the principal and his staff to fail to grow on the job. Regardless of teachers' marital status, the educational leader is concerned with ways and means of improving learning experiences for children through in-service activities of teachers.

Some suggestions to the principal for improving his working relationships with married teachers are to:

1. Try to understand their home situation, including the knowledge that they are, in many cases, trying to raise a family, keep a husband happy, and teach, all at the same time. On top of this, some are taking college courses for additional credits and degrees.
2. Treat them as career women who understand their commitment to perform at a high level as teachers.
3. Work out suitable time schedules for meetings, then take care not to go beyond the announced dismissal time because many of these women have family schedules to meet.
4. Evaluate their work in terms of the job being done and be cautious about letting their outside problems weight your evaluation, although they must be taken into account.

The Male Teacher in the Elementary School

There appears to be no evidence that men of any age are preparing in large numbers for elementary school teaching. Economic conditions, war conditions, and other factors have had some slight impact. Draft deferment for male teachers led some men to choose elementary teaching in lieu of army service. Teacher Corps volunteers brought men into preparation programs for elementary teaching. Currently the oversupply of men at the secondary level, particularly in social studies and English, has led to retraining efforts for these individuals. Occasionally one still hears of the young man who is doing an outstanding job with primary children, but at this writing there is still no evidence of a male take-over of elementary education, as in some European countries. It is safe to say that a large number of male teachers in the elementary schools are looking forward to a career in elementary administration or some central office position.

Children need contact with male teachers, and principals should make every effort to recruit men to balance their staffs. Boys especially need contact with male teachers, even at the first-grade level. An attitude toward school itself as being feminine in nature is sometimes listed as a cause for a boys' failure in school. Suffice it to say that we should work toward a balance of contacts for both boys and girls.

IN-SERVICE DEVICES

As he studies the needs of the community and the school, a leader must be able to look forward. To meet the challenge of continuous change, the principal searches for new and improved in-service education devices which will facilitate professional growth of his staff. Almost alone, the principal sets the tone in his building by his own personal commitment and actions. When interaction between principal and staff is informal and mutually respectful, he can involve his staff in many activities which promise growth in skills and knowledge.

While content is important, we have been guilty of placing too much emphasis on accumulation of facts and not enough on skills of learning. Boys and girls need to know how to find, analyze, and accurately report and use data. This makes it imperative that the principal do everything possible to help teachers become aware of and skillfull with all available tools for improved teaching, especially in the areas of skill acquisition, pupil-teacher interaction, and human relations. Thus the problem remains one of the principal's knowing how to choose those activities which will be meaningful to his staff. Among the in-service devices from which the principal may choose are:

1. The before-school conference;
2. Professional days during the school year;
3. Faculty meetings;
4. The interest group;

5. The curriculum committee;
6. University courses;
7. Participation in the student-teaching program;
8. Participation in a university-intern program;
9. The conference method;
10. The use of audio-visual techniques;
11. Development of teachers' creative ideas;
12. Team teaching;
13. Working with teachers' professional organizations; and
14. The role-playing technique.

The Pre-school Conference

Schools in many states now employ teachers to work for periods longer than the usual 180 teaching days. This innovation has brought with it varied plans for using the additional days in the school year. In this way the pre-school conference as an in-service educational device was initiated. Although the usefulness of this device frequently depends upon the number of days assigned for the conference, it is important that the staff understand the purposes of these meetings, held before the children actually come to school. Although the length of the conference varies from one day to two weeks, the pre-school conference was originally thought of as a device to enable teachers and administrators to plan their year's work. Recently, modifications have been made by some school systems in the direction of utilizing the conference as an integral part of the in-service education program.

The principal may or may not be directly responsible for organizing the pre-school conference; that is, this responsibility may be the supervisor's or the curriculum director's if the conference is a system-wide activity. However, if it is not the principal's direct responsibility, his function will usually be to serve in whatever capacity he is asked. If it is his duty to organize a pre-school conference for his own school and staff, he needs to give careful thought to developing a cooperative approach for organizing and administering this in-service education device. In either case, his knowledge of the organization of a pre-school conference can be helpful.

The principal, whether a member of the planning committee or directly responsible for the conference planning, will find that planning the most effective use of the conference time is a central problem. Some promising practices concerning the pre-school conference may guide the principal's thinking as he develops plans for the conference. These are:

1. Plan the conference during the preceding spring while teachers are available.
2. Use teachers' problems as the basis for conference activities.
3. Have teachers elect a central planning committee.

Leadership Through In-Service Education

4. See that all groups are represented in the planning—primary and intermediate groups, specialists, etc.
5. Set up a leadership workshop during the summer for those who are to serve as group chairmen.
6. The conference should be held for not fewer than three days.
7. Work to develop a warm social climate permeated by a permissive, informal atmosphere.
8. Teachers should receive full compensation for conference work days.
9. Use community resource persons as needed, and consultants from universities and publishing companies.
10. Plan activities that will keep the conference moving toward it objectives.
11. Schedule sufficient time for individuals and groups to achieve objectives.
12. Provide for materials which will be needed by the groups
13. Plan recreational activities suitable for all ages.
14. Develop a cooperative plan for evaluating the effectiveness of the conference in terms of its objectives.

Professional Days

For those schools unable to pay teachers for pre-school in-service planning for a significant block of time, there is a steady movement to lengthen the school year by contract with teachers and set aside two to five days during the school year for "professional days." These special days usually take two forms: (1) days designated in the calendar of the school as in-service education days for the entire staff, and (2) those days negotiated by teachers with the board of education to conduct the business of the local teachers' professional organizations. The first is quite common and always involves the principal and his staff in the planning and in the day itself. The second is not common, but where it is a negotiated item the principal is usually not involved since in most instances he is not permitted membership in the classroom teachers' organization.

When a professional day is set aside for in-service education, the principal exerts leadership efforts to involve his staff in a cooperative effort to plan and use the day to best advantage. Usually a steering committee representing the staff, composed of volunteer teachers and administrators, makes the arrangements for the day and, working through the building representatives, relays this information to the staff of each school. Often there is a choice of activities planned to meet the special needs expressed by teachers or administrators to the steering committee. When a total system plans professional meetings, there is more chance that paid specialists can be secured than if one building tries to finance this alone. It is, of course, manifestly impossible to plan such variety of programs or such exciting programs that every teacher will be thrilled to attend, yet the principal has a responsibility to urge each teacher to take advantage of and contribute to the planned activities. He should offer his services to the steering committee and suggest ways to make each day as meaningful as possible. His main responsibility is to cooperate with the steering committee in implementing plans.

Faculty Meetings

A common complaint of teachers concerns the poor quality of faculty meetings. These complaints are generally a reflection of poor administration. Faculty meetings are called for many useful purposes, but when the principal exhorts teachers about their failures, the meetings usually degenerate into uninspiring and tension-producing administrative sessions. If the principal uses the faculty meeting with discretion, he has at his disposal one of the best techniques for in-service growth. Thus, when the whole staff works together, the results should be representative of the group's thinking and readily acceptable to all.

Faculty meetings may be held for (1) administrative purposes, and (2) in-service growth. Our concern here is with the second purpose. Faculty meetings that provide in-service growth must have a purpose common both to teachers and principal. Such a purpose may be identified at the beginning of the school year. With the purpose established, a faculty committee responsible for the year's program should be elected by the staff. This committee, working closely with principal and teachers, should be responsible for preparing and submitting an agenda before each meeting. Continuous and systematic evaluation should be made as the year's program unfolds.

Obviously, such a procedure can produce better teacher morale than a situation in which teachers have no voice in planning the meetings. However, even committee-made plans should be flexible. The agenda should be subject to change at the beginning of all faculty meetings. The staff may feel that an item at the bottom of the agenda is important and needs early consideration,[6] or a new item considered urgent may be suggested.

Although the program committee may suggest a time for meetings, it is important that all teachers be heard concerning this question, so that a consensus can be gained. Research indicates that after school is the optimum time for faculty meetings. However, other times for holding meetings are before school in the morning, during the noon hour, in the evenings, and on Saturdays. Most authorities agree that faculty meetings should be held during school time, but the problems of scheduling meetings on school time depend on the size of the school, its location, and community mores. It may be desirable to hold meetings starting at two o'clock one afternoon a month and dismiss the children. This is an administrative function which requires careful planning with the central staff as well as the board of education.

If there is a lay advisory council working with the curriculum director or the board of education, its help should be enlisted in formulating plans for the use of available time for in-service education. Any time planned for in-service activities or for parent-teacher conferences must take into account any state law requiring a minimum number of hours that students must be in attendance for the school to qualify for state funds. Parents have sometimes complained to both local and state authorities when schools have used released time for professional meetings, parent-teacher conferences, etc.[7] The same reasoning holds true for planning released time for students in order to hold any in-service meeting. Another factor for concern is the large number of cases in which both parents of a child work, causing hardship when the child is released early and the parents must provide extra or outside help for supervision.

Many states now require a specific amount of duty-free time for each teacher for lunch. In schools where children are dismissed for the noon hour, there may still be time for staff meetings during this period, but this practice may be on the wane with the advent of busing, federal or state lunch programs, free lunches for indigent or disadvantaged children, and other programs that require supervision for the children. In most elementary schools there is no one time of day, from the moment children enter until they leave, when all teachers are available for a meeting.

The principal, working with a committee of teachers or team leaders, should strive to make every faculty meeting as interesting and meaningful as possible. He should avoid using any more time than absolutely necessary for administrative trivia, the kind of information that can and should be put in a bulletin. In a team-teaching situation, total staff meetings become less important, for the smaller group comprising the team has many of the same learning characteristics as a small group of students: common goals, close interaction, group-centered planning, identified leadership or specialty skills. Teams are usually adaptive to change because they have already made a significant change in their teaching patterns by joining a team. There are times, however, when the committee and/or the principal need to schedule a total staff meeting, and these occasions include such activities as:

1. Listening to a consultant or specialist discuss a program that cuts across grades or teams.
2. Discussion of programs or activities that involve the whole school.
3. Hearing the superintendent or business manager explain the financial matters of the school district.
4. Seeing a demonstration of new equipment that is being considered for purchase and that will be used by all.
5. Discussion of purchasing priorities related to curriculum development.

6. Presentation and discussion of instructional evaluative instruments that will be used through the entire school, as, for example, a cumulative reading checklist begun in kindergarten and used each year as a device for continuous evaluation and reading placement.

This list is merely suggestive. The principal, through his committee, should strive for variety with purpose, as much interaction as possible, and some critical evaluation sessions on a periodic basis in a constant endeavor to improve the faculty meetings.

The Interest Group

This approach to teacher growth is based on the psychological concept that for learning to be effective, the learner must have a deep and abiding interest in that which is to be learned. The principal who utilizes this approach may find some teachers unwilling to participate in an in-service program, yet he can assume that teachers who have a mutual interest will work together to seek a solution to the problem which concerns them.

Curriculum committees, study groups, and other organizations function in many schools as interest groups. This form of in-service growth must be entirely free of coercion by the principal. Membership in the interest group must be voluntary and the activities cooperatively planned. The interest group should be explored critically to determine its values and limitations, not only as an individual school device, but as a system-wide approach to in-service growth of teachers and administrators.

The Curriculum Committee

Improvement of instruction should be the goal of all in-service programs. Through the curriculum committee, teacher growth is enhanced and the ultimate goal achieved. This committee is specialized, and usually consists of some of the best teachers in the school system. It may be made up of a representative from each school in the system if the committee is designed to serve the entire system. However, the principal may find it desirable to limit the organization only to his own school. Regardless of the breadth of the committee representation, its task is to develop or to study certain aspects of the instructional program. For example, this committee may be studying the scope and sequence of the language arts program in grades one to six. Then the committee would have members representing all grade levels, as well as citizens from the community, and specialists in language arts serving as consultants. All aspects of pupil growth relative to the area under study would be considered.

Curriculum committees in modern school systems usually meet regularly throughout the school year. In some systems these committees are retained for eleven months so they can write a report of their findings. The principal and staff should determine the mechanics and operations of such a committee to meet best the needs of the school. The following case study shows the effectiveness of a district-wide curriculum committee in meeting the specific needs of teachers by providing specially-designed college level courses.

In 1967 the curriculum director, working through the principals and the local teachers' association, asked for teacher volunteers to form a Power Steering Committee for the local district. The original concept was that this committee would be responsible for helping in the development of specified curriculum areas within the local district. This concept grew, however, when the teachers comprising the committee found they had the opportunity and freedom to structure more sophisticated activities. The main objective of the Power Steering Committee was to find out what teachers considered the most pressing needs for in-service activities and to structure activities to meet those needs. Each building in the district had at least one representative on the committee, and it was this representative's responsibility to survey the teachers in his building and report to the committee. The committee discussed the teachers' feelings and needs and proposed possible solutions. The committee soon found that they would have to move beyond the local scene and seek university asssitance to meet the expressed needs of teachers. These needs had not been difficult to identify once the teachers felt free to express themselves through their peer group on the Power Steering Committee. Once a particular need was defined, a subcommittee was formed, made up of teachers from the steering committee with a particular interest in the proposed area plus volunteers from any building. This subcommittee then worked with the curriculum director to secure a university instructor, enlist teachers in the course, and write preliminary specifications for the content of the course. One of the strong points concerning the work of a subcommittee, the point most liked by teachers, was that once the course for which they were responsible was finished and evaluated, their responsibility was automatically over.

During the first four years, the Power Steering Committee made available to teachers one course in learning disabilities of children, two consecutive courses in the teaching of health (part of a long-range plan to implement the S.H.E.S. Health Program in all area schools), one class in audio-visual techniques, and three consecutive courses in the teaching of reading. All the courses were made available to teachers through the help and cooperation of personnel from Miami University, Oxford, Ohio. These classes have been well attended and successful because the specifications for instruction have been written by the teachers themselves, and instructors were most cooperative in following the teacher-designed specifications. Each subcommittee used a step-by-step process in structuring a course. First, after a need was identified, each building representative made a more detailed survey of teachers' feelings about a proposed course and enlisted as many as possible on a tentative basis. The second step involved asking the county supervisor's assistance in further identification of detailed needs, and the third step was to bring the university instructor into the planning. The instructor, the subcommittee, and the curriculum director then formulated plans for the course. At the first class meeting these plans were discussed with the teachers attending, and once more their opinions were considered. At any time during the course, upon mutual agreement, areas of concern could be added or deleted, or new activities could occur that were not originally planned. This provided an atmosphere of much instructor/teacher interaction. Even the type of marking, whether pass/fail or traditional letter grades, was agreed upon by the class and the instructor.

The response to these courses suggests that teachers are more willing to invest their own time and money in university courses if the courses are tailored to their needs and if they have a direct voice in writing the specifications for the courses. It also seems evident that there is a greater transfer from these courses to the needs of children in the classroom. After the audio-visual course, for example, there was a noticeable increase in the use of audio-visual equipment and in the making of teacher-made materials. This entire process is based on the theory of functionalization, for the university extension course fulfills its function by meeting the special and specific needs of a group of teachers; the special knowledge and skills learned by the teachers enables them to function more professionally in the classroom; and interaction patterns in the classroom improve with the increased professionalism of each teacher.

The principal does not have an authoritarian image in any of the activities mentioned above. He becomes the facilitator, possibly a member of a committee, and often a classmate in one of the university courses. The curriculum director states that this method of promoting teacher growth through involvement in planning and implementing in-service activities is the most valuable and productive idea ever promoted in the Madison Township schools. Teachers like this procedure because they can voice their opinions throughout the entire process, because they receive university credit which may affect salary, and because the courses are tailored to their needs.

From the administrator's standpoint, this device of using a teacher committee to plan and implement special courses cuts down significantly on the amount of time that would ordinarily have to be allocated for handling details. The administrator has a one-to-one relationship with the chairman of the Power Steering Committee, acts as adviser, liaison with the university, or in any other capacity that will foster the teacher-directed activities. It is doubtful that the process will work unless the director is willing to delegate authority and minimize the traditional hierarchy. The experience of this school system indicates that the more we expect of teachers, the greater their response to the challenge.[8]

Student-Teaching Programs

A major problem facing teacher-preparing institutions is that of locating good schools where student teachers may profit from a directed-teaching experience. The changing concept of the university laboratory school and the greatly increased numbers of student teachers make it mandatory that student teaching be done off-campus and preferably on a full-time basis. This type of student teaching provides an opportunity for public schools to participate in a program which should enhance teacher growth. The principal can give leadership here by contacting colleges and universities to obtain student teachers in his school. The writers have known some teachers who were reluctant to accept responsibility for assisting with the preparation of students for teaching, but the results have most often been gratifying to the cooperating teachers. Teachers who work with student teachers are intrinsically motivated to prove their worth. They often remark about the new ideas they receive from the student teachers; thus the experience becomes one of mutual growth.

Many principals have reported increased professional growth on the part of the entire staff as a result of having student teachers in the building. New ideas are brought from college and university campuses to the participating school, theory is tried, and practical learning is gained. Student teaching may thus serve as a promising source of in-service growth. Most universities now offer credit courses to teachers who want to learn the techniques of working with student teachers in their classrooms. Some universities also offer teacher's the opportunity to attend one or more meetings at which there is a sharing of ideas about what is expected of the student teacher and of the classroom supervising teacher. In addition, most universities remunerate the classroom supervising teacher, with cash, or, more often, a certificate to cover the full cost of one or more college courses. The interactions set up between college-level supervisor, classroom-teacher supervisor, and student teacher have helped teachers overcome their feelings of inadequacy concerning their ability to cooperate effectively with the student teacher and the university. A teaching team offers much greater opportunity for student-teacher growth than does the self-contained classroom. There is much more contact at the adult level in the areas of planning and instruction, and the opportunity to interact with many more students. An additional growth factor is present for teachers, also, since the addition of a student teacher to the team brings more ideas, interaction, and increases the necessity for careful planning to include the student teacher in as many of the activities of the total team as possible.

University Interns

The elementary principal should selfishly become involved in teacher education. He recognizes that many benefits will accrue to the total educational program through the presence of preservice teachers in his school. The preservice intern, coming out of a modern teacher education program, has had many participation experiences with children from the beginning of her training. Many of these experiences border on what formally was called student teaching. Now the teacher intern finds herself not just playing the role of teacher, but assuming the teacher's role. The intern might be assigned to varied roles, ranging from a self-contained classroom to staff differentiated assignments. In either case the intern would work as a team member and thus would be in a decision-making situation. The intern would not only learn from the experienced teachers with whom she is teamed, but would also bring to the school environment new ideas about teaching, learning, and use of media. The intern would be in the school for not less than a semester and thus would have the opportunity to try a wide range of teaching behaviors. When the principal works with the university on setting up the program, he must insist on sufficient time to test these teaching skills. Short-range experiences might serve a purpose during the sophomore and junior years, but the intern teacher needs to be in the classroom long enough to test her skills and assess her accomplishments with the learners. Thus the experience builds on to the intern's preservice training by providing the opportunity for alternative choices in developing "master" teacher behaviors. The principal readily recognizes the inherent contributions which the interns make to the children, his staff, and the community.

Conference Method

The principal can use a personal conference with a teacher as a very effective method for promoting professional growth. All principals use this method, whether informally or as a formal evaluative instrument, either on their own initiative or as mandated by the local school district. If the principal's interpersonal relationships with his staff are on a high level, the evaluative instrument, no matter what its format, can be a steppingstone to a rich and rewarding conference experience for both teacher and principal. Today most teachers' organizations, usually through their negotiating committees, are demanding a voice in the development and use of any evaluative instrument. This need not be regarded as a threat to the administration, for a teacher-designed and accepted evaluative instrument is much the same as one prescribed by the administration—it is only another key to open the communication door. Any instrument, used cooperatively, can be successful for structuring and guiding the principal/teacher conference.

Audio-Visual Techniques

Involving teachers in the use of audio-visual techniques for self-evaluation of the teaching-learning situation offers some fascinating possibilities. Audio-visual techniques for evaluation of many areas of the elementary school are limited only by the creative imagination of the principal and his staff. When an adult hears a tape recording of his class presentation, or sees and hears himself through the medium of film or video-tape, he is usually quite critical of his performance. Often the teacher is shocked to "see" that the interaction he thought he had elicited from pupils was not really there, and that the entire "presentation" was just that, a presentation with little or no involvement of pupils, with the teacher's doing most of the talking. Video-taping a teaching situation, when voluntary on the part of the teacher, can give a sharp, objective look at the characteristics of a teacher's performance, revealing personality traits, tone of voice, effectiveness in questioning, mannerisms, ability to involve pupils, tendency to be desk-bound versus ability to move freely among class members, and his overall effectiveness in helping students establish goals and move toward them.

Some definite techniques are already offered for structuring this type of self-evaluation. One, known as micro-teaching, is a short lesson, usually ten to twenty minutes, built around one teaching skill, and video-taped for the teacher to critique. For the student teacher, the supervising teacher and college supervisor usually offer suggestions and criticisms. In an actual teaching situation, it is usual for this activity to be completely voluntary and for the teacher alone to critique her taped presentation. Usually only the teacher has the option of asking others to observe her video-tape. She may keep it for future reference as a means of checking her own progress, or she may erase it. The Far West Laboratory for Educational Research and Development in Berkeley, California, is one group developing this technique. They "sort out the specific skills that go into the complex art of teaching. We're trying to demonstrate that good teachers are taught, not born."[9] The group conducted one experiment in the area of teacher-questioning techniques, with about forty-eight teachers participating. Video-tapes made several weeks after the original micro-teaching showed that questioning techniques improved. The first tapes showed that teachers answered their own questions an average of 8.8 times during the 20-minute lesson; post-tapes showed they answered themselves only 1.3 times.

At a recent Ohio Education Association-sponsored workshop which focused on the topic "Indicators of Quality Education," two researchers from the Institute of Administrative Research at Teachers College, Columbia University, gave the participants a look at an instrument known as *Indicators of Quality,* which is not yet available for general use.[10] The instrument has been used in nearly 20,000 public school classrooms, but only under the careful guidance of the Institute and only with trained personnel for classroom observation and scoring.

The Institute's research indicates that on a scale of activities listed in order of effectiveness in the teaching-learning situation, small group activities rank first, while question/answer activities rank tenth; yet question/answer is used 16 percent of the time in the typical classroom while small group activity is used only 6 percent of the time. Principals and other administrators have to make an enormous effort to help teachers learn and use classroom techniques that increase effectiveness of the teaching-learning situation.

Table 1
What Classroom Techniques Are Most Effective

The following classroom techniques were observed during studies made by the Institute of Administrative Research, Teachers College, Columbia University. The activities shown at the left are listed in order of their effectiveness in the teaching-learning situation as measured by the Institute's Indicators of Quality. The figures show the relative frequency these activities were being used in the classroom.

Elementary Classes		Secondary Classes	
Type of Activity	Frequency of Use	Type of Activity	Frequency of Use
Small Groups	6%	Small Groups	4%
Laboratory Work	1	Individual Work	14
Individual Work	14	Laboratory Work	5
Discussion	8	Discussion	11
Pupil Report	2	Pupil Report	2
Demonstration	3	Library Work	—
Library Work	1	Demonstration	4
Seat Work	30	Rehearsal	1
Other	10	Other	9
Question/Answer	16	Television	—
Television	1	Question/Answer	19
Movies	2	Seat Work	11
Test	3	Movies	3
Rehearsal	1	Test	7
Lecture	2	Lecture	10

Audio-visual techniques promise to be effective in helping administrators accomplish this task.

A study by Foster shows that teachers recognize and acknowledge that they do not teach as well as they know how. Each of the 213 experienced elementary teachers who participated in the study readily admitted that he was not teaching as well as he could, and placed part of the blame for inferior teaching upon himself. Foster says "They stated that numerous means for improving their teaching were presently available and within their power to accomplish; that is, that they could make certain instructional improvements immediately with working conditions remaining as they are."[11] The study showed the following reasons for not teaching to capacity:

Table 2
Reasons for not Teaching to Capacity

Reason	205 f	Teachers %
Insufficient time spent in planning and preparing	78	38.0
Insufficient teacher-pupil planning	52	25.4
Fatigue and lack of energy	51	24.9
Insufficient grouping for instruction	40	19.5
Lack of knowledge of subject matter	26	12.7
Demands of home life	25	12.2
Failure to provide for individual differences	23	11.2
Insufficient time spent in working with individual pupils	22	10.7

If the principal believes that personal interest and involvement are requisite to purposeful action, he must make an all-out effort to help teachers change attitudes and behavior, for these changes make possible the improvement of the daily interaction in the classroom and the continuing process of professional growth through education in service.

Encouraging Teachers' Creativity

On any staff, there are always imaginative and creative teachers, and in them lies a wealth of in-service potential. Through encouragement of these creative people, the principal has a unique opportunity to encourage instructional changes through innovative practices and ideas. A teacher's creative idea, proved in her own classroom and possibly in those of her teammates, may be given much wider distribution than the local school. The creative teacher is the one who continually brings to her teaching situation new ideas that make her teaching more interesting and produce more student/teacher interaction, creating more opportunities for learning. The principal should be alert to recognize creative ideas, and encourage the teacher to keep developing the idea until it becomes a finished product that reaches or exceeds her original concept. Nothing boosts a teacher's ego so much as knowing that what was once an idea has been developed into a workable and useful instructional tool. However, the principal and the teacher should not stop at this point. If the idea works in one situation, and is a valuable device for use in the classroom, there is every reason to believe that it can be just as valuable in many classrooms across the nation. The principal should assist the teacher in contacting commercial educational publishing companies to have the device or idea published. Educational publishers are putting great emphasis on teacher-developed ideas.

The Team Approach

Team-teaching structures are as varied as the schools in which they operate, yet the focus of each is on the improvement of teacher-student interaction and the direct benefits that may accrue to students through group planning. Bair and Woodward state,

> The diagnostic, planning, and evaluative procedures employed in the teaching-learning process, when developed by a team of teachers, are generally superior to those developed by a single teacher. In most team teaching projects there is a basic assumption that a group of professionals whose minds are focused on the same problem will usually arrive at solutions superior to those offered independently by the same individual.[12]

They also declare that "team teaching provides a superior vehicle for teacher training which ultimately results in improved instruction."[13] The principal's role starts with planning and organizing team structure, proceeds to selection of teachers, and moves on to help the team state and define basic goals and delineate instructional methods and grouping patterns. For in-service purposes, the team, by its very structure, is goal-centered and self-directed; the principal functions in some ways as a member, in other ways as an ex-officio member in an advisory capacity. In either capacity, he sends a constant flow of ideas and suggestions to the team and continues his main responsibility of supporting their efforts to improve instruction. In a team, there is strong pressure for each member to act responsibly and to teach professionally, which leads to many team meetings and discussions. Every device mentioned in this chapter can be used for in-service educational needs of a team; but if the team is operating as described above, evaluation is taking place at every phase of the instructional program, which reduces the need for pressure from the principal toward involvement in in-service activities. Bair and Woodward list three items concerning satisfactions of team participants:

> 1. The team members find great personal and professional satisfaction in the opportunity to work closely with a number of other people;
> 2. The flexible arrangement of grouping children, especially the crossgrading, has been advantageous to children and has contributed to the efficiency of instruction;
> 3. There continues to be a stong sense of pioneering towards goals that seem extremely desirable.[14]

If the purpose of in-service education is to encourage teachers to establish and move toward goals, certainly items 2 and 3 indicate a strong inclination for teams to function in this manner. The principal who can forget hierarchy and "join the gang" as a team member has probably realized that built-in incentives work very successfully to increase in-service activities, without undue pressure on his part.

Teachers' Professional Organizations

Professional organizations representing teachers' interests are just beginning to visualize their role and responsibilities in the areas of teacher competencies and in-service education. Most of their efforts have been directed toward increasing teacher benefits, rather than looking critically at the professionalization of teaching. This is understandable when we realize that teachers have been underpaid and overworked, and we are now in a period of teacher militancy to force adjustment of these conditions. Once demands for improved benefits, both salary and fringe, have begun to be answered, the administration should expect greater cooperation from professional organizations in efforts to answer such questions as "Why don't teachers teach as well as they know how?" There is a great reservoir of professional skills and talents latent in the leadership of teachers' organizations, and hopefully this can be tapped to provide in-service assistance at the level of greatest need—the teacher's. Although the principal is usually not permitted to be a member of the local teachers' organization, he should offer his full cooperation to the organization in promoting any device which will further the in-service program, whether in his own building or in the overall school community.

Role Playing

Role playing is a recognized psychological technique for involving a personality in acting out moods, feelings, frustrations, or situations. It is a calculated and often carefully-structured attempt to humanize interpersonal relationships by taking on a role in which one is sensitized, and becomes more emphatic, to another's problems and situations. It is often used with children in school, particularly in the area of social studies, but is often overlooked by principals as a fascinating possibility for in-service education. Role playing as a device to be used with teachers is obviously for the purpose of getting teachers to act out or react to problems and concerns as perceived by either the teachers or the principal. The following account describes how role playing was used in a contrived situation as structured by the principal, with assistance from a willing teacher, in one of the author's schools. This role playing situation was created because the principal felt that some teachers were using certain statements of a negative nature in the classrooms—statements and comments that were consciously or unconsciously aimed at "putting down" a child in the presence of his peers, an obvious holdover from the authoritarian teaching of the past. This particular role playing situation was planned to be short, part of a regular staff meeting, heavily emotional, and to involve the principal and one teacher, one quite popular with the staff. Most of the meetings were informal, with lots of banter and chit-chat before, and often during, the meeting. At the meeting for which the role playing was planned, the principal set a serious tone by asking the teachers to review with him the items on the agenda concerning teacher attitudes toward children. The week before, each teacher had been given a list of suggestions for positive ways of interacting with children in the classroom. When the teacher-fellow conspirator entered the meeting late, as planned, the principal interrupted the meeting and chided her, none too gently, for being late. She immediately retorted with a rather sharp answer that raised eyebrows. The principal continued with his comments and questions for a few moments, but directed his next question at this teacher concerning one of the items on the list. In a petulant, almost angry voice she replied, "I really don't know the answer, I haven't had time to read the thing. I've been so busy with my class I just haven't had time for that stuff." The principal, in a rather loud voice said, "You were expected to read it, like everybody else in this room." The teacher, in an even louder voice, and looking directly at him, said, "I told you, I've been so busy with my kids I just didn't have time to do it." Then, in a very angry voice, the principal said, "We'll not discuss it further here. I'll see you this afternoon immediately after school." The principal kept to the agenda items for a few more minutes, accompanied by dead silence from the entire staff. Then, putting aside his papers, leaning back in his chair, he looked at every member of the group with a smile and then asked, "Tell me, what happened between Marty and me just a few minutes ago?" There were audible sighs of relief, smiles began to appear, tension quickly dissipated, and from then on the meeting was a lively one. Questions and comments came rapid-fire, and from the reactions it was determined that (1) even though the principal was right in asking for promptness and the reading of a required assignment, he was wrong in handling the situation emotionally and angrily; (2) the teachers all felt sympathetic with the teacher, not the principal; (3) the peer group (teachers) reacted by shutting the principal out; (4) the items on the agenda were completely ignored or forgotten because of the emotional tension; (5) the teacher did not lose status, but the principal did; and (6) even though the teacher's tone of voice and choice of words were not appropriate, the peer group was still on her side. The principal turned the staff's attention to the fact that the same reactions could be expected of children when a teacher used punitive verbal tactics in the classroom. He also pointed out that as an adult the teacher had some recourse, she could "answer back," while a child in a classroom seldom would dare to do so even though he might be emotionally very upset. Hours later, during the noon hour, one of the teachers said to the principal, "I'm still mad at you, even though I know it was a put-up job," but they laughed together about it. Role playing used for a specific purpose can serve as a means to an end, getting teachers involved in understanding the importance to learning of the emotional climate in a classroom. Immersing oneself in a "role" increases the chances for understanding and empathy. Even though it is play-acting, it has a direct transfer, through the role playing teacher(s), to structuring the emotional classroom climate which is accepting of human weaknesses as well as strengths.

EVALUATING THE EFFECTIVENESS OF IN-SERVICE EDUCATION

Educational leadership must not advocate the use of in-service educational devices without first examining their effectiveness. All efforts exerted toward promoting teacher growth are based on the hope that this growth will reach the classroom level; that is, the effects of the growth must be realized in improved learning experiences for children. A National Education Association Research Summary lists nineteen in-service practices, reports favorably on the growth resulting from in-service efforts, and lists and describes some common barriers to in-service programs.[15] The principal should recognize the need for cooperative evaluation of the staff's efforts to grow through in-service programs or devices and, with the staff, choose the programs or devices which offer the greatest possibility of meeting the particular needs of their local situation.

SUMMARY

In-service education is concerned with helping teachers keep up-to-date with changing educational knowledge, skills, techniques, and attitudes. Continuous personal and professional growth for the teacher are essential in improving learning experiences for children as well as in improving the staff's ability to function as a unit. The principal's role is paramount in leading teachers in in-service activities. He must provide the leadership for those activities that will lead to teacher growth based on mutual understanding of the teacher's need.

The principal's basic responsibilities for in-service education are: (1) to establish favorable working conditions for his staff; (2) to provide leadership in helping his staff attack problems; (3) to assist in implementing the plans; and (4) to help evaluate the results.

Some of the devices used for group in-service activities are (1) the preschool conference; (2) the faculty meeting; (3) the interest group; (4) the curriculum committee; (5) college and university courses; and (6) participation in student-teaching programs.

SUGGESTED READINGS

Anderson, Robert H. *Teaching in a World of Change*. New York: Harcourt, Brace & World, 1966.

Association for Supervision and Curriculum Development. *The Supervisor: Agent for Change in Teaching*. Washington, D. C.: ASCD, National Education Association, 1966, pp. 1–10.

Carr, William G. "The Changing World of the American Teacher." *The National Elementary Principal* 47 (April 1968): 14–19.

Curtin, James. *Supervision in Today's Elementary Schools*. New York: Macmillan, 1964, Chapters 7, 10.

Goodlad, John I. "Educational Change: A Strategy for Study and Action." *The National Elementary Principal* 48 (January 1969): 6–13.

Leiper, Robert R., ed. *Supervision: Emerging Profession.* Washington, D. C.: Association for Supervision and Curriculum Development, National Education Association, 1969, Parts I, IV.

Pharis, William L. *In-Service Education of Elementary School Principals.* Washington, D. C.: Department of Elementary School Principals, National Education Association, 1966.

Shuster, Albert H. "Principals and Teachers for Nongraded Schools: Pre-Service and In-Service Education." *The National Elementary School Principal* 47 (January 1968): 10–14.

Spears, Harold. *Curriculum Planning Through In-Service Programs.* Englewood Cliffs, N. J.: Prentice-Hall, 1957, Chapters 7, 8, 11.

Swearingen, M. E. "Identifying Needs for In-Service Growth," *Educational Leadership,* March 1960.

Wood, Thomas C. "The Changing Role of the Teacher—How Does It Affect the Role of the Principal?" *The National Elementary Principal* 47 (April 1968): 32–37.

Notes

1. Lee Wilborn, "In-Service Education," *National Secondary School Principals' Bulletin,* 39 (April 1955): 140.

2. Ibid., p. 141.

3. Robert Shannon, "A Style for In-Service Education," *The National Elementary Principal* 48, no. 4 (February 1969).

4. Albert H. Shuster, "The Advantages and Disadvantages of the Collegiate Certificate in Virginia," dissertation, University of Virginia, 1955.

5. Courtesy of the Tiffin Elementary School, Chillicothe, Ohio.

6. Kimball Wiles, *Supervision for Better Schools,* 2d ed. (Englewood Cliffs, N. J.: Prentice-Hall, 1955), p. 184.

7. See, "Schools in Dilemma Over Parent-Teacher Conferences," *Ohio Schools,* March 12, 1971, pp. 10, 32.

8. The authors are indebted to Mr. Carl Noffsinger, Assistant Superintendent in charge of Curriculum, Madison Township Schools, Trotwood, Ohio, for his description of the structure and operation of the Power Steering Committee.

9. U.S. Office of Education, "Research and Development: Advances in Education" (Washington, D. C.: Gov. Printing Office, Supt. of Documents).

10. OEA Seminar, "Measuring the Quality of Education, *Ohio Schools,* February 12, 1971, pp. 15–17.

11. Walter S. Foster, "Teachers' Opinions: Their Implications for In-Service Education," *The National Elementary Principal* 45, no. 5, (April 1966): 48.

12. Medill Bair and Richard G. Woodward, *Team Teaching in Action* (Boston: Houghton Mifflin, 1964), p. 12.

13. Ibid., p. 14.

14. Ibid., p. 195.

15. National Education Association, "In-Service Education of Teachers: Research Summary 1966 – SI" (Washington, D. C.: E.R.I.C. Document No. Ed 022 728), Research Division Report No.-RS-1966-SI.

9

Developing Guidance Services

Increased problems which plague all schools, many of which are socioeconomic problems, are reflected in addition of specialized pupil personnel services to school systems. A 1968 report[1] states that an increase in resource personnel was made available for the *first time* to elementary schools as indicated by the percentages shown below for the last five years of the report (1963-1968), among them:

Specialist in Reading	27.7	Psychologist or	
School Librarian	26.1	Psychiatrist	14.9
Specialist in Guidance	16.0	Specialist in Testing	12.3
Specialist in Speech	13.6	Visiting Teacher	12.1

The many aspects of and all services inherent in a total developmental guidance program are now more readily accepted as specialized functions of the elementary school. In many respects, good teachers have always been guidance counselors, and their concerns combined with those of knowledgeable parents and administrators have pointed up the need for more highly prepared, specialized personnel who relate themselves particularly to the elementary school. Educators have long been writing that one of the goals of the school is to develop each individual to the extent of his potential. From teacher-training institutions to television and the popular press, great emphasis is placed on early childhood education, making teachers and others conscious of the need for understanding the distinctive traits and characteristics of each child. Schools must make use of this public awareness and provide specialized personnel in order that curriculum experiences can be planned to help children achieve the goal of accepting more and more responsibility for self-direction as they mature.

The superstructure of a guidance program has been framed for the secondary school, but this was done without consideration for the quality of the foundation, as it were. Secondary school guidance programs are being appraised by various accrediting agencies and state departments of education without regard for the quality of the elementary school program from which the children have come. The writers have no intention of criticizing the guidance operations, or efforts to improve them, at the secondary school level, but they do believe that many problems stemming from social, educational, and emotional maladjustment can be remedied before youth reach high school if adequate guidance services are made available at the elementary school level. Many life patterns, habits, and attitudes are firmly set at earlier ages than was formerly believed. Some researchers contend that as much as half a child's lifetime knowledge is gained by the time he is six to eight years old. Time and money spent on guidance at the earliest possible age is the best investment schools and society can make. Frequently, by the time the child reaches the secondary school and sixteen years of age, the school will lose the child. That is, he may be one of the thirty-five percent of those children who drop out of school. Krugman very ably states the case for more adequate guidance services and personnel for elementary schools when he says, "Life doesn't begin at age fourteen."[2]

In discussing the initiation of a guidance program with a general supervisor of a public school, one of the authors was told that after careful consideration by the administrative staff the decision was reached to provide such services only at the twelfth-grade level. Needless to say, many problems go unresolved until it is too late in those school systems where guidance services are considered the function of secondary schools. Furthermore, this concept has grown out of the early emphasis on vocational guidance in our high schools. If our purpose is to help each child gain the most from his school experience, guidance should extend beyond mere vocational counseling. Thus emphasis on providing guidance services in the elementary school demands at least two imperatives: (1) the principal's understanding of his function in the elementary school, and (2) his leadership in promoting the value of guidance with his staff and the community. This chapter is largely concerned with the following aspects of these two imperatives: first, the principal's role in guidance; second, the scope of guidance services in the elementary school; third, ways of administering and evaluating the guidance program.

Since there are many misconceptions about the meaning of guidance and related activities, certain terms are defined here to assist the reader in understanding the concepts adhered to by the authors. Guidance activities may be thought of as *all those experiences the child has under the direction of the school, which assist him in realizing his potential for becoming a self-directed individual.* This definition suggests the comprehensive nature of guidance. It also suggests the need for some type of organization which

Developing Guidance Services

will enable the child's learning experiences to be continuous and sequential in nature. Obviously, this need calls for an organized guidance program which is not distinct and separate or simply attached to the instructional program, but which is an integrating force that facilitates learning and instruction for the teacher as well as for the child. Since the definition of guidance is comprehensive in scope, the guidance program should be planned to encompass the many ramifications inherent in the meaning of guidance. Thus both organized services and unorganized efforts of the school may comprise the guidance program, although the latter is frequently carried out within the framework of classroom teaching.

The guidance program, then, consists of a number of organized services which may be identified, initiated, and evaluated, and which must also be administered in order to be effective.

SCOPE OF GUIDANCE SERVICES

These services must be broad enough in scope to accomplish the purpose of guidance as defined above. Each child must be able to benefit from the available guidance services. Also, the services must be broad enough to provide for the many kinds of problems children face as they grow toward self-direction and responsibility. To accomplish this aim the program must utilize the entire school staff and, in addition, must bring in specialists for cases that need the help of professionally-prepared persons such as physicians, psychiatrists, specialists in perceptual-motor skills, and specialists from the courts, the county health department, and the county or regional board of education. Most of the writings researched by the authors strongly favor a team approach to developmental guidance, and in the team, the teacher is a vital member, both as a contributor with essential information and insight about the child, and as a learner who gains much from the professional opinions and suggestions of specialists working as team members. Thus a good guidance program constantly seeks and develops needed resource personnel to assist in analyzing and helping children solve their problems at the earliest stages in their growth and development, and reaches out into the community in its efforts to provide these needed services.

Contrary to the common belief that guidance is a service primarily for those individuals with major problems, its real function in the elementary school should be preventive in nature, although obviously it must also be curative. The program should attack causes of poor educational, social, and emotional adjustment, as well as health and physical needs, in order to prevent minor obstacles from becoming major problems.[3]

Gordon summarizes the functional meanings of guidance in five points:

1. Guidance is the organization of information by the school about the child and his community for the purpose of helping the child learn to make wise decisions concerning his own future.
2. Guidance is the organization of life experiences within the school situation so that the child is provided with situations in which he feels completely accepted, in which he is enabled to "take stock" of his potentialities, accept his limitations without threat, and develop a realistic picture of himself and the world around him.
3. Guidance is the provision for satisfactory group experiences in which successful leadership and membership roles are learned and in which the group is able to set goals and solve problems dealing with interpersonal relations.
4. Guidance is the provision of opportunities for the child to understand and value his uniqueness and his relatedness to others.
5. Guidance is the provision of the above experiences and opportunities for all children.[4]

A Philosophy of Guidance

In keeping with the theme of this book, the leadership role of the elementary school principal is manifested by his ability to lead his faculty in developing a guidance point of view. The staff must think together concerning their role in helping every child discover and develop his potentialities. Children, of course, need experiences in learning in order to face difficult situations and to make wise choices and decisions themselves. As teachers study children and their behavior, they should gain new insights into those factors related to good mental health as well as to other aspects of personality development. The principal who leads his staff to consider these aspects helps teachers discover their role in this process, and encourages them to formulate a philosophy of guidance.

The principal of the modern elementary school can utilize many devices to focus his staff's attention on the problems of pupil adjustment. Some of these devices are:

1. Various group conferences,
2. School bulletins,
3. Workshops in child study,
4. Individual conferences,
5. Visits to schools with exemplary guidance programs,
6. Working as part of a guidance team (for which the principal must be willing to provide duty-free time),
7. Judicious use of the many excellent audio-visual materials made available by many groups, including Mental Health, State Departments, NEA, and several of the special divisions of the NEA.

To illustrate the use of several devices to encourage staff interest in guidance, the following incident describes how a principal of a California school, who believes in orienting new teachers, was effective in helping them develop a sound philosophy of guidance.

> A number of new teachers were coming to me with questions such as, "How do you answer a parent who asks you to recommend a tutor when you believe the child is doing as well as can be expected?" "When it is near grading time, how do you determine what is satisfactory work for a given child?" These are common questions, and I realized that other staff members also might like to discuss them with someone. After talking it over, we decided to organize a workshop.
> Every Friday morning from 8:10 to 8:50 throughout the year the new teachers got together to discuss their problems and share their ideas on guidance practices. Attendance was not required, but most of the teachers came regularly because of their interest. I served only as a guide to the group, occasionally bringing up a problem, or supplying information, or helping to point up conclusions once they had been reached. The teachers soon warmed up to each other and felt free to raise questions and contribute their ideas. All sorts of problems came up, problems involving guidance theory and practice, child development, discipline, parent conferences, self-understanding.
> At the last session, the teachers made some observations about the value of the workshop. By talking and listening and sharing ideas, they had grown in ability to handle classroom situations and to guide children. They had acquired more self-confidence. They no longer felt constrained to cover up their problems for fear of losing face. They saw that other new teachers faced identical problems and had the same anxieties. They relaxed and became more secure in their relations with pupils. And finally, they expressed the belief that the guidance philosophy of the school had taken on a deeper meaning for them, one that probably could not have been acquired through lectures or the usual teachers' meetings. This meaning had come to them out of the reality of the workshop situation. Finally, they asked that the workshop be continued in the fall, not only for the benefit of new staff members, but for several of them who expressed a desire to participate again.[5]

It is apparent that the principal who demonstrates this kind of leadership must already have developed a sound personal guidance philosophy through preparation and experience. Furthermore, the example indicates how administrative action actually can lead to professional advancement.

Principal's Role in Guidance

The quality and quantity of the guidance services found in an elementary school should be related by the educational leader to the understandings and values attached to these services which also comprise his personal guidance philosophy. Although the extent of the principal's role in guidance depends largely upon the size of the school operation, his responsibility for having a sound program is not lessened. He has a basic responsibility to pupils, and he must be alert to provide those services which will benefit them as they grow and mature.

In the small school, the principal, if adequately prepared, may be called upon to render many of the services of the guidance specialist. However, the principal must guard against working with children who are seriously maladjusted, since they need professional help which he is not qualified to render.

Basically, the principal has four responsibilities which require leadership directly related to his guidance function: (1) identifying present services; (2) initiating and extending additional services; (3) organizing and administering all guidance services; and (4) evaluating the effectiveness of the guidance program. To clarify further the principal's leadership function, we will discuss each of these responsibilities briefly. Item 4, evaluating effectiveness, is discussed at the end of the chapter.

Identifying Present Services. The guidance-conscious principal should carefully study the operation of his school to determine what services are currently offered. He may, for example, find that some teachers are keeping progress charts of their pupils' achievement as well as samples of their work. Such a practice, if found to be of value to the teacher and pupil alike, may be the basis for a general faculty study to determine whether this practice can become school-wide.

A further study of cumulative records may reveal that the machinery is available for employing or establishing a pupil-inventory service, or perhaps that the service is not being utilized to the best advantage. That is, only routine information such as marks, age, height, and weight may be recorded. These and other factors which are identifiable evidence of the effectiveness of a guidance program serve also to develop an awareness on the part of the principal and his staff for determining the use of tools and techniques, as well as the kind of services that are being rendered or should be offered by some staff members to aid in pupil adjustment. In short, as the principal discovers the guidance activities which are being carried out by various staff members, he determines ways of initiating further steps toward expanded guidance services.

Initiating Guidance Services. One of the major responsibilities of the principal is that of promoting improved guidance services. As indicated, unless the principal is aware of this need, he may not be conscious of what services are actually being rendered by his staff. Therefore, merely to identify guidance activities currently in use does not necessarily lead to improvement of those services. It often happens, however, that identifying guidance functions leads to initiation of an expanded program. The principal should recognize two broad categories of guidance concepts, one conducted by the teaching staff, and one a cooperative team venture in which teachers and principal work with specialists to diagnose and remedy childrens' problems of growth and learning. The first concept is limited by teachers' lack of time and training. Already involved with many instructional programs and demands, and averaging over forty-seven hours per week of instruction and preparation, teachers are in most cases unable to assume much responsibility for an in-depth developmental guidance program. This is not to say that the program does not revolve around them, for it does. They are in most cases very cooperative and anxious to do all they can to help solve children's problems. But it does tell us that they cannot provide the specialized services necessary for a comprehensive guidance program.

Using the first concept, Hatch pointed out in 1951 that there were at least six starting activities that could lead to initiation of a guidance program by the teaching staff:

1. A case conference.
2. Filling an obvious need for a given service.
3. A study of the guidance tools and techniques.
4. The application of one tool or techinque, followed by a staff discussion of the results.
5. Arranging visits to schools having one or more outstanding guidance services.
6. Starting a complete program with one grade.[6]

To initiate all or any one of these approaches requires much skill on the part of the principal. He must determine the readiness of his faculty for such action. He should also evaluate his own preparation to determine his leadership fitness for developing these areas into an organized guidance program. If the principal does not feel his own preparation is adequate to direct the thinking of his faculty, he then must call in resource persons. The visiting teacher, supervisor, or high school guidance director may contribute to initiating the guidance program. One must remember that a poor beginning may lead to delay of the next step. For the activity to be successful, the school staff must first see its worth. It would appear wisest, therefore, to select only one of the areas listed above for faculty study and to follow it through to completion before beginning work in a new area. For example, the staff might decide it would like to initiate study of a testing program as one aspect of the guidance services. As this study is made and the tests are administered, scored, and interpreted carefully, teachers may decide that additional information is needed about pupils that is not revealed by the testing program. Although the testing program serves a purpose in determining mental ages, competence in basic skills, etc., additional information may seem desirable. As the staff members discover how each service contributes to their understanding of children and thus leads to improved instruction, they should become ready for further direction in building the guidance program. Therefore, if each experience leads the staff toward gaining satisfaction from the study and *finding useful that which they have developed,* they should be more willing to continue studying the need for improving and extending guidance services.

The second concept, that of the team approach, allows the principal to visualize an open-ended guidance program of great depth. The increasing complexity of the principalship makes it mandatory that the principal concentrate on management and supervision, delegating authority as much as possible, but providing leadership for setting goals and maintaining direction. He must make every effort, working with teachers, parents, community and board of education, to secure the most competent and willing specialized and professional help possible to assist in solving the problems of growth and development. He cannot do it himself; therefore, he must first visualize and then begin to build a guidance structure and team that will do the job. The literature provides many excellent patterns for building guidance programs, so there is an abundance of ideas and directions available to the discerning principal.

Teachers, parents, and the general public are now sufficiently aware of the importance of high-quality early childhood education that the time is ripe for requests for specialized guidance personnel to be given serious consideration by boards of education, regardless of the size of the school. As reported at the beginning of this chapter, there has been a significant increase in the number of specialists added to school staffs in an effort to meet children's needs. The trend will continue as parents realize more fully that teachers, however willing, are unable to do the task of the specialist. Pupil services will not just appear, however. The principal and his staff must sell the idea of the urgent need for such services if society's many problems are to be realistically attacked where it will do the most lasting good and cost the least. Ferguson says,

> In-school people and the community which we serve often are not clear where pupil services fit in. This is not unreasonable, but it is a challenge. We are quite new in the educational scene and not too many of our specialists have long tenure on the job. Other phases of the school program have much deeper traditions and are better understood. Also, since we come from a variety of disciplines, not necessarily native to the educational institution, confusion is possible in attempting to understand our contribution. Again, the challenge and the burden are for us to clarify pupil services. We need to make crystal clear to people what kinds of services we can provide with the backgrounds which we bring to the school, and why these services are necessary

in the educational enterprise. We are subject to the psychological phenomenon that people not understanding something tend to be suspicious of it. When we are better understood and people are more familiar with what we can bring to the situation, acceptance will increase.[7]

Organizing and Administering Guidance Services. Developing a comprehensive guidance program is a process of selection and implementation. The principal, with his staff, must strive to develop pupil-personnel services to their optimum, using all the money, time, and talent available to build the best developmental guidance program possible. The principal must identify each aspect of the desired program, interpret the needs to his staff and the public, obtain assistance from every possible source, organize the team, and continually coordinate the team's efforts. He must delegate authority wherever and whenever possible, but he must carry the major load of coordinating the guidance services, as well as maintaining his leadership in continuous efforts to expand and improve pupil services. Many schemes have been worked out in elementary schools for coordinating the guidance services. Three such plans are (1) appointment of the guidance counselor or a teacher; (2) establishment of a guidance council using some combination of teachers, parents, and specialists; and (3) establishment of a team, using all available personnel including specialists, recognizing that the classroom teacher occupies the key position in the total guidance program. Obviously, if a single teacher is delegated this responsibility, she should have special preparation, sincere interest, and a desire to serve in this capacity. A council, too, requires leadership, and this could be voluntary, delegated, or rotated, so long as there is continuity. The team approach encourages the involvement of more people, with many possibilities for leadership from administration, staff, or specialists. Regardless of the plan chosen, close cooperation is required between the principal and the individual, council, or team if the program is to serve the children's best interests.

One pattern showing the relationships between teachers, counselor, specialists, pupils, principal, and advisory committee is found in figure 7. This organizational pattern reveals the need for understanding relationships if cooperative efforts are to produce results. The principal must be even more concerned about helping all personnel understand relationships when the new area of professional specialists is added to the pattern, since it involves a mixture of many people, each a little jealous of his field, and each not fully understanding the other areas. The principal's insistence that each role be understood as well as possible is crucial in establishing and maintaining a team structure that serves the guidance purposes. Each special role, if used properly, provides support to all the rest.

The authors believe that the organizational pattern for guidance services shown in figure 7 will serve smaller schools where specialists are not yet available. However, a different pattern must be visualized when specialists are added to the pattern. Figure 8 shows the organizational pattern expanded to include the specialists. This pattern clearly shows the following:

1. It is pupil-centered, with all guidance activities surrounding and concentrating on the pupil.
2. Administrative responsibility for all personnel from the school and special areas.
3. School personnel and all specialists under the administrative direction of the principal.
4. The Advisory Council, whose members can come from any group including community and specialists, acts in a cooperative/advisory capacity.

― ― ― Cooperative Relationships
——— Administrative Relationships

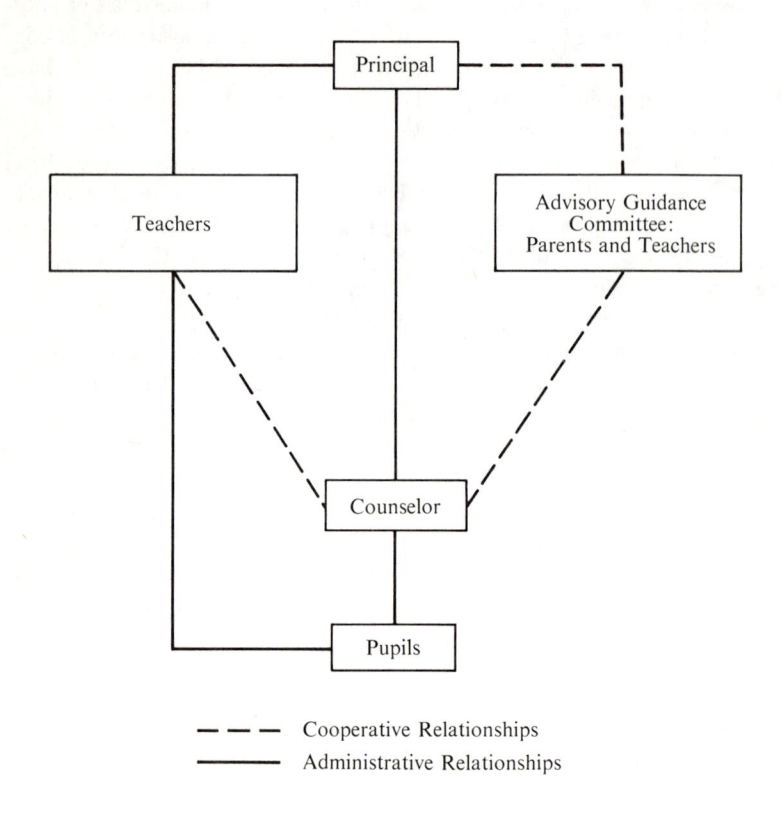

Figure 7

Organizational Pattern for Guidance Services

Developing Guidance Services 223

5. The team concept of guidance services is delineated, yet the structure does not limit the possibility of various kinds of teams.

The enlarged pattern, showing the inclusion of specialized personnel, whether on the school staff or on call, points up the belief of most leaders in the elementary guidance field that the problems of children are too many and often too specialized to be handled by the classroom teacher alone. The pattern shows that teachers are still central in the efforts to solve or remedy problems because of the teacher's direct relationship to and responsibility for the pupil.

- - - - Cooperative Relationships
———— Administrative Relationships

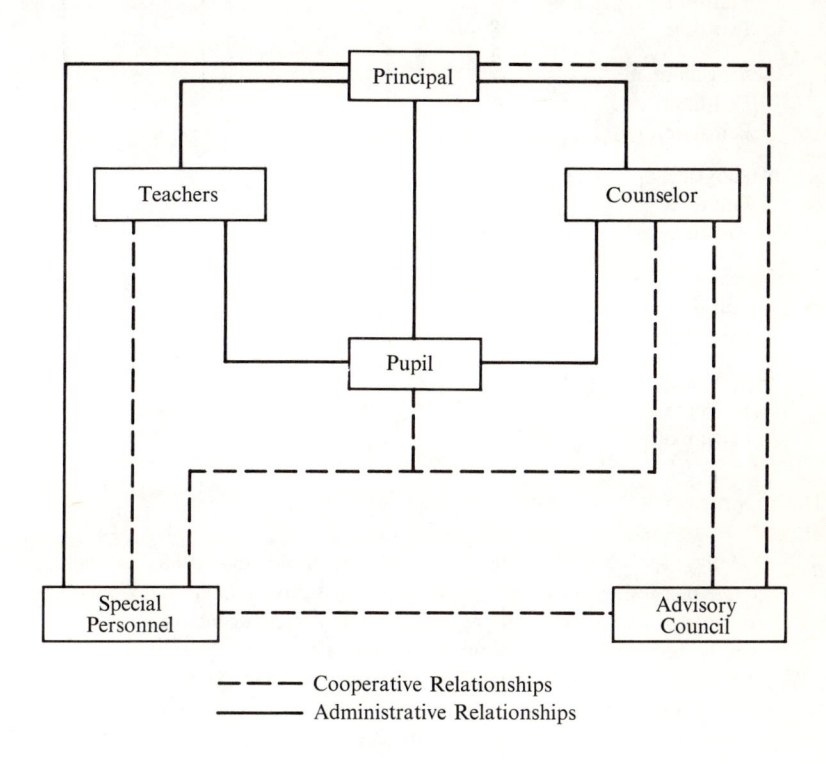

Figure 8

Expanded Organizational Pattern for Guidance Services

Research concerning the addition of specialists to elementary school staffs is somewhat encouraging. For example, the following statistics showing special personnel available in elementary schools, either on a full- or part-time basis, are taken from a previously reported research study[9]:

Personnel	Total Sample Percent
Teacher of homebound pupils	
Full-time	6.9
Part-time	47.4
Curriculum specialist	
Full-time	8.5
Part-time	31.7
Guidance specialist	
Full-time	7.7
Part-time	32.4
School librarian	
Full-time	27.3
Part-time	34.2
Audiovisual specialist	
Full-time	7.7
Part-time	35.5
Specialist for exceptional children	
Full-time	10.8
Part-time	23.3
Speech and hearing specialist	
Full-time	7.6
Part-time	57.6

The report also states:

> One may speculate that the gains between 1958 and 1968, as well as the increasing percents for the past five years, reflect the growing problems of the school systems and the many socio-economic problems recently becoming acute in many communities. The question may be raised on whether or not the number of specialists is keeping pace with the extent of the new and unique problems in elementary education, especially those that fall heavily upon the principal.[10]

It is evident that these services are beginning to be recognized as a necessary part of the elementary school; however, real statesmanship is required of the principal if professional personnel and services are to be secured and approved by the community and the board of education.

As the principal leads, the guidance program expands in terms of number of services offered. Yet for these guidance services to be effective, they must be efficiently organized and administered. What, then, are the services which comprise a good guidance program?

A PROGRAM OF GUIDANCE SERVICES

The effectiveness and success of a developmental guidance program depends heavily upon teacher attitude. Many authorities point to the classroom teacher as the key factor in the guidance program. There is only empirical evidence concerning teacher attitude and little or no research on this, but, considering the usual necessity for in-service activities concerning any improvement in program, the principal should recognize that he must conduct a planned and continuous in-service education program with every step or enlargement of the guidance program. Militant teachers state quite frankly that they will not assume further responsibilities in many areas unless they have a voice in the selection, structure, and implementation of those responsibilities. Teachers are also frank to admit, as they grow professionally, that there are areas of guidance for which they have no preparation and with which they cannot cope. Here again the principal's responsibility is to define the goals, and structure activities to inaugurate, implement, and improve programs to reach those goals. He must work to eradicate the old concept that incidental guidance is good enough. The modern elementary school has staggering responsibilities to today's children, and the more we learn about our children's and society's needs and problems, the more principals and staff should become aware that the crucial attitudes, learning skills, and social skills of life cannot be left to chance.

The principal who is developing a program of guidance services must recognize the relationship between guidance and teaching, since both processes are compatible and are based upon the fundamental principles of democracy. Obviously, for either the guidance process or the teaching process to be effective in the classroom, highly-qualified teachers must be in charge of instruction. This is the goal of all school leaders.

The classroom teacher does play a key role in the guidance program, and on the whole teachers recognize this as an area of responsibility and concern. A study by Witmer, using the stratified random sampling technique in Florida, involving forty-five schools and 556 elementary teachers in grades kindergarten through six, shows significant findings of teacher attitudes toward guidance practices as reported by the teachers. We have summarized his conclusions:

1. The teachers in the public elementary schools of Florida appear to accept the guidance function in education as a major responsibility of the classroom teacher for meeting children's varying needs.
2. The elementary teachers seem to make greatest use of such guidance functions as using information in the cumulative records; identifying the needs of exceptional children; helping children explore the world of work, their educational interests and opportunities; serving as a

source for personal and social information; helping children with learning and adjustment problems; understanding child growth and development; and promoting a psychological climate in which there is mutual trust and acceptance among the teacher and the pupils.
3. Certain guidance principles and practices appear to have greater value than others for meeting the varying needs of pupils. Those practices which have greatest value use the information in the cumulative records; identifying exceptional children such as the slow learners, intellectually gifted, and the emotionally disturbed; helping children explore the world of work; serving as a source for personal and social information; helping children with learning and adjustment problems; helping pupils in areas in which they excel or show special interests; helping children who need essentials in health, clothing, and food; and helping children examine their attitudes and feelings toward themselves and matters in everyday life. The most important team function is working with parents of normal and exceptional children.
4. The elementary teachers see only limited use and moderate value in interpreting certain appraisal data to the pupils.
5. The elementary teachers recognize the need for additional guidance services in the elementary schools, since the value they ascribe to guidance principles and practices is significantly greater than their use of these same principles and practices.
6. A majority of the elementary teachers see the need for improving most of the guidance principles and practices, largely through providing additional time for the teacher and through the assistance of an elementary specialist.
7. The elementary teachers appear to accept the role of a guidance specialist for complementing the guidance function of the teacher.
8. The teachers desire assistance from an elementary specialist largely in the areas of appraisal or child study, counseling with children, consulting with parents, and in coordinating the guidance function with other school personnel, the parents, and the community.[11]

The guidance program should not be considered an either/or choice. Even though many elementary schools are still without the services of specialized personnel, the point to be made here is that when specialists are present, there is a need for cooperative teamwork if all pupils are to gain the greatest amount of good from their educational opportunities. The greatest obstacles to incidental guidance services stem from the lack of relationship between one service and another and the lack of time for and training in guidance fundamentals on the part of the classroom teacher. Generally, no one person is sufficiently skilled in the integration of the many values gained from the services available to be able to bring about the greatest good. This is pointed

Developing Guidance Services 227

up more strongly in one study which states, "Teachers tend to develop a feeling of helplessness due to their inability to cope with the mental health hazards which confront their children."[12] This fact calls for preparation, at the college level, of personnel who can perform the necessary specialist services at the elementary level, and also for continued development of the necessary attitudes and skills among present administrators and teachers. During the past decade, the Federal Government has recognized this need and provided funds under the N.D.E.A. Act to train a variety of elementary guidance specialists. The kind and extent of guidance services which are made available depend upon the size of the school and recognition by the community of the need for funds for such services.

There is general agreement among authorities about what areas of services comprise a good guidance program, and practically no difference in point of view toward these services or the grouping of services. The authors agree that the following services are important for the elementary school developmental guidance program:

1. Pupil-inventory service
2. Informational service
3. Counseling service
4. Referral service
5. Placement service
6. Follow-up service.

These services seem desirable for enhancing and facilitating pupil adjustment through the school program. Since guidance is concerned with helping the individual make wise choices and become more self-reliant as he matures and takes his place in adult society, the above services seem to be essential. Organized and systematic procedures must be employed for teachers to gain significant insights into the more profound differences among individuals. Also, these six services must become unified and integrated into the total school program so that teachers may adjust curriculum experiences to fit the child. Teacher, principal, parents, nurse, physical education teacher, psychologist, counselor, and others must all contribute to the goal—behavior modification which leads to better adjustment of the individual.

Pupil-Inventory Service

The heart of any guidance program is the pupil-inventory service. Authorities agree that to do a relevant study of a child, the collection, appraisal, and interpretation of all pertinent information about that child is a necessity. Only if the child's history and life patterns can be opened up for examination, using information from observation, tests, sociograms, anecdotal records and other devices, can teachers or specialists suggest possible solutions to the child's problem. The principal's role here is to lead the staff in discovering what information is the most useful. Teachers criticize principals who compel them to collect a great deal of information they do not feel is usable. Even though the principal believes certain information is helpful, he must refrain from arbitrarily insisting that it be collected, to prevent resentment against the guidance program. To reiterate, the successful program is one in which teachers believe their activities are useful and meaningful. Thus, when teachers gather information about pupils through their own efforts, such as written observations and anecdotal records, and then have help in interpreting this and other data, they are motivated to continue their efforts to assist in pupil adjustment. The greatest motivating factor for any teacher is to see a child make a change for the better after the data about him have been correctly interpreted and applied.

Authorities differ little as to what information is useful in the pupil-inventory. The following items seem to provide the most necessary information:

1. Personal data
2. Home environment
3. Prior scholastic history
4. Health history
5. Testing data
6. Out-of-school activities
7. Interests and hobbies
8. Special aptitudes
9. Anecdotal records.[13]

The extent to which useful information is accumulated about each pupil in these areas depends upon the ability of the principal to lead his teachers in seeing the usefulness of such information. One need only scan the records of the average school to see the tremendous need for improving and extending the amount of information recorded.

Pupil Records. Essential to the value of the pupil inventory is an efficient system of records. However, there is a wide range of differences in school records now in use. There are even distinct variations in the number of different records used in schools within the same system. Teachers can become overburdened keeping endless and seemingly useless records. Since records are a necessary aid to effective operation of the school program, the elementary school leader must help devise the best possible record system, one which is efficient and satisfies the needs of all who need information about pupils, both in the present and the future. All data to be used as evaluative information by teachers and/or specialists, accumulated by developing the individual inventory service, are brought together in a cumulative record.

Developing Guidance Services

The cumulative record. The cumulative record is the sum of all the records kept through the individual inventory service, which includes the areas of information listed above. These data are usually kept in a folder known as the cumulative or personnel record. Some sources list eight areas of information. These are listed here, with each heading divided into sub-areas, to serve as a guide to the principal interested in improving the type of information contained in cumulative records.

A. Family background.
  1. Names of parents or guardians.
  2. Occupations of parents or guardians.
  3. Marital status of parents—divorced, separated, etc.
  4. If both parents are living, which one student lives with, and address.
  5. Economic condition of the home.
  6. Language spoken in the home.
  7. Number of siblings.
  8. Attitude of family toward the individual and other members of the family group.
B. Personal Data about the student.
  1. Name and age.
  2. Personal appearance.
  3. Color and race.
  4. Place of birth.
  5. Religious affiliation.
  6. Dated picture of student if possible.
C. General health status.
  1. Past illnesses.
  2. Daily schedule kept by pupil of his health habits; food included in daily diet, amount of sleep, exercise, etc.
  3. Absences and tardinesses.
  4. School examinations (physical).
  5. Physical handicaps, if any.
D. Personality traits and work habits.
  1. Continuous record of developing interests.
  2. Behavior diary—kept by teacher over a period of time with regular notations made and dated.
  3. Autobiographies.
  4. Reports of interviews.
  5. Teachers' observations of work habits, etc.
  6. Reports of visits to the home, from the parents, correspondence, etc.
E. Participation in out-of-class activities.
  1. Summer activities.

  2. Hobbies.
  3. Clubs and activities in school.
  4. Spare-time activities.
 F. Special aptitudes, interests, abilities.
  1. School grades.
  2. Results of standardized tests.
  3. Interest tests.
  4. Teachers' observations and anecdotal records.
  5. Honors and awards.
  6. Special abilities, such as music, art, etc.
 G. Work experience.
  1. Part-time work experience.
  2. Summer jobs.
 H. Vocational preferences.
  1. Student's expressed goals and purposes.
  2. Questionnaires—e.g., What would you like to be when you grow up?

  The cumulative record, including reports and information from teachers, guidance counselor, parents, and all involved agencies and specialists, should contribute to the school's understanding of the student, and enable those concerned to make wise decisions, to help the child improve his social, emotional, and academic adjustment. Cumulative data should be such that it assists the entire guidance team in planning better for the student's educational, emotional, and vocational needs.

  The principal should work continuously to improve the quality of the recorded information. In-service education programs may be developed around the cumulative record. As an illustration, one of the writers took a group of student teachers to a nearby school for the purpose of examining the school's records. The object was to find what information in the records would be useful to teachers. The principal of Mountain Bluffs elementary school greeted the group, and invited them into his office. He identified a file where all cumulative records were kept, and removed one to familiarize the group with the folders. The principal then gave the group free access to the file. As the student teachers looked through the records, they were astonished to find the large number of statements which were actually insignificant. One such statement was, "He tends to be lazy and sleeps a lot in school." This same statement was repeated for six years about this student. Nowhere in the record was there evidence that teachers had tried to find out why.

  This illustration points up the strong need for leadership on the part of the principal who is concerned with improving pupil records. Some of the procedures which a principal can use to improve records are:

Developing Guidance Services

1. Direct teachers into activities which will help them evaluate statements found in the records.
2. Help them analyze statements for objectivity.
3. Lead them into using objective statements for planning a course of action.
4. Assist them in evaluating the results of using good anecdotal records.

Health Records

If recent data coming from many sources is an indication of the enormity of the problem, health problems of children and young adults must receive greater attention and call forth much more effort at prevention and remediation than is now the case. One report indicating the high percentages found says that:

> During the first four months that PEG (Program for Elementary Guidance) was in operation about 85 per cent of the youngsters referred for guidance and counseling were found to have some kind of problem—physical, mental, social, or emotional—that was health oriented. This was not a complete surprise. The Trotwood-Madison Schools, in conducting Head Start programs through two summers, had become aware that, among Head Start students, many serious health problems existed; necessary dental care, for instance, during the course of one such program, had amounted to $8500. But the extremely high percentage of youngsters with health-oriented problems turned up by PEG—and the fact that these youngsters, to a large extent, came from the general school population—was a surprise.[14]

Health information is vital since it has a direct relationship to the pupil's progress in school. Adequate cumulative health information should be recorded so the school can be informed of any changes in a child's health which may result in modifications of his school progress and adjustment. It is equally important for the teacher to observe her children regularly and carefully for symptoms of the various childhood diseases, as well as the more serious diseases. Children with symptoms of tuberculosis and rheumatic fever have been known to go unnoticed for months. For the child's sake, early referral to the nurse or a note or call to parents when something seems physically or mentally unusual about the child is far better than a "wait and see" attitude. Careful study of the child's health record and alert observation will contribute to better understanding of the child's behavior; then the guidance team can go into action to muster all the help possible to direct a personalized program to the child's needs.

Few teachers are trained in any way to recognize even the most common diseases. Working with the school nurse, the county or state Department of Health, or such community agencies as the Red Cross, the principal can, through in-service activities and the use of various audio-visual media,

232   *Developing Guidance Services*

help his staff become acquainted with behavior and physical symptoms that are indicative of mental or physical ill-health. Teachers should be cautioned not to pursue indications of mental problems beyond the detection stage, but to refer the child, through the principal or the guidance counselor, to his parents and/or specialists for professional diagnosis and assistance.

Records of Progress

These vary greatly in format, but the principal and his staff should be most concerned with the content. Content ranges from the traditional (listing the basal readers in sequence by title, pages covered, and number of library books read) to the modern concept, which places far greater emphasis upon the skills employed in learning a subject, with such skills marked on a Skill Checksheet for the subject. (See Checklist of Language Arts Skills, figure 9). This type of reporting pupil progress assists teachers in diagnosing and prescribing for each student, assists students and parents in understanding exactly where strengths and weaknesses lie, and gives a much more objective picture of individual pupil progress. It does, however, require analysis processes and instruments that are much more sophisticated than the traditional method, and it requires much planning and in-service work on the part of the principal if such reporting procedures are to be understood and adopted by the staff.

Figure 9
Checklist of Language Arts Skills–Quest Team (5th & 6th Grade)

Shilohview Elementary School
Madison Local School District
Trotwood, Ohio

_____ TO _____
DATE   DATE

NAME

R—Weak—needs review and reinforcement
I—No skills—needs introduction and teaching
S—Satisfactory—regular program will be adequate
M—Has mastered skill—needs no more practice

	FIRST YEAR				SECOND YEAR			
	R	I	S	M	R	I	S	M
READING SKILLS:								
Recognition of sight vocabulary								
Recognition of consonant sounds								
Recognition of vowel sounds								
Knowledge of syllabication								

Developing Guidance Services

	FIRST YEAR				SECOND YEAR			
	R	I	S	M	R	I	S	M
WORD STRUCTURE:								
Root Words								
Prefixes								
Suffixes								
Ability to use context clues								
Ability to use synonyms and antonyms								
COMPREHENSION:								
Ability to understand meaning								
Word								
Sentence								
Paragraph								
Recall of main idea								
Ability to give supporting ideas								
Ability to recognize the sequence of ideas								
Ability to draw conclusions								
Ability to evaluate material read								
SPELLING:								
Learns assigned words								
Spells correctly in written work								
WRITTEN LANGUAGE:								
Word usage								
Capitalization and Punctuation								
Sentence Development								
Paragraph Development								
ORGANIZING AND REPORTING SKILLS–SRA								
Form of report								
Sticking to the point								
Order in the paragraph								
Quality in the paragraph								
Notetaking								
Outlining								
LISTENING SKILLS:								
E.D.L. Level completed								
A____ B____ C____ D____								
E____ F____ G____								
SPEAKING SKILLS:								
Good enunciation								
Work usage								

COMMENTS:

READING INVENTORY—QUEST TEAM (5th & 6th Grade)

NAME _____

_____TO_____
DATE   DATE   ACHIEVEMENT TEST SCORES _____

MATERIALS USED:

S.R.A. BOX# _____

 _____orange _____brown _____gold _____aqua
 _____olive   _____green _____tan   _____silver
 _____blue   _____purple _____red   _____rose

S.R.A. BOX # _____

 _____orange _____brown _____gold _____aqua
 _____olive   _____green _____tan   _____silver
 _____blue   _____purple _____red   _____rose

INDIVIDUALIZED READING:

 Pacemakers_____ Total Books Year 1_____ Total Books Year 2_____
 Scholastic_____ Total Books Year 1_____ Total Books Year 2_____

SCOTT FORESMAN: GINN:

   TEXT WORKBOOK   TEXT WORKBOOK
Open Highways 4 _____   Roads to Everywhere _____
Open Highways 5_____   Trails to Treasure_____
Open Highways 6 _____   Wings to Adventure_____
Ventures_____
Vistas_____
Calvalcades _____
Wide Horizons _____

WEBSTER PRACTICE READERS: CHARLES E. MERRILL:

A _____ B _____ C _____ D _____   Uncle Ben _____
E _____ F _____ G _____   Uncle Funny Bunny_____

READERS DIGEST:

 1 2 1 2 1 2 1 2
 3 3 4 4 5 5 6 6

OTHER SUPPLEMENTARY BOOKS: _____
_____
_____
_____

It is the observation of the authors that almost without exception the staff that has worked together and adopted this modern concept of skill and work habit analysis as a basis for reporting, as well as for prescribing instructional needs, has found itself in a challenging, exciting, and rewarding professional growth pattern. The principal helps his staff attain such professional pride by advocating the concept, providing the materials and time for research and evaluation, spreading information to administration and parents, and providing every possible in-service opportunity to help teachers structure and implement the necessary materials and methods for the new method. In most instances involving use of the Skill Checksheet, one advantage immediately stands out—it is multipurpose. Since the Skill Checksheet shows *both* the materials covered by the student and his *growth in skill* with that subject, it can be used for counseling with the student concerning his individual progress, as the actual report or basis for a report to parents, as a drop-in sheet for the cumulative record for analysis of progress, and as one definitive item to be used in placement decisions.

Records of Parents' and Teachers' Conferences. To help each child make continuously improved adjustments, from the time he enters school, information is needed beyond that available from the child alone. Information pertaining to the child's early life, unusual illnesses, family circumstances, special interests or talents as observed and reported by the parents, give added insights for understanding the pre-school child. The observed attitude of the parents toward the child also may help to better understand his behavior in school. An example of a counselor contact record is given in figure 10. Such records are necessary to enable the counselor to fulfill his obligations for communicating with the staff, parents, specialists, and students.

Anecdotal Records. Teachers and counselors alike are coming to appreciate the value of recording anecdotes. There are, of course, inherent weaknesses in the direct observation method of securing data. This method of gathering information about a pupil was originally used largely in observing overt behavior related to a child's deportment. However, the anecdotal method of record keeping can make invaluable contributions toward understanding certain aspects of the child's life. Over a period of twelve years, a complete developmental picture of the child's interests and abilities can be accumulated.

Paramount to developing anecdotal records is teachers' willingness to spend the necessary time observing and recording information. The principal must not move into this phase of the guidance program too rapidly; that is, he must know when his staff's philosophy has developed to the point where their interest in children goes beyond the academic. The principal might utilize a consultant to work with his staff in developing necessary

FIGURE 10[15]

Name _____ Room _____ Grade _____

Interview No.

( ) Referral   1.   5.
( ) Voluntary   2.   6.
( ) Called in   3.   7.
( ) Other   4.   8.

Reason _____

Nature of Problem

			Parent
Educational	*Personal-Social*	*Vocational*	*Interview*
( ) attendance—tardy	( ) interests	( ) information	( ) home visit
( ) scholastic failure	( ) emotional	( ) placement	( ) school visit
( ) skill deficiency	( ) home family	( ) choice	( ) phone
( ) under-achievement	( ) discipline		
( ) study habits	( ) social conflict	*Referral*	
( ) _____	( ) financial	( ) remedial reading	
	( ) health	( ) speech therapist	
	( ) _____	( ) nurse	
		( ) psychologist	
		( ) _____	

Teacher Interview _____

skills and techniques for this endeavor. At this point the staff may see the value of taking time to record observations. The alert leader moves slowly with his staff, however, and perhaps suggests that they first study and record observations of one child. As teachers recognize the value of the procedures and become more experienced, they will become adept at methods which will save time for them in recording anecdotes.

The principal should lead his staff in developing a special form for recording anecdotes, which should be as simple as possible. As teachers record their observations, the question will no doubt arise as to how many observations per week should be recorded. Although no common agreement seems evident among authorities in this field, the teacher who finds the procedure valuable is usually not concerned with number. To make the most use of anecdotal records, they should be adequately summarized at the end of each year and recorded on a summary form. This practice eliminates bulkiness in cumulative records, to which teachers generally object. The summarizing process requires professional skill and should be done by those staff members who possess the necessary competence. It should not be entrusted to clerical office personnel.

Developing Guidance Service

Staff members must know what constitutes a good anecdote. At least two principles are important: (1) continuous striving toward objectivity is essential, and (2) positive behavior of pupils should be recorded. The first principle is particularly important because teacher's opinions or assumptions may creep into the report. Prejudgment of pupil action can have a detrimental effect on pupil adjustment, so if teachers record positive forms of behavior, the anecdotes are more likely to furnish basic insights.

The cumulative record is no better than the quality and quantity of information it contains. The principal proves his leadership ability by helping his staff grow toward better understanding of the value of such records.

The Case Conference. The case conference is a technique for bringing to bear on an individual's problem the collective thinking of all those who have contact with, or are concerned about, the individual and his adjustment. The principal, if qualified, may lead his staff or a portion of his staff in a case conference. Since the success of the conference depends upon the information obtained in the pupil inventory or in a case study, teachers need a chance to test the usefulness of the information gathered. They are then in a position to see the need for deleting or adding certain information. In this respect, the principal may well use the case conference as a technique for in-service education. Success here may also relate to the leaders' ability during the conference. Although the principal is generally responsible for arranging the conferences, the responsibility for conducting them may be delegated to any member of the guidance team qualified to give leadership. If a case study has been turned over to a guidance team, the conference should result in some constructive program of action for aiding the pupil's adjustment.

THE GUIDANCE COUNSELOR

The expanding consciousness of the need for elementary guidance, and the ever-growing number of schools starting developmental guidance programs, has created a need for well-qualified elementary guidance counselors. Certification requirements of most states include teaching experience, work experience, and a master's degree with training in some or all of the following areas: counseling, child growth and development, individual and group conferences, parental conferences, interpreting test data, knowledge of test procedures, psychology, community resources, and knowledge of occupational and educational information.

A successful developmental guidance program demands time and skill on the part of many people, but must be coordinated by one person. The many examples and quotations throughout this book concerning the many responsibilities of the elementary principal should make it very clear that he cannot fulfill the role of guidance counselor. It is his responsibility as an administrator to bring to his school every person whose talents and skills can help improve and enlarge the school's programs. In most instances, when a guidance program is inaugurated or improved, the first additional person the school asks for is a guidance counselor. The guidance counselor's training and experience enable him to lift from the principal's shoulders the details of conducting guidance functions for the school. Administratively, the principal uses his authority as well as his human relations skills to coordinate all guidance activities, but a competent guidance counselor should be able to handle the paper work and administer the day-to-day correlation of guidance activities. The following comprehensive breakdown of the services a guidance counselor can render, as listed by the elementary counselors of the South-Western City Schools, reveals some of the many valuable ways the guidance counselor can serve the school, the students, and the community.[16]

Services to Teachers

If the counselor is to function as a resource person, he must adjust his schedule so as to be available when teachers are free. In other words he must make himself available to teachers wherever they happen to be.

Below are some of the services the counselor will provide teachers:
The counselor

1. assists teachers in developing sound guidance programs in the classroom.
2. provides necessary information about pupils to assist the teacher in planning and conducting the classroom work.
3. helps the teacher develop and use individual and group guidance techniques.
4. works with teachers to determine the causes for student underachievement.
5. supervises test administration and interpretation.
6. helps teachers in the orientation of students to new activities.
7. provides teachers with life-adjustment information necessary in the guidance-orientated classroom.
8. serves as a resource person to provide teachers with information about the world of work.
9. helps teachers plan and implement units about the world of work.
10. helps the teacher to understand the reasons for pupil behavior and to develop and use appropriate classroom procedures to effect the childrens' adjustment.
11. aids in the identification of gifted children and those in other special categories and provides teachers with the information which she may use to help these children to develop to their full potential.

12. helps teachers prepare case studies.
13. arranges and participates in teacher-parent conferences.
14. assists teachers in recording the developmental progress of students.
15. participates in in-service training of teachers.
16. provides teachers with information about special services available to them.
17. acts as a referral agent for children in need of special services.

Services to Administrators

The counselor
1. provides information about pupils which will help the administrator plan the instructional program of the school.
2. helps administrators interpret and use the results of tests and other appraisal techniques.
3. cooperates with administrators in the planning, organization and administration of testing programs.
4. advises administrators of the need for preventive and remedial programs.
5. helps the administrator to understand the reason for pupils' misbehavior and assists in developing procedures for the improvement of pupil adjustment on both an individual and a group basis.
6. assists in the development of sound pupil personnel policies within the school.
7. helps arrange and participates in parent group guidance activities, such as orientation to junior high school, interpretation of test results and counseling of parents of gifted children.
8. helps arrange and participates in parent-administrator conferences.
9. assists in planning in-service guidance programs for the professional staff.
10. helps develop wholesome, desirable extracurricular activities appropriate to the various physical, mental and social stages of child development.
11. provides information about the needs of pupils necessary to curriculum development and planning.
12. advises school administrators on matters affecting pupil welfare.

Prudent administrators will avail themselves of the services of the elementary counselor to the fullest extent. However, the counselor must comprehend his role in the light of a helping relationship and understand that help can only be offered; it can never be forced on administrators.

Caution should be exercised on the part of the counselor and the administrator to prevent the assumption of the other's role. Each has a distinct role; the administrator should concern himself with instructional leadership; the primary concern of the counselor should be guidance functions.

Services for Specialists

During the last ten years there has been an increase in the special services offered to pupils in the elementary school, such as health services, speech therapy, psychological services, remedial reading, etc. Each specialist may have need for various services from the elementary counselor. Listed are some services of the elementary school counselor in his role—relationship with other specialists.

The counselor

1. counsels with individual students upon the recommendation or referral of a specialist.
2. participates in case studies with specialists.
3. provides the specialists with information about students who have special needs.
4. helps interpret special needs to the parents of these children.
5. acts as a referral agent to specialists.
6. assists children to understand, accept and adjust to their special needs.
7. helps specialists contact community agencies for referral of children in need of special help.
8. participates in the orientation of children to special activities.
9. aids in the administration of tests and interpretation of test results to specialists.

Many of the communication problems between school and home can be alleviated with the guidance counselor in a unique position to aid in this improvement, since at the heart of all communication is the desire to inform parents of the child's individual progress and achievement. Problems of elementary children may be rooted in conditions in the school or in the home, and the counselor/parent conference, in which the counselor has the opportunity to convey the school's concern for the child and assess the parents' attitude, is quite often the most successful way to secure parents' cooperation. The counselor may also be able to organize and direct group meetings with parents on any number of topics concerned with the school's activities and programs. In-service activities with teachers, in cooperation with the principal, should also be a basic responsibility of the guidance counselor. Development of the most comprehensive guidance program possible should be the desire and aim of every elementary school.

Information Service

This service makes available to pupils that information which is not usually accessible through classroom instruction. To provide such a service, the principal should lead his staff in discovering areas of information needed and desired by various age groups; the availability of such information may also give strength to the instructional program. Three phases of the information service are commonly recognized by guidance authorities: (1) occupational, (2) educational, and (3) orientation. Much has been written about these three phases of informational service, and ample material is available for the reader interested in pursuing this point further. The purpose here is to help the principal gain an overall perspective of his leadership function in improving the guidance program.

Occupational Information. Hill[17] has stated that an increasingly significant volume of research during the past two decades casts serious doubt on the wisdom of postponing vocational guidance until adolescence. This aspect of the guidance service is one in which the classroom teacher can play an important role. The interested principal should direct study of certain curriculum experiences to determine which areas or units might incorporate certain pre-occupational information for children in the elementary school. For example, the sixth grade may study "The World at Work," and thereby obtain occupational information through meaningful experiences. Although this should not be considered to fulfill the occupational function of the informational service, it should acquaint pupils with materials and sources of information, and provide the tools for solving their own problems as needs arise. An additional function of the information service is to accumulate a variety of materials, such as books, magazines, catalogs, pamphlets, current occupational data, filmstrips, and films, which will help pupils in solving their problems. Many of those who drop out of school do so soon after completing the elementary grades. These are the pupils who need current occupational information which may facilitate their vocational adjustment.

Educational Service. Briefly, the educational service should help the child gain an understanding of himself and of opportunities for further training. Information about secondary schools, vocational schools, apprentice training, and higher-education requirements and opportunities should be available.

This may be accomplished through an orientation program for children who complete the elementary school and matriculate in the middle school or junior high school, or the senior high school. The principal should cooperatively plan with his teachers for excursions to vocational schools and various cooperating apprentice-training industries. Units can be taught which help the children determine educational requirements for entrance into a chosen field of work. In addition, where high school handbooks are available, children may study the program offered and determine their own courses, with guidance, and carefully plan the continuation of their educational activities with their parents and teachers.

Orientation. Orientation is another phase of the information service. This aspect of the information service is sorely needed, so the leadership role of the principal must be emphasized here. Until recently, practically nothing had been done to orient pupils when they moved to new school environments. The pupils' failure to adjust to the new environment and the lack of foresight on the part of school leaders led to many pupils' dropping out of school at the ninth-grade level. Whether the pupils are entering first grade, moving from sixth grade to the first year of junior high school, or going to senior high, the principal is responsible for helping them adjust satisfactorily to the new school situation. Smith points out several areas of information that pupils need when entering secondary school from the elementary grades. These areas, listed here with some modifications, are:

1. The plan of the school plant,
2. The curricular offerings,
3. Policies governing school attendance,
4. Policies and opportunities relating to part-time jobs,
5. The nature and purposes of co-curricular activities.
6. History and traditions of the school, and
7. Community agencies offering services to pupils.[18]

The elementary school principal, together with the secondary school principal, must bear the responsibility for developing a sound orientation program. In one situation known to the writers, a high school has been built to replace six smaller schools. These small schools have been used to develop enriched elementary school centers, while the new school organization is based on a seven-five plan. Essential to the pupils' adequate adjustment to this new large high school is the orientation program. The following description explains this school's program.

> The high school has a standing faculty committee known as the orientation committee. This group meets with the principals from the six elementary schools to plan the program. The high school principal is an ex officio member of this committee. The committee plans for such activities as the following:
>
> During the early spring of each year, the seventh-grade pupils, through regular class activities, focus on plans for their high school education. The music supervisor administers a music aptitude test which helps to determine which children will be selected for various music experiences, such as string classes and other instrumental opportunities. Since the eighth grade is the first year of a five-year high school, guidance services are emphasized, including a complete testing program during that year. During the time designated as Orientation Day, all of the county's seventh-grade children are taken by bus to the consolidated high school. Here they are greeted by various student leaders and school officials in an assembly program. The core approach at the eighth-grade level is explained to them by the curriculum director, and the principal briefs them on registration procedures.

Developing Guidance Services 243

The school handbook is distributed and other pertinent information disseminated.

Following this general assembly, the pupils are divided into small groups to tour the school plant. Student leaders serve as guides, and then take the pupils to lunch in the school cafeteria. Opportunities are available to hear briefly about the co-curricular activities, the guidance program, etc. The day concludes with a presentation by the band and school orchestra.

This orientation program is not presented to serve as a model, but simply to illustrate what one school is doing about the problem. Each school must plan for its needs in accordance with local conditions and limitations. Thus each school and each situation will demand its own particular kind of orientation program.

Coordination of guidance services between elementary and secondary schools definitely leads to better school articulation. Principals, through planning with their staffs, can provide the needed machinery for inter-working committees, which in turn can focus attention upon the total educational process rather than upon its segments. Both guidance and instruction begin when a child enters kindergarten, but guidance should continue under school supervision even after a child leaves high school.

All phases of the guidance program may be facilitated by teachers at all instructional levels, focusing attention on the needs and problems of all youth. Elementary teachers can learn from secondary teachers what information is most useful to them. Elementary teachers can also learn about their former pupils from the secondary teachers, which may help them improve upon teaching-learning experiences in the future.

COUNSELING AND THE PRINCIPAL

As the elementary school principal helps to develop an improved guidance program, he is faced with the problem of providing a counseling service. Some authorities believe that incidental counseling by classroom teachers is sufficient. This means counseling for which there is no plan or preparation by either the counselor (in this case the classroom teacher) or the counselee. Others advocate that a specialist trained in counseling techniques should be employed as a counselor. The philosophy developed by the principal and his staff should determine how this service will be rendered in their school. However, the professionally-trained elementary school counselor can provide valuable help to the principal, teachers, and parents which will improve their counseling skills and thus assist the child.[19] The need is for teachers and principal to acquire these professional skills.

The principal of every elementary school is a counselor, if only by the nature of his position. He conducts both individual and group interviews, which are basic counseling devices. In fact, the individual conference is the primary vehicle of the counseling process.[20] For example, the principal may counsel with a pupil concerning his absence from school, which may be due to the pupil's inability to adjust to the school environment. Such situations call for individual counseling. *School counseling, then, may be defined as any situation which brings the principal, teacher, or counselor together with one or more people for the purpose of solving an individual or group problem.*

In other cases the principal may be called upon to hold a group conference. This technique requires skills in the group process as well as a keen understanding of children. In one elementary school with which the writers are acquainted, the following incident took place:

> Five boys had been caught smoking behind the stage in the auditorium. They were sent to the office by the custodian who caught them. The principal gave each boy the opportunity to discuss his reaction to breaking the school rule. He asked each of them to relate the dangers of smoking behind the stage, as well as the effects of smoking on growing bodies.
>
> They agreed with the principal that the rule concerning smoking was a good one and that they were sorry they had broken it. One boy pointed out that they could stay in each day after school for one week, and the other four agreed. The principal told them that since they were aware of the need for the rule and were ready to live by the rule, punishment would not be necessary. He dismissed them with a smile and a pat on the shoulder, urging them to remember the things they had discussed.
>
> In a few weeks, the boys came back to the office to see the principal. This time they asked the principal if they could make some posters for Fire Prevention Week concerning the dangers of fire from smoking. They principal readily consented and felt that he had gained new insights into understanding boys.

The principal utilized counseling techniques in the group conference or interview when he: (1) let each person have an opportunity to discuss his situation; (2) directed thinking toward dangers involved in the problem; (3) used the non-directive approach toward consequences of action; (4) established a friendly relationship and a permissive atmosphere; and (5) followed the conference by constructive action.

The principal is called upon many times for individual and group counseling. Some problems which commonly require counseling techniques are:

1. Admission of transfer pupils,
2. Behavior problems beyond teacher control,
3. Special education needs of handicapped children,
4. Arrangements for gifted pupils,

Developing Guidance Services 245

5. Health problems,
6. School adjustment problems,
7. Poor educational achievement,
8. Family problems affecting school relations,
9. Absenteeism, and
10. Problems requiring the services of special community agencies.

Although this list does not identify all the areas in which the principal may be called upon to counsel with pupils, it does show the need for professional counseling skills and services. In a very real sense, then, the principal is a counselor. Even if the services of a trained counselor are available, the principal probably should be the first contact for the pupil after the classroom teacher.

SUMMARY

Although great strides have been made in providing increased services to help teachers understand children and special service personnel to help children understand themselves, much remains to be accomplished. Although good teachers have always rendered some guidance functions, they have neither the training nor the time to get involved in problems beyond their capabilities. The principal has a definite leadership role in helping his staff to understand the need for guidance services in the elementary school. He has the additional task of helping the staff define the services which will best aid pupils and the teachers in their respective roles.

With the advent of the team approach to instruction, the principal must be able to visualize a guidance program that is open-ended and of great depth. Teachers, parents, and the general public are now much more aware of the importance of high-quality elementary education and are more interested in supporting the need for guidance personnel to complement this program. As guidance programs develop, a system of records becomes increasingly important. These records are meaningful if teachers have shared cooperatively in developing the system to contain information they consider pertinent.

Finally, the principal must give leadership in evaluating the guidance program. Unless this program can prove its worth, parents may be unwilling to support its expense. Some techniques for evaluating effectiveness of a guidance program are (1) use of a questionnaire to parents and former pupils, (2) planned observation, (3) analysis of adjustment problems, and (4) use of the section "Pupil Services," *Minimum Standards for Ohio Elementary Schools,* Revised 1970.

SUGGESTED READINGS

Brison, David W. "The Role of the Elementary Guidance Counselor." *The National Elementary School Principal* 43: 41–46.

Frost, Jack M. and James A. Frost. *Elementary Guidance Handbook, A Book of Process.* Rev. ed. Grove City, Ohio: South-Western City Schools, 1966.

Fullmer, D. W. and H. W. Bernard. *Counseling: Content and Process.* Chicago: Science Research Associates, 1964, pp. 207–27.

Haring, Norris G. and E. Lakin Phillips. *Educating Emotionally Disturbed Children.* New York: McGraw-Hill, 1961.

Hill, George E. and Eleanore B. Luekey. *Guidance for Children in Elementary Schools.* New York: Appleton-Century-Crofts, 1969.

Hummel, Dean L. and S. J. Banham, Jr. *Pupil Personnel Services in Schools: Organization and Coordination.* Chicago: Rand McNally, 1968.

Johnston, Edgar G. "Elementary School Guidance." *The National Elementary Principal* 46 (April 1967): 38–39.

Krugman, Morris. "Why Guidance in Our Elementary School?" *Personnel and Guidance Journal* 32 (July 1954): 270.

Noffsinger, Carl E. "Health Education in the Trotwood-Madison Schools." *Ohio's Health* 30, no. 7 (July 1969).

Pullen, Milton V. "When There Are No Guidance Specialists—Guidelines for Principals." *The National Elementary Principal* 43 (April 1964): 19–21.

Sigel, Irving E. "How Intelligence Tests Limit Understanding of Intelligence." In *Children: Readings in Behavior and Development.* New York: Holt, Rinehart, and Winston, 1968.

Notes

1. *The Elementary School Principalship in 1968 . . . A Research Study* (Washington, D.C.: Department of Elementary School Principals, National Education Association, 1968).

2. Morris Krugman, "Why Guidance in Our Elementary School?" *Personnel and Guidance Journal* 32 (July 1954): 270.

3. Raymond N. Hatch, *Guidance Services in the Elementary School* (Dubuque, Iowa: William C. Brown, 1951), p. 14.

4. Ira J. Gordon, *The Teacher as a Guidance Worker* (New York: Harper, 1956), pp. 3–5.

5. Adapted from a bulletin of the California State Department of Education, *Good Guidance Practices in the Elementary School* (Sacramento: California State Department of Education, 1955), pp. 3–5.

6. Hatch, *Guidance Services,* pp. 104–5.

7. Dr. Donald G. Ferguson, "Patterns of Excellence in Pupil Services," Pupil Personnel Services Workshop: Developing a Team Approach to Pupil Services, Florida State Department of Education, Tallahassee. Sponsoring Agency—Pinellas County Board of Public Instruction, Clearwater, Florida, E.R.I.C. # ED 032 579, pp. 9–10.

8. Adapted by permission from *Organization and Administration of Guidance Services* by Edward C. Roeber, Glenn E. Smith, and Clifford E. Erickson. (New York: 1955), McGraw-Hill, p. 33. Copyright 1955.

9. *Principalship in 1968 . . . A Research Study,* p. 76.

10. Ibid., p. 77.

11. J. Melvin Witmer, "The Teacher's Guidance Role and Functions as Reported by Elementary School Teachers." American Personnel and Guidance Association, Washington, D. C. (From a paper presented at the American Personnel and Guidance Association Convention, Las Vegas, Nevada, April, 1968) E.R.I.C. # ED 030 890.

12. Louis Kaplan and J. David O'Dea, "Mental Health Hazards in School," *Educational Leadership* 10 (March 1953): 352.

13. See the following sources for further discussions of information needed for guiding pupils: Division of Research and Guidance, Los Angeles County Schools, *Guidance Handbook for Elementary Schools* (Los Angeles: California Test Bureau, 1949); Dean L. Hummel and S. J. Bonham, Jr., *Pupil Personnel Services in Schools: Organization and Coordination* (Chicago: Rand McNally, 1968).

14. Carl E. Noffsinger, "Health Education in the Trotwood-Madison Schools," *Ohio's Health* 30, no. 7 (July 1969).

15. Jack M. Frost and James A. Frost, *Elementary Guidance Handbook, A Book of Process* Rev. ed. (Grove City, Ohio: South-Western City Schools, 1966), p. 55.

16. Frost, *Elementary Guidance*, pp. 16–17.

17. George E. Hill and Eleanore B. Luekey, *Guidance for Children in Elementary Schools* (New York: Appleton-Century-Crofts, 1969), p. 351.

18. Glenn E. Smith, *Principles and Practices of Guidance,* p. 169.

19. Hill, *Guidance for Children,* p. 203.

20. Glenn E. Smith, *Principles and Practices of Guidance,* p. 262.

10

Pupil-Personnel Policies

A good pupil personnel program is built upon a sound guidance program, which makes available the information needed about each pupil. The elementary principal can use this information, if he has a thorough understanding of child growth and development, in developing policies which will benefit the pupils. These policies are in the areas of placement, classification for learning, marking, promotion, testing, and follow-up. This chapter shows how the principal can capitalize on the growth of his staff in developing guidance services, and how he may give direction for improving policies which affect pupil-personnel practices.

EDUCATIONAL PLACEMENT

Since guidance is a function of all school personnel who coordinate efforts to afford pupils opportunities for developing potential, the educational placement service must rely upon the other pupil personnel services to be effective. That is, there must be an available source of accumulated information, as well as an organization to administer these services. The principal and his staff must work closely with parents in placing each youngster in each situation, whether it be in a given grade, a class for special education, art or music classes, or the like.

Classifying Pupils for Placement

Policies for placing children for instructional purposes may be established by school board policy or by the superintendent's or principal's edict. Regardless of the source of policy-making, the principal as an educational leader must seek to discover with his staff and the parents how improved placement procedures can facilitate pupil adjustment. Basically, the principal is concerned with two kinds of pupil classification for instructional placement: (1) classification of the overall school population into classroom groups, and (2) distribution of children for special education needs.

Organizing School Population. Many schemes have been devised for arranging children in workable groups. Children have been and still are being classified for teaching in at least three ways: (1) according to ability, (2) by chronological age, and (3) in relation to readiness for reading. Various other plans have been developed and tried since the advent of the "lock-step" graded system. The platoon organization, the Winnetka plan, the Dalton plan, team units, multiage groups (6, 7, 8), and departmentalization are a few such plans that could be mentioned here. However, the guidance-conscious educational leader must look beyond mere administrative procedure in his search for the most effective division of the school population into classroom groups.

The elementary school principal should review with his staff the objectives of the school and then determine the appropriate plan for grouping children with their teachers. The plan of organization should bear directly on the outcomes anticipated from the educational program.

The writers, after an extensive review of research, are inclined to align themselves with multiage grouping for the basic school organization. To date, research has not clearly indicated a better plan, but philosophical considerations point to the many advantages of the multiage group. The philosophy is consistent with the aims of public education. In modern educational planning, however, one must be cognizant of the need for flexibility within the classroom unit. Children may be grouped within the unit according to the best plan for enhancing the teaching-learning situation: teamed for some activities, or self-contained for others, depending upon the purpose to be achieved. For some activities, interest grouping may be appropriate, while for others, grouping by ability or choice of friends may best serve the learner. It is desirable that the principal provide leadership in helping teachers and parents see the necessity for flexible grouping within a classroom in order to attain basic educational objectives for all. *This in no way implies that the level of inspiration or achievement should be permitted to dwindle to mediocrity.*

Currently, administrators are seeking ways to add special teachers for remedial classes. Efforts need to be redirected toward providing additional teachers to achieve a team balance of specialists and generalists. When the children are working at their own level of achievement or are individualized, the need for remedial teachers decreases. When special-education children are grouped with the multiage group, the special education or E.M.R. teacher becomes a part of the team.

Classification for Learning. One of the most difficult tasks facing the elementary school principal is that of classifying children for learning. Many pressures are imposed upon the principal for special classes for the gifted, the mentally retarded, and the physically handicapped. Here the principal needs all possible help from the various school specialists. Classification of children can be based only upon a cumulative index relating all facets of the child's personality to his present level of growth. Some parents resent their children's being placed in classes for the mentally retarded, while others insist that their children should be in a class for the gifted. Leadership skills are needed here to help the principal plan with teachers and parents the best program possible for each child. When children are heterogeneously grouped and are instructed on an individualized basis, the need for special grouping lessens. This is not to say that children are not deployed for certain portions of the day for the particular need which they might have. The mentally retarded might be redeployed for the purpose of increasing attention span at one activity, etc.

The Mentally Retarded Learner

Growing public recognition of the necessity for providing education for handicapped children is occurring. The term *handicapped* as used here refers to any child who is educable, but for whom a special class is necessary. That is, a child may be handicapped because of mental retardation, or may have some physical impairment which requires special instruction and facilities.

Samuel A. Kirk describes the various degrees of mental retardation as follows: (1) the educable mentally retarded, (2) the trainable mentally retarded, and (3) the totally dependent mentally retarded.[1] The principal of a small school needs to recognize his responsibility to these children, although he may not be as fortunate as the principal of a large school or a school in a city system. Provisions must be made to teach the mentally retarded to enable them to become self-supporting. Many of these children, under special classroom conditions, are capable of learning to read at about the fourth-grade level; some are also capable of learning to write and compute fundamental processes in arithmetic.[2] The principal's greatest responsibility here is two-fold: (1) to provide for special teaching, but also to provide that these children associate with regularly-classified children, and (2) to classify the children for training so they can be redeployed in this manner. The former requires recognition of the problem and use of leadership skills in arousing community support for the plan. The latter requires the ability to gather sufficient data through pupil inventory and use of specialized personnel and consultants in making the classification. Where special classes are available, either in the school or elsewhere in the school system, the principal and staff may work together to identify these children early in the school program so they may attend such classes for certain portions of the day.

For the principal of the small elementary school or of a school where team units are not functioning, the problem is more complex. All too frequently, these children are "sitters" who are just waiting to pass the compulsory attendance age so they can drop out of school. The alert principal may find it feasible, however, through staff study of the problem, to enable his teachers who have one or more mentally retarded but educable children to have fewer normal pupils in their classes, and thus compensate for the time and effort needed to assist the handicapped pupils. In this way the handicapped would not take time away from the whole class, particularly if the teachers are moving toward individualized instruction. Regardless of the plan for the organization of teaching, special assistance may be needed in developing real learning experiences for these boys and girls so their time is not just taken up with seat-work. Channing and Kennedy have shown that approximately 80 percent of these children become self-supporting, and under ordinary conditions can hold jobs and function as citizens without supervision.[3] Principals, then, must find better ways for adapting instruction to the limited abilities of these children. Ideally, specially-prepared teachers are needed to serve as team members; however, the concerned principal and teacher, through their interest and initiative, may develop their own abilities in this kind of teaching.

The Physically Handicapped

Physically handicapped children pose similar problems of classification. Expert diagnosis is needed here to determine from what situations the children may best profit. City systems which provide special classes for the physically handicapped are becoming more numerous. Yet the principal must take responsibility for having these children identified early in their school experience. Delay in initiating some plan for screening these pupils may result in lack of interest, or academic retardation. Many authorities point out the need for physically handicapped children to be grouped with similar children, so they can develop the attainable aspirations of children within their peer group. Children during their growth years are quite sensitive; thus the mental-health aspect should be carefully considered when these pupils are placed in groups. The handicapped child, if placed with normal children, may aspire to participate fully in physical activities, only to feel frustrated because he is handicapped. The same child in his peer group will develop a sense of security as he gradually becomes able to participate in such activities to a limited extent. These facts point up the need for school leaders to be conscious of such problems, and unwilling to let them go unsolved.

The Gifted Child

Another challenge to the principal's leadership is that of classifying gifted children in a way that enables them to develop their greatest potential in mass education. No one wants to see the most promising minds wasted, for modern civilization cannot afford such extravagance. This situation presents three challenges for public education:

1. To be sure that giftedness does not go unrecognized;
2. To provide appropriate instructional and guidance programs so that giftedness can come into its full favor to serve itself, the contemporary society, and timeless culture;
3. To protect the gifted person from cultural isolation from his contemporaries.

These challenges must be met, and the principal's recognition of them can be reflected in the staff's efforts to improve the curriculum. Decisions must be made by the staff and the community concerning action upon these challenges. Decisions must deal with questions such as: Should the gifted be segregated for instructional purposes at the elementary school level? Can the gifted be adequately cared for in the regular instructional program of a heterogeneous classroom? Do gifted children show significant educational achievement gains when they are homogeneously grouped? Is society willing to sacrifice a chemist, a physicist, an Edison, or a Shakespeare because of civic ignorance of or apathy to the problem of the gifted child? What attitudes develop within groups when gifted pupils are homogeneously grouped for learning in the elementary school?

The guidance services of the modern elementary school can be valuable in identifying gifted children. However, the principal's responsibility goes beyond identification of the gifted. Action in meeting these children's needs becomes paramount. Many schemes have been tried, and some are being used on a nationwide basis, to meet the challenge of the gifted child. For example, the city of Cleveland has for many years conducted a program known as "major work groups" for gifted children. Ample professional literature is available to help understand this problem. It is mentioned here only as an aspect of the pupil personnel program, pointing to some possible suggestions for the principal in working with his staff and community to meet the challenge. When the gifted child is a member of a team teaching unit, he can be redeployed for certain "Quest" type learnings. That is, the gifted child in science might spend a portion of his time working alone, or with another child with similar interests and a teacher, on special science projects.

A survey of educational literature reveals at least six different ways to meet the problem of educating gifted children, including:

1. Homogeneous grouping.
2. Enrichment in regular classes.
3. Additional opportunities such as clubs, creative works, research, and other extra-curricular activities.

4. Assignment of additional responsibilities to the gifted.
5. Special provisions created by the teacher.
6. Individual projects.

The principal must seek to provide for the gifted child in light of his particular school situation. For example, in the education of the gifted in regular classroom groups, it seems wise to consider such factors as identification of the real needs of the gifted, size of the class, facilities and resources available, quality of the teaching personnel, availability of special teachers or supervisors for assistance, etc. Each school and community must evaluate its potential before arriving at a decision as to how to best meet the needs of the gifted child.

If the guidance program is to help pupils make satisfactory educational and vocational adjustments, the principal must use his leadership role in developing the placement services within his school.

THE TESTING PROGRAM

The elementary principal may operate within a system-wide, established testing program, or he may have a single program for his individual school. Standardized tests may be used for many purposes: (1) to make a school-wide survey of achievement; (2) to gain better understanding of an individual pupil, or (3) to help the individual pupil gain a better understanding of his own strengths, weaknesses, and interests. Such information should become a part of the individual inventory, which must be used with discretion. The significance of the information will depend upon many other factors which should have been observed, such as interest, maturity, home background, and experiences.

On the other hand, testing information may assist the teacher in modifying curriculum experiences. For example, a test of the gifted child may indicate the need for higher-level materials; for the slow learner, perhaps a slower pace in mathematics. Therefore, if the testing program is to help the learner make a better adjustment, the resulting information should become part of the pupil inventory, to be treated as a single index in the record. Like other data gathered, it gives meaning only when it becomes part of the total indices.

Planning a Testing Program

A testing program begins with whatever tests are currently being used. Initiation or expansion of the program depends upon teachers who recognize the need for additional information which may be gained through objective tests. *Only to the extent that test information is useful to teachers in helping pupils are the expenditures for tests justified.* The following steps may help in expanding or initiating a testing program:

1. A survey should be made of tests presently in use.
2. An analysis of how teachers use the test results should be studied.
3. The staff and parents should plan what additional information is needed which is not currently available. (This may be done through a committee approach.)
4. The testing program decided upon should be initiated gradually.
5. The testing program should be evenly distributed. No one grade should carry a heavy load.
6. The program should be considered comprehensive in nature, encompassing grades 1 through 12.
7. Tests should be used that can be machine scored.
8. Costs should be weighed against values derived.
9. Tests should be selected for specific purposes.
10. A complete testing program from any one company should not be justified only on the basis of facilitating clerical work.
11. Tests selected should be appraised by consulting sources such as the *Mental Measurement Yearbooks*.
12. Test results on a school-wide basis should be revealed annually through newspaper releases and other reports.

If initiation of a testing program is a cooperative endeavor, the principal usually need not fear the outcomes. The dangers lie in faculty acceptance of a program on the basis of the principal's strong persuasion, rather than on the merits of the plan. The need for a careful, cooperative plan before the first test is ordered cannot be emphasized too strongly. One national research study[5] reveals that 50 per cent of the schools studied were not satisfied with their present testing programs. They wished to include more individual tests in their programs. The principal must have a committee charged with continuous evaluation of the testing program, although modification must be gradual. No sudden change to a completely new program of tests should be initiated in any one year or grade. Greater satisfaction with the testing program will result from continuous, cooperative evaluation.

IMPROVING MARKING SYSTEMS

A point of departure for understanding more clearly a system of marking is the widely-accepted view that a child should be appraised in terms of *his own* achievement in relation to his ability. To state it simply, he does not compete with anyone except himself. Therefore, no matter how the mark or score is given, the teacher, the child, and the parent know that it represents an evaluation of how well the child is meeting educational objectives in light of his abilities and capacities. If one accepts this principle, it is clear that school personnel face an evaluation task embracing several

Pupil-Personnel Policies

approaches and calling for different skills and instruments to determine educational growth and development. The principal helps bring about unity in and acceptance of the marking system by defining the terms and organizing a system that meets with total approval.

Defining Terms

The principal may accomplish his first task by achieving agreement on a set of guiding principles which spell out a meaningful system of marking. Herrick and his co-workers[6] suggest a set of principles which we adapt here:

1. Marking should be related directly to progress in those areas of human behavior already defined in the educational goals of the school. There should be purpose in marking.
2. In marking, teachers should consider the wide variations in a child's growth patterns to reveal and encourage progress toward goals.
3. The evidence used for determining progress or achievement should be clearly related to the area under examination.
4. Marking should embrace a range of characteristics no greater than the range of available data. In other words, teachers should make no evaluative decisions if they are not prepared, or lack sufficient data about a particular phase.
5. Marking should have diagnostic and constructive implications.
6. Marking should be a cooperative endeavor involving teachers, students, and sometimes parents.
7. Marking considers the welfare of the child by respecting his integrity, and is something people do *with* the child.

Modern Concepts of Marking

Assigning marks or scores to a child's work, achievement, or development is both an administrative and a staff problem. Inconsistencies of marking or grading practices, both on a day-to-day and a long-range basis, have pointed to a need for careful study and revision of existing practices. The principal may continue to prove his worth as a leader by working with staff, pupils, and community in developing a satisfactory system of marking. He must be the professional consultant who gives direction to an examination of the present marking system, if it needs analysis. Although there is a wealth of evidence and material available in many research studies,[7] the purpose here is to present some accepted modern concepts of marking or scoring to help the principal and staff analyze their current practices, as well as to suggest some data which can point the way for improved systems of marking.

The actual mechanics of marking seem to be a chronically unsolved problem. The use of the traditional numerical mark in mathematics, for example, is objective, but in almost universal disfavor among professional educators today. Even the letter system of marking is widely disapproved because of its comparative approach and emphasis on revealing standings among pupils. Other variations of marking include "satisfactory" and "unsatisfactory," and so on. School personnel and citizens may further explore these various marking systems, but only the commonly accepted approaches to this problem can receive attention here. Marking or scoring must provide more than a mere report to the child and parents. The principal should be ready to lead to some definite and formal marking system, cooperatively developed and based on accepted principles.

Organizing a Marking System. Although the next section suggests definite ways of reporting to parents, the purpose here is to indicate how the principal may organize his school marking system to obtain a complete picture of the individual child. The organization of this program may be divided as follows:

1. The principal and teacher collect evidence to be placed in a cumulative file. In the strict sense of the word, the child is not assigned a *mark* or *score,* but evidence is available that describes many things about him (e.g., test scores of various types, and other strictly confidential items reserved for school personnel use only).

2. Evidence is assembled by the teacher, kept in her files, and shared by both teacher and child. The teacher may decide that certain information should be withheld from the parent either permanently or temporarily. The child receives a "mark," in that some evaluation of a skill, habit, or attitude is given to him for definite purposes, leading ultimately, it is hoped, to improved behavior.

3. Reporting to parents is the commonly accepted marking or grading procedure. This information is a three-way sharing of information concerning a child's work and progress, and is expressed by a mark.

4. When teacher and parents confer about the child, some information may be withheld from the parent for purposes of protecting the child's welfare. Although no actual mark is given, the principal may ask for written, filed reports of such meetings for future reference in the overall appraisal of the child.

It may be seen that a marking system can be thought of in the light of these four areas, yet the commonly considered viewpoints of marking are usually narrowed down to the third area.

Reporting to Parents

School personnel have the responsibility of informing parents about the educational status of their children. The preceding discussions should assist the principal and staff in deciding how to convey the proper information about the child to the parents in an economical and expedient manner. Having organized a marking and evaluation program in terms of the four areas mentioned, the principal may find his next step—organizing a system for reporting to parents—easier. Three approaches may help in developing a reporting program.

Formal Written Reports. The usual report card or mimeographed form is sent periodically to the parent for examination and signature. This practice has a distinct advantage if the marks or scores have been given proper meaning and follow sound principles of evaluation. Highly important is the parents' understanding of the meaning of the marks. Another device is a letter sent by the teacher to interpret educational progress. The letter below illustrates this approach to reporting. As is always true in trying to convey an idea or impression, communication presents a problem. Teachers, however, through a series of good in-service education meetings, can learn to write accurate reports to parents. The report shown below clearly points up some of Mary's strengths as well as some of her weaknesses. This kind of information conveys far more than one mark. This technique of reporting pupil progress should be supplemented with a teacher-parent-pupil conference at least three times a year. It should be noted that children attend this school for five weeks in the summer as a part of an extended year program.

Ohio University Elementary School
Athens, Ohio
Child's Progress Report[8]

Date: August 8, 1971

To: Mr. and Mrs. W. W. Smith

Mary has been interested in contributing to news and sharing. She had worthwhile contributions but spoke in such a little voice many times that it was difficult to listen to her.

Mary benefited from both the Earth and Store units. She is easily distracted, and her poor listening habits caused her to have confused concepts at times. She was usually eager to help but somewhat immature and dependent in carrying out responsibilities. The same can be said of her participation in seasonal activities.

Mary's work habits show average improvement. The summer showed gain in her listening habits, but she still needs reminding. She is improving in keeping her notebook more organized. She still requires considerable guidance in following directions. We have tried to help her achieve more independent ways of working.

Mary is better accepted by the group and she is learning to accept them and her status in the group.

Mary's reading is a little above average. Her handwriting is average in speed and better than average in legibility. Her spelling is good average, and she shows more independence in learning to spell. Her progress in the use of phonics is average. She is dependent on group work or adult help in her use of capitalization and punctuation. She contributed ideas for the information in the Store Book. These were group-composed. When she was needed to compose individually and more independently for friendly letters and stories she frequently did not succeed. A letter to Anne Jones at the end of the summer school showed success and was one of the first to be sent. She showed some poetic ability in describing what she saw on her way home.

In numbers Mary is taking more interest and is trying more. Tests indicate she is doing a little below average for her grade. Her daily work shows better understanding and more skill, but there are still misunderstandings in her concepts. She needs to develop more understanding of time, and money, and measures. Taking time to guide the incidental number learning in her daily activities with a view toward understanding is helpful to Mary.

The music teacher believes that Mary has some confused ideas about the printed page. These are caused, at least partially, because she does not listen to explanations. Her attention span seems very short. She is improving in her ability to concentrate and desire to improve. Mary sings well, but usually learns songs by hearing the others work them out.

It has been interesting to work with Mary this year. Mary will go on to fourth grade in September.

Name *Mary Smith* Grade *3* Teacher *Miss B. White*
Days of School *177½* Days Present *170* Days Absent *7½*
Times Tardy *5* Principal *H. H. Doe*

Conferences with Parents. Written or telephoned communications are effective ways to report a child's progress. However, no device can supplant the conference period with parents, led by the teacher, and in some instances the principal, if he is needed to assist the less effective faculty member. The teacher may reserve the conference period for showing exhibits of the child's work which may be too bulky to send home or which need explanation. The teacher may use samples of the child's work as a focal point for discussion. To some extent the explanation of standardized test scores is used cautiously to strengthen a point in appraising the child. The principal needs to know which tests can be discussed with parents and in what ways, and should encourage staff sensitivity to this problem.

The principal can render definite leadership service to his staff by calling attention to or developing with them the techniques of conducting a good conference, as discussed in Chapter 5. Careful planning and preparation for parent conferences will insure better results. For the teacher who has not had successful experiences in parent-teacher conferences, the principal might plan some role-playing as a technique to help the teacher gain confidence in using the conference for reporting to parents. It is often useful to include the child in the conference. When the child is included, he should be the one to summarize his progress and to indicate the things he needs to improve. The instruments or techniques in this area of communication are to be used by the whole staff, but the principal's leadership efforts can bring them into focus.

Establishing Rapport with Parents. An area of concern in reporting a child's progress is a knowledge of what the parent wants in evaluation. Awareness of and sensitivity to parent's needs, desires, and feelings should result in more effective procedures and strengthen school-community relations. It has already been noted that parents should participate as widely as possible in establishing evaluative procedures and in reaching decisions that affect the child's educational welfare. The principal and teacher may now establish rapport more effectively by developing the following skills in working with parents:

1. School personnel need skill in creating good teacher-pupil relations. There should be genuine interest and faith in children. Skill in working with people develops when an individual makes the effort to communicate his thinking and feelings about the people he is leading. The principal may give positive direction to his staff by evaluating behavior in terms of this area and providing ways and means for improvement.

2. School personnel need skill to convey to parents certain feelings of adequacy and achievement derived from their child's progress. In effect, parents need a somewhat vicarious experience of achievement through the child, but more especially, they need to know something of a positive nature about his growth and development, regardless of recognized limitations in abilities and capacities. Evaluations should not degenerate into false praising of achievement, but some strong points can be found to commend in almost every child. Recognition and awards are to be made honestly and with integrity, but some way must be found to give them to all children.

3. School personnel need skill in communicating effectively with parents.

4. School personnel need skill in helping parents understand how well the child is acquiring competence in the basic skills. Many parents are concerned chiefly with what progress has been made in certain skill subjects. Closely related to skills of communication is the problem of helping parents see the picture in meaningful, significant language at their level of understanding. The school administrator reveals leadership by discovering with teachers what the parents want to know particularly and helping to get this information across.

IMPROVED PROMOTION PRACTICES

As elementary school personnel recognize the need for improved guidance opportunities, the school's promotion policies should be carefully scrutinized.

Teachers who learn the values which accrue to them and their pupils through effective guidance services may not be satisfied to continue outmoded promotion practices.

The Principal's Leadership in School Promotion Policy

The elementary school faces complex problems in policy making to regulate children's progress through the grades. These policies should reflect organization and administration that fosters continuous and smooth progress for every pupil according to his pattern of development. Research findings give evidence of promotion procedures which insure satisfactory results. Many elementary school principals may profit by understanding and accepting such findings; they may demonstrate positive leadership for faculty and community personnel by effecting certain changes in organization and administration.

The school administrator must not view the problem of promotion in an isolated fashion; that is to say, the promotional practices in his school are distinctly related to all phases of the educational plans; i.e., classification of pupils, number of students in a class, the philosophy of teaching methods, the administrator's approach to his job, and many other factors. Perhaps the most important single item is the leadership provided by a principal who solves promotion problems by employing administrative policies and educational practices that help the teacher and parent see these relationships and reach satisfactory answers. The principal may find the following two approaches helpful in giving leadership to his school:

1. The principal needs to know what promotion policy is best for his elementary school. Perhaps the personnel will have to survey many present educational practices within the school to discover whether a general overhauling of outmoded organizations and policies is needed. Answers are needed to these questions: Are there philosophies concerning promotion, acceleration, and retardation for the present-day elementary school? Does research suggest a basic philosophy with regard to promotion? What do recent trends in promotion theory suggest for the elementary school?

2. The second approach for the principal in working with the promotion problem is that of taking steps to assist his staff in employing promising practices grounded in educational research. Suggestions below may stimulate the principal to organize and administer a promotion program superior to his present one. In every situation the principal is reminded to work cooperatively with faculty and parents in agreeing upon a program appropriate to the school.

The elementary school principal needs to put into practice certain functions to insure sound promotion procedures in his school. On the basis of research evidence and in the light of recent trends, the following four functions point the way for the school executive in giving leadership in this important area. These functions suggest ways to arrive at more progressive practices, to help in crystallization of philosophy, and to point out more effective methods of creating a better learning environment for the child.

The Exploratory or Appraisal Function. The principal is first concerned about the greatest benefits that will accrue to the child, regardless of any preconceived notion about promotion or retention. He and the staff need to give attention to these problems in terms of the exploratory or appraisal function. That is to say, careful consideration is given to each pupil before definite recommendations are made for promotion. The staff should raise the following questions to guide them in this function:

1. Has a complete study been made of the child's total development?
2. Has the trend of the child's growth patterns been accurately determined in terms of intellectual, emotional, social, and physical characteristics and achievements?
3. Has an appraisal included a study, through diagnostic devices, of the causes of any difficulties encountered? Any predictive judgments?
4. Has the age-grade status been determined to show "normality"? Will the pupil profit from promotion or retention?
5. Has consideration been given to new experiences to be encountered? If he is to be promoted or retained, will there be an adequate variety of experiences for him?
6. Have conferences been held with parents and various school personnel?

The principal encourages his staff to think along these lines when they approach promotion problems. Having explored and appraised the situation with regard to the individual student, school personnel are better prepared to consider the second function.

The Corrective and Remedial Function. The staff is now faced with the practical task of taking corrective and remedial steps to insure that every child will be guided in the best possible ways. The detailed data gathered as a result of the exploratory or appraisal function help to provide a basis for wise decisions in improving the child's educational program. Some specific corrective and remedial steps are:

1. Enrichment programs for the gifted pupils who are expecting to go beyond the public school;
2. Improved programs for all children, especially for superior children who may be denied opportunities for higher education;
3. More attention to children's readiness for school;
4. More staff concentration on research findings and educational literature; and
5. Positive and definite aid to the pupil in light of what is known about him and his difficulties.

It is evident that this second function requires that the school staff be concerned with ways to help the child profit more from educational experiences. In addition, the faculty should study ways to correct their own promotion practices within the school, with major emphasis on actual classroom activities. The principal may help the individual teacher identify and initiate many other ways of improving each situation.

The School Survey Function. The concern of school personnel in this function is to survey and study the actual organization of the primary and intermediate grades. Entrance and progress problems are complicated, and require constant surveillance to determine whether existing plans harmonize with approaches that have already been tried. Schools that are moving into nongraded programs need to look at the child's readiness for each sequence of learning. Individualized instruction and nongraded-school organization imply a continuous progress program or no failure philosophy.

This function is especially difficult to put into practice without full cooperation from all school personnel. Actually, this function implies development of a basic elementary school organization that should provide the best possible way for each child to progress through the grades. The emphasis is on surveying the individual school plans currently employed, studying research findings, and thus arriving at an optimum organizational method for the school.

The Action-Program Function. This fourth function is largely the responsibility of the principal. He must initiate plans of action to meet the needs of each pupil in the most adequate and satisfying manner. The exploratory or appraisal activities, together with corrective and remedial procedures for improving instruction from the pupil-progress viewpoint, provide the basic data and framework for an action program in handling promotion problems. Even the survey function has contributed further understanding of the grade organization which can assist the staff in constructing an effective and progressive action plan.

Any action program is to be geared to the one fundamental principle of furthering educational opportunities for children. Since many plans of action have been tried, and a number of plans remain to be tested, the principal may benefit from research evidence in helping the staff produce a plan that will incorporate these policies recommended for promotional practices:

1. No child is retained at the end of the school year.
2. Provide a rich school environment designed around individualized learning for each pupil.
3. Involve parents in evaluating pupils in the light of their age, mental maturity, social and emotional adjustment attitudes and achievement.
4. Provide for initial differences in children when they enter school and study development of differences as children progress.

5. Study and express in writing a promotion philosophy based on research evidence.
6. Provide enrichment programs for all children within the framework of the curriculum.

Thus all four functions contribute to the thinking of principal and staff. It becomes obvious that a promotion program based on the above criteria can be developed only by a guidance-minded staff and leader. A basic philosophy of action is predicated on the simple formula that no child faces failure, since each pupil will progress with children his own age through a curriculum adjusted to his abilities and potential.

SUMMARY

The principal needs the various informational records kept by teachers in developing plans for placing or classifying pupils. He must classify pupils for instructional placement in two ways: (1) according to the total school population by instructional groups, and (2) according to special education needs. The latter requires leadership in developing programs suitable for the educable mentally retarded, the physically handicapped, and the gifted child.

Although follow-up activities in the elementary school are not the same as those in the secondary school, they should be equally important. Curriculum revision should result from the school's efforts to determine those areas in which they have failed to meet pupils' needs. Cooperative efforts, led by the principal and his staff in working with secondary school teachers, may lead to helping pupils become more successful.

The elementary school principal must recognize the need for teachers to plan cooperatively for the school's testing program. Efforts to coerce teachers into accepting the principal's testing program may result in loss of respect for an instrument which might be of immeasurable value if used discriminately.

The principal recognizes the relationship between the guidance services of his school and its marking and promotion practices. He leads by initiating improved promotion policies. He must demonstrate leadership in at least four functions: (1) the exploratory and appraisal, (2) the corrective and remedial, (3) the school survey, and (4) the action program.

Another important aspect of the pupil-personnel program is the development of a satisfactory means of reporting pupil progress. There are at least four approaches to this problem: (1) formal written reports using symbols, (2) a personal letter interpreting pupil progress, (3) anecdotal reports, and (4) a combination of the first with the second or third approach.

SUGGESTED READINGS

Anifson, R. C. "School Progress and Pupil Adjustment." *The Elementary School Journal* 41 (March 1941): 507–14.

Arthur, Grace. "A Study of the Achievement of Sixty Grade One Repeaters as Compared with that of Nonrepeaters of the Same Mental Age." *The Journal of Experimental Education* 5 (December 1936): 203–5.

Bloomers, P. and W. H. Coffield. "Effects of Non-Promotion on Educational Achievement in the Elementary School." *Journal of Educational Psychology* 47 (April 1956): 235–40.

Boyle, Barbara. "Promotion or Retention: Some Recent Research." *Teachers College Journal* 34 (October 1962): 29–30.

Chansky, N. M. "Progress of Promoted and Repeating Grade One Failures," *Journal of Experimental Education* 32 (Spring 1964): 225–37.

Dobbs, Virginia and Donald Neville. "Effect of Non-Promotion on the Achievement of Groups Matched from Retained First Graders and Promoted Second Graders." *The Journal of Educational Research* 60 (July-August 1967): 472–75.

Funk, H. D. "Non-Promotion Teaches Children They Are Inferior." *The Education Digest* 35 (November 1969): 38–39.

Glasser, William. *Schools Without Failure*. New York: Harper and Row, 1969.

———. "The Effect of School Failure." *The Education Digest* 35 (December 1969): 13–17.

Goodlad, John. *The Non-Graded Elementary School*. Rev. ed. New York: Harcourt, Brace and World, 1963.

———. "To Promote or Not to Promote." *Childhood Education* 30 (January 1950): 212–15.

———. "Research and Theory Regarding Promotion and Non-Promotion." *Elementary School Journal* 53 (November 1952): 150–55.

———. "Some Effects of Promotion and Non-Promotion Upon the Social and Personal Adjustment of Children." *Journal of Experimental Education* 22 (June 1954): 301–28.

———. "Ungrading the Elementary School." *National Education Association Journal* 44 (March 1955): 170–71.

Holt, John. *How Children Fail*. New York: Pitman, 1964.

———. "I Oppose Testing, Marking, and Grading." *Today's Education,* March 1971, pp. 29–31.

Kamii, Constance and David Weikart. "Marks, Achievement and Intelligence of Seventh Graders Who Were Retained (Nonpromoted) Once in Elementary School." *The Journal of Educational Research* 56 (May 1963): 452–59.

Reinherz, H. and C. L. Griffin. "Second Time Around Achievement and Progress of Boys Who Repeated One of the First Three Grades." *School Counselor* 17 (January 1970): 213–18.

Sabatino, D. A. "Psycho-Educational Study of Selected Behavioral Variables with Children Failing the Elementary Grades." *Journal of Experimental Education* 38 (Summer 1970): 40–57.

Shane, Harold. "The Promotion Policy Dilemma—Standards for Children or for Subjects." *National Education Association Journal* 42 (October 1953): 411–12.

Notes

1. *Proceedings of the Fourth Annual Conference on Crippled Children* (Richmond: Virginia Council on Health and Medical Care, 1955), p. 41.

2. Ibid., p. 42.

3. Ibid., p. 44.

4. Committee on Exceptional Children and the Reporters of *Exchange* Magazine, *How to Educate the Gifted Child: A Collection of Practical Suggestions* (New York: Metropolitan School Study Council, 1956), introduction by Donald Ross.

5. S. C. Huslander, "Assisting Youth Adjustment in Elementary Schools," *Personnel and Guidance* 32 (March 1954): 394.

6. Adapted by permission from *The Elementary School*, V. E. Herrick, J. L. Goodlad, F. J. Estvan, and P. W. Eberman, pp. 379-81. Englewood Cliffs, N. J.: Prentice-Hall, Inc., 1956. Copyright 1956, by Prentice-Hall, Inc.

7. See John W. Rothney, *Evaluating and Reporting Pupil Progress* (Washington, D. C.: Department of Classroom Teachers, National Education Association, 1955).

8. This is an actual report received by a parent. Names and other identifying information have been changed.

11

Administering the School Office

Important to the effective operation of a school is the principal's attitude toward the non-instructional aspects of his job. For some principals, the administration of these areas of school operation provides an excuse for restricting themselves to only incidental involvement in the instructional phases of their tasks. Others may be interested in the instructional program to the neglect of the non-instructional phases of school administration. It is important that the principal be an effective organizer and administrator as well as a supervisor of instruction. Undoubtedly, many elementary school principals are doing a more effective job of administering the non-instructional phases of school operation because of their inadequacy in dealing with curriculum and instruction. But the good leader budgets his time and administers in such a way that the non-instructional phases of school operation facilitate instructional progress. If principals are to take the lead in developing a good school program, there is a fundamental need for understanding the organization and management of the office. Two phases of the program are discussed here: (1) the functions of the school office and (2) the improvement of office organization and service.

FUNCTIONS OF THE SCHOOL OFFICE

The principal's office may be a nook between two classrooms or an elaborate suite of offices. In either case, the office is the hub around which revolve the numerous activities of the school. Parents, children, staff members, central office, business representatives, and others all request contact with the office and make demands upon the time of the principal and his secretary. Despite the fact that the office handles numerous and increasingly complex details, little has been done to improve this medium of public relations.

Although modern buildings generally provide improved accommodations for the principal, much can still be done to improve the functions of the school office, whether it is a fine, modern one or a make-shift arrangement at the end of a blind hallway.

One real obstacle to the principal's most important job, that of supervision and improvement of instruction, is the heavy demand made on his time by routine administrative and clerical duties. Even when done efficiently, these demands are enervating, and take time and energy that should be given to leadership of the professional teaching staff, and all others whose goal it is to contribute to the instructional program. With the ever-mounting demands of paperwork, one almost expects the elementary principal to be literally crushed under the weight, but according to a 1968 research study made by the Department of Elementary School Principals, National Education Association, this is not the case.[1] This study showed that teaching principals averaged 9 percent of their workweek given to clerical tasks in 1958, and exactly the same percentage in 1968; supervising principals gave an average of 14 percent of their workweek to clerical tasks in 1958, and again the same percentage in 1968. This would seem to indicate that more secretarial help was available, and this was verified by the study, which showed that 40 percent of the total sampling had the equivalent of full-time secretarial help in 1958, while 50 percent had this equivalent in 1968. It must also indicate that principals are becoming more adept at handling routine details, since in the decade spanned by the study there are many more complex details to handle; the average principal seemingly expedites them in such a way that they still take no more time from his instructional supervision than they did in 1958.

As revealed in this same study, even the physical facilities in which to conduct the routine matters of an elementary school leave much to be desired.[2] Of the total sampled, almost 16 percent rated their office and facilities exceptionally good, and more than 34 percent rated them satisfactory. Significantly, however, 34 percent of the teaching principals *had no office*, while in the supervisory group this was true of only 4 percent. Obviously, there is still much to be done in improving the elementary office and supplying secretarial help to handle the routine details so the principal may spend a significantly greater portion of his time in supervision, in-service activities, and attempts to up-grade the instructional program.

The usefulness of the school office depends on the principal's vision of the total educational program. The principal who envisions the office as strictly "off limits" for his staff, except when he summons them to conferences, has a narrow view of its relationship to the total educational program. One can gain insight into a school's philosophy by sitting in the outer office waiting to see a principal: a child comes in for chalk, and the secretary hands it to him with a smile, or tells him that next time he must have a note from the teacher; children come in for lunch charges, and the secretary treats them courteously, or lets them know by her voice that this is a nuisance; a teacher makes a request and the secretary makes a note, or reminds the teacher to go through channels and put it in writing; an irate parent demands to see the principal, and the secretary treats this parent calmly and courteously, or reacts in a negative way that upsets the parent even more. The secretary is the key, and her first responsibility is to make that first contact with a child, teacher, parent, or any visitor, as positive and pleasant as possible. The principal's contact with them is greatly eased if the secretary meets people of any age with humor, courtesy, and dignity, listening to each of them, screening out those whose problems she can answer and sending to the principal those who need his personal help. Usually endless details pile up on the secretary's desk in the midst of phone calls, yet the secretary must be, first and foremost, proficient in public relations, not only on the telephone, but in face-to-face contact with all ages and all kinds of people. The functions of the principal's office are many and varied, and becoming more so as additional local programs and state and federal monies and programs move into the schools. Proficient secretarial assistance, paid if possible, volunteer if necessary, must be provided for the principal who really wants to improve his school.

The principal should maintain the office along the lines of a control center to relate every person, all materials and equipment, and space and time, to the total educational program. The wide range of responsibilities are difficult to categorize into broad areas since there is so much crossing of lines, but detailed and firm management of all of them minimizes friction, expedites the use of materials, frees teachers from as many routine details as possible, develops good public relations, and attempts to relate all office activities to improvement of instruction. The following list of office activities is by no means inclusive, since each school is individualistic, but it does itemize most of the major responsibilities of the elementary school office. Neither is the list an attempt to itemize in order of importance, since each principal will see these responsibilities in a different light. Since our greatest concern should be for children, however, the areas where they are particularly vulnerable should come first. The principal of the smaller school may not have all these categories to deal with, but principals of larger schools have all these and more:

1. To serve as communication center.
2. To care for ill or injured children.
3. To act as liaison with all outside agencies concerned with children's welfare.
4. To schedule, supervise, and record emergency drills according to state laws.
5. To work with staff and children to devise and maintain necessary rules and regulations.

Administering the School Office

6. To help the bus supervisor establish routes, instruct students and parents in safety rules and regulations; to schedule field trips for instructional purposes.
7. To establish safety rules and procedures for children who walk to and from school.
8. To supervise the lunch program.
9. To schedule all special personnel and correlate their work with the entire instructional program.
10. To schedule and supervise the work of all volunteers.
11. To expedite the use of instructional supplies and textbooks.
12. To expedite the use of audio-visual materials and equipment.
13. To promote the use of the Learning Center and Preparation Room as instructional tools.
14. To keep records:
    a. For the federal government, the state, the regional center or county office, the central office, and the school itself.
    b. For cumulative records for each student.
    c. For data processing.
15. To promote the use of budget control as an aid to instruction.
16. To account for receipts and disbursements.
17. To serve as liaison for school parents' organization and for community resources.
18. To serve as a medium for public relations.
19. To work with the business office or supervisor of maintenance to maintain and improve the physical plant and site.
20. To supervise the work of salaried non-certificated personnel.
21. To schedule use of the building for after school hours.

Some implications of the responsibility of the school office for each area will be discussed, but the depth of responsibility for each one must be decided by the individual principal, or he must follow the guidelines or dictates of the central office. Specific suggestions for handling particular areas are included, but the principal must constantly search for more efficient ways to manage the multitude of details that crowd in on him. As schools become responsible for larger numbers of children from varying communities and as instructional programs become more complex, so does the responsibility of the office increase to keep all areas in perspective, to make each one as vital a part of the learning process as possible. Many times the principal can and does delegate leadership authority in a particular area, but he is still responsible for supervising all areas and all activities.

The School Office Serves as a Communications Center. The school administrator visualizes his office as the nerve center of the school, and attempts to organize its services to enhance the total school program. Since he is conscious of the many factors affecting teacher and pupil morale, he cheerfully welcomes everyone to his office. Effective interaction with school office personnel creates a feeling of teamwork, rather than an impression that the office is an obstacle to securing help when needed. Through oral and written communications, the principal helps school personnel and the public see the relationship between the many functions of the office and effective operation of the total school program. He uses the communication functions of his office as a means for improving educational opportunities.

During the school year, thousands of oral and written communications come from the principal's office or are channeled through his office to everyone connected with school activities. The success of the school literally depends on the principal's ability to communicate, and he must constantly strive to improve his communication skills. For example, the modern school office requires much correspondence, all of which should be directed toward school improvement. Whether they are letters to parents containing school information, to business houses to secure school supplies, or to one of many diverse groups from the central office up to the federal government, each is an important function of the school office. The principal, then, must be expert at letter writing, since the letters may be used to evaluate his school operation. Carelessness resulting from lack of time or to inadequate training on the part of the school secretary are poor excuses for ineffective communication.

The telephone is a demanding instrument, but the principal and the secretary can control its demands and make good use of it by following certain procedures. A capable secretary can screen many incoming calls, as well as limit the number of outgoing calls. Too often an incoming call takes precedence over some activity going on in the office, even a conference, and this should be controlled. The secretary should be expected to (1) screen incoming calls, answer those she can, and make notes for the principal or teachers to return calls; (2) relay calls to the principal if he is free; (3) make appointments for him and note them on his appointment calendar; (4) respect his privacy when he is in conference and not interrupt with a telephone call; (5) be courteous but as brief as possible with every telephone conversation; (6) relay immediately to the principal any threatening telephone call regardless of what he is doing. Telephoned bomb threats are increasing, and the principal must call upon his immediate superiors at once for help and support in responding to such situations. Even though many of these calls are hoaxes, most districts insist that the building be evacuated and searched before students re-enter.

The public address system in most buildings is limited to necessary announcements that can better be done vocally than in writing. It is easy to misuse this device. Announcements should be made only when necessary; they should be brief; they should be made at the time most convenient for most

Administering the School Office 271

classrooms; when directed at children, they should use the simplest words possible; they should not be repetitive; they should be announced by chimes to alert each room; they should contain humor where possible; they should not always be made by the principal.

Caring for Ill or Injured Children. This responsibility always entails first aid *only*, and does not involve the practice of medicine. An ill or injured child is handled with routine or emergency procedures until parents can be contacted. It is then the parents' responsibility to see that the child receives the necessary medical attention. The office should have an established procedure to insure that proper attention is given. Although there is no set procedure, the order of action should look something like this:

A. Illness
 1. Make child comfortable
 2. Take his temperature. If temperature is elevated, call parents and ask them to come get the child.
 3. If temperature is not elevated but child is obviously ill or has symptoms of a communicable disease, call parents and ask them to come get the child.
 4. If there is minor upset, such as a headache, let the child rest and check him occasionally.
B. Accident
 1. Follow prescribed first aid procedures.
 2. Contact parents immediately, at home or at work.
 3. If parents can not be contacted—
    a. Call the emergency number listed by parents.
    b. Call the family doctor listed by parents.
    c. Call local rescue unit or police for assistance.
    d. Go with child to treatment center (doctor's office, clinic, or hospital) and stay with him until parents arrive.
C. Routine
 1. Have posted near each phone
    a. Local police number.
    b. Local rescue unit number.
    c. Local fire station number.
 2. Have on hand
    a. Ice bags. Ice is excellent for first aid. It will reduce swelling, help stop minor bleeding, and relieve pain. It is the best first aid help available. Use it freely, as there is no possible way it can be misconstrued as medication.
    b. Splints, bandages, liquid soap. The new plastic inflatable splints will immobilize a broken limb and give it full protec-

tion. They are easy to use and inexpensive. Most first aid procedures allow cleansing of a minor wound with liquid soap and bandaging with sterile bandages.
c. Have posted in clinic a chart giving instructions for recognizing symptoms of the common communicable diseases such as mumps, measles, chicken pox, pink eye, impetigo, etc. If there is suspicion of infectious disease, the nurse or principal should ask parents to take the child to a physician for a medical opinion.

A good school secretary soon learns to detect the child who fakes illness. If a child persists in this behavior, a word to the principal is in order, for he will often find upon investigation that there is a classroom situation or a personality conflict bothering this child. Sometimes just talking it out will ease the situation; sometimes referral to a counselor is necessary; sometimes the teacher can quickly and easily solve the problem when she is made aware of it. To enable the secretary, principal, nurse, or an aide to make the contacts listed when a child is ill or injured, the office obviously must have the necessary information on file. The office should *insist* that the child's information form or health record be completed in full by parents, giving the telephone number of the home, the parents' number at work, an emergency number such as a neighbor or relative who lives close by, preference of a local doctor, and preference of a hospital. A special precaution is given here. *Mark in some special way* easily recognized by school personnel the information cards of those children whose parents, because of religious beliefs, have stated that they do not want medical treatment of any kind for their children regardless of the severity of the illness or accident. What to do? If one of these children is seriously injured, contact the parents immediately, or get the child home if possible. The principal must decide whether a child's life depends upon his immediate actions and act accordingly. In the case of severe injury, such as concussion accompanied by unconsciousness, a broken limb, or a cut artery, it is the opinion of the authors that the principal should seek immediate medical help after every effort has been made to contact parents without success.

There appears to be legal support for the principal's actions in the case of accidents but not support for expending school funds beyond the initial cost of first aid. The following case is cited:

> A pupil in a public school in West Virginia had been severely burned. Immediately after the accident the chief local administrator called a physician to attend to the child. At the request of the board of education the physician continued to provide service for the child. The Supreme Court of Appeals of West Virginia ruled that school funds could not legally be used to provide medical services of the type and extent in this instance.

Administering the School Office 273

However, the court case in West Virginia, while refusing to expend school funds, did point out that boards must be deemed to have implied authority to assume responsibility for first-aid services rendered to a pupil who is injured or becomes ill while engaged in school activities.[3]

Many school districts now have a trained nurse on the staff. Often, however, the nurse is on duty in a particular building for only a day or two per week. The secretary and the principal provide for care of ill and injured children the rest of the time. In some areas the Red Cross will train and supervise mothers who volunteer to staff the school clinic. These volunteers are trained in first aid procedures, qualified to handle minor injuries and illness, and cautioned to bring to the attention of the principal those situations that require his decision. These volunteers often assist the school nurse in maintaining up-to-date health records for each child, making parental contacts to remind them that certain immunizations, sometimes required by law, have not been done.

Office Responsibility for Emergency Drills. Every state has strict rules governing emergency procedures, and the individual school's routine for building evacuation, accounting for students, marking date, time, and results, must conform to these limitations. Usually, emergency drills are required at least once a month during the school year. The principal's responsibility is clear—he shall devise procedures to evacuate pupils and personnel as quickly as possible; he shall post rules and regulations concerning such procedures; he shall inform teachers and students of the requirements; he shall hold drills at specified intervals; and he shall record the date, time of day, and evacuation time of each drill. He should work with staff and students to expedite such procedures, but only he can answer to the state's authorized representative for fulfillment of the requirements.

Scheduling Special Personnel and Correlating Their Work. The problem of scheduling and correlating the work of special personnel is one of human relations, promoting understanding between full-time staff members and the special personnel who serve the building, usually on a part-time basis. This demands communication, lots of it, and special efforts to promote the uniqueness of each special program, while correlating the specialities offered by each program with the ongoing instructional program. Having special teachers in the building on a part-time basis, as in the fields of music, art, and physical education, makes communication difficult between the classroom teacher and these special teachers. It is also difficult for the special teachers to meet with classroom teachers in order to correlate the efforts of both for the benefit of students. The principal must see that such meetings do happen, if possible, on a scheduled basis. Scheduling is always a problem, an ever-growing problem that becomes more complex as we add more programs in the elementary school. Large groups such as band and vocal groups often end up in some odd rehearsal space—perhaps even the boiler room. There is just not enough space in most elementary buildings for all the activities we would like to pursue for the children's benefit. There are not enough nooks and crannies that afford some semblance of privacy where adults can work with small groups of children. Even finding a quiet spot for the counselor or the psychologist is sometimes difficult. The principal's office is often used for such activities if no other place is available. A new suggestion for housing special programs and their personnel is given in chapter 12, with a discussion of the principal's leadership role in making maximum use of all auxiliary services. It is the responsibility of the principal to schedule, correlate, and supervise the work of all special personnel.

Expediting Use of Instructional Supplies. This function of the school office is a basic responsibility of the elementary school principal. Nothing is more discouraging to teachers than to have to go through an abundance of red tape or to feel that they must apologize for needing materials. If the principal has established the machinery for determining (prior to budget-making time) the anticipated needs of his staff during the year, supplies should be on hand for the opening of school. A staff-developed policy for using supplies can help teachers appreciate the costs involved and may lead to greater concern for and better use of such materials.

Although many school systems purchase supplies through the purchasing agent at the central office, more freedom is being extended to individual school staffs in determining their own needs. One practice allots a fixed amount of money per pupil for instructional supplies. Such a practice permits the principal to prepare a more accurate budget and assures teachers of getting whatever they need. The principal must, of course, work within the framework of central office policies concerning such matters.

The Department of Elementary School Principals, National Education Association, in a 1968 research report,[4] had responses from 2,292 elementary schools to the question, "What best describes your individual role in selecting instructional materials for your school?" The report noted that:

> In the total sample 54.2 percent of the principals believe their role in selecting instructional materials is to work with their staffs in listing the materials needed for the school's program. More than one third report that the decisions on instructional materials are made largely by school system committees with little opportunity to make changes; 7.4 percent report that the central office makes the decisions.[5]

There was a singificant difference in the method used for selection of instructional materials when tabulations were made by the size of school systems:

Administering the School Office

> In the larger school systems (3000 or more pupils) the decisions on instructional materials are likely to be made by school system committees or the central office. In the smaller systems (300-2,000 pupils) a surprising 75.3 percent of the supervising principals report that instructional materials are largely determined by the school faculty and the principal working together.[6]

The section of the report concerning selection of instructional materials supports the assumption that more school systems are granting more authority to principals and their staffs in selection of materials, for the concluding statement says:

> In general three pertinent conclusions can be made: (a) in the decade (1958–1968) there has been a marked decline in the proportion of supervising principals reporting that the selection of instructional materials is handled by the central office; (b) there has been substantial increase in the proportion of supervising principals reporting that decisions on materials are made largely by school system committees; (c) the pattern of selection of materials by faculty-principal cooperation in the individual school continues to be the dominant pattern although reported by a slightly smaller proportion of all supervising principals in 1968 as compared with the total group in 1958.[7]

Practices in issuing textbooks vary from state to state as well as from system to system. At least four plans for distribution of textbooks are operating throughout the nation: (1) state ownership and free usage; (2) school board ownership and free usage; (3) school board or individual school ownership and rental to pupils; and (4) pupil purchase. There may also be variations on these four plans. Regardless of the plan in use, the principal must take some precautions. The principal is responsible for an accurate accounting; records in most cases are furnished by the central office, and they must be kept up-to-date. If books are rented or sold within the school, an inventory should be readily available, as well as an accounting of funds. The principal should carefully check books received against orders placed to avoid shortages.

Expediting Purchase and Use of Audio-visual Equipment. The principal has a responsibility to purchase the best-quality equipment possible for use in his building. This may be a problem if the central office, through bid procedures, will order certain items because of a low bid, only to find that in actual use a particular item will not withstand normal hard usage in the classroom. Here again, it is the responsibility of all the administrators in a district to work with the central office, ask the help of persons skilled in the audio-visual field, and set up criteria for the purchase of audio-visual equipment. Once this is done, and approved by the board of education, the business office has official backing to control the quality of all items submitted for competitive bidding. When a particular item of equipment is needed for a program, and when it is the only item that will exactly meet the needs of the program, the principal should not hesitate to insist that only this item and not a substitute be purchased.

Equipment which will not take normal classroom usage, consistently needs repair, and has too much down-time, can readily be identified, and such items are then listed with the business office as unacceptable for future bidding or purchase.

Many schools now combine with neighboring schools or districts to form a purchase group which can, through large group purchasing, save substantial amounts of money for each school and district. What items are put up for bids depends upon group need, but they range from pencils and paper to projection bulbs and all types of audio-visual equipment. If top-quality items of any kind are to be obtained by bidding, the purchase group should also prepare quality and reliability criteria for such items. Since purchasing through bidding is usually done once a year, the principal, through an inventory sheet, can easily add the consumable items used during the year, such as projection bulbs, and have facts to back up his requests for the coming year.

There should be a quantity of projection bulbs for every projector on hand at all times, for nothing is more irritating to a teacher than to plan a program in which a specific piece of projection equipment is to be used, only to find that there are no bulbs on hand and the one in the machine has just burned out. Keep in mind that equipment out of repair is useless and results in low teacher morale.

EQUIPMENT CHECK-OUT FORM					
Date & time to be used	Type of equipment	Place to be used	Name of person	Date returned & person returning
1-6-71 2:10 p.m.	Sound Projector Screen	Auditorium	R. Finch	1-6-71 R.F.
1-15-71 8:00 A.M.	Opaque Projector	Classroom 101	C. Myor	1-16-71 C.M.
1-19-71	Film Strip Projector and Screen	Room 203	B. Stevens	

Figure 11

An Equipment Check-out Form

How much the audio-visual equipment is used depends on the principal's attitude. If he feels that normal use causes too-frequent breakage or breakdown, his attitude obviates much classroom use, since teachers will be uneasy over the possibility of breaking something. It is the authors' opinion that the school office must keep records that will facilitate use of all materials by everyone in the school. In fact, if a philosophy of education advocates that children shall be as deeply involved in the learning process as possible, the audio-visual equipment and concomitant materials must be available to students as well as staff. Many students handle audio-visual equipment casually and competently because they have grown up with it and accept its use as a matter of course.

Keeping Records. Keeping records in the elementary school office is a necessity, often a time-consuming chore for the principal, but one that must be done with or without additional administrative or secretarial help. The objective of all record keeping is to supply information concerning any particular part of the total operation of the school, for use within the building, as required by the central office, as required by state or federal government agencies, or to assist local official government agencies concerned with the welfare of children. Records properly kept can reveal many facets of the school's operation, can furnish information for compiling comparative data, and in many instances, particularly through budget control, can be used as a means for improving the instructional program. Records normally fall into two categories: (1) those kept for financial and attendance purposes (attendance is tied with finances because most states allocate money to schools according to the average daily membership), (2) records that expedite ordering, storing, and distributing equipment and materials.

Special programs funded by the state or federal government require accurate record keeping of personnel involved in the programs, and to account for materials and equipment used, with particular emphasis on accurate and detailed information for evaluative procedures. True, the central office, which usually designates the curriculum director as the supervising administrator because many programs are school-wide, usually maintains most of the necessary records, but information about each program must be supplied by the local school. Since many of the programs are structured to involve teachers and parents, more and more principals, parents, and staff members are becoming involved in writing proposals, applications for funding of programs, supervision of programs within the school, and, of course, evaluation of each program. Any program funded by agencies or foundations outside the local school district will require accurate record keeping. Again, the simplest method is the best, the only requisite being that accurate information is available when needed. One of the simplest and most accurate methods known to the authors makes use of the common three-ring notebook. For every program requiring continuing correspondence and record keeping, a notebook is marked with the title of the program and kept up-to-date either by the principal or his secretary. It is a simple matter to keep all information for a particular program in the appropriate notebook by punching each page as it comes to the principal's desk, including correspondence, record sheets, lists of staff and student personnel involved in the project, inventory sheets, observations, evaluations, and other pertinent information. Not only does such a simple system keep all information filed accurately, it also keeps all the information about the program in sequential order, which makes it easy to locate information. Schools using this system keep a separate notebook for such things as budget allocations, lunchroom information and regulations stipulated by state or federal programs, building maintenance, and others.

Regardless of the system of record keeping the principal is required or chooses to use, inventory procedures are necessary. If inventory cards or sheets are specified and furnished by the central office, the principal must work with these, but there is no reason why he cannot make suggestions for simplifying procedures and reducing detail work. Regardless of its source, any inventory sheet serves to (1) assist in budget control, (2) itemize, (3) act as running inventory, (4) become a basis for future orders. The one illustrated can also (1) allocate equipment to specific areas, (2) keep track of accessories such as projection bulbs, (3) serve as identification and verification of cost for insurance purposes, and (4) indicate all repair costs, which may well affect future purchases. Remember that if the "control card" system or something similar is used, the cards themselves act as an inventory check in combination with the teacher-request card, eliminating a special inventory sheet for instructional materials, supplies, and testbooks unless the central office requires one.

SECURING SUBSTITUTE TEACHERS

Many schools today have teacher contracts which include sick leave, personal leave, and emergency leave for a specified number of days; and for any day a teacher chooses or is forced to be absent because of illness or emergency, a substitute teacher must be secured. When a teacher plans a personal leave day in advance, which is usually the case with this special leave, it is suggested that the principal consult with her concerning her preference for a substitute to take her place. Often teachers know the substitutes and have one or more they feel can competently replace them. This also gives teachers the opportunity to call the substitute and talk over plans and details. In case of teacher absence in a team group, the substitute has help available at all times, making it much easier to conduct the class as planned by the absent teacher.

The local school district usually has an adequate list of substitutes from which to draw. The teacher who will be absent usually notifies the principal,

DESCRIPTION OF EQUIPMENT	MAKE (BRAND NAME)	MODEL NUMBER	SERIAL NUMBER	COST (1967)	SCHOOL CODE	LOCATION IN BUILDING
Overhead Proj.	National	36	03739	$110.00	OP22	Alpha Team

TYPE OF LAMP USED	LAMPS ON HAND			REPAIR DATES AND COST		
DXX	9			4/3/69 Fan Motor $19.50		

DESCRIPTION OF EQUIPMENT	MAKE (BRAND NAME)	MODEL NUMBER	SERIAL NUMBER	COST (1965)	SCHOOL CODE	LOCATION IN BUILDING
Record Player	Enco	309	0527	$65.00	RP16	Miss Smith Room 9

TYPE OF LAMP USED	LAMPS ON HAND			REPAIR DATES AND COST		
None	—			3/7/70 Overhaul $9.00		

Figure 12

A Sample Audio-visual Inventory

and he in turn secures a substitute. Another method is also now being used. Some schools maintain a master list compiled by the main office listing all available substitutes, their preference of schools, days of week available, and preferred subject and grade level or team. Duplication of calls to one substitute is avoided by having a secretary on the school switchboard one or more hours before school time. After a call from a principal or teacher, this secretary secures substitutes from the master list and directs them to the right building. If this plan is not in use in your district, the administrators in the district might discuss the possibilities with the superintendent and the board of education. Most schools using this plan have the switchboard secretary report early and leave early, thus avoiding additional cost. This plan also saves many early-morning calls on the part of principals.

Part of the principal's before-school preparation should be to secure the list of possible substitutes, some of whom he will already know. If at all possible, interview in advance any person who hopes to substitute in your building. For some emergencies this may not always be possible, but most persons who desire to substitute usually want to visit the building and see firsthand the physical conditions in which they will be working. This seems to be especially true of open-space, team-teaching buildings. During the interview be sure to tell the prospective substitute at what hour in the morning she can expect to be called and by whom. In your files for all prospective substitutes, have the answers to such items as:

1. Name, address, phone number.
2. Certificate number and date.
3. Days of the week available.
4. Grade-level or team preference.
5. Subject preference.
6. Reference from previous experience.

Once the principal knows a substitute and something about her abilities, it is suggested that he add to the above list comments from teachers and his own observations concerning her competence.

THE PRINCIPAL'S PARTICIPATION IN BUDGET MAKING

School superintendents are beginning to permit wider participation in budget making. The elementary school principal should become informed about good budgeting procedures. If the principal finds he is able to share in the budget-making process, he must be aware, first, of the philosophy of the school budget, second, of the need to understand budget components, and third, of budgetary operational procedures.

The School Budget

Many school administrators prepare the annual school budget behind the closed doors of their offices. Although school administrators use numerous other undesirable schemes in preparing their budgets, much improvement has been noted in the budget-making process. In a recent survey of elementary principals, it was found that an increasing number of principals are being involved in the budget-making process.[8] DeYoung set the stage for a philosophy of budget making by his use of the equilateral triangle—the base depicts the educational program prescribed by the community, one side represents the financial plan, and the other the plan of expenditures.[9] A school's budget reflects the extent to which a community is willing to tax itself for the desired educational program. A philosophy of budget making which bases its expenditures on the educational program deemed satisfactory by a community requires good educational leadership.

The principal whose administrative superiors welcome his support in preparing the budget has an opportunity to demonstrate a higher degree of professional leadership than the principal who is not permitted to participate in budget decisions that vitally affect his school. Principals may readily interpret the failure of higher administrators to involve them in budget procedures, at least those directly affecting their own buildings, as lack of confidence in their ability and lack of respect for their judgment. Gross and Harriott, in a study concerning the EPL (Executive Professional Leadership) of the principal, say:

> Just as teachers are exposed to principals who offer strong or weak professional leadership, so, in turn, principals may be given variable professional leadership by their superiors. Higher administrators who themselves conform to a professional leadership definition of their role can serve as models for the principal in his efforts to lead. In doing so, they show their principals that the obstacles can be overcome and demonstrate effective strategies and techniques to this end. Therefore, we assumed, other things being equal, that principals' own professional leadership will be directly affected by experiences of this kind with their superiors, and we developed the hypothesis that: the greater the EPL displayed by the principal's immediate administrative superior, the greater the EPL of the principal.
>
> Our findings provided support for the hypothesis. Approximately one-quarter of the principals reported that their superiors infrequently helped them to understand the sources of their important problems or made principals' meetings a valuable educational activity. A similar portion described their superiors as not usually taking a strong interest in their professional development. And it was these principals who on the average had the lowest EPL scores.[10]

The principal who gives strong and enthusiastic support to his staff and involves them deeply in the allocation of funds by working with grade levels or teams, reflects his confidence in them and his respect for their professional judgment. Such a group, comprised of principal and staff, can wield strong influence upon higher-echelon administrators and the board of education in speaking out for the kind of instruction they believe children should have. It is not suggested that this is a power play, but rather that a school organized in such a way has cohesiveness and purpose that command respect.

Two related trends are affecting the role of the elementary principal in regard to professional leadership of budget management. First, larger school systems, seeking to escape the problems of bureaucracy, are moving toward decentralization of management, allowing individual principals to make more decisions regarding their own school, staff, and budget. From an operational standpoint, this enhances his role as coordinator of all special personnel, encourages increasing participation in selection of teachers, allows principal/teacher/community involvement in local school decisions, and increases his responsibility to manage the budget. Second, principals themselves, by grouping together for professional purposes, are presenting a more united front in efforts to solve problems. The following excerpt illustrates how one group organized to promote self-renewal projects, including requests for budget allocations to assist in the self-renewals:

> At its annual convention in January of 1967, the Association of Elementary School Administrators (AESA) of Los Angeles launched a long-range program of self-renewal. A study of educational funding practices in the Los Angeles Unified School District was presented, and this led to the development of an audiovisual presentation to the Board of Education entitled *The Crisis in Elementary Education: An Introduction to a Master Plan for Elementary Education*. Printed copies of the report were left with each Board member on the date of presentation, November 27, 1967, so that the facts would be available to him as needed. Between the convention and the board report a two-pronged program of education was launched. One was aimed at the support division of our school district at the director level. The other was geared for the public through KNXT, the CBS television outlet in Los Angeles. Both built an awareness of elementary school needs. AESA is now preparing the second board report to illustrate the concept of self-renewal at the school site. An important part of this presentation will be the request for budget allocations which will enable the self-renewal process to begin.
>
> Has the role of the elementary principal in urban schools changed in the past ten years? You bet it has! It will continue to change as we conscientiously and courageously speak to the importance of elementary education in our public school systems, responsibly practice the unique role of middle management, and enthusiastically involve our faculties, children, parents, universities, business communities, governing boards, and anyone else who will help in the exciting process of self-renewal.[11]

Components of the Budget

To facilitate the compilation of community and staff requests for improved educational services, the principal should be familiar with the various sections of the budget. The following headings are commonly used: (a) personnel services (salaries and wages); (b) supplies (textbooks, library, art, industrial arts, fuel, janitor supplies, office supplies, classroom supplies, etc.); (c) materials and maintenance (buildings, grounds, buses, furniture); (d) equipment replacement (buses, educational equipment, maintenance equipment); (e) contract and open-order service (water and sewer, electricity, telephone, tuition to other districts, freight charges, repairs to buildings); (f) fixed charges (insurance, teacher retirement, workmen's compensation, auditor and treasurer's fees, etc.); (g) capital outlay (improvement of site, equipment, old buildings, equipment offices); (h) interest on loans.

Obviously, the principal who is working to improve educational opportunities must be realistic and recognize that budget items must somehow be financed. Although several sources of income contribute to school receipts, local taxes carry the load in most communities.

The Principal's Duties in the Budget Operation

The principal, like the superintendent, must be a watchdog of budget expenditures in his school. If sufficient cooperative planning by the school staff goes into the budget-making process and teachers are informed of the extent to which their requests are approved, the principal need not gain the reputation of trying to save money which has been appropriated for a specific need. However, he must be aware of his responsibility to the public as well as to his staff, and try to prevent waste and inefficiency.

In many school systems, control of the budget rests with someone in the central office, even though the program of every individual school is affected by budget allocations and procedures, and each principal is involved automatically with budget problems. How much he is involved covers a wide range. At the low end of the scale his involvement may be only clerical, keeping track of requisitions, purchase orders, and materials delivered for his school. At the high end of the scale, the principal may be heavily involved in budgetary procedures and allocations, including working with the central office and the board of education to develop a philosophy of budgeting that will support present instructional programs and furnish incentives toward improvement. It means working with staff within the building to schedule budget allocations for improving the instructional programs, which means that allocated funds can serve as a base upon which the principal and his staff can furnish funds for program development within the limits of each budgetary item. A necessary requisite for such involvement is a philosophy among teachers, administrators, and the board of education that all items of the budget concerned with the instructional program be allocated on a per pupil basis, thus allowing exact amounts for each allocation to be known by the principal and his staff. Teachers, principals, and central office administrators, when working with the board of education toward adoption of budgetary procedures, should state that when budget allocations are adequate, the pressure is taken off individual schools to support programs through fund drives. The reduction of such fund drives fosters better community relations.

Accounting for Receipts and Disbursements. This function of the school office must not be considered lightly by the beginning principal or even the experienced one. Even the smallest elementary school handles thousands of dollars each year. In states where there are no public statutes to control activity funds, the principal's personal responsibility for these funds is even greater than for funds from the board of education.[12] There is little doubt that most principals are honest, but due to faulty handling of school accounts and an attitude that school funds are the concern of the principal only, some administrators have moved on to other positions leaving behind some question in the minds of the former staff as well as the community concerning school funds:

> Mr. Drew came to his new position as principal of the Fair Hill School. Upon arriving at his office, he found a personal check, written by the former principal, lying on the desk. A note was appended stating that this was the balance in the school account. At the opening of school Mr. Drew informed his staff of the funds the teachers had to work with that year. They were dismayed to find that the balance in the school account was much less than their expectations. They were sure there must be some mistake, since they had raised at least four times that amount last year. However, they agreed that they never did know exactly how much money was in the account, since they were not informed or invited to see the financial records.

Such doubts as pointed out above are not ill-founded. The preceding principal was no doubt honest, but he failed to use a satisfactory plan for accounting for school funds. The following discussion points up some of the safeguards the principal must use in handling school funds.

School Receipts. There is no reason for modern schools to use inadequate procedures for safeguarding the school's funds. All income should be accounted for by a duplicate receipt showing source of the funds, date received, amount, and signature of the person who received the funds. Such a receipt is shown in figure 13. Many types of receipts are available from various commercial school supply houses. Receipt forms may also be duplicated and stapled together by schools which lack funds for purchasing receipts. Regardless of the source of the receipts, the important point is that the person depositing money with the principal be given an official receipt, the money deposited to the correct school account as stipulated by

Administering the School Office 285

the clerk of the business office, and a copy of the receipt kept at the local school. When a receipt is given to a parent who is paying for some item for a child, such as fees for supplies, it is a wise precaution to put both the child's name and the parent's name on the receipt, since many children have family names different from that of a brother, sister, step-brother or step-sister, or even different than the adults they live with. The same receipt illustrated can be used for deposit to any fund drive, such as Parents' Association, by using the line marked Fund.

Bookkeeping methods and forms for organizing and handling financial accounts are usually furnished by the central office, but if they are not they can be purchased from an office-supply firm. The office should be equipped with an adequate safe where money is kept until deposited. However, it is a good practice to deposit money daily if it amounts to ten dollars or more. Use of the night deposit box at the local bank is frequently advisable. This permits the principal to deposit immediately any large sums that may have been collected at a school fund-raising function. Some schools are built today without safes to force daily deposit of funds with the business office or the local bank as a deterrent to break-ins and thefts. Some districts require that all deposits be made through the business or clerk's office for accounting purposes and safety, and the principal is not permitted to use bank facilities. It is not a wise procedure to divide money among several teachers to be taken home for safekeeping after a school activity. Such practices can lead to embarrassment or even loss of stature if some mishap should occur. If the principal's banking privileges are restricted, he must make

```
┌─────────────────────────────────────────────────────────────┐
│      MAPLE GROVE ELEMENTARY SCHOOL OFFICIAL RECEIPT         │
│                           Date  2-10-70                     │
│   Received of   Louise Zimmerman                            │
│     Five                                  Dollars $5.00     │
│                                                             │
│   For (Fund)  _____          │
│   For (Child)   Jane Brownell                               │
│   Account   Student Fees                                    │
│                          Signed   E. Jarrell                │
│                                      Principal             │
└─────────────────────────────────────────────────────────────┘
```

Figure 13

A Sample Receipt

prior arrangements for night banking deposit through the business office, and follow up the next day with the required school deposit slip. If the school has a safe, no sizeable amount of money should be left in it overnight or over the weekend; if there is no safe, money must be deposited daily through the prescribed procedures. This practice does reduce the chance of mistakes or theft.

Disbursements. The principal should be able to account for all disbursements of school funds. The disbursements should be paid by school check as directed by the business office or the clerk of the board of education. Usually the principal, for any disbursement, does not handle the money or the checks, but sends his request for payment of an account through channels, usually in the form of a purchase order. The clerk or business manager attaches an official board number to the purchase order if funds are available in the particular account specified. The principal's office is responsible for keeping running accounts of each budget allocation, making sure that ordered items match the budget description, checking each item when it arrives, and informing the business office or clerk that the item is satisfactory and that a check should be sent to cover that particular purchase order. Usually disbursement procedures require a written request, with a copy retained in the school files, for any money to be paid from any budget account, including the principal's fund or the school activity account. This is a safeguard the principal should welcome, since it usually relieves him of many banking and accounting procedures and protects him fully since all expenditures are fully accounted for and double-filed.

Liaison for Parents and Community

More and more, parents are becoming involved in school programs, primarily as volunteer aides in the instructional program. Parents' organizations related to the school deserve much credit for enrolling personnel for these activities, and the principal, acting as liaison, is responsible for instruction, scheduling, and supervision of volunteers. In one school known to the authors there are 197 families represented and more than 100 mothers volunteer their services each week, serving as aides to classroom teachers, doing clerical work, acting as guides for visitors, tutoring individual children, and many others. The office, from which comes or through which flows the constant stream of information concerning all the activities of the school, is the communication and coordination center for all school activities, whether these activities involve children, teachers, paraprofessionals, or volunteers. The parents' association is an important companion to most elementary schools, and the beneficial activities sponsored by enthusiastic parents' groups are beyond counting. The principal, in his role as administrator, schedules and correlates the activities of the parents' organization with the ongoing school activities.

How much the moms and dads of the parents' association contribute in time and talent to the school depends upon the principal's view of their usefulness to his school. As liaison, the principal's responsibilities toward parents' organizations fall into two categories—one, correlating the activities and programs of the parents' organizations and the staff for the children's benefit, and two, encouraging and guiding the organization and individual parents toward volunteer services in the instructional programs.

Judicious use of community resources can be richly rewarding for a school, and the literature contains numerous references to various ways principals and teachers may utilize community resources. In the field of social studies, particularly, the possibilities are limitless. In every school community there are parents, friends of the school, small businesses, professional people, and many others who can add a personal touch to a particular topic being studied by students, bringing to them a richness, a depth, a warmth and reality that cannot be obtained in any other way. Schools have found that individuals representing every facet of the community eagerly accept invitations to come to the school and share their experiences with young children. The office serves as liaison for these individuals or groups, sending invitations, scheduling time and place, providing audio-visual aids, etc. The principal often has the pleasure of forwarding letters of thanks from a speaker or group to the students, or from students to a speaker or group. The school should have a file of available community resources; not just speakers, but also places of interest, businesses that welcome tours, historically significant places, and others. With the help of teachers and parents to add notes that may be of interest in planning an activity, this file can be kept up-to-date without difficulty.

Public Relations

The school office is frequented by many visitors, and the prevailing climate or working atmosphere in the office is likely to remain with each visitor when he leaves. Equally important, however, are the physical factors of the office layout. Many psychological studies point out the effects of a physical factor, such as color, upon the attitudes of visitors to an office. A good social climate and an attractively painted office, neatly arranged, enhance the public's attitude toward the school, the principal, and his staff.

As noted earlier, the secretary is the key to public relations so far as office visitors are concerned. First impressions are formed by a combination of the physical appearance and the reception given them by the secretary or the principal. The secretary is often the buffer between parent and principal or between parent and teacher, and as such has a vitally important role in human relationships.

Public relations spreads far beyond the walls of the school, and the principal and his staff have a responsibility for improving public relations through positive associations with children and parents. It has been said that the best school public relations device ever found is the child who goes home from school feeling successful and happy, and eager to return to school the next day.

The Need for a School Secretary

An important addition to the elementary school staff is the office secretary. This position has developed as a result of parents' and superintendents' recognition of the fact that a principal's professional ability, preparation, and experience are wasted if he is required to spend his time at clerical duties. The growing importance of the school secretary's position is recognized increasingly by state education associations, some of which have established departments of school secretaries. Such groups of employees are making notable efforts to improve school operations.

No national pattern determines when a school is large enough to warrant an office secretary. Smallenburg[13] recommends employing a full-time secretary when school enrollment reaches 400, and one full-time and one half-time secretary in schools above 800 in enrollment. The enrollment factor, however, cannot be used as the sole criterion. Modern schools require clerical services of a somewhat different nature from those of traditional schools. Teachers who use an informal instructional approach require many more materials. In addition, modern schools keep and use more information about children, so their record systems are more detailed. Some authorities have pointed out that the socioeconomic levels of the community may also influence the functions of the secretary, since schools located in underprivileged areas require more and different services.[14]

In many instances, the teaching principal as well as the supervising principal will require the services of a secretary. In one investigation it was found that teaching principals spend less time in administration, supervision, pupil personnel, clerical, and community activities than do supervising principals.[14] Since 85.6 percent spend 40 percent or more of their workweek teaching, it is quite obvious that other functions must be cut to a minimum.

The contention, then, is that the addition of a full- or part-time clerk to the school enrolling fewer than 400 pupils, when the principal is teaching full-time, will result in more efficient administration and improved classroom teaching. Thus, in summing up factors for determining the need for an office secretary, one must include: (1) the school's philosophy of education; (2) the teaching time of the administrator; (3) availability of office space and equipment; (4) school enrollment; and (5) the socio-economic level of the community.

Functions of the Office Secretary. It has been emphasized that the office in the modern elementary school must serve the whole school. Essential to the achievement of this end is the use of the teamwork approach in carrying on the functions of the school office. The teamwork approach helps the secretary feel she is a vital part of the school staff, and that the success of the office in fulfilling its function is largely her responsibility.

The secretary must have the kind of personality which is acceptable to most people. The human relations function of the office secretary in a public school is vitally important, since she greets many people whom the rest of the staff never see. In addition, she answers the telephone innumerable times and answers endless questions from children throughout the day. Her constant contact with pupils requires understanding and appreciation of children.

The functions of the office secretary could be classified according to the following categories: (1) human relations, (2) communication services, (3) records and filing, (4) assisting the principal with purchase procedures, storage, inventory, and disbursement of materials, (5) bookkeeping and financial records, (6) telephone service, (7) keeping schedules and appointments, and (8) duplicating and mimeographing.

The principal can improve the secretary's effectiveness and at the same time give her a feeling of security by: (1) defining her duties through a job-analysis program, (2) setting up evaluation periods to review her work, (3) reviewing daily the demands of her work, (4) identifying problems for which she will seek solutions, and (5) delegating certain authority with responsibility.

The Teachers' Secretary. A somewhat novel idea, but one of much value in improvement of instruction, is the addition of a teachers' secretary to the staff. The teachers' secretary is a comparatively inexpensive addition to the staff if the principal and the school board measure the increased teacher morale resulting from this service. Teachers have many uses for typing, duplicating, and other clerical services. Preparing and duplicating seatwork in arithmetic and other subjects is one service that can be provided by a teachers' secretary. The principal who recognizes these needs and provides for them encourages teachers to improve instruction. One school system has found that the use of teachers' secretaries pays off in building teacher morale and in improving the use of instructional aids. Mound, Minnesota, has been using the teachers' secretary successfully for a number of years.[15]

It is readily apparent that the principal must be aware of the many factors involved in adding such a person to the staff:

1. All work submitted by teachers should be carefully scheduled.
2. No teacher should monopolize the secretary.
3. Policies concerning the teachers' secretary's work should be developed cooperatively by the staff and the secretary.
4. The principal should not use the teachers' secretary unless she is completely free of other work. No teacher's work should be held up because of the principal's needs.

SUMMARY

The successful school leader recognizes the importance of efficient office management, since the office facilitates the instructional work of the school. The office operation in a modern elementary school has at least six functions. These are (1) to improve the educational program, (2) to keep records, (3) to serve as a center for communications, (4) to expedite distribution of instructional supplies and textbooks, (5) to account for receipts and disbursements, and (6) to be responsible for public relations.

The school leader attempts continuously to improve the office organization and its services. He uses the best practices found in business and industry, since office functions everywhere are basically the same.

The modern school has an office secretary who, with the principal, employs a teamwork approach to improving the school's program through the services of the office. Some factors which should be considered in determining the need for an office secretary are (1) the school's philosophy, (2) the teaching time of the principal, (3) the availability of office space, (4) the school's enrollment, and (5) the socio-economic level of the community.

SUGGESTED READINGS

Cox, Robert T. and William A. Pearson. "Physical Features of the Principal's Office." *National Elementary Principal* 40 (October 1960): 17–19.

French, Marilyn. "Ten Ways to Get Along With Your Boss." *Today's Secretary* 59 (January 1957): 22–23.

Kirlin, Vernon L. "The Office Without a Secretary." *The National Elementary Principal* 40 (October 1960): 33–36.

Lawson, Douglas W. *School Administration Procedures and Policies.* New York: Odyssey, 1953, Chapter 9.

McLaughlin, Hugh W. "When A Visitor Enters Your Office." *The National Elementary Principal* 41 (May 1962).

Nash, Robert L. "Good Office Help." *National Elementary Principal* 33 (May 1954).

Stolliker, John E. "Handling Receipts in California School Districts." Doctoral dissertation, University of Southern California, 1963.

Notes

1. *The Elementary School Principalship in 1968 . . . A Research Study* (Washington, D.C.: Department of Elementary School Principals, N.E.A., 1968.)

2. Ibid., p. 70.

3. E. Edmund Reutters, Jr. and Robert R. Hamilton, Jr., *The Law of Public Education* (Mineola, N. Y.: Foundation Press, 1970), p. 231.

4. *School Principalship in 1968.*

5. Ibid., p. 81.

6. Ibid.

7. Ibid., p. 82.

8. *School Principalship in 1968.*

9. Chris A. DeYoung, *Budgeting in Public Schools* (New York: Odyssey, 1936), p. 7.

10. Neal Gross and Robert E. Harriott, "The EPL of Elementary Principals—A Study of Executive Professional Leadership," *The National Elementary Principal* 45, no. 5 (April 1966).

11. Douglas H. Naylor and James V. Traughber, "As We See It," *National Elementary School Principal* 47, no. 5 (April 1968).

12. Will French, J. Dan Hull, and B. L. Dodds, *American High School Administration: Policy and Practice* (New York: Rinehart, 1951), p. 508.

13. Harry Smallenburg, "Assignment of Clerical Assistance in Elementary and Secondary Schools," *American School Board Journal* 110 (February 1945): 38.

14. *School Principalship in 1968.*

15. Based on a communication from Dr. La Vern Krantz, former superintendent, Mound, Minnesota.

12

Administering Auxiliary Services

The auxiliary services of any school are established and organized to enhance the instructional program, and to meet special needs. The dictionary defines auxiliary as "that which helps or aids; acting as an extra help." In this context, auxiliary services refers to services to children performed by persons other than the classroom teacher or principal. Since some auxiliary services may seem quite remote or unnecessary to the inquiring layman, the educational leader will need to gauge public opinion carefully. He must not hesitate to initiate beneficial programs, but for their success, he must have the support of his school community, especially in programs that involve paraprofessionals or volunteers. He must be willing to spend time and energy explaining to parents that programs such as these do attain sound educational objectives. He should make use of research to verify his statements.

For many principals, auxiliary services present certain perplexing problems and are considered an undesirable aspect of the principalship. When auxiliary services are properly organized and managed, however, they produce opportunities for improving pupil growth. The alert principal will readily see the relationship between auxiliary services and the total educational program.

AUXILIARY PERSONNEL

All auxiliary personnel—professionals, paraprofessionals, volunteers—must feel that they are a necessary part of the total school operation. The principal can help his auxiliary staff achieve this attitude by (1) arranging for space and time for their programs, (2) showing interest in their problems and concerns, (3) encouraging their participation in policy-making decisions, (4) applying motivating factors to encourage their growth and involvement, (5) helping them relate their special skills to the childrens' needs, and (6) helping them interrelate with staff, students, and other auxiliary personnel. He shows his respect for them by his willingness to involve them in school problem-solving procedures, and accepting their particular talents as unique and positive contributions to child growth and development.

If the principal uses the job-description approach[1] with auxiliary personnel, he should know each person's duties and render assistance by clarifying these duties through mutual understanding. His goal must be to develop a teamwork approach through clarifying duties of and relationships between instructional personnel and auxiliary personnel. There are five categories of auxiliary personnel: (1) certificated personnel; (2) salaried non-certificated personnel; (3) paraprofessionals (special certifications); (4) volunteers; and (5) agencies of government concerned with children's welfare, whose personnel are usually specialists in their fields. The educational family tree is constantly developing new branches of service to children, and as communities become aware of the vital needs for preventive techniques during early childhood, more and more of these services will be added. Many of them will move from the volunteer-staffed category to programs staffed by specialists, certificated specialists who are on the salary schedule and whose professional talents are fully utilized. No one can predict with certainty what the future will bring in the way of auxiliary services in elementary schools, but it is safe to say that as dedicated professional educators identify the need for new services, programs will arise to meet those needs. The following list indicates the auxiliary personnel and services available to children in thousands of elementary schools across the United States, although many children are still without many of these services:

Group A—Certificated Personnel
1. Guidance counselor
2. Psychologist
3. Speech therapist
4. Art and music teachers
5. Physical education teacher
6. School social worker
7. Reading specialist (local or federal program)
8. Other federal programs requiring certificated teachers
9. Librarian

Group B—Salaried non-certificated personnel
1. Nurse
2. Lunchroom personnel
3. Bus drivers
4. Maintenance personnel

Group C—Paraprofessionals (sometimes with special certification)
1. Teacher aides
2. Library aides
3. Tutors
4. Perceptual motor skills (body management) instructor
5. Supervisors of pupils, such as lunchroom

Group D—Outside personnel and services
1. Central office of local school district
2. County office or regional district office
3. Government agencies
4. Service organizations or agencies
5. Local community service organizations
6. Individuals

Each auxiliary program's unique qualities and services must be correlated with the total educational program, given as much emphasis as possible to utilize its potential, but not allowed to dominate. The principal's role is to balance these services, to guide teachers and parents to full utilization of each program to meet the needs of a child, or a group of children.

This section concerns some of the common problems and conventional safeguards involved in administering the auxiliary services. The principal who utilizes proper leadership skills will find that his actions result in an efficient organization and management of auxiliary services, which will produce valuable experiences in group living both for children and for school personnel.

The Guidance Counselor

The guidance counselor is a specialist in helping the professional staff identify problems that block or inhibit learning. His role in this respect is rapidly gaining the support of teachers, public, and state departments. Elementary guidance counselors are now required to be certified in many states, and their particular services to children are constantly being more clearly defined. Such services go far beyond testing, for the guidance counselor is the liaison between the child and all other auxiliary services and personnel. Role differentiation must be clear between the guidance counselor and the school psychologists. Their functions are not one and the same, but they do complement each other. The guidance counselor and guidance services are discussed fully in chapter 9.

The Psychologist

The principal must be aware of the job description of the school psychologist and should evaluate his work to determine the extent to which he accomplishes the identified tasks. The psychologist is primarily a diagnostician.

His chief role in the elementary school should be to diagnose learning disabilities. The school fortunate enough to have a psychologist on the staff or on call, who establishes rapport with children referred to him, has an educational ally with great potential for improving a child's self-image. The psychologist who hopes to be successful in an elementary school situation must go far beyond the traditional "testing" program. At times he must be a counselor, for teachers, students, and parents, for if he cannot interpret to the concerned parties his test results and his suggestions for improvement, his efforts are in vain. He must be one of the guidance team members contributing to recognition, diagnosis, and remediation of childrens' problems, working with the guidance counselor, teachers, nurse, social worker, and any other adults, whether school staff or outside personnel, to help meet the needs of a particular child or a group of children. He should be included in the in-service education activities, asked to interpret to the staff members and parents his role in diagnosing problems and the follow-up procedures expected of parents and staff.

The psychologist should be skillful in counseling parents according to his assessment of a child's psychological needs. Working alone, or with and through the guidance counselor, he must be able to relate to parents psychological findings concerning the sensitive areas of mental retardation, extreme hypertension, lack of gross motor development, retardation in perceptual motor skills, recommendation for slow-learner classes, neurological impairment, indications of mental illness, and other findings which are usually difficult for parents to accept. Often it is a blow to their pride to hear that their child has an impairment. They may be able to accept it intellectually but often have difficulty accepting it emotionally. The psychological assessment is worthless unless all adults concerned with the welfare of the child work as a team to understand the problem, sympathize with the parents and the child, and do all within their power to see that school programs are geared as much as possible to the child's needs and that parents are referred to outside specialists or agencies that offer the necessary services.

As the school staff becomes more aware of children's psychological needs and more informed about psychological malfunctions, there is a growing demand for professional psychological services. Teachers stand on firm educational ground here, for there is ample research evidence to show that habits, psychological as well as others, are set at a very early age, and that early detection of problems is vital for remediation techniques to be most successful.

When a psychologist is available, it becomes the principal's responsibility to maintain a priority list of children to be scheduled for conferences, to provide space and time for the work of the psychologist, and to correlate his activities with all other special personnel, the staff, and the instructional program. Any guidance program that hopes to be well-rounded and provide adequate services to children must include the services of a psychologist. In turn, the psychologist must consider himself a member of the team and must be willing to counsel and discuss with the team the educational needs of a child and his assessment of the child in relation to those needs. Valett says:

> . . . it is quite obvious that the findings from individual child study and psychological evaluation do carry implications for improving learning. Through his concentration on the individual pupil, the school psychologist is able to obtain much objective data which, when professionally interpreted and presented to those concerned, can have a significant effect on curriculum.[2]

The Speech Therapist

The principal must coordinate the work of the therapist with the teachers in his building. The speech therapist is a member of the school's team and the principal must facilitate this service by providing work space, scheduling adequate time, and building a cooperative relationship between teachers and therapist. The speech therapist may also need to call in other auxiliary personnel to assist with certain kinds of problems.

Coordinating Music, Art, and Physical Education

Music, art, and physical education teachers are listed as auxiliary personnel because in many instances they serve more than one building within the district. Even if they are assigned to one building full-time, they are often looked upon as "special" teachers by the rest of the staff. The principal's responsibility is to correlate the activities of these teachers with the classroom instructional programs through encouragement, communication, and in-service activities, whether they serve his building on a part-time or full-time basis. Much has been written about correlation of music and art programs with classroom instructional programs, but physical education is traditionally so separated from the instructional activities that very little has been accomplished in teaching children something of life values or attitudes toward lifelong recreational activities. Many devices have been tried to dovetail music and art programs with instruction. School practices range from tight scheduling of music and art with no connection with classroom programs to leaving these teachers completely free of schedules hoping that, as consultants, their services will be better utilized in correlating music and art skills and activities with the teachers' objectives in classrooms. This last method has not been too successful in most cases because teachers either do not see the value of music and art experiences for their students or they do not take time to confer with the art and music teachers for assistance in instruction, or because they resent the fact that there is no scheduled period when they are free to leave the room while the art or music teacher takes the class. Although the authors cannot quote a survey, it is suspected that the solution lies somewhere in between, with music and art teachers scheduled for classes most of the time but allowed a planning period or time to meet with staff on a cooperative basis for development of program ideas.

The principal's job is to involve the special teachers in grade-level or team-level meetings working toward use of all media to improve instruction, to encourage them to initiate special projects, and to encourage classroom teachers to use the talents and skills of these teachers toward improvement of instruction.

Physical Education Serves All Children. Some educators and communities are beginning to take a sharply critical look at the physical education programs offered to elementary children. They say that most programs have the wrong aims or are conducted for the physically-adept minority, that high-pressure competitive sports serve the ambitions of instructors or parents, and do little to enhance the physical development of elementary school children. Many dedicated physical education teachers agree that elementary school gym instruction desperately needs improvement.

One of the high priorities of the physical education instructor should be education of the whole child, with emphasis on perceptual motor skills. Piaget, the noted Swiss child psychologist, has demonstrated that a child's earliest learnings are motor oriented as a result of large-muscle activities such as running, jumping, reaching, and that these are vital to later intellectual growth. Youngsters lacking coordination skills must be identified at the earliest possible age, and proper instruction given to children who are lacking in motor development or have perceptual-motor-skill handicaps. This is rightfully the province of the physical education teacher, who should be a leader in developing such programs. Even though the American public is strongly oriented toward competitive sports, this should not deter the principal from working with his community, his staff, and the physical education instructor to revitalize the elementary physical education program.

The School Social Worker

Elementary principals lack time to consult with parents about children's problems. The telephone is a valuable time-saver, but a telephone conversation cannot take the place of a face-to-face conference. In many instances the conference should take place in the child's home rather than in the school office, for this is the opportunity to meet the parents on their ground and see the child as a member of the home and family. Few principals can find time during the school week to schedule home conferences, and fewer yet have the time or energy to conduct such conferences after school hours. Some boards of education and superintendents discourage the principal's leaving the building at all during school hours, even for professional reasons.

One professionally certified position added to the staff, that of school social worker, can help solve the problem of home/school contacts and add a valuable dimension to home/school/community relationships.

The professional social worker is skilled in the areas of personal contact, counseling, home visits, referrals to social agencies where necessary, and can give a personal touch to home/school relationships, not only because of training and background, but because the job description specifies that this shall be his full-time work. Children with negative social attitudes, families in trouble that affects their children, attendance problems, parent-education programs, potential drop-outs, conditions that cause children mental or physical distress—these and many other areas can be the responsibility of the social worker. The responsibility cannot be his alone, however, for the principal and other members of the guidance team must share in identifying problems, counseling, suggesting solutions, and supporting agreed-upon action. There is no question that early remediation of childrens' problems contributes significantly to reducing social problems, and the school is fortunate indeed whose community and board of education realize the importance of such activities and provide for them by adding a social worker to the elementary staff as a full-time assistant.

The Reading Specialist

Reading was among the first specialized areas to be added to many elementary schools. Even before federal money was available, many schools had convinced their communities that it was not possible to conduct a reading program to meet the needs of all children with a thirty to one pupil/teacher ratio. Consequently, reading specialists began to appear on elementary staffs. When federal funds became available, many more specialized personnel were added to the instructional staff, with the hope that different programs and techniques might be offered to children with reading difficulties. The perceptive principal and staff recognize that the special reading teacher is one of a team, the *guidance* team, and that the staff and the guidance team must work together to make adequate diagnoses of reading difficulties and problems be made. Often the reading specialist found himself in deep water when testing showed problems in perceptual motor skills for which he had no training. These skills had to be improved if there was hope for improving the child's reading. Other problems became evident, the same ones mentioned before—hypertension, brain damage, dyslexia, neurological impairment, lack of motor skills and others—and the reading specialist found he needed far more knowledge and many more materials than books and workbooks to begin to solve some of the problems.

The principal whose staff includes a reading specialist should encourage this specialist to obtain at least a working knowledge of the handicaps that can stall or stop reading progress. He should also encourage his participation as a member of the guidance team, one whose skills of diagnosis and instruction fit into the total pattern when analyzing a child's instructional needs and prescribing instructional changes to meet that child's needs. Again the principal's responsibility is that of coordination and cooperation, helping the staff see the special strengths of the reading specialist and helping the reading specialist combine his strengths and skills with all other adults for the benefit of children.

DEVELOPING THE MULTI-MEDIA CONCEPT OF THE LIBRARY

Many agencies and professional associations believe the library must become a multi-media instructional center for teaching children the skills of learning. Such titles as Multi-Media Center, Instructional Media Center, Learning Center, Resource Center, etc., are revealing, since they imply more than the traditional book-oriented library and instead, advocate the concept of multi-dimensional educational audio-visual materials and equipment. Since the terms Instructional Media Center or Instructional Materials Center seem to encompass all that should be included in the expanded library, the initials IMC will be used for identification.

The basic purpose of the IMC is to broaden the students' opportunities for exposure to many materials related to the instructional program and to increase the number of available approaches to basic concept understanding. By increasing the available approaches, we also increase the possibilities for a student to have successful experiences with multi-media instructional materials, and since success breeds success, the student is encouraged to seek further experiences through the IMC available resources.

Elementary schools in this nation furnish leadership in many areas, including that of developing IMC's for improving the learning environment and opportunities; yet we still lag far behind the fields of science and technology. Davis says:

> When we look around and discover that the majority of schools are operating about the same way they operated at the turn of the century, we realize that ours is an evolution rather than a revolution. However, change is coming with the growing realization that children who merely learn to manipulate memorized rules, are inadequately prepared for the future. Educators are becoming aware of the fact that teachers must place an emphasis on cognition rather than regurgitation, on research rather than rote. To meet the changing needs of society, schools must create an atmosphere that encourages exploration and discovery.[3]

Elementary schools are again taking the lead in developing the concepts and content of the IMC, which is basically structured to offer children the opportunity to learn the "how-to" skills. There are many patterns of internal organization concerning IMC development, but three basic patterns predominate: (1) the local IMC within each building in the district, structured and staffed to meet the needs of that particular building, and for the use of the teachers and students within the building; (2) the centralized IMC maintained for the entire district and from which materials are disseminated to local schools; and (3) a combination or variation of the first two patterns, usually with certain materials and equipment contained in local schools and certain more expensive equipment or materials housed in a central IMC. All three plans have merit, and determining which will best serve the district depends on many factors, including money, administrator/teacher decisions, and available personnel.

Services of the Elementary School IMC

With the advent of new teaching methods, scientific studies in child growth and development, and many curriculum innovations, the stage was set for the emergence of the elementary school instructional media center. It can be said that this service was born of necessity. Only in recent years, however, has the IMC begun to find its place in the elementary school.

The modern elementary school recognizes the importance of the library services in a good school program. For example, inquiry teaching in the modern school has created a need for a wealth of materials—books, magazines, pamphlets, bulletins, pictures, maps, charts, and other instructional aids. If these materials are to be used effectively and economically, they must be catalogued, housed, and maintained. New materials must be selected, and obsolete or worn-out materials discarded.

The heuristic, or discovery, approach now being used as the basis for many commercial programs as well as in revitalized classroom instruction adds to the necessity for the above-mentioned materials, in addition to appropriate audio-visual equipment and materials. Today's elementary children will eventually have to know how to use many kinds of information retrieval systems, so today's schools must teach the skills of learning, the "how-to" skills, the work-study skills at levels appropriate for the learner. The IMC must be open to all of the children all of the time, and the librarian must assume the role of research assistant, helping the children feel that the IMC is the right place to search for additional information for the classroom or for personal use. Drummond says:

> Children need time to explore the many possibilities within the library. And they need this time when they are ready, when they have reached that point in their thinking and in their need to know. Neither the librarian nor the teacher can be clairvoyant about this. The time needed to explore and develop an idea through books and other library materials should be decided by the learner. Again, this provides him with another opportunity for decision making.[4]

Newer methods of teaching, then, have brought about greater demands on the schools' instructional programs; thus the IMC becomes an essential feature of any good elementary school. Not too long ago the library was looked upon primarily as an aid to reading. In 1955, Jacobs stated the common purposes of a room library, central library, and the public library in the school's program. These purposes were:

> To open up to children the values of being able to use books to meet their needs both practical and recreational,
> To extend children's acquaintance with various types of reading matter,
> To refine taste in reading,
> To whet children's appetites for increasingly more mature literature,
> To guide children in their techniques of book selection,
> To teach children responsibility for book care,
> To acquaint children with appropriate new publications,
> To stimulate children to learn to read by reading.[5]

Jacob's list is still appropriate for books, but must be greatly expanded to meet the definition of expanded services offered by an IMC. For example, as teachers and students pursue their teaching-learning interactions, there should be easy access to all the school can afford to furnish in the way of equipment, materials, and informational sources. This affords the opportunity for children to learn how to use the card catalog, indexes, encyclopedias, filmstrips, sound or silent films, tape recordings, records, dictionaries, projectors and players, teaching machines, transparencies, and other devices for research or personal pleasure. The search for information can be accelerated and simplified when the entire resources of the IMC are made available to all students.

The IMC must be available to students at all times. We will see later that one of the areas frequently served by volunteers in elementary schools is the library or IMC. Of course, it is best to have such areas staffed by professionals, but when this is not possible, the principal may have to resort to the use of volunteers for staffing. Many schools do so quite successfully. The principal and staff, working with a group of dedicated volunteers, can provide for the *use* of materials and equipment and books even though there will be a minimum of instruction from a professional concerning their use. This in no way implies that volunteers can or should replace the professional media specialists. The principal must work to add such personnel to his staff. But volunteers can do all the clerical tasks, read for story hour, help students select books and find information. This practice, however, adds to the work of the principal because he must work with a number of volunteers on a part-time basis rather than with one or two professionals or paraprofessionals who could significantly reduce his work load. If the school has a librarian, her clerical work can often be handled by volunteers, freeing her to work with children in the instructional areas. Regardless of how the IMC is staffed, it can fulfill its purpose only if it is open and available, and, as Drummond says, "If it is perceived as a natural extension of classroom learning opportunities, it will become an authentic research center where pupils may go whenever they feel the need."[6] Many children in the modern elementary school learn early in life the value of the instructional media center. They learn to develop skills in finding materials to solve their problems, and they become increasingly capable of utilizing the IMC resources for activities which result in pleasure and in increased knowledge and skills for more effective community and personal living.

The Need for Classroom Libraries. To some principals and teachers, the classroom library has become an either/or situation. There is a need in the good elementary school for both the central IMC and the classroom library, as well as for a children's library in the public library. Teachers need certain reference materials—books, magazines, etc.—in their classrooms when pupils are developing units, enriching their learning, or extending their acquaintance with new materials, but to put a set of books or other materials out of circulation by placing them indefinitely in a classroom is not economically or educationally sound. Teachers need materials of many levels to care for the range of abilities within their classes. Therefore, schools which have central IMC's can improve their services by simplifying the processes which teachers use in checking out large quantities of material for classroom use. These materials may include supplementary readers and other textbooks which can be shelved separately in the IMC. The important point is that the IMC must have a large enough variety of materials and be administered in such a way that teachers can get the material they need when they need them. Thus the central IMC serves the classroom by providing revolving classroom libraries as needed. The teacher should, of course, have certain books, such as dictionary, encyclopedias, etc., to keep in the classroom; the point is that the principal's leadership must help teachers see the instructional values of the central IMC and its component, the classroom library, as a single entity.

Physical Requirements of an Educational Media Center

Modern education programs must be housed in school plants which accommodate the broad range of learning activities. The educational media center should accommodate the resources and services which comprise the media program. A functional design with an inviting appearance, good lighting and good acoustical treatment, and temperature and humidity control are prerequisites.

Location. The center should be so located in the building that it is easily accessible, and can be opened without opening the rest of the school building.

Administering Auxiliary Services 303

Such a location makes this learning resource available during the school day and also available to serve the children and community before and after school hours, on Saturdays, and during vacation periods.

Staff. The American Library Association recommends one full-time media specialist for every 250 students or major fraction thereof. Such staffing provides the optimum in individualized media services to students and teachers. Additional supportive staff is needed in the form of media technicians and media aides. To attempt to operate a center without an adequate supporting staff results in costly expenditure of professional time for routine clerical and technical tasks.[7]

Pupil Expenditures. Media centers must be kept up-to-date with new collections of materials and proper maintenance of equipment. A per pupil expenditure equal to six percent of the national average for per pupil operational cost is recommended.[8] (The estimated national average for per pupil expenditure for 1970–71 was $690.) Thus approximately forty dollars per pupil would be spent for materials for both the local school and the district media center.

Required Space. The American Library Association recommends for schools with less than 1,000 pupils the following space allocations:

Functions	Special aspects	Space in square feet
Entrance Circulation and distribution	Displays and exhibits, copying equipment, card catalogs, periodical indexes	800–1000
Reading and browsing Individual viewing and listening	No more than 100 students should be seated in one area	Space based on 15 per cent of student enrollment at 40 sq. ft. per student[a]
Individual study and learning Storytelling (elementary schools	30–40 per cent of seating capacity for individual study areas, equipped with power and capability of electronic and response	The instructional program in some schools may require that $1/3$ to $3/4$ of the student population be accommodated in the

[a] Schools with fewer than 350 students should provide space for no less than 50 students.

Functions	Special aspects	Space in square feet
Information services	systems and television outlets; area should be ducted for power and coaxial distribution Where carrels are used, suggested size is 36 in. wide and 24 in. deep, equipped with shelving and media facilities, including electrical power, television and response outlets Linear and other types of shelving for all types of materials	media center(s)
Conference rooms	Movable walls to allow for combining areas Electrical and television outlets and acoustical treatment One room, acoustically treated, with typewriters for student use	3–6 rooms with 150 sq. ft. each
Small group viewing and listening	In addition to space provided for conference rooms Electrical and television inputs and outlets, permanent wall screen, and acoustical treatment	200
Group projects and instruction in research	Flexible space, the equivalent of a classroom area, equipped for instructional purposes and needs	900–1000
Administration	Office space for 4 professional staff members Media program planning area	600–800

Administering Auxiliary Services

Functions	Special aspects	Space in square feet
Workroom	The amount of space recommended will have to be increased if centralized cataloging and processing services are not available from a system media center	300–400
Maintenance and repair service	Major service to come from system center	120–200
Media production laboratory	Sinks, running water, electrical outlets	800–1000
Dark room	Light-proof and equipped with light locks	150–200
Materials and equipment storage for production	Necessary temperature and humidity control	120
Stacks	Stacks for overflow books and audiovisual materials	400–800
Magazine storage	Space for back issues of magazines, readily accessible for use	250–400
Audiovisual equipment: distribution and storage	Decentralized storage in large schools	400–600
Center for professional materials for faculty	Designed as a teachers' conference room Adjacent to media production laboratory	600–800

Optional space (determined by school program)

Television Studio	A soundproof studio with ceilings 15 ft. high and doors 14 ft. by 12 ft.	40 ft. by 40 ft. studio with necessary control space

Functions	Special aspects	Space in square feet
Storage	For television properties, visuals, etc.	800–1000
Office with work space	Place back-to-back with television studio	1200
Radio	May be near television facilities	20 ft. by 25 ft. studio with necessary control space
Computerized learning laboratory	Facilities to have response capability	900–1000
Storage and control center for remote access		900–1000

Required Equipment. In addition to standard library equipment and furniture, the media center must have certain other equipment to facilitate a multimedia approach. Individualized instruction, team teaching and the like place responsibility for learning on the learner. Recommendations made by the American Library Association are:[9]

	Basic	*Advanced*
16mm sound projector	1 per 4 teaching stations plus 2 per media center	1 per 2 teaching stations plus 5 per media center
8mm projector (only equipment for which materials exist at the appropriate school level should be procured)	1 per 3 teaching stations plus 15 per media center	1 per teaching station plus 25 per media center
2×2 slide projector remotely controlled	1 per 5 teaching stations plus 2 per media center	1 per 3 teaching stations plus 5 per media center
Filmstrip or combination filmstrip-slide projector	1 per 3 teaching stations plus 1 per media center	1 per teaching station plus 4 per media center
Sound filmstrip projector	1 per 10 teaching stations plus 1 per media center	1 per 5 teaching stations plus 2 per media center

	Basic	Advanced
10×10 overhead projector	1 per teaching station plus 2 per media center	1 per teaching station plus 4 per media center
Opaque projector	1 per 25 teaching stations or 1 per floor in multi-floor buildings	1 per 15 teaching stations plus 2 per media center
Filmstrip viewer	1 per teaching station plus the equivalent of 1 per 2 teaching stations in media center in elementary schools	3 per teaching station plus the equivalent of 1 per teaching station in media center in elementary schools
2×2 slide viewer	1 per 5 teaching stations plus 1 per media center	1 per teaching station plus 1 per media center
TV receiver (minimum 23 in. screen)	1 per teaching station and 1 per media center where programs are available	1 per 24 viewers if programs available, in elementary schools
Microprojector	1 per 20 teaching stations	1 per 2 grade levels in elementary schools 1 per media center
Record player	1 per teaching station, K-3 3 per media center 1 set of earphones for each player	1 per teaching station, K-6, plus 5 per media center 1 set of earphones for each player
Audio tape recorder	1 per 2 teaching stations in elementary schools plus 2 per media center	1 per teaching station plus 10 per media center in elementary schools 1 set of earphones for each recorder
Listening station	A portable listening station with 6-10 sets of earphones at the ratio of 1 per 3 teaching stations	1 set of 6-10 earphones and listening equipment for each teaching station and media center

	Basic	Advanced
Projection cart	1 per portable piece of equipment, purchased at the time equipment is obtained	
Projection screen	1 permanently mounted screen per classroom plus additional screens of suitable size as needed for individual and small group use. The permanent screen should be no smaller than 70×70 with keystone eliminator.	
Closed-circuit television	All new construction should include provisions for installation at each teaching station and media center. Older buildings should be wired for closed-circuit television with initiation of such programs.	
Radio receiver (AM-FM)	1 per media center plus central distribution system (AM-FM)	3 per media center plus central distribution system (AM-FM)
Copying machine	1 per 30 teaching stations plus 1 per media center	1 per 20 teaching stations plus 1 per media center
Duplicating machine	1 per 30 teaching stations plus 1 per media center	1 per 20 teaching stations plus 1 per media center
Micro-reader (some with microfiche attachment)	Equivalent of 1 per 10 teaching stations to be located in the media center	Equivalent of 1 per 5 teaching stations to be located in the media center
Micro-reader printer	1 per media center	3 per media center
Portable video tape recorder system (including cameras)	1 per 15 teaching stations with a minimum of 2 recorders per building	1 per 5 teaching stations with a minimum of 2 recorders per building

Administering Auxiliary Services

	Basic	Advanced
Light control		Adequate light control in every classroom and media center to the extent that all types of projected media can be utilized effectively
Local production equipment		Per building: Dry mount press and tacking iron Paper cutters Two types of transparency production equipment 16mm camera 8mm camera Rapid process camera Equipment for darkroom Spirit duplicator Primary typewriter Copy camera and stand Light box 35mm still camera Film rewind Film splicer (8mm and 16mm) Tape splicer Slide reproducer Mechanical lettering devices Portable chalkboard

Items for special consideration		Large group instruction
		  The following equipment should be available for each large group instructional area:
		
		10 × 10 overhead projector, auditorium type: large screen with keystone eliminator: 16mm projector, auditorium type (consideration should be given to the possible use of rear screen projection)
		
		Television
		  A complete distribution system of at least six channels should be available in a building so that: broadcast TV 2500 MHZ, UHF, or VHF can be received; signals can be distributed to

Basic	Advanced
	each room from the central TV reception area and/or from a central studio; signals can be fed into the system from any classroom; signals are available simultaneously
	$3^{1}/_{4} \times 4$ projectors If still used by teachers at the school building, there should be 1 per school building plus 1 auditorium type per each large group instructional area.
	Equipment to make tele-lecture available

Administering the IMC

The usefulness of the IMC in any school, even when well organized, depends upon the leadership ability of the principal and his conviction that the IMC is essential to the educational program. If the organization of the school is such that children are not free to use the IMC, its services are of little value. Although each school situation varies according to size of enrollment, accommodations of the IMC, qualifications and working hours of the librarian, etc., certain objectives should be kept in mind by the principal for making the library functional. These objectives require pupils to have (1) some specific library instruction each school year; (2) freedom to use the library each day as required by classroom instruction; and (3) freedom to use the library daily for personal use. Further, the librarian should have the opportunity to function in a guidance capacity.

As a school develops an IMC, certain administrative policy regarding factors other than housing should be established. Acceptance of the IMC concept as an aid to learning and use of its varied equipment and materials places responsibility upon the principal for developing a cooperative approach with the librarian and teachers in selecting, purchasing, housing, and distributing materials. The principal who is working to develop, or has developed, an IMC, should seek further to formulate with his faculty a philosophy of education that gives direction to the basic purposes and functions of such a program. The following statements suggest some principles in establishing such a philosophy:

1. The IMC embraces every kind of instructional aid and teaching method that appeals to sensory experience. It is not restricted to precise categories

of materials, equipment, or procedures. Rather, it includes all materials and procedures that answer instructional needs.

2. The materials to be purchased and concentrated in the IMC should depend upon instructional and recreational needs as specified by the staff and principal.

3. Audio-visual materials are aids to instruction to be used in specific situations. They should also be available for research and personal check-out by students.

4. It is a responsibility of educational leadership to help teachers become aware of the scope and value of the IMC materials; through in-service education to keep them familiar with standard procedures and newer developments as they become available; and to help and guide them in testing instructional methods and teaching apparatus.

5. The acquisition of instructional aids implies the acceptance by administrators of full responsibility for housing, maintaining, distributing, and replacing them; it implies too that the administrator will be constantly on the alert for better instructional aids and equipment.

6. The administrative procedures involving IMC materials and equipment must be clearly stated, so that teachers and students will know who is responsible for what.

7. There should be constant in-service activities involving the staff and the librarian concerning maximum use of the IMC by students.

HEALTH ENVIRONMENT AND HEALTH SERVICES

This section concerns itself with two of three aspects of the school's health program—*health environment* and *health services*. The third aspect, *health education* is discussed in Chapter 7, "Curriculum Development."

There is little question today about the school's responsibility for protecting and promoting children's health. Modern professional educators recognize health services as a functional aspect of the school program. Intellectual pursuits are often of little value to the child who is suffering from malnutrition or otherwise poor health. Children learn best when they have healthy bodies and minds, and when they have a healthy, wholesome environment in which to live and play.

Only as the principal acquaints himself with children's health needs can the health program best serve its purpose. If he is unaware of the effects of health on learning, he may make the mistake of initiating devices which are detrimental to a good health program. Thus the first function of the health service is to provide a wholesome, healthful school environment, free from injurious influences. In developing such an environment, the principal should work with committees of parents, students, and staff members. These committees should make periodic inspection tours of the building, playground, and the neighborhood to discover unsafe conditions. Physical factors which require attention are (1) unprotected street crossings, (2) bicycle riding on playground, (3) lack of handrails on stairways both indoors and out, (4) school buses backing and turning, (5) insufficient trash containers or trash not disposed of properly, (6) insufficient supplies in restrooms, (7) lack of restroom privacy and sanitary napkins for older girls, (8) poor lighting in rooms, (9) poor ventilation in rooms, (10) unprotected glass doors or windows, (11) poor drainage of playground area, (12) lack of equipment or space for healthful exercise, (13) tables and chairs at wrong height for comfortable work, (14) inadequate emergency materials and equipment.

Although many other factors can contribute to an unwholesome environment, these fourteen items will serve as a guide for committee consideration. A good school atmosphere characterized by a warm, friendly social attitude emanates from the principal's office and permeates the entire school. Teachers and pupils reflect their feelings through their attitudes and relationships. Thus, the school which reflects warm, friendly relationships between school personnel and pupils provides an environment conducive to learning and living.

Principal's Role in School Health Services

The second function of the school health program is to provide or to utilize *health services which will enhance pupil health and welfare*. Many schools now provide certain health services for children right at school. Others provide only limited health services, or none at all. Obviously, the principal must accept the prevailing philosophy of the community toward school provision of health services and facilities. However, the principal whose school does not utilize the available community agencies should seek to improve his program of health services through this medium. The nurse, whether school employed or a staff member of the county health department, is the liaison between principal and community agencies.

Role of the School Nurse

In the first year of Title I of the Elementary and Secondary Education Act of 1965, about 4900 nurses became staff members of public schools across the United States. This same legislation made it possible to add almost the same number of nurses to schools in the 1967-68 school year. There is much variation in the quality and requirements of state certification programs for school nurses. There is a growing trend toward more demanding certification requirements, some of which reflect interest in having the school nurse assume health education responsibilities as well as responsibilities for health services. Even the titles of certification are revealing—New York State describes it as "Nurse-Teacher Certification;" Illinois calls it "Teacher-

Administering Auxiliary Services 313

Nurse Certification." Responsibility for health services still takes priority. Kepler and Thayer say:

> For the nurse, school health services continue to be the key emphasis, and she cannot do full-time formal classroom teaching and still meet these service demands. The allocation of her time should be jointly planned by the nurse, the principal, and such other persons as the local situation indicates.
>
> Consideration should be given to the health needs of a particular student and community population, available resources, size of pupil load, and auxiliary assistance. The trend toward employment of school health secretaries and aides will free the nurse of routine nonprofessional duties so that she can also participate in the educational aspects of the health program.

The basic aspects of school health services are encompassed under six major headings:

1. Emergency service for injury or sudden illness.
2. Health appraisal for each child.
3. Screening programs performed by school.
4. Encouragement to seek recommended treatment.
5. Planning for handicapped children.
6. Prevention and control of disease.

Emergency Services. Procedures for emergency services have already been discussed. Even though a nurse may be on duty and may even be given the authority to call parents concerning ill or injured children, it is still the responsibility of the principal to make a final decision. If there is no nurse available, the principal or his secretary must follow the prescribed procedures. It cannot be overstressed that this is a very sensitive area in connection with parental emotions, and the principal should avoid problems by insisting that certain procedures, based on county board of health or state regulations, be followed by any person who gives aid to an ill or injured child. The nurse and the principal should communicate with parents at meetings or through written bulletins, preferably both, to inform them of these procedures and enlist their aid in promoting health and safety for all children.

Health Appraisal. For school purposes, health appraisal starts with the before-school examination and should be followed by periodic examinations by the school, a physician, or a clinic. A cumulative health record should be maintained for each child. This includes records of state-required or board-of-education required immunizations, observations and recommendations resulting from school health screenings, notations and recommendations concerning special health problems, and notations from any member of the staff concerning a child's emotional, mental, or physical health.

Screening Programs. School health-screening programs are aimed at early identification of health problems, followed by recommendation to parents to secure professional assistance in specialized areas of health, both mental and physical. Screening programs include vision, hearing, dental, tuberculosis, and day-to-day observations by nurse and teachers.

THE LUNCH PROGRAM

The majority of modern schools provide lunch program facilities for those children who cannot go home for lunch. Educators and health authorities have learned a great deal about improving the facilities for preparing, serving, and eating foods as a result of early efforts in rural schools.

The lunch program in the modern elementary school is an important operation and an integral part of the education program. The principal's philosophy toward the relationship of this service to the total school enterprise can largely determine the value children will receive from the lunch program's operation. Consistent with all other leadership functions of the principal is his ability to use the lunch program as a means of furthering school objectives such as health, social effectiveness, economic efficiency, group relations, aesthetic appreciations, etc. To accomplish these ends, the school staff, pupils, and parents must understand the inherent values in the concomitant learnings derived from cooperative efforts in the lunch program.

The lunch program, whether funded locally or in combination with the state or federal government, offers two distinct opportunities to the elementary school. A lunch program that consistently offers tasty, nutritious lunches to teachers and students, at a nominal price, is a strong positive factor in maintaining morale. Nothing brings more complaints to the school office faster than meager or poor-quality lunches. Second, for those schools serving the Type A hot lunch, federal and state regulations require that each lunch be nutritionally balanced. This offers the staff an opportunity to include the lunch in the educational program because of its direct connection with good nutrition and health. The principal is not actually in charge of preparing the lunch, since this is managed by a lunchroom supervisor, a dietitian, or a head cook, but he is in charge of scheduling teachers and students for lunch time, and for supervision of students during lunch time. Serving lunch is one school operation that must stay on schedule, since it affects all other schedules, even to the point of dictating what other schedules will be. Since this is the most important break in the school day, the principal should work closely with his staff to set up schedules and regulations that will help make this time as pleasant and relaxing as possible. Scheduling supervision of students during lunch, whether in a separate dining room or the usual multipurpose room, must be done carefully so that all teachers have equal responsibility. In states where a duty-free lunch period is required, the principal must work his schedules around this requirement. Most schools solve this problem by having two teachers team up. While one is on duty with both classes in the lunchroom, the other has a duty-free lunch period, and they then trade places. Others solve the supervision problem by having paid aides, if the system can afford them, or having volunteer mothers supervise the lunchroom. Use of volunteers always gives rise to the question of responsibility and liability. The principal must know the laws of his particular state regarding use of paraprofessionals and volunteers in the areas of supervision of students. Until states enact laws to protect school volunteers from liability, the principal should have a strict rule that volunteers do not handle discipline problems, but refer them immediately to a teacher or the principal. Such a rule should be in writing, and reviewed periodically with all volunteers.

Some modern open-space schools have eliminated the problem of scheduling students to a lunchroom area, which in most instances means the multipurpose room, by providing mobile serving centers which are taken to each pod or team area at a specified time during the noon hour. The students are served, eat in their own area, and return their trays to the mobile center. In almost every instance the mobile serving center is stocked from a central kitchen, and food is brought by truck to the local school in insulated containers to maintain proper temperatures. Many boards of education are investigating the money-saving possibilities of such units. The need for a preparation kitchen in each local school is eliminated, the cost of lunch tables is eliminated, and the number of needed lunchroom personnel is reduced. From the principal's standpoint, there is the added advantage of freeing the multipurpose room for use during the total school day. Normally the multipurpose room is required for the lunch program for up to two hours each day, preventing its use during this time for physical education or other large-group activities.

Elementary schools are increasingly asked to provide more services for more children. Often such programs are required by the state, with no provision made for additional funds or personnel to operate the program and assist in the paperwork. One such area is that of providing food services for indigent or culturally disadvantaged children. If this includes providing breakfast, it means that the principal or his delegate must be at school long before the usual opening time to supervise the program. If this includes free lunches or partial pay lunches, it means working with outside agencies such as welfare, family and childrens' services, and others to correlate information, keep records, and complete the required reports. All these activities require time on the part of the principal or his secretary, require that forms be sent home to obtain family information, require that the office be involved with partial pay slips, free lunch slips, and other details. The secretary can handle many of the details, but the principal must set up the program and help work out details.

The U.S. Department of Agriculture reported that for the year 1970, over 20,000 school districts were required to file policy statements on free and reduced-price lunches for needy children being served by the lunch programs.[11] All schools that filed were operating under federal and state regulations and had shared 674 million pounds of food purchased under the commodities-distribution program. Since each district averaged four schools, this means that over 80,000 individual schools were involved in 1970 in the Type A hot lunch program. In Ohio, for example, 3,049 schools served almost 145 million Type A hot lunches to school children.

The increasing concern for adequately meeting at least part of the nutritional needs of children through school programs, both for poor families where food is scarce and for affluent families whose children are allowed to choose poor diets, has influenced more states to legislate certification requirements for food service directors or supervisors. The food service manager may in many cases be required to have a degree in food service operation, a teaching degree with special qualifications in school lunch-program management, a certificate as a dietitian, or a combination of two or more requirements. Most districts have one such head for the lunch program for the entire district, while the program in each individual building is under the management of a head cook.

Administering the School Lunch Program

The educational leader with the responsibility of lunch-program operation will find this a time-consuming task. Therefore, if the lunch program is not operated through a central management system, the principal should employ a lunch-program manager and the manager's responsibilities should be made clear to him at the outset. If the lunch program is to serve the school properly, the manager should

1. Be friendly and like children;
2. Be responsible for purchasing all food;
3. Submit a monthly statement of the cafeteria operation;
4. Plan menus with high nutritional standards in compliance with state and federal standards;
5. Cooperate with teachers in classroom health projects;
6. Have an annual physical examination, including a chest x-ray.

The principal must delegate authority to the manager for efficient operation of the lunch program and maintenance of rigid health standards, but he must not neglect his supervisory duties, which require careful checking of this operation. He is charged with the responsibility of administering the total school program, and he must be continuously alert to the lunch-program operation.

Financing the Cafeteria. The principal must see that the lunch program manager is bonded by the school board for the maximum amount of the balance in the lunch program's account at any one time. A sound policy is to see that the balance does not exceed two months' operating expenses. As in the case of other auxiliary services which require pupil purchases, the lunch program should not be considered a profit-making enterprise in the school.

Many school systems now include the lunch-program operation in the school budget and place it in the same category as school transportation. Many states have set up a division or department of school lunches in the state department of education. Most states now maintain school-lunch subdivisions in their state departments of education organizational patterns. Schools participating in the National School Lunch Act[12] usually receive direct assistance and supervision from their state departments of education. This service helps in preparing financial statements and provides supervisory assistance in developing and maintaining standards for good health practices. Federal funds are distributed through the state agency which has been established to distribute funds to the participating schools and to supervise health standards.

A well-balanced school lunch, attractively served, can result when the school board accepts the responsibility for paying the salaried employees of the lunch program. Although the principal is obliged to operate within the framework of established policy, he should seek to free the lunch program of unnecessary financial burdens so that the quantity and quality of the servings can be improved, and so that the cost per lunch can be brought within the range of all students. Obviously, cost will depend upon volume of sales.

The Lunch Program and the Educational Program

The lunch program in the modern elementary school emphasizes the health practices and teachings of the school. The writers have visited elementary schools where teachers were attempting to improve children's health habits, but a visit to the washroom revealed that the school was without soap or towels. It was later discovered that the school board made no provision for these necessities, because they believed children only wasted the towels. Other schools are similarly working at cross-purposes in their attempts to improve the health of children. It is not uncommon to find soft-drink and candy machines stationed in a school building where the staff members are trying to teach good nutritional habits to children. Poor scheduling of the noon hour in some schools may cause children to rush to the lunchroom line; consequently, handwashing may be completely neglected. Also, the shortness of the noon period may cause children to eat too quickly. These detrimental practices usually reflect a lack of quality in the administrative leadership of the school.

Every effort should be made to create a wholesome, healthy environment throughout the school and particularly in the lunchroom. The lunchroom should be attractively decorated and neatly arranged. Odor is usually a major problem in makeshift lunchrooms, so adequate facilities should be installed to reduce cooking odors.

The classroom teaching of good eating habits and health standards should be associated with actual practice in schools which have lunch programs. Units concerning various phases of health, such as nutrition, may be selected and cooperatively planned. Teaching good food selection will be a meaningful learning activity if it is augmented by a survey of food selection in the school lunch program. If pupils are given no choice in selecting food for their lunches, a useful activity for them might be to find out which foods are not consumed and are returned on the plates. If the lunch is served cafeteria-style, a group of children might make a check of food selections at the end of the line. Many opportunities are readily available for improved health teaching based on real and meaningful problems identified in the lunch program. The principal who gives leadership in this kind of instruction should also seek to determine the extent to which school health policies are operating at cross-purposes with the instructional program.

TRANSPORTATION IMPROVES EDUCATIONAL OPPORTUNITIES

The nation's school buses transport more than fifty percent of all children attending school. In 1950-51, there were 120,000 buses transporting 7,300,000 pupils to and from school.[13] The latest figures available (1967-68) show an increase to 17,130,873 pupils.[14] This figure includes all pupils transported at public expense. School bus registrations were up to 262,204 for the same period.[15] Such a daily operation requires the cooperation of pupils, parents, teachers, principals, bus drivers, maintenance crews, and a host of other personnel.

Bus Transportation Serves the Instructional Program

Scheduling of bus routes, maintenance of buses, hiring of drivers, and all the many other details of providing safe and efficient student transportation is usually not the direct responsibility of the principal, but he is immediately and directly involved in the operation because of his responsibility for the students. Since the buses of any particular district transport all children who live beyond a specified distance from each building, bus transportation is a factor which can be used or misused in the problems of segregation, geographical distribution, defacto segregation, and all the other human problems thrust upon the schools. Power groups use the issue of busing as a weapon to force change, and the principal may feel that his ability to respond to challenges in this area are limited by conditions beyond his control. It is imperative that all principals in a district work together, and, with parents, board of education, and central office staff, form policies and establish goals to establish that all children in the district shall have equal educational opportunities. If this means bus changes, the administrators must assume responsibility for changing geographical school lines, or changing bus routes, or making any other changes necessary.

The bus situation is made more difficult in areas where school population is rapidly expanding, as in suburban areas near large cities, for it involves planning for constant change. It means changing routes when buildings become overcrowded and the geographical distribution of students must be altered. For the office, it also means the staff may have to be reassigned within the building or possibly to another building, changing records of bus routes, moving instructional materials, changing student and adult personnel records; in short, dealing with the myriad details involved in moving hundreds, perhaps thousands of students. Double sessions, forced upon some districts by increased school population, makes many additional demands upon the principal for supervision of buses and children. There is no one answer, no panacea, but a group of administrators working together can and do find solutions to the problems. Year-round schools, now contemplated by many schools, will not ease the bus problem, but will complicate it even further. Administrators are going to have to call upon computers for assistance in handling the details.

Bus supervision by the principal should involve close cooperation with the bus supervisor to see that routes run on schedule, that safety rules are followed, that information about student conduct be discussed with drivers and children and that information about all these matters be sent home to parents or discussed at parent meetings. It also means handling discipline problems brought to the principal by the bus drivers. The principal should make it a point to relay to the driver the disposition of the case, either personally or in writing. Bus drivers have little contact with the principal and need reassurance that their problems are being dealt with as efficiently as possible.

State laws regarding bus inspection by Highway Patrol officers have strengthened the physical safety factors by enforcing standards of bus maintenance and mechanical condition. In-service programs, required physical check-ups, and required training for bus drivers, and helping drivers understand the techniques of handling large groups of children with efficiency and kindness contribute to an effective school transportation program. In spite of sensible rules and good training, drivers occasionally grow careless, and the safety practices they have been taught, as well as those taught in the classroom, are completely disregarded. The principal should inform the superintendent and/or the bus supervisor when drivers do not meet legal requirements. He should also inform them immediately when a bus is crowded beyond legal limits. In many states, the driver is held responsible for an overloaded bus if he is stopped for a routine inspection or is involved in an accident. In many instances drivers put pressure on the board of education to relieve an overcrowded condition quickly, and in some cases refuse to transport pupils under such conditions. It is all to the good that conscientious drivers put such pressure on the superintendent and the board of education to provide adequate busses to meet required safety standards. The principal should know what his state requires regarding bus transportation, and work with his community, the bus drivers, the bus supervisor and the central office to see that the regulations are followed.

SCHOOL HOUSEKEEPING

Working with the Custodial Staff

It usually does not take a beginning principal long to recognize the importance of the custodian's position. As housekeeper of the school, he is a key member of the staff. The health and safety of pupils and teachers and the cleanliness of the building depend mainly upon the custodian. The principal who understands the value of the custodian's work must help his staff and custodian build a strong spirit of cooperation. Perhaps the best suggestion that can be made here is to involve the custodian in faculty meetings which deal with the school's philosophy of discipline, instruction, health attitudes, etc.

The custodian must be made to feel a part of the school organization. If he can see the importance of his work to the total school program and its effective operation, he will find real satisfaction in his position and will take pride in his work. The principal can give leadership to this task when he understands the custodian's duties and appreciates the magnitude of his job. The following letter contains many suggestions for developing a good working relationship with the custodian:

An Orchid Letter to the New Principal

After the school board hired you, I inquired about what you might be like as our principal . . . I was anxious about how you might regard the custodian. I wondered if you would sort of think he was only another ignorant, and sometimes stubborn, "problem child." . . . But you seemed to understand my job when you said at your staff meeting

—remember, you invited me to come, and it was the first time I ever had been asked to join the teachers and the principal in talking over problems that weren't mine alone; and I had a chance to be among you in my dress-up clothes and without a broom in one hand and a dust cloth in the other—that I was your "assistant in charge" of operation and maintenance of the school plant.[16]

Facilitating the Work of the Custodian

The principal leads by helping his teachers understand the many requirements of the custodian's position. Since some teachers may infringe upon the custodian's time and good will, it is important to have all requests channeled through the principal's office. Only when the teaching staff and the custodial staff understand how each depends upon the other can optimum services be achieved. The principal facilitates the work of the custodian by

1. Having children in rooms equipped with tables and chairs place chairs on their tables at the close of school;
2. Directing teachers to have paper on the floors picked up and placed in containers;
3. Seeing that classrooms are not left with books and other supplies scattered on the floors;
4. Securing doormats for all entrances to reduce the amount of dirt carried into the building;
5. Obtaining the supplies which the custodian needs to do his job;
6. Assisting him in scheduling his work;
7. Making it possible for him to attend workshops sponsored by state departments of education, state universities, etc.

Supervising Custodial Personnel

Most school systems of any size have a maintenance director whose responsibility is to employ custodians, train them, help them set up building-maintenance schedules, supervise their overall activities, and, usually with the assistance of the principal, evaluate their overall effectiveness. Even though the principal may not be involved in hiring the custodian, it is still his responsibility to blend the work of the custodian with all the other activities that affect the instructional program. The principal should at least, however, have the opportunity to interview prospective custodians before a final selection is made.

In schools where the custodian does not work directly under a maintenance supervisor, the principal works closely with him to plan a schedule of work which will help save time and allow more work to be accomplished. There should be a daily schedule for cleaning toilet rooms and drinking fountains, vacuuming the entire building, emptying waste cans, dusting chalk trays, etc. As the principal plans with the custodian, a daily, weekly and monthly cleaning schedule can be developed. In addition, a schedule for vacation periods can be worked out the cleaning areas which cannot satisfactorily be cared for with children present, such as windows, walls, shades, etc.

The principal may also discover that the custodian can be of service to him in determining public sentiment toward the school's program. The custodian talks to many people with whom the principal has little or no contact. He is often acquainted with older families in the community, and they respect his opinion not only of the school, but also of the principal. Thus the quality of his relationship with the principal will no doubt be reflected in the public relations which the custodian establishes with reference to school operations.

PARAPROFESSIONALS—NEW BRANCHES ON THE EDUCATIONAL TREE

Use of paraprofessionals in new career positions in public schools is increasing. In 1968, there were more than 200,000 teacher aides in the United States, and it is estimated that this total may reach one and one-half million by 1977. Reports from a number of states concerning the role of the paraprofessional as a teacher aide in the classroom indicate distinct improvement in children's learning where such aides are employed. This is particularly true when the school system provides an upward-mobility program, usually in connection with university training, which encourages the aide to learn on the job and at the same time work toward becoming a professional. In a study made for the Office of Economic Opportunity, Bowman and Klopf made the following observations:

> The sponsors of the demonstration programs believed that even if there were no shortage of teachers, the introduction of more adults into the classroom would enhance the quality of education—adults selected on the basis of their concern for children and their potential as supportive personnel rather than primarily on the basis of previous training. They saw, too, great possibilities in the professional-nonprofessional team in enabling the teacher to differentiate the learning-teaching process to meet the individual needs of pupils, as diagnosed by the teacher. They saw, too, in this multilevel team approach escape from rigid structuring in the classroom—for example, more freedom of movement, more small groupings, more independent activities than would be feasible for one teacher, often operating under difficult teaching conditions. In fact, the teacher might, with this assistance, be able to experiment with innovative techniques which he had long been wanting to inaugurate.
>
> These values are universal—that is to say, they might be realized through the effective utilization of auxiliaries in any classroom regardless of the composition of the school population or the socioeconomic background of

the auxiliaries. The proponents of this new development in education saw the possibility of multiple benefits, in all school situations, such as:
1. *To the pupil,* by providing more individualized attention by concerned adults, more mobility in the classroom, and more opportunity for innovation;
2. *To the teacher,* by rendering his role more satisfying in terms of status, and more manageable in terms of teaching conditions;
3. *To the other professionals,* by increasing the scope and effectiveness of their activities;
4. *To the auxiliary,* by providing meaningful employment which contributes at one and the same time to his own development and to the needs of society;
5. *To the school administrator,* by providing some answers to his dilemma of ever increasing needs for school services, coupled with shortage of professionals to meet these needs—*a* solution, not *the* solution, and certainly not a panacea;
6. *To family life,* by giving auxiliaries, many of whom are or may someday become parents, the opportunity to learn child development principles in a reality situation;
7. *To the community at large,* by providing a means through which unemployed and educationally disadvantaged persons may enter the mainstream of productivity.[17]

Without exception, reports from schools using auxiliary personnel refer to three crucial areas in implementing and maintaining programs involving paraprofessionals: (1) a thorough preparation and orientation program, preferably involving university personnel; (2) adequate supervision and support; and (3) continuous in-service education. Some school systems found out the hard way that inadequate or hurried preparation and orientation was detrimental to the program, and caused human-relations problems that could have been avoided had the administration been more thorough in these areas. The three areas seem to be the same required for the principal to work successfully with professional staff, and there are indeed many similarities. The difference lies in the *kinds* of activities involved. Auxiliary, according to Webster's New World Dictionary, means one who will "help, assist, give aid and support to," and this supportive role is under the direction of and in cooperation with the professional staff and the administration. Adequate preparation and orientation of the paraprofessional for his role in the school situation does not always occur, and some observers say this is true because too often the programs are instituted on a crash basis, brought about by urgent needs or hurriedly put into effect when funds suddenly became available. These observers feel that preparation should be not only for the non-professional, but even more importantly for the teachers and other professionals with whom the auxiliary personnel will be associated. But the problem of defining the role of the professional and the paraprofessional, and redefining each role as programs develop, is only one part of the challenge. The most important aspect which must be defined is in the area of human relations, understanding and acceptance of the role of each person with whom one works. Since both the professional and the auxiliary enter into new roles, the complex human relationships touch very sensitive areas, especially when paraprofessionals are recruited from socioeconomic or racial groups different from the teaching staff. Possible difficulties should be discussed frankly by the administration, university personnel, paraprofessionals, and the professional staff in training sessions, thus avoiding many doubts and concerns because definite specifications of roles and functions are provided for each participant.

Planning must be wide-range, encompassing each individual or group that will be involved with or affected by contact with the auxiliary personnel employed to participate in the instructional program. Action on the part of the administration must be specific, detailed, and geared to the *beginning* competencies of paraprofessionals, but with possibilities and paths for improvement clearly defined. Bowman and Klopf say:

> Administrative action that is needed as prelude to the introduction of auxiliary personnel in a school setting includes:
> 1. Authentic involvement of all school personnel as well as students, parents and community in the planning.
> 2. Development of a basic rationale for auxiliary participation on the team.
> 3. Functional analysis of educational tasks with a view to establishing new staffing patterns.
> 4. Selection and recruitment of school personnel primarily on the basis of potential capacity rather than previous academic training.
> 5. Establishment of new career lines not only for auxiliary personnel but for the total educational system, with new leadership roles at various occupational levels and increased motivation for career development throughout the system.
> 6. More flexibility and imagination in the use of time, space and material resources.
> 7. Clear allocation of roles, responsibility, and accountability for the initiation and maintenance of effective team functioning.[18]

The second necessary function, that of providing adequate supervision and support, is the direct responsibility of the principal. He must first have a philosophy concerning the role of the teacher aide. Is this a potential solution to teacher shortages? Is the program there to make use of available federal money? Or does he see such programs as essential aids to instruction? Many city schools, for example, are keenly interested in experimental programs to make their schools more responsive to the needs of the inner city, the ghetto, the underprivileged, and the poor. There are barriers to these dreams of making schools responsive to human needs through the use of paraprofessionals. One article makes the point that teachers often resist such programs:

> The teachers' resistance to the idea of an aide in the classroom is rooted historically in the teacher's perception of his classroom as his autonomous bailiwick, where he may enjoy relative isolation and power. An aide is easily perceived as infringing on this isolation and autonomy. Some teachers have informally confessed that they often view the aide as a "spy from the community." Not only does the aide then embody a personal infringement of a private domain, but there is the suspicion that the aide is there to report back to all in the community all of the teacher's activities and inter-personal relationships with the children in the classroom. It is feared this reporting may bring recriminations from the parent. If the teacher holds this perception of "being invaded," he is then constrained to place the aide in a position of relative isolation and impotence in the classroom. The aide is then given chiefly menial tasks—housekeeping, monitoring, etc.
> There is another source of teacher-tension in the use of aides. That is the movement toward increasing professionalization that has swept through teacher education. The aide development is sometimes seen as weakening the hard-fought battle for qualified teacher training, with its resultant increases in salary and stature.[19]

The structure of supervision should be such that all major decisions about the work of the paraprofessionals should be made in a team situation involving all concerned with the success of the project. If each individual has respect for that which can contribute to a child's education, the first essential for successful programs, that of mutual trust, can be established. Bowman and Klopf elaborate upon this theme:

> The introduction of auxiliaries into a school situation requires drastic change—a whole new web of interaction. It may shatter trust not only of one another but even of self.
> The auxiliaries, themselves, may experience a blizzard of conflicting impressions. They will need time and assurance as they develop new ways of responding to situations.
> Teachers and other professionals, on the other hand, may feel as if strangers were trespassing on their private terrain—their classrooms, their hallways, their offices. They will have no less a need for time and assurance as they give up the one-to-thirty or one-to-forty interaction with students which has been time-honored and with which they feel comfortable.
> Learning to function in a new way is especially complicated when mature adults with a wide range of background, competencies and life experiences

are being asked to interact within the same universe. It is possible only in an atmosphere of mutual trust. Hence, trust formation is the *sine qua non* of team training.

Mutual trust cannot be decreed. It can only develop through free and open communication. This may involve confrontation. It inevitably requires a slow and sometimes painful process. However, the outlook is not bleak, since team training, sincerely conceived and appropriately executed, can and indeed has in many instances succeeded in developing a sense of the magnitude of the common task and a belief in the sincerity of those who work at it together.[20]

Schools that structure programs using auxiliary personnel who live in disadvantaged environments are endeavoring to improve home/school/community relationships. Employing persons from the neighborhood and providing incentive for upward mobility helps bridge the gap between the culturally disadvantaged child and the typical teacher who has little knowledge and less understanding of what it is to be disadvantaged or poor. An auxiliary from his own neighborhood can often relate to a child in ways that are familiar and non-threatening. Such a person can help the child adjust to the strange world of the school. He may also serve as a model to motivate the child, since his very presence in the school as a member of the instructional team gives him status that can say to the child, "You can make it here. These people are for you. I made it and so can you." The auxiliary person from the child's neighborhood can also interpret to the professional teaching staff the reasons for a child's non-performance in school. The auxiliary aide may also be extremely helpful in interpreting to parents and children the goals of the school and the possibilities of success for each child in the learning-teaching process.

It is not possible in this brief narration to present all the possibilities for using paraprofessionals in elementary schools. It is strongly recommended that the principal who wants to use paraprofessionals in his school study the available information about the funding, structure, training, and job descriptions of programs using paraprofessionals as salaried auxiliary personnel. One significant factor should be mentioned, that of increased effectiveness of classroom teachers when a competent aide is available. This is exemplified in an excerpt from a report concerning a program in the Greenburgh Central School District No. 7, which states:

> It is interesting to note that where experienced (or second year) teacher-aides are working that the role of the teacher with whom the aide works has changed. The teacher has become a more proficient diagnostician. The requirement of assigning a child to an aide for reinforcement has demanded a more definitive approach to specifically what the child should be learning. Another way of stating this is that after a lesson has been taught exactly

what will the teacher expect Johnny to have learned. The teacher has moved from the role of being "everything to everyone" and has combined her professional knowledge and skill with a non-professional's warmth and "know-how" of reaching children. This is not to infer that the teacher lacks these assets but with classes of twenty-five and a goal of equality of opportunity no one individual can reach all children in any one day or week. The change in teacher receptivity to aides has been dramatic. Where suspicion and distrust existed there is now faith and cooperation. Teachers of grade levels who do not have aides have expressed a very vocal request for them for the next school year. Significantly, parents have become the greatest supporters for the aide program, and an organized group of parents now plans to bring pressure to bear on the Board of Education to have the aide program expanded through local support. The aide project has become accepted enough to be on the list of our local teachers' union organization as to groups who should be organized for the next school year.[21]

VOLUNTEERS

Although the foregoing remarks concerning the role of the paid paraprofessional have been confined primarily to the use of such persons in the classroom, we have not meant to imply that salaried auxiliary personnel are not useful in other school areas, particularly as library aides, tutors, teachers of body management, and supervision. Volunteers can be used for service in the same situations, but the ground rules for volunteer participation are different and the role of the volunteer is significantly different from that of the paid aide, because the volunteer is not a school employee paid for services by contract. In some ways volunteers must be treated differently, perhaps more carefully, than the paid aide since the desire to work and serve children comes from within, and they offer their services because of personal motivation, not because of a paycheck. In many respects the two roles are alike; they demand careful planning and orientation, they must be organized and structured with the full cooperation of the teaching staff, constant in-service education is a necessity, and evaluative techniques must be accepted and used by all.

It is estimated that volunteers can take over about thirty percent of the routine tasks performed each school day by teachers. None of the positive factors mentioned are nearly as important as the fact that using volunteers or paid paraprofessionals tends to reduce the ratio of children to adults, thus increasing the chances for interaction, better diagnosis of problems, and all other positive factors concomitant with lowered pupil/teacher ratios.

Choosing volunteers and paraprofessionals is not an easy task, since few, if any, references or personality inventories are available, and the basic question of whether or not the person under consideration can relate to children and to the teaching staff can often be answered only by observing the person in action. Many schools have lists of requirements for volunteers, defined by the principal in cooperation with the professional staff and/or the parents' organization. Once a decision to use volunteers is made, the principal must support the volunteers and continue activities to integrate them and their activities into the school programs. Most volunteers offer their services with the best of intentions, but since they are human, the risks of failure are the same as for any other adult attempting to learn a new role. One basic difference between the paid aide and the volunteer is that the volunteer sees his services as short-range and for a limited time, while the the paraprofessional striving toward increased professionalism tends to see his role as long-range and relatively permanent.

A word of caution is given here—since volunteers come to the school expecting to work, the easiest way to lose them is to have nothing for them to do. Conversely, the best way to keep volunteers is to make sure their tasks are within their abilities, and are needed and wanted. Made-up "busy work" is just as destructive to the morale of the volunteer as it is to the child in the classroom. The depth and range of voluntary services is limited only by the imagination of the principal and his staff. Mutual respect and understanding between volunteers and the teaching staff for their respective roles in enriching children's educational experiences is the basis of a successful volunteer program for which the principal should strive. Maturity of outlook, creative imagination, commitment to service, a warm personality acceptable to children, ability to team with peers to improve instruction; these are some of the characteristics that should be looked for in those who volunteer their services to the school. Service roles in the schools, by volunteers and paraprofessionals, can fulfill many functions if mutual trust and appreciation can be established. Yarmolinsky says, "The future service role is at best an expression of mutuality, of mutual recognition of human capacities and human needs. As urban society makes possible greater mutuality of service among its citizens, it enables them to fulfill their possibilities as men."[22] Schools can be instrumental in tapping the potential service possibilities of citizens within the school community.

SPECIALIZED RESOURCE PERSONNEL AND AGENCIES

Bureaucracy and red tape notwithstanding, the plethora of agencies, companies, service groups and individuals offering assistance to the school for the welfare and education of children is truly amazing. The principal may, through direct contact, or through contact via county office and official agencies, enlist the aid of many organizations and specialized personnel. The local situation will determine what agencies, service organizations, and individuals are available, and the principal, with the assistance of others who know the community, should list these and the services offered. Many groups and individuals offer money and services willingly if needs are explained. They should not be taken advantage of, but neither should their help be neglected because it takes time to make contacts and follow through. Also, any service rendered to a school or a child in the school should be acknowledged with a thank-you note or phone call from the principal.

Cooperating with welfare, probation, health, and law enforcement agencies for the welfare and protection of children is becoming an increasingly important aspect of the principal's responsibilities. Increasing violence, school break-ins, child beatings, vandalism to teachers' cars, increasing numbers of children in foster homes, families on welfare, children on free lunch or breakfast, vandalism to school property—all these and many more cannot be handled by the school alone, and the principal must seek help outside the school. If a guidance counselor is available, activities that involve cooperation with an outside agency are often delegated to him, but the principal must be kept apprised of each situation since he is the only one who can take official action. Usually his signature is the only one acceptable for official reports. In the future, in-service education of principals must include more skills of human relations if he is to work effectively in understanding his community and its people, understanding the pressures put on children by home and school, understanding ways he can keep the organizational climate healthy, and realizing that the best investment of time and energy is spent in the development of human resources. We now recognize many things that warp or stop child growth and development, and if the school is not equipped to offer corrective or preventive services, there are many social services of the community that offer resources, skills, and personnel. There are many laws that protect children from abuse or harm, from their own parents as well as other adults, and the principal must occasionally invoke the law for a child's protection. He should move cautiously but firmly if he sees a condition that merits such action, seeking the best advice of the school's legal counsel and the assistance of the proper authorities. Often, once the evidence makes the condition apparent, an agency acting in official capacity will assume full responsibility for further action on the case and its disposition.

SUMMARY

The auxiliary services of the elementary school have been established to enhance or complement instruction. Leadership on the part of the principal is essential to keep these services in balance so that each can make its greatest contribution. In some modern schools, the principal has little or no control over the activities of the custodian, transportation, and food services, but these schools are in the minority, and one preparing for the principalship needs to be aware of his role in relation to personnel who perform these functions.

Also under the jurisdiction of the principal are such professional people as the guidance counselor, school psychologists, speech therapist, social worker, and reading specialist. The principal is also concerned with paraprofessionals such as clerical aides, instructional aides, etc. In addition, the principal must coordinate the work of the television and/or the education media specialists.

The principal's function in supervising the lunch program becomes a major responsibility even if he has a competent lunchroom manager. He must be aware of the health and safety practices in the lunchroom. Rigid health standards must be adhered to. The lunchroom must be attractively decorated, and the food appetizing.

The principal who is responsible for transportation usually is involved in (1) supervising bus operations at his school, (2) recommending changes in bus schedules in order to effect safety, economy, and efficiency, (3) supervising bus drivers, (4) promoting pupil behavior, (5) scheduling supervision by teachers or aides during loading and unloading periods, and (6) keeping reports required for the central office.

The modern library extends its services into the entire media area. The educational media center is truly the heart of the school, as it serves as the learning center to complement individualized instruction.

The principal has a major role in helping his staff—teaching and nonteaching—as well as the pupils to understand each person's position and how each is dependent upon the others. The principal works closely with the custodial staff to help them schedule their work for greater efficiency. As the principal leads, he helps the custodian gain a new understanding of his position through a recognition of how the total school operation depends upon his work.

SUGGESTED READINGS

American Association of School Librarians. *The Elementary School Library*. Washington, D.C.: National Education Association, 1966.

Bard, Bernard. *The School Lunchroom: Time of Trial*. New York: John Wiley, 1969.

Brown, Richard. "How to Keep Discipline on a Bus." *School Management*, November 1965.

Cooper, Charles R. "An Educator Looks at Busing." *The National Elementary Principal* 50 (April 1971): 26–31.

Hensarling, Paul. "How Good or Bad is Your Food Service Operation?" *School Management*, February 1966.

Kilander, H. Frederick. *School Health Education*. 2d ed. New York: Macmillan, 1968.

Lowrie, Jean E. *Elementary School Libraries*. New York: Scarecrow, 1961.

———. *Providing School Library Service for the Culturally Disadvantaged*. Chicago: American Library Association, 1965.

Martiney, Roy. "How to Set-up a Bus Safety Program." *School Management*, November 1965.

Mayshark, Cyrus and Donald D. Shaw. *Administration of School Health Programs: Its Theory and Practice*. St. Louis: C. V. Mosby, 1967.

National Conference on School Transportation. *Selection, Instruction, and Supervision of School Bus Drivers*, Washington, D.C.: National Education Association, 1964.

National Education Association, Safety Education Commission. *Minimum Standards for School Buses*. Washington, D.C.: The Association, 1964.

Olivero, James L. and Edward G. Briffie, eds. *Educational Manpower: Bold New Venture*. Bloomington, Indiana: Indiana University Press, 1970.

Saxe, Richard W. "About Principals and Custodians." *The National Elementary Principal* 46 (April 1967): 23–30.

White, Dan A. "Does Busing Harm Urban Elementary Pupils." *Phi Delta Kappan* 53 (November 1971): 192.

Yeager, William A. *Administration of the Noninstructional Personnel and Services*. New York: Harper & Row, 1959.

Notes

1. See chapter 14 for guides to job analysis.

2. Adapted from Robert E. Valett, *The Practice of School Psychology; Professional Problems* (New York: John Wiley, 1963), pp. 253–55.

3. Harold S. Davis, "Organizing a Learning Center" (Cleveland, Ohio: Educational Research Council of America, 1968), p. 1.

4. T. Darrel Drummond, "The Learning Center—A Chance for Every Child," *National Elementary Principal* 50, no. 1 (September 1970).

5. Leland B. Jacobs, "Three to Teach Reading," *Library Journal* 80 (September 15, 1955): 1928.

6. Drummond, "The Learning Center."

7. *Standards for School Media Programs* (Chicago: American Library Association, 1969), pp. 12–15.

8. Ibid., p. 35.

9. Ibid., pp. 45-49.

10. Mabel B. Kepler and Virginia E. Thayer, "The Qualified School Nurse Vitalizes Health Education," *The National Elementary Principal* 48, no. 2 (November 1968).

11. *School Lunch Journal,* February 1971.

12. Public Law Number 396, passed by Congress in June 1946.

13. *Pupil Transportation,* 1953 Yearbook of the Department of Rural Education (Washington, D. C.: National Education Association, 1953), p. 17.

14. Kenneth Simon and W. Vance Grant, *Digest of Educational Statistics 1970.* National Center for Educational Statistics, U.S. Department of Health, Education and Welfare. Document catalog No. HE 5.210:10024-70, September 1970, p. 36.

15. Automobile Manufacturers Association, Inc., "1970 Auto Facts and Figures."

16. Letter read by Wayne P. Marshall at a district custodian's meeting, Grand Island, Nebraska, reported in *The School Executive* 74 (August 1956): 56.

17. Garda W. Bowman and Gordon J. Klopf, "Auxiliary School Personnel: Their Roles, Training, and Institutionalization." ED 026 713. Based on a Nationwide Study of Teacher-Aides, Teacher-Assistants, Family Workers, and other Auxiliary Personnel in Education. Conducted for the Office of Economic Opportunity, Bank Street College of Education, New York, New York. October 1966, 22 pages.

18. Garda W. Bowman and Gordon J. Klopf, "Training for New Careers and Roles in the American School." ED 028 146. Bank Street College of Education, New York, New York. Sponsoring Agency—Office of Education (DHEW), Washington, D. C., January 1969, 18 pages.

19. National Commission on Teacher Education and Professional Standards, "Descriptions of Paraprofessional Programs in Education." ED 027 259. New York University, New Careers Development Center, January 1969, 38 pages.

20. Bowman and Klopf, "Training," p. 3.

21. "Descriptions of Paraprofessional Programs."

22. Adam Yarmolinsky, "The Service Society," *National Elementary Principal* 48, no. 6 (May 1969).

13

Planning and Organizing

Many school executives are competent and skilled administrators because they give particular consideration to planning and organizing their time, duties, and even thinking. Perhaps the elementary school principal can improve his overall effectiveness if he is challenged to move in this direction and provided with some definite aids to assist him in attaining such skills. The modern principal needs first of all to understand the problems of his particular school and how to find time for thoughtful planning of his many administrative duties; second, the principal can employ certain techniques that will assure better planning and organizing practices; and finally, the year's work as a whole should be planned well in advance.

MEETING THE NEEDS OF THE PARTICULAR SCHOOL

There are some 70,879 public elementary schools and 14,900 parochial schools in the United States, and these vary widely in size and type of organization.[1] It is presumed that each institution is striving to meet the needs of the children from the local school district, and that the principal is attempting to administer his school and provide leadership to meet these needs. It takes skilled leadership working with time, talent, tenacity, and teachers to lift a school or a school system from mediocrity to superiority. Each school is a unique combination of program, principal, and all other cooperating personnel, unlike any other school. Yet, despite recognized differences, administrators face common problems which call for certain leadership skills. The purposes of this section, therefore, are (1) to compare some problems of the small school with those of the larger school, (2) to suggest how the principal may find time for giving leadership, and (3) to discuss the role of the assistant principal.

Small School Versus Larger Institution

The list below indicates the problems faced by the principal of the small and the large school. Suggestions are made for meeting each problem, and the elements common to both the small and the large school are cited. The differences between schools may be great and the problems more complex in one type of school than in another, but the differences usually are a matter of degree and not of kind.

Problems of the Small School Situation

1. Staffs are inadequately trained to handle pupil personnel problems.

Problems of the Larger School Situation

1. Too many guidance problems to cope with; time too short; guidance staff overloaded with cases.

Comment: In each case, guidance is a real problem. In one type of school no trained guidance persons are available; in the other kind of school too many cases appear. In both instances guidance is not being supplied, but for different reasons.

Suggested solutions: Combine with other schools to provide psychological aid, speech correction, dental and physical examinations, and special classes for the exceptional child; use outside consultants more widely; organize a carefully integrated program with other agencies.

Suggested solutions: Use consultant services; organize a carefully integrated program with other agencies; utilize total staff more widely in a better-organized program.

2. Inadequate facilities, equipment, and instructional aids hamper the educational program.

2. Facilities are adequate, but teacher loads preclude optimum use for best advantage.

Comment: Both of these are legitimate problems in the smaller school. The only common element in this situation is that facilities in each school may be inadequate, or not fully exploited when available, in which case neither school is giving the students full advantage of these things.

Suggested solutions: Give leadership in helping teachers discover and invent ways and means of supplanting shortages; use community resources more widely; work toward better support by patrons; call upon supervisors' aid.

Suggested solutions: Give leadership to staff by suggesting better uses of facilities; develop with them better policies and techniques of use; work out more systematic schemes of organization; provide workshop experiences or extended training periods for more effective use of facilities.

3. The principal is too busy teaching and has little or no clerical help; this rules out leadership activities; the principal may not be professionally trained.

3. The principal is too busy with office routine and needs additional clerical aid; his administrative duties prevent proper leadership work.

Planning and Organizing 335

| Small School | Larger School |

Comment: The teaching principal will have little or no time to give leadership, especially if clerical duties occupy a great deal of his time. On the other hand, the principal who is occupied with the many details of a larger school faces the same situation in that he too is unable to give leadership.

Suggested solutions: Put a supervisory principal in charge of two or more of the smaller schools, use faculty committees more widely; appoint a vice principal; secure office help through community or patron help; use some pupils in a limited fashion.

Suggested solutions: Learn to delegate responsibilities; appoint a vice principal; use community or patron help; use faculty committees; use some pupils in a limited fashion.

4. Staff personnel not used to democratic type of control; lacking in community leadership; training inadequate; teacher loads excessive; turnover is high; principal has little contact with teachers.

4. Same items as mentioned in other column; more emphasis here on coordination and cooperation factors as problems.

Comment: Every principal faces staff problems as described. However, training and turnover problems are not generally as serious in the larger, better paid city school systems. The principal of the smaller school often faces a situation in which poorly trained faculty members constitute his most difficult problem. Perhaps his own administrative training and experience will be below par.

Suggested solutions: Take the staff from where they are and gradually develop group participation in decision making; help them to recognize where community leadership is needed and point out how they may serve; work out in-service programs suited to their needs; find causes of turnover and seek aid in finding answers; use student and patron aid to relieve the pressure on the teacher during the day; consider teacher-aide use.

Suggested solutions: Use the same approaches suggested for the smaller school. Concentrate on coordination of activities.

5. Curriculum problems arise because of inadequate staff preparation, poor facilities, and the like, including problems of improving instruction.

5. Curriculum problems arise because of scheduling difficulties, crowded facilities, etc.

Comment: It is clear that both small and large schools have difficulties in the area of curriculum. Usually the smaller schools face difficult situations because of inadequate staff preparation and facilities.

Suggested solutions: Wide use of curriculum specialists seems to be the

Suggested solutions: Better organization and exploitation of existing facilities and

Small School	Larger School
immediate answer; an aggressive in-service education program should be continuous; teacher should be led to see the total educational program.	staff talents; teachers should see the total educational program through workshops and in-service plans; teacher morale should be developed.
6. There is a definite need for better public relations work because of misunderstandings as to the school's objectives, its program, etc.	6. Public relations is a real program in schools of this type.

Comment: Regardless of the size or type of school, the principal needs to have communication with the community. Ways and means of informing patrons and citizens will not vary greatly in either type of school.

Suggested solutions: The principal may utilize the various devices and techniques at his disposal in meeting this need.	*Suggested solutions:* The principal may utilize the various devices and techniques at his disposal in meeting this need.

These six categories point up the common problems for both large and small schools. The list of categories might be extended or broken down into greater detail, but it should be noted that in every instance, the principal can take definite and positive steps. Every administrator needs help and guidance in performing his duties, and, while school environments are completely different, the job must still be done. For example, the principal of the smaller school is busy teaching in the classroom, while the city-school administrator is engaged in detailed desk work. For entirely different reasons, each is unable to give proper leadership. Therefore, the real crux of the problem seems to be centered in the time factor and in administrative help for the principal.

Finding Time for Giving Leadership

Administrators of elementary schools generally complain that there is not enough time to give proper leadership to the school. To discharge these leadership functions would require full-time assistants and superior clerical help. Also, no teaching duties can be imposed if genuine leadership is expected. Unquestionably, these conditions do not exist to any serious extent in *all* schools of the smaller or larger types, and larger schools frequently have a better administrative situation. A recent research study shows the following:

> Comparison among the DESP surveys does not give an optimistic impression of the gain in the number of assistant principals in the country as a whole. In three surveys the percents reporting no administrative assistants have been: 1948, 81 percent; 1958, 87 percent; and 1968, 91.6 percent. The percents reporting one *full-time* assistant principal have been: 1948,

Planning and Organizing

16 percent; 1958, 7 percent; and 1968, 8.4 percent. While these percents are not strictly comparable, the general trend implies that the assistant principalship has not gained substantially as a recognized part of the elementary school staff.

Whether or not the principal has an assistant principal is clearly related to the size of the school system. In the largest school systems (25,000 or more pupils) 24.2 percent of the supervising principals had full-time administrative assistants. The proportion declines steadily to only 2.4 percent in the smallest systems.[2]

Real help will result for the time-pressed principal if he can see more clearly a way to solve this difficult problem. Some suggestions are now offered, together with a general approach to the problem, to encourage more effective leadership.

First, the principal needs to develop a systematic account of just how he uses his time. He needs to develop a priority system based on carefully planned long-range and short-range objectives. Evidence indicates that principals spend too much time "putting out fires" rather than attacking the source of a problem. A priority system should reveal those areas that are receiving an undue portion of his time, and bring into focus the problems that are left unattended. The principal may think he knows how he is using his time, but he needs to be positive. Second, after such an account has been developed, the administrator will be in a better position to organize his time systematically. Perhaps there is duplication of effort, imperfect scheduling, and so on. The principal should be able to identify accurately what is to be done and plan ways to do it. Then he is prepared to take the third step of planning techniques and procedures to meet his situation. The planning outlined above will help the principal do something constructive about finding time to accomplish his objectives. For example, if he is a teaching principal, he will schedule a portion of his teaching time in advance by securing the services of a relief teacher, or by reorganizing his classes to leave them under other supervision for part of an hour.

It is suggested that the principal use a visual method of recording his activities over a period of time as a check upon his various professional activities. The following chart can be adapted to include as many items as desired, and the code can be altered to suit the situation. Such a chart, kept for a period of weeks, can effectively show priorities the principal gives to certain areas, and can even be an effective method for convincing the board of education to consider employing an assistant principal.

Methods by which the principal may plan the best use of his time are many and varied. He needs to weigh values carefully when confronted with a specific situation. He will often find that an undue portion of his time is consumed by irrelevant items. Again, the principal who learns to delegate

TIME	MONDAY	TUESDAY	WEDNESDAY	THURSDAY	FRIDAY	NOTES
8:00	MTG–ST	MTG–TM	CON–A	MTG–TM	CON–P	
8:15	MTG–ST	MTG–TM	CON–A	MTG–TM	CON–P	
8:30	MTG–ST	MTG–TM	OF	MTG–TM	OF	
8:45	OF	TL–S	CL(D.L.K.)	OF	CL(N.D.)	
9:00	TL–P TL–S	MTG–PRO	CL(D.L.K.)	OF	CL(N.D.)	
9:15	OF	MTG–PRO	WR	OF	OF–PRE	
etc.		MTG–PRO			OF–PRE	

CODE TL (Telephone)
       P (parent)
       S (school)
       O (other)

    SA (salesman)

   MTG (meeting)
     ST (staff)
    TM (team)
    GL (grade level)
   PAR (parents)
   PRO (professional)
    AD (administrative)
   CM (committee)
     D (discipline)

    CL (classroom visit)
  CON (conference)
     T (teacher)
     P (parent)
     C (child)
     A (auxiliary personnel)
     O (other)

  PRE (preparation of materials)

   OF (office details—records, orders, reports, etc.)

   WR (writing—letters, brochures, flyers to parents, staff notes, schedules, etc.)

Figure 14

The Principal's Calendar

responsibility will find more time for leadership functions. Better communication with faculty and parents will often give him more opportunities to accomplish objectives. With better-informed persons, he will need to spend less time presenting ideas and making decisions, and delegating responsibility is the greatest time saver.

Using time to the best advantage is a problem that cannot easily be solved. It is strongly recommended that the principal consider the statement, "Never write when you can talk," and use a dictation machine or a tape recorder to make notes. Any principal, even if he is a full-time teacher, can make

Planning and Organizing 339

quick verbal notes and save much time by using a small portable tape recorder and record his concerns, problems, and ideas for transcription into useful notes. Later, these notes can be sorted out and given priority for consideration. Recording meetings and conferences is also helpful. Another suggestion is that the principal ask teachers and parents to write out their problems, which is a perfectly legitimate way to seek understandings which will help lead to solutions, by forcing them to put their concerns in writing. In doing so, people often discover that much of the talk about the problem was irrelevant and the real reasons for the problem are difficult to define. Often just putting it in writing will lead the teacher or the parent to come up with some possible solutions, or will show that the problem was not what they originally suspected. However, there is another device that the principal can use in overcoming the time problem: the appointment of an assistant principal.

Role of the Assistant Principal

The role of the assistant principal will depend upon his status in a given school. Regardless of the size of the school, however, an assistant principal can be appointed, and can be an asset to the institution. In the small school the principal, with permission from the central office, may take several steps to bring about such an appointment. First, he will discuss the merits and even the disadvantages of making this appointment. He will be most emphatic in pointing out the benefits both to the faculty and to the student body. He will be careful to show that an assistant principal will be a teacher, but at the same time will play a definite role in the principal's office. Second, after the faculty shows a thorough understanding of the need for and the functions of this position, a staff committee may be selected to review the qualifications and experience of the likely candidates. The principal will, of course, make the final decision, but he will work closely with this committee. When the faculty members feel they have a definite part in the selection, there will be more likelihood of getting better cooperation from the group. Should the committee recommend a person who is obviously unqualified to be an assistant principal, the administrator can show good leadership by helping them see that a better selection might be made. If criteria are set up by the group before recommendations are made, the right person generally will be selected. Finally, after the selection is made, the newly-appointed assistant should be properly presented to his colleagues. Reaffirmation of the need, together with a complete description of the scope and duties of the office, may again be briefly stated. Such an appointment may be made even if a salary increment cannot be furnished for the assistant principal. Usually there are ambitious, capable faculty personnel who are willing to assume this office without additional salary, even while teaching regular classes. This does not imply that the school board should be unwilling to pay for this service, however.

A 1969 survey of the elementary principalship stated that:

> Years ago, many of those with the title of assistant principal received only their regular salaries as classroom teachers. If that was typical practice at one time, it was no longer true in 1968-69.
>
> In the total sample only 4 in 100 (4.3 percent) of the respondents reported that the basis of payment was their regular salaries as classroom teachers. Twenty-three in 100 (22.8 percent) were paid a flat amount above their regular salaries as classroom teachers; 35 in 100 (34.8 percent) were paid on an "index schedule" related to the schedule of classroom teachers; and 38 in 100 (38.2 percent) reported that their school systems had developed a schedule especially for assistant principals.[3]

In the larger schools, the assistant principal assumes a position of great importance. He is usually an administrator with training and experience comparable to that of the principal. Although in many large schools, unfortunately, the assistant principal is thought of as the discipline officer, he should be permitted to perform in a broader way to supplement the work of his superior officer. Perhaps the role of the assistant principal may be most effectively described by indicating what part he plays in the administrative picture. The assistant principal is an executive who:

1. Works closely with teachers on instructional problems.
2. Writes proposals for school innovations and seeks approval for them from the principal.
3. Supervises and evaluates the attempted innovations.
4. Uses a guidance approach in dealing with children referred for discipline.
5. Provides resource materials and aids for improvement of instruction.
6. Gives a sense of confidence and security to the staff by assuming control of the school in the principal's absence.
7. Provides the principal with briefs, summaries, reports, etc., to keep that administrator abreast of certain functions and developments.
8. Supports the on-going program of the school.
9. Aids in conservation of school materials, funds, supplies, etc.
10. Increases the effectiveness of administrative acts by stimulating motivation, guidance, and enthusiasm on the part of the staff.
11. Releases the principal from certain routine chores to allow him to give better leadership.
12. Serves as a sounding board for the principal in planning sessions before decisions are made or ideas put into action; helps him to be sensitive to certain people's points of view, etc.

Planning and Organizing

13. Uses his knowledge of administration processes to build teamwork within the school.

The assistant principal in the larger school may be appointed directly, or the principal may use the same techniques as in the smaller school for making the appointment. A school of any size can use an assistant principal if the principal and others accept the philosophy that an additional person can strengthen the school's management team. If wise planning and democratic processes are employed in appointing this person, the assistant principal will add immeasurably to the overall effectiveness of the administration. It is important that the entire staff recognize the appointment as a benefit to the school.

IMPLICATIONS OF LEADERSHIP TODAY AND TOMORROW

One of the most important tasks of the elementary school principal is to understand how he may conduct himself more efficiently. It is always overwhelming to view the list of demands made upon the administrator. To be able to perform satisfactorily and to carry out the wide variety of functions necessary for good school management entail responsibilities that often seem never-ending and sometimes insurmountable. The inexperienced and insecure executive may read with understanding how he is to function as a leader in various skill areas, yet he may still feel that to discharge these duties will require superhuman abilities and tireless energy. In the face of his many tasks the administrator may have to gloss over certain responsibilities or avoid completely many leadership activities.

Therefore, we feel the principal needs three additional skills to insure his acceptance as an educational leader and to insure that he will be able to translate what he *knows about* leadership into positive plans of action. These three skills may be stated simply.

First, the principal must know what good planning is. He will have to know how to plan and to check on the planning he has done. Second, the administrator must be an organizer. His knowledge and understanding of good organizational techniques should enable him to know how to organize and to determine whether the administrative machinery is available for carrying out his plans. Third, he must be able to evaluate and constantly realign his administrative patterns in light of his own and others' evaluation of himself and his school. He must read, analyze, interpret, and adapt to his own situation those ideas and goals he identifies as beneficial to his school's program. These three skills will help the principal practice the leadership activities he has studied and analyzed. Without planning and realistic organization, the administrator will be unable to render his most effective service to his school. Finally, he should be aware of trends and promising practices for his profession.

Developing Skills of Efficient Planning

An executive must learn how to plan if he expects to earn the label of an efficient and able administrator. It is true that many decisions are made or steps are taken that seem to depend on expediency or upon making a choice among relatively simple alternatives. Experience and training may assist in making such choices, even where little or no planning seems to be involved. Yet, to give a group intelligent and wise leadership, the administrator must accept the thesis that the long-range view requires an understanding of planning techniques as well as a knowledge of how to project these skills through a series of steps that will lead to a choice or decision. Planning becomes an important tool, regardless of the size of the school or the scope of the office of the principalship. Whether the administrator inherits a favorable school situation from his predecessor or moves into a difficult one, he has a responsibility for giving continued good leadership, or greatly improving it for a still better educational program. He has choices to consider, predictions to make, and outcomes to be concerned about. In short, he has much long-range planning to do and many immediate decisions to make.

The principal may conceive of planning as his responsibility for laying out a course or structure by which decisions can be made. It is his duty to organize and shape the course of the work to be done or goals to be reached. Through his planning of activities, he leads individuals and the staff toward attainment of mutually-recognized goals. Perhaps the nature of administrative planning may be understood more completely through an examination of some of its characteristics:

1. Planning is concerned with the improvement of the educational program. Either the overall or the specific plan for gaining educational goals will be formulated. Purpose is present in planning.
2. Planning is a comprehensive process. The principal is concerned with immediate problems and at the same time endeavors to envision future actions. His planning calls for use of many details, techniques, and persons for bringing about the most desirable results.
3. Planning is a continuous process. Amidst changing conditions the administrator knows that he must subject his planning procedures to rigorous scrutiny in the light of newer and better plans. Evaluation of school plans is a periodic activity.
4. Planning is a cooperative matter. Plans are developed with staff personnel in accordance with the philosophy of the personnel-oriented administrator.

A Guide to Better Planning. The steps to take in setting up a planning experience may be considered under three headings. Although these three steps are comparatively clear and simple, the emphasis will center on how the personnel-minded principal proceeds through each step of the planning.

Step One. The principal will develop with the group some purposes and objectives which call for planning. Beginning with their concerns gives the planning purpose and significance for all. The plan should always be consistent with the values and philosophy of the school. Successful planning at this stage depends on how well the principal helps the group understand what is being attempted. The principal should take the staff members into his confidence and give them reasons and implications which will lead to better understanding and genuine desire to participate in planning process. If the principal is planning independently, it is still important that purposes and objectives be clearly stated. He encourages free expression and group thinking at all times.

Step Two. The principal will plan ways to attain goals and determine who is to be involved and who is to have definite responsibilities. The planning at this stage will also consider scheduling and time factors. Action planning is expressly concerned with finding the best possible methods of attack; individuals should know what to expect and what is expected of them. Specific procedures will be brought out in the planning process. Perhaps at this stage of the planning he can help people arrive at different concepts of the group and its purposes, or help them to make decisions and assignments, arrive at judgments, and so on. The principal's planning must take into consideration the amount of responsibility his group is able and willing to take. He may need to give considerable direction in shaping the actual planning procedures if his group has not fully accepted this personnel approach. Of course, he keeps in mind that he is working toward greater faculty participation.

In discussing the method of attack and identifying individual responsibilities, the principal may find his planning process materially strengthened. If he feels a need to supply greater feelings of security at this stage, the planning should center on providing the details needed for successful realization of aims. For example, the principal may lend assistance in the planning by helping locate materials to be used; acquainting personnel with sources of usable materials; arranging for charts, books, maps, films, and other supplies; discovering resource persons; or providing business and industrial information useful for certain learning experiences. Finally, the *when* and the *where* are worked into the planning process, with definite time schedules or commitments decided upon.

Step Three. Many plans have been made which include what is to be done, how the plan will be carried out, and who will be responsible for various procedures. Even a compelling time schedule encourages the individual or the group to work. Yet some situations require a third stage of planning, which deals with evaluative activities. The principal gives very definite leadership when he helps the staff review how well the planning has been done. This phase of planning is simply a process of looking over the plans before they are actually carried out. To evaluate plans at this stage may call for re-thinking or revision, and may lead to even better planning. The procedure will eliminate needless effort and reduce failures to a minimum. Such questions as these may be asked: Are all data included? Have all alternatives been stated? If the plans lead to failure, what course may be taken? On the basis of this plan, what other decisions or actions might be expected? The administrator may apply to planning the principles of evaluation for the purpose of *weighing a given plan to discover how it may be strengthened before carrying it out.* A planning session led by the principal of one school will indicate how an administrator used this particular skill:

> Mr. Roberts began the new school year with great expectations. Several additions to his faculty gave him new strength in those grades which he felt needed better teaching. In a workshop experience with them, he asked the staff to help him in planning some professional programs of an in-service nature. He helped them to see what could be done and left them to define a plan that would be of their own choosing. After serious discussion, the group believed that they wanted to improve their own skills by knowing more about teacher-student sharing techniques in the classroom. The principal received this plan with enthusiasm. The group went to work and wrote up an outline of a plan that called for systematic aid in this area. The principal read it over approvingly, noted some changes to be made in terms of time especially, and decided to let the group think it over before putting the plan into operation. Several weeks later they examined the original plan once more and agreed that they ought to limit their work, at the beginning, to the area of language arts. This evaluation proved beneficial in many ways, as they found out later, especially in getting down the details of putting the plan into action. With the principal's help they were able to work out a realistic plan of this kind, and by the second semester were actually able to put it into effect.

PLANNING THE YEAR'S WORK—SHORT- AND LONG-RANGE PLANS

Because of increasing recognition of the importance of the elementary school principalship, there has been a steady increase in the length of the contract year to allow time for planning and preparation. The 1968 DESP research study states, "Approximately half (47.2 percent) of the total sample reported

Planning and Organizing 345

that they were employed each year for ten but less than eleven months. Twenty-one in 100 are employed for less than ten months; 14 in 100 for eleven but less than twelve months; and 18 in 100 reported a twelve-month term."[4]

In planning for the school year, the principal must anticipate endless details and at the same time plan to achieve the broader, overall objectives of his school. His planning, then, requires foresight in order to give careful attention to details prior to the initiation of plans. The details of planning the year's calendar, opening and closing school, requisitioning teaching materials, janitorial supplies, arranging for pupil activities, etc., are part of this task.

The broader plans relate to directing the school along the course which leads to achievement of school and community objectives. These plans may involve such leadership functions as planning for professional growth of his staff, initiating improved school services, and working with teachers, parents, and pupils in curriculum revision and the like.

Planning for the School Year

The principal of a small school employed for only the teaching days may find it wise to avoid procrastination, and do much of his planning during the preceding spring. The principal who does not chart his course for the school year before opening day will find that endless details pile up and some matters are left undone.

The principal needs a guide or calendar planned in advance for the school year. Every event, activity, or function which affects the principal or his school should be planned in advance and placed on that calendar. An illustration is given in figure 15.

The principal should also maintain a weekly-daily calendar with space for notes, on which he should list activities and schedule for each day, reminder notes and comments, and the time schedule for activities. Only in this way can he keep track of the hour-by-hour details for which he is responsible. Having space for notes is extremely valuable, since the notes will serve as constant reminders for important points he wants to remember about schedules and activities.

Such an accounting is necessary to show the principal how his time is being spent in administrative, supervisory, or clerical duties.

Cooperative Planning. It has been stated that cooperative planning is the key to good school administration. The modern educational leader recognizes the need to involve people in the planning process. A committee of teachers and parents representing the many interests of the community may, during the summer or the week before school opens, assist the principal in planning the activity calendar for the year. For example, the annual Halloween party for the community usually held in the school gym, the fall concert presented

Figure 15

Typical School Calendar

Aug. 29	Sept. 5	Sept. 12	Sept. 19
M 29 Pre-school con-	M 5	M 12	M 19 Ten-day report
T 30 ference	T 6 School opens	T 13	T 20 due
W 31 (all week)	W 7	W 14 Principal's	W 21
T Sept. 1	T 8 Faculty meeting 8:00 A.M.	T 15 meeting 9:00 A.M.	T 22 PTA Exec. Comm. 2:00 P.M.
F 2	F 9 Assembly pro-	F 16	F 23
S 3	S 10 gram	S 17	S 24
Sept. 26	**Oct. 3**	**Oct. 10**	**Oct. 17**
M 26	M 3 Attendance re-	M 10	M 17
T 27 PTA 7:30 P.M.	T 4 port due	T 11	T 18
W 28	W 5	W 12 Principals'	W 19
T 29	T 6	T 13 meeting,	T 20 PTA Exec. Comm.
F 30	F 7	F 14 Central Of-	F 21 2:00 P.M.
S Oct. 1	S 8	S 15 fice	S 22
Oct. 24	**Oct. 31**	**Nov. 7**	**Nov. 14**
M 24	M 31	M 7	M 14
T 25 PTA 7:30 P.M.	T Nov. 1	T 8	T 15
W 26	W 2	W 9 School Board	W 16
T 27	T 3	T 10 inspection	T 17
F 28 Attendance re- port	F 4 School carnival	F 11 State Education Association meeting	F 18 Band concert
S 29 Halloween party	S 5	S 12	S 19
Nov. 21	**Nov. 28**	**Dec. 5**	**Dec. 12**
M 21 PTA Exec. Comm. 2:00 P.M.	M 28	M 5	M 12
T 22 Thanksgiving	T 29 PTA 7:30 P.M.	T 6	T 13
W 23 vacation be-	W 30	W 7	W 14
T 24 gins	Dec.1	T 8	T 15
F 25	F 2	F 9	F 16
S 26	S 3	S 10	S 17
Dec. 19	**Dec. 26**	**Jan. 2**	**Jan. 9**
M 19	M 26	M 2 School opens	M 9
T 20	T 27	T 3	T 10
W 21 Christmas holi-	W 28	W 4 Deadline for	W 11
T 22 days, 1:00	T 29	T 5 teacher	T 12
F 23 P.M.	F 30	F 6 budget items	F 13 Budget due
S 24	S 31	S 7	S 14

by the school orchestra, the Lions' Club Amateur program, the P.T.A.'s bazaar, and the school carnival, all need to be planned and scheduled. When a community shares in planning the school's master schedule, there is less chance that conflicts will occur between school activities and community affairs. Such conflicts disrupt school and community relations and should therefore be avoided.

For the internal activities of the school, such as safety patrol meetings, student council meetings, and other student activities, a faculty-student committee will be of much help to the principal in planning regular meetings.

Planning and Organizing 347

Figure 16

Daily Calendar

Monday 18 January

8:00 Staff meeting

9:00 Short assembly for all boys—Quest team with Jr. Hi coach.

10:00 Barb & Jeannette—Field trip—check buses.

6:00 County AESP-YMCA Bldg.

NOTES

Mon.—Staff mtng. Judy & Kay report on workshop

Call J.N. to sub. Thurs.

Have secretary type materials for student com. & math consultant.

Get early entrance forms from Carol.

Thursday 21 January

Teachers not due in until 8:30

12:30 Conf. with student com. about special project.

3:00 to 4:00 Consultant on math.

Tuesday 19 January

8:00 Joyce & Kathleen from county office meet with Alpha team.

9:00 Mrs. Walton to ask about early entrance to first grade.

1:00 Assembly—Skills team presents program.

Wednesday 20 January

Mary visits McNeal school—J.N. will sub.

8:00 Team meetings.

9:00 P.T.A. Council

12:30 Conf.—J.K. (Team chairman)

7:30 pm Combined P.T.A. school council.

Friday 22 January

C.C. subs. for Nancy

Soc. St. Committee

9:00 Conf. with Mr. & Mrs. Orman, Guidance counselor, & psychologist.

10:00 Elem. Prin. meeting.

Some Before-School Duties

As indicated, it is desirable that the principal be employed for a period longer than the usual 180 teaching days. The principal should begin his duties at least two weeks prior to the opening of school. The principal may or may not have responsibilities connected with a system wide conference prior to the opening of school. If he has such responsibilities, these should get immediate attention. Some of the most important duties which need the principal's early attention are:

1. Checking class registrations and assignments; assigning additional registrants for placement.

2. Inspecting building against summer maintenance list to determine readiness for occupancy.
3. Checking school supplies received against requisitions submitted.
4. Determining class enrollments for best possible room assignments. (Consider age of children, size and location of room, etc.)
5. Meeting with the custodian to check his supplies, the readiness of heating equipment for operation, and the building work schedule.
6. Checking textbook stock against anticipated needs. Re-order immediately if necessary.
7. Preparing a bulletin for distribution to teachers concerning routine administrative duties.
8. Checking to determine whether all teachers have adequate living arrangements.
9. Arranging conferences with new and beginning teachers.
10. Preparing a schedule showing division of responsibilities.
11. Preparing an agenda for the initial meeting with the faculty.
12. Giving careful attention to opening remarks or address to faculty.
13. Allocating A-V equipment to rooms, teams, or grade levels. If equipment has been color coded, as suggested in another chapter, this becomes an easy, routine task.
14. Checking to see that the lunch program is ready to start. Make sure the manager has the schedule for all groups.
15. Having library or I.M.C. ready to operate first day, if possible.
16. Obtaining a map of bus routes, changes in schedules, etc. Assigning new children as they enroll.
17. Working with principals and the bus supervisor to change geographical boundaries if necessary to balance school population in several or all buildings. Letting parents know of these changes through newspapers or letters.
18. Having all supplies, equipment, materials, textbooks, and workbooks, as agreed upon the previous spring in planning meetings, allocated to rooms, teams, or grade levels, ready for use so that instruction may begin the first day.

Planning for Opening Day

The success of a good school administrator on the opening day of school may determine to some extent the success of the school's program. A carefully-planned opening day for the school will eliminate some of the confusion that arises in schools which lack strong leadership. For example, if teachers are given adequate instructions in bulletin form before the opening day, they will probably have an opportunity to clarify these instructions prior to that time, sparing many needless trips to the office.

Planning and Organizing 349

The principal should review with his staff whatever forms must be submitted by classroom teachers to the superintendent's office or the state department of education. Essential to the success of completing these routine matters is providing the staff with information concerning the purposes of such forms. Teachers who are uninformed about administrative requirements may not recognize the necessity for carefully gathering the necessary data.

The principal who is fortunate enough to have a clerk can assign her the responsibility of preparing entrance cards for new pupils and for those who were in attendance the previous year. In the absence of a regularly-employed clerk, this task must be done by someone else. One such form used in many schools is shown in figure 17. This card becomes a permanent record in the principal's office. It provides an up-to-date account of enrollment and a close check on pupil personnel.

The principal should plan to spend the first day of school in the school office. He should anticipate the many demands which will be made upon his services during this day. He will need to avoid conferences with teachers, pupils, parents, or sales representatives which might require large portions of his time. Situations will arise that require on-the-spot decisions. However, the discerning principal will attempt to anticipate the consequences of each decision. That is, he must not make hasty judgments simply to clear the office; rather, he should arrange for future conferences on those matters that require more time than he can give on the opening day. His primary purpose on the opening day of school is to see that teachers and pupils attend to their many routine duties and assignments.

School should open and close at the regular time on opening day so that ample time will be available for both formal and informal functions. Teachers should plan initial informal activities when routine matters are completed. The principal may plan for this by having the staff briefly discuss, at a faculty meeting prior to the opening of school, some of the worthwhile activities that children can participate in during the opening day. Such sharing may prove of value to inexperienced teachers, as well as to a few teachers who have been prone to waste this time.

Facilitating the Closing of School

Leadership is needed in closing school in the spring just as it is needed in opening school in the fall of the year. Rush and confusion should be held to a minimum. If the principal has planned with his staff the various activities and reports which are a vital part of the closing of school, he can find many ways to alleviate troublesome days for teachers and pupils alike.

Many schools now provide work days for teachers when the children are not present. Such a procedure at the end of the school year will provide

Figure 17

Registration Record
Madison Township Elementary Schools

DEAR PARENTS:

WE ARE REQUIRED TO HAVE A COMPLETE RECORD FOR EVERY CHILD ENROLLED IN OUR SCHOOL SYSTEM. PLEASE FILL IN THIS REGISTRATION FORM FOR YOUR CHILD AND RETURN IT TO THE SCHOOL IMMEDIATELY. WE MUST HAVE THIS INFORMATION IN ORDER TO COMPLETE YOUR CHILD'S RECORDS. THANK YOU.

Director, Pupil Personnel

BUILDING _____ DATE_____

CHILD'S FULL NAME _____ TEACHER_____ TEAM___
                Last First Middle

SESSIONS ATTENDED____BUS NO. IN___ BUS NO. HOME__ GRADE__

DATE OF BIRTH _____ PLACE OF BIRTH_____
            Month Day Year   City County State

NUMBER OF SISTERS OLDER_____ YOUNGER_____

NUMBER OF BROTHERS OLDER_____ YOUNGER_____

LAST SCHOOL YOUR CHILD ATTENDED NAME_____

    ADDRESS_____ CITY_____

===

WE MUST HAVE EXACT INFORMATION AS TO WHERE THIS CHILD LIVES AND WITH WHOM

_____ OR _____
(House No.)   (Box No.)   (Street or Road)   (City)

BETWEEN_____ AND _____
       (Street or Road)   (Street or Road)

_____ _____ _____ _____
(Zip Code) (Residence Phone) (Emergency Phone) (Name of person at
                                                            emergency phone)

CHILD LIVES WITH: (Circle which ones)

FATHER MOTHER STEPFATHER STEPMOTHER GUARDIAN OTHER

FULL NAME OF PERSON CHILD LIVES WITH:

_____ _____
(Name of Father, Stepfather, or Guardian)   (Occupation)

_____ _____
       (Company Name)   (Business Phone)

_____ _____
(Name of Mother, Stepmother, or other)   (Business Phone)

Planning and Organizing 351

Fig. 17—*cont'd.*
HEALTH RECORD

Has your child been vaccinated for Smallpox? Yes___No___Scar? Yes___No___

Immunized against Diphtheria, Whooping Cough, and Tetanus? Yes___No___

Number of Polio shots your child has taken: 0 1 2 3 or more___.

Does your child wear glasses? Yes___No___

Does he wear a hearing aid? Yes___No___

In case of emergency do we have permission to take your child to the doctor? Yes___No___

Do we have permission to take your child to the hospital in case of emergency?

Yes___No___ Which hospital? _____

Family doctor _____
                (Name)   (Address)   (Phone)

Alternate doctor_____
                (Name)   (Address)   (Phone)

Parent signature_____

time for teachers to make careful evaluations of pupils' progress. In addition, teachers can complete report cards and have things in readiness for the last day the children return to school. Some of the duties which the principal should prepare for prior to closing school are:

1. Arranging for transfer of pre-registration information for pupils leaving school to attend junior high school.
2. Preparing for the closing assembly or other closing events by informing pupils and parents in advance.
3. Having all equipment used by teachers returned and checked for summer storage.
4. Preparing a comprehensive bulletin with detailed instructions to teachers concerning attendance reports, etc.
5. Arranging for the auditor to audit financial accounts and turn the records over to proper school officials.
6. Having all permanent records completed, filed, and stored in a safe, fireproof vault for the summer.
7. Making arrangements for cleaning and repairing all audio-visual equipment during the summer months.
8. Planning a pre-enrollment day for new children entering school next fall.
9. Re-checking maintenance needs which have occurred since requests were sent to the superintendent's office in the early spring.

10. If leaving town for the summer, providing the superintendent with a summer address.
11. Arranging with teachers dates for special trips that demand long-range planning because of limited accommodations, such as camping, outdoor education, overnight trips made as part of a social studies unit, etc. Many times, unless dates are confirmed well in advance, there is no chance to make such plans after school starts in September.
12. Planning with grade levels or teams for instructional arrangements for September—class assignment, teacher assignment, team areas or team structure, grouping of children, change of grade or team location, teacher changes, etc.
13. Deciding with staff matters concerning children with special problems.
14. Hiring necessary teachers as early as possible and requesting that they visit the school to meet their future fellow teachers before school is out.
15. Planning recognition of those leaving because of maternity, sabbatical, retirement, advancement, or relocation.
16. Making sure teachers have orders in for materials and equipment agreed upon at planning meetings.
17. Making arrangements to have as many unfinished psychological referrals completed during the summer as possible.
18. Checking all office equipment, including the Public Address system, and requesting repairs where needed.

A MODERN IMPERATIVE

The principal must be able to adjust his professional life to *crisis situations*. He must be able to live with and learn from both minor and major crises. He must prepare himself and his staff to understand the principles of human behavior and the stresses and strains which bring about crisis. Together the principal and his staff should be prepared to meet a crisis when it arises. Many situations in which the principal finds himself or his school are highly emotional, and unless handled in the highest professional manner possible, can lead to unfortunate, even dangerous, results. The principal should create opportunities for his staff to discuss possible crisis situations and ways to meet them. Role playing, acting out crisis situations and noting reactions and suggestions, is a highly effective means of involvement. The discussion and role playing must involve the question of how best the principal and staff can react *as people* to a crisis situation.

Even a minor disturbance can turn into an explosive situation if not handled properly. It is imperative that every adult involved strive for a calm, professional, objective attitude in dealing with crisis situations. The adult who cannot control his own emotions is not only avoiding a solution, but is complicating the problem. He should remove himself from the scene and let others take over. For example, the most effective means of dealing with highly emotional parents and students, no matter whether their provocation is legitimate or not, is simply to listen. These people need an opportunity to talk out their frustrations, and the school, especially the principal, is the usual scapegoat. Do not accept such encounters as a threat to one's position or personality. Most often it comes down to the fact that the principal is the target because he is the head of the school. The principal will not last long in the principalship if he looks at every criticism, attack, or emotional outburst as a personal affront.

When the principal prepares himself and his staff to meet crises, and when those that arise are treated calmly and objectively, there is less likelihood that a confrontation will precipitate a major crisis. Long-range planning such as this pays dividends in smoother school operation and less psychological stress for all.

SUMMARY

Principals of smaller schools may gain help as they come to see that many of their problems do not differ substantially from those of the larger schools. The most common reason for lack of leadership in any school seems to be the press of time, but all executives will find they can be more systematic in budgeting and using time, regardless of the size of school.

The greatest challenge to the elementary school principal who strives to give better leadership is in planning and organizing. Sound planning facilitates creation of an organizational structure to carry out plans. The basic three-step approach to planning includes (1) developing purposes or objectives; (2) deciding on ways to attain these goals; and (3) providing evaluative procedures to test plans before organizing for action. Leading from the planning stage, the principal follows again the basic three-step approach by (1) organizing the situation in terms of a structural framework consistent with the planning aims; (2) selecting specific functions designed to reach the objectives and organizing them into an effective pattern; and (3) completing the process of organization by creating a definite arrangement of positions and responsibilities for individuals.

SUGGESTED READINGS

Borgeson, Fritz C. "Preparing the Principal for Leadership." *The National Elementary Principal* 32 (April 1955): 14–16.

Dawson, Barbara. "The Principal is Always There." *Arts and Activities* 52 (October 1962).

Department of Elementary School Principals. *The Elementary School Principalship in 1968: A Research Study*. Washington, D.C.: National Education Association, 1968.

Hockman, Thomas. "The Assistant Principalship — The Assistant's Role." *The National Elementary Principal* 42 (February 1963): 36–37.

McIntyre, K. E. "The Block of Time Program." *The School Executive* 74 (April 1955): 49–51.

National Association of Elementary School Principals. *The Assistant Principal in Public Elementary Schools–1969: A Research Study*. Washington, D.C.: National Education Association, 1969.

Sessions, Eldon B. "Standard of Efficiency Chart Will Determine Work Load." *School Management*, April 1966.

Smith, M. F. "The Teaching Principal Is False Economy." *The Nation's Schools* 74 (May 1955): 66–67.

Notes

1. Kenneth Simon and W. Vance Grant, *Digest of Educational Statistics, 1970*, National Center for Educational Statistics, U.S. Department of Health, Education, and Welfare, Document Catalog No. HE 5.210:10024–70, September 1970, p. 44.

2. *The Elementary School Principalship in 1968 . . . A Research Study* (Washington, D.C.: Department of Elementary School Principals, NEA, 1968).

3. *The Assistant Principal in Public Elementary Schools–1969. A Research Study* (Washington, D.C.: National Association of Elementary School Principals, NEA, 1969).

4. *School Principalship in 1968*.

14

Staff Relations and the Principal

The administrative behaviors identified in chapter 3 are the keys to developing staff relationships. The principal should be cognizant of the fact that from the time he makes the first contact with a prospective teacher, he sets the stage for developing some kind of staff relationship. The extent to which he demonstrates sensitivity to teacher needs will have much to do with the quality of rapport that emerges in his professional contacts. As a member of the middle-management team, the principal sometimes finds himself in frustrating and disturbing situations. He must carry out orders handed down by the chief school officer and at the same time maintain a warm working relationship with his teachers. Complaints to the superintendent's office about a teacher will find their way to the principal. The principal today must have a knowledge of the forces which affect teacher-teacher and teacher-principal relationships.

REASONS FOR TEACHER MILITANCE

The days of placid teacher organizations seems to be a thing of the past. Following World War II, teachers expected Americans to move quickly to remedy the poor conditions under which teachers were employed prior to and immediately after the war. But the inequalities continued into the fifties and sixties. Stinnett points out that teachers have simply become irritated beyond tolerance because the American people have failed to provide them with a fair share of the economic wealth of an affluent society.[1] Minney identified four causes for teacher militance: (1) economic injustice; (2) teachers' desire to participate in decision-making; (3) changes in the teaching force; and (4) larger-size school districts.[2]

Economic Injustice

Prior to and during World War II, the public schools were grossly underfinanced, when the largest part of our funds was deployed to the war effort. Teachers' salaries fell far behind those of people with equal training in industry and, in fact, part of the teacher shortage during and following the war was the result of large numbers of teachers going into defense plants for higher income. When the war ended there was not the expected correction of inequities in teachers' salaries, although some school systems did make a determined effort to improve salaries in order to compete with industry. "Moonlighting" was the order of the day, as teachers, particularly men, sought after-hour jobs in order to meet their budget needs.

During the middle 1960s, salaries continued to be a major issue. Carr wrote "the teaching profession is more insistent than ever on professional salaries."[3] The struggle continues today for improved teacher salaries, as shown by the increasing number of teacher strikes across the nation.

Teachers and Decision Making

Teachers have sought participation in decision making for many decades. In 1951, Chase[4] found that teachers were more satisfied with their positions in situations where they shared in the decision-making process. Teachers are not only interested in sharing in policy making which affects them, but they want and have gained the right to collective negotiations for salaries as well as for conditions under which they teach.

Changes in the Teaching Force

Two factors have contributed to the changing composition of the teaching force: (1) the upgrading of educational preparation required for teacher certification, and (2) an increase in young people, including men, who are entering the teaching profession.[5] Between 1946 and 1966, the number of teachers holding a bachelor's degree increased from 35 to 93 percent.[6] Teachers today are better educated and younger than ever. They take the meaning of democracy more seriously, for they seek an improved environment where mutual trust between teachers and administrators will prevail.

Larger School Districts

Larger school districts have resulted from efforts to provide better education more economically. State laws based on the number of pupils in an attendance area have reduced the number of small school districts across America significantly. With these larger school districts have come greater communication problems and larger numbers of employees, which has tended to depersonalize the teacher. Bigness has, in a very real sense, added to the problem of teacher militance. Barbash states that the more employees, the more problems, and the more complex the problems.[7] In large-school situations, it is not unlikely that employees feel more militant since they are often a long way from personal involvement in the decision-making process.

Elementary school principals are in a unique position to be close to their teachers and to deal with their problems in a face-to-face situation. With increasing unionism and the advent of strong teachers' associations, relations can become strained. But there is reason to believe that the principal can work closely with his staff to maintain a high level of rapport.

COLLECTIVE NEGOTIATIONS

The very nature of the principal's position places him in situations that require him to answer to many publics. He must answer to the superintendent, the board of education, the taxpayers, the teachers, parents, and children. His position requires him to be a leader in educational development, manager of a teaching and non-teaching staff, personnel director for interviewing and hiring his staff, and a budget efficiency expert, among many other responsibilities. There is now a new responsibility added to the many already identified for the elementary principal—that of collective negotiations.

There are many opinions concerning the principal's role in teacher negotiations. On this issue, he finds himself caught between management and the teaching staff. He is, without a doubt, the man in the middle. If he is drawn into being part of the management team, his role as an instructional leader is in jeopardy. Action has been taken in many states to exclude the principal from the professional classroom teachers' associations and unions. In some cases, neither the board of education nor the teachers have decided to which side the principal belongs.[8]

Although the National Education Association advocates that "principals can and should function within the same local as teachers without conflict of interest, some guidelines have indicated that classroom teachers may desire representation independent of principals."[9] Principals have definitely been excluded from participation with teachers in the locals of the American Federation of Teachers.[10] Even in this new role the principal finds himself in a unique position—a relatively independent agent. State laws governing public employees differ widely across the country, from including teachers and principals in statutes governing public school personnel in collective negotiations to including them with all public employees. Rhode Island law completely excludes principals from the bargaining units.

Effect of Collective Teacher Negotiations on the Principal

The National Conference on Professional Negotiations, sponsored by the Department of Elementary School Principals, indicates that the principal's prestige and status increase if he aligns himself with the board of education, but there is also the fact that this alignment might cause a breakdown in his rapport with the faculty. If principals align themselves with teachers, the following benefits might accrue: (1) better communications, (2) greater mutual respect, (3) less autocratic behavior, and (4) better teacher understanding of the principal's problems. On the other hand, certain negative results might occur: (1) the principal's relationship might be jeopardized by his role in grievance procedures, and (2) the relationship gives an overall appearance of too great idealism.[11]

The elementary school principal is finding that teacher negotiating teams have negotiated away some of the powers originally given to the principal by the board of education. Such factors as class size, pupil discipline, teacher assignments, promotions, and transfers were powers once given to the principal, but they have now been negotiated into teacher agreements. Redfern points out, however, that "the principal has been charged with the responsibility for making final decisions and is accountable for them."[12] Certainly, if teachers are going to negotiate for such things as teacher-pupil ratio, teacher assignments, etc., negotiations may result in maintaining the status quo. Differentiated staffing, team teaching, and other arrangements, might not be possible under certain teacher-board of education agreements.

Finally, Minney, in an extensive analysis of the principal's function in collective negotiations, concludes that the leadership role of the principal has been greatly diminished by the negotiating process. He feels the reasons for this condition are:

> (1) an effective and equitable role for principals has not been clearly formulated and activated; (2) the traditional chain of command has been discarded as teachers have taken their grievances directly to the authority which ultimately has the power to finalize decisions—the board of education—administrative team; and (3) teacher organizations are using the powers which are inherent in the negotiation process as a means of enforcing their demands for an effective voice in regulating all facets of the educational program.[13]

An Equitable Role for the Principal in Collective Negotiations

The principal, obviously, has an important stake in teacher negotiations. He possesses certain expertise which must be utilized in any bargaining situation affecting his school. King has identified at least four methods for utilizing the principal in the negotiating process:

> 1. A joint review with principals (or principals' representatives if in large cities) sitting with the superintendent or the board to cooperatively review, analyze, and evaluate the demands of teacher negotiators in terms of positive or negative effect on school management and quality of education. The joint review becomes the basis for the board-superintendent response in negotiations.

2. Representatives of a principal-supervisor team may be permitted full fledged membership on the board's negotiating team.
3. Representatives of a principal-supervisor team may sit in on three party conferences with board and teachers.
4. A series of teacher-administrator negotiation units may work on various areas and transmit conclusions to superintendent or board to be worked out with teacher negotiators.[14]

Perhaps the principal's role in collective teacher negotiations is best defined as that of consultant to both the board of education and the teachers. His expertise is best recognized when he advises negotiating teams—management and teaching—concerning those conditions of employment that directly affect the operation of the educational program. To accomplish this role, he must gain the respect of teachers for his understanding of a quality education program. But, in addition, he needs to be constantly cognizant of problem areas and seek to work these out with his staff before they become conditions for negotiation. The need for negotiation stemmed in the first place from failure of administrators to act wisely and promptly to alleviate poor working conditions. The next section of this chapter, which deals with the job analysis approach, is still another means of developing better understanding of both the principal's and the teacher's role in the educational process.

THE JOB-ANALYSIS APPROACH TO EFFECTIVE ADMINISTRATION

If the school organization is to achieve one of the main goals of personnel administration—the effective utilization of teaching and non-teaching personnel—the principal has a personnel tool at his disposal in the job-analysis procedures. This tool is the procedure by which a principal acquires accurate knowledge of the individual jobs in the school organization. Job analysis is a method for studying, in an orderly and systematic way, the duties, requirements, and skills of a job.[15]

Although job analysis has been widely used in industrial settings is no reason for principals to disregard this procedure for improving the selection of personnel for his school. Perhaps there is no better way for the beginning principal to gain a thorough understanding of the duties and functions of each person who works in his building than through a carefully administered job analysis. The elementary school principal must be aware that the job analysis program is not a study of abilities, aptitudes, and characteristics of the staff personnel. Yet, as will be noted later, job analysis can be used in evaluating an individual's capabilities in terms of performance. It has also been suggested that a modification of the job-analysis approach, when used to study both the teacher's and the principal's roles, will serve as an excellent in-service device to enhance teacher growth.[16] The personnel-characteristics requirements for a position certainly help identify the kind of person who should be placed in that position. With the advent of team teaching and differentiated staffing, a job analysis as suggested here may help strengthen the school organization and the educational program through improved teacher understanding of their roles.

The principal should keep three things in mind when approaching the task of job analysis. First, he must be systematic and accurate in securing the proper data. Definitions and guide manuals should be clearly formulated, understood, and reviewed so that data will have common meanings. Second, he must take the responsibility for compiling the information in clear, usable forms or reports. Third, he needs to know how he can use the information to best advantage.

With the growth of public school education, administrators have found it difficult to keep up with details, such as changes in teaching and non-teaching positions. The elementary school principal seldom has complete records of what the modern team-level positions call for in terms of teaching duties, working conditions, physical demands upon the teacher, and to some extent, even the education and specific skills needed to perform satisfactorily in the classroom. In addition, the roles of various teacher aides need to be analyzed according to the job requirements.[17] Local conditions will of course modify these factors. Equally important, there are often no specific terms spelled out either for staff members or for administrators to assure that each party has the same concept of the various issues and problems at hand. Achieving these common understandings is crucial to school personnel, since incomplete or inaccurate information about jobs can lead to gross misunderstandings. In a study carried out in one city district, great differences were found to exist concerning what teachers believed principals were doing with their time.[18] Role clarification is needed to enable the entire staff to exert its energies toward common goals based upon mutual understandings.

For the purposes of the elementary school principal, job-analysis procedures may be further defined as orderly and systematic studies of the characteristics, duties, and responsibilities of a specific school position. Job analysis of the total staff will yield information of three kinds significant to the principal:

1. *Job description*. This is a statement setting forth the characteristics, duties, and responsibilities of a specific job in the school.

2. *Job specification*. This is a written record of the minimum requirements or standards which must be met by an applicant for a specific job.

3. *Job relationship*. This sets forth the progression of incumbents on jobs ("promoted from . . . ," "promoted to . . . "). In some instances, rela-

tionships may also be shown to jobs in other departments of the school or system which require the same or similar characteristics of skill or training on the part of the staff member.[19]

Uses for the Results of Job Analysis

The question may well be asked, why should the principal need a formalized investigation and write-up of job duties, working conditions, and other requirements? Many principals and other individuals feel competent to describe a job within a particular school, and can do so informally. With changing hiring requirements, new emphasis in preparation, different concepts of differentiated staffing, and new tasks to be performed, however, the personnel-minded principal may find it desirable to standardize descriptions of school positions according to the duties involved.

The principal will find a job-analysis program helpful in at least four areas of school administration. Each of these areas uses the job-analysis procedure to obtain information for furthering the educational objectives of the elementary school and for giving leadership status to the principal.

Recruitment. When a prospective candidate for teaching must be informed of the skills and abilities needed to enter the teaching profession, such occupational information from the elementary school principal may be viewed as a recruitment device. Further, the principal will have at hand the necessary job descriptions and specifications when he tries to work out a cooperative program in his school and community, and perhaps at the state level, to recruit teaching candidates. A comprehensive job-analysis information file supports the principal in an intelligent marshalling of all resources in the teacher recruitment program.

Selection and Placement. The employment of an individual usually requires examination of the skills, abilities, and training of many people in order to select the one teacher suitable for the job opening. Looking at it in another way, it is "placement," or an examination of the various teaching duties and requirements to enable placing a specific person in the classroom for which he is best suited. Although college programs and state certification requirements are specific (although not nationally in agreement) for nearly all teaching positions, it is still essential to have at hand factual information about the teaching positions in a particular school. With job analysis yielding basic operating knowledge of the teaching duties and hiring requirements, many misjudgments will be avoided at the employment stage. Misunderstandings after selection and placement will be lessened by adequate explanation and mutual understanding of job-analysis data.

To help select and place teacher applicants efficiently, some school systems use selection tests in the areas of aptitude, intelligence, personality, and the like. Job knowledge should be the primary aim of any such test.

Preparation. The principal may readily see the relationship of job analysis to the preparation of teachers. He knows the skills, habits, and content needed for teaching success in his particular educational program. He is in a position to furnish guidance to the prospective teacher, to evaluate intelligently an applicant's record in terms of continued training, and, probably more important, to furnish leadership for staff improvement based on factual information.

Merit Rating. Although job analysis is concerned only with the characteristics and demands of the teaching positions, and not with those of teachers in the classroom, the principal may be called upon to determine the value of a teacher's performance. Job analysis can reveal the kind of performance required and thus give a basis for teacher evaluation. The teacher's job becomes clarified through job descriptions, and items for rating his performance can be listed on some kind of a merit-rating form. His performance can be appraised in terms of his success in discharging these specified educational duties.

Making a Job Analysis

The success of a job-analysis program depends on careful selection of the analyst and the method used to introduce the need and value of the work to be done.[20] The principal may conduct his own program, but he will need the support of his entire staff and immediate superiors. All individuals included in the analysis must have the opportunity to assist in developing plans and procedures to insure ultimate acceptance of the program.

There are three basic methods of gathering information for job analysis:[21] (1) Use of the questionnaire with administrators, college of education personnel, and with the state department of education. A tabulation of data collected from one or all of these sources is necessary to get certain basic information concerning minimum requirements for a teaching position. Additional data about staff positions may also come from the local level in particular situations. (2) Interviews with key personnel. The information gained from these persons will furnish important data from realistic sources. Key persons include those individuals who are in typical and representative positions and are able to furnish the appropriate information. (3) Observations made by the analyst. The person who is compiling the data may get firsthand information by seeing the person on the job and making written records of what he sees. This device enables the analyst to support his data by actual visitation or observation.

Much of the necessary information may be secured from the central administrative office, but the principal should check to see that those files are up-to-date and satisfy the needs for which he is making his job analysis. A checklist is furnished below to guide the principal in preparing for the analysis.[22] He must include in the analysis those items which will best meet his special needs.

1. *The name or title of the teaching position.* This naming of the correct job title is usually a simple matter. It should be done, however, for the sake of accuracy and understanding. For example, the teacher leader of the language arts team is labelled as such, while an "acting principal" title in a school may be included in the analysis to indicate a temporary status during a given period. Every person should know what each job is properly called.

2. *The classification title.* Usually there is little need for any standardized grouping of the jobs in the school. If it is necessary to precisely relate the jobs within a system, or even within a single school, perhaps there is some justification for stating titles in a certain terminology in order to define or clarify the classification within the system or school. Most principals will find that giving each position a title such as educational aide, assistant teacher and senior teacher will be sufficient.

3. *Location of job.* Again, in a large school it may be useful to write a series of precise statements regarding the location of the job. This means describing the functions of the department, division, or level in which the job is found. Usually an organizational chart serves the purpose of showing how the teaching position or non-teaching job fits into the organization. In some instances unnecessary duplication of work may be spotted or a re-allocation of assignments may be called for. The principal of the average school has little difficulty in writing up this item, since his school plan usually does not call for a complex form of organization.

4. *Personel problems.* In some instances, the principal may find it necessary to study a job on which there have been excessive resignations or absences. If some sort of pattern seems apparent, his analysis may assist him in his future recruiting selection, and in-service problems. He will also be in a better position to eliminate the causes of personnel problems.

5. *Teaching or work performed.* The principal cannot describe all of the teaching and auxiliary services performed. Yet he should attempt to estimate the time spent on certain functions to suggest, for example, that on a given Tuesday the teacher is not expected invariably to give 15 percent of class time to reading. In addition to the time estimates, some ideas should be given as to how, why, and with what materials a particular job is done. Caution should be observed in trying to list and pin down each item too precisely, but the principal may make a rough notation of each of these items of work performed.

6. *Supervision given and received.* Frequently there are individuals who have supervisory jobs in the elementary school. The principal will note who is being supervised, the specific kind of supervision, and to whom the supervisor is responsible. The exact duties and functions of such persons should be listed to give the principal a clear perspective of each position.

7. *Level-of-position difficulties.* The school executive should be aware

of the difficulties involved for each level of position. Such difficulties generally fall into several categories under which specific information for each position may be listed: *Responsibility*: Is there any specific knowledge required particularly for this position? *Initiative*: What special abilities are necessary to meet certain requirements, solve new problems, and so forth? *Mental alertness*: Do changing situations or conditions demand a particular degree of attentiveness? *Judgment*: Does the staff member need to make many independent decisions based on objective data and observation of the situation? *Dexterity*: Will the individual need to have qualities of quickness, deftness, and exceptional coordination to meet specific situations? *Accuracy*: Is a particular degree of precision necessary for a standard performance? *Miscellaneous factors*: What other factors or special combinations of factors should be listed or defined? It is in this way that the principal analyzes particular position difficulties to learn what factors, including physical requirements or demands, are needed for a certain position.

8. *Salary schedule.* The central administrative office will provide these data if a salary schedule is available. How the staff member is to be paid should also be listed.

9. *Length of workday.* There should be clear understandings as to working hours for each position.

10. *Standards of performance.* Some positions in the school may lend themselves to the setting of performance standards (i.e., custodial and cafeteria jobs, and the like). The definition of standards for each teaching station poses a serious problem. However, the principal should not avoid this responsibility. *Perhaps the best approach will be to get each faculty member involved in defining standards of performance for the school as a whole and standards of performance for each grade level.* The principal should organize this phase very carefully and involve all personnel responsible for teaching in every grade. Performance standards should be realistic and clearly formulated.

11. *Job relationships.* Often in a city-wide program there are possibilities for promotion or transfer. In such cases the type of information gained from defining job relationships can be valuable; such information can also be of assistance in the in-service program.

12. *Uses of teaching aids and equipment.* Does the position require the use of special machines, tools, equipment, or material? Certainly all positions use many teaching aids, but the principal is concerned with listing the more technical items as well as the more commonly used ones.

13. *Working conditions.* Although many principals would like to see improved facilities in the school, the essential consideration here is the listing of any specific conditions which are peculiar to a certain job. For example, the heating engineer's job may require special attention, while the first-grade teacher would be listed as having normal working conditions even though there might be room for some improvement.

14. *Previous experience and preparation required.* The colleges and universities, local authorities, and state departments of education will define the training and preparation needed for teaching positions. Non-teaching jobs may have some specific requirements to be described in the current analysis. The principal should list the training and preparation requirements of all positions in the school.

15. *Selection methods.* If the principal has the opportunity of selecting his staff, he should work out selection methods for teaching and auxiliary jobs, subject to approval from higher levels. Such items as interviews, tests, references, and so on should be clearly described to aid him in making his selection for a particular position.

The principal may wish to extend this list in preparing to collect data for a job analysis. In a small school it may be unnecessary to put what is already known into writing. Yet, in spite of the simplicity of an organization, a job analysis procedure that covers all or most of the above-described items can be a valuable and enlightening experience to the principal and his staff.

Preparing Usable Forms for the Job Analysis

The kind of form used for obtaining information will depend upon the needs and scope of the analysis to be made by the school.[23] After the decision has been made concerning the items to be covered in the analysis, the principal should use a work sheet to record his information. This form should be worked out thoughtfully, and each item must be carefully defined. He should either devise some kind of guide manual, with explanations and definitions, or make sure that the form itself contains explicit information. The former procedure is considered preferable. Having prepared forms which are suited to his needs, the principal is then ready to be specific in collecting his information. To aid the principal in setting up usable forms for collecting and assembling data, four patterns are furnished here. The information called for in these four forms covers the items deemed most important by many principals, but the forms may be adapted to meet particular objectives and needs.

(Identification Form)

JOB ANALYSIS SCHEDULE
FOR
MAIN STREET ELEMENTARY SCHOOL

Date_____

I. *Job Identifications*

    1. Title of Position _____
    2. Number of such positions in school _____Male_____Female
    3. Alternate title(s) _____

4. School system classification of position _____
   (Refer to systems manual for classification of position).
5. Location of job_____ Salary schedule_____
6. Working conditions _____
7. Teaching or work performed _____

   _____
   _____
   _____

8. Supervision given or received _____

   _____

   (Continue Items 7 and 8 on additional sheets, if needed.)
9. Length of workday _____

Reviewed by_____ (Signed)_____
                                                (Analyst)

(Personnel Form)

JOB ANALYSIS SCHEDULE
FOR
MAIN STREET ELEMENTARY SCHOOL

Date _____

II. *Personnel Form for Position*
   1. Experience: None_____ Acceptable_____
   2. Preparation Data:

      | | *Minimum* | *Deficiencies* |

      College _____
      University _____
      Local Requirements_____
      State Requirements _____
      Specific Requirements_____
      Comments: _____

   3. Position Relationships:
      Promotions possible from _____ to_____
      Transfer possibilities from _____ to_____
   4. Level-of-position difficulties _____
      Responsibilities_____
      Knowledge _____
      Initiative _____
      Mental alertness _____
      Judgment _____
      Dexterity _____

Staff Relations and the Principal 367

      Accuracy _____
      Miscellaneous _____
5. Any combination of factors needed or desirable? _____
_____
              (Use supplementary sheets, if needed.)
6. Standards of performance _____
      School requirements _____
      Grade level or term requirements_____
      Non-teaching position requirements _____
              (Related to Point 4 of Personnel Form.)
      Comments_____
_____
_____

7. Teaching aids and equipment uses _____
_____

8. Selection or hiring methods_____
_____

9. General Comments: (Indicate if there are any special personnel problems involved.) _____
_____
_____

Reviewed by _____ (Signed)_____
                                                              (Analyst)

(Physical Demands Form)

JOB ANALYSIS SCHEDULE
FOR
MAIN STREET ELEMENTARY SCHOOL

                                         Date_____

III. *Physical Demands Form for Position*
    1. Physical Activities:
       Normal expectation _____
       Specific requirements _____

    2. List any detailed physical activities needed for:
       Grade level teacher: Conducts own physical education class
       (Non-teaching)
_____
_____

    3. General Comments:_____
_____
_____

Reviewed by_____ (Signed)_____
                                                              (Analyst)

(Personnel Characteristics Form)

JOB ANALYSIS SCHEDULE
FOR
MAIN STREET ELEMENTARY SCHOOL
Date_____

IV. *Personnel Characteristics Form for Position*

Indicate the amount of each characteristic required of the individual in order to do the job satisfactorily. Place the appropriate symbol after each characteristic.

    N—Not required for satisfactory performance
    C—A medium to low degree required
    B—An above average degree required
    A—A very high degree required

A. Physical Characteristics
    Rapidity of work_____
    Strength of arms_____
    Dexterity of hand _____
    Keenness of vision _____
(and so on—the principal will determine in advance how many physical requirements need to be listed since most teaching personnel will not require any particular degree of physical proficiency, except for areas such as physical education and the like.)

*B. Teaching Characteristics
1. Personal traits:
    Personal appearance _____
    Social adaptability (manners, etc.) _____
    Emotional stability _____
    Dependability _____
    Cooperation with pupils and school personnel _____
    Enthusiasm, drive, etc. _____
    Initiative, resourcefulness _____
    Vitality, health_____
2. Teaching competencies:
    Understanding of very small children _____
                    small children _____
                          youth _____
    Knowledge of principles of teaching _____
    Knowledge of subject matter_____
    Command of oral English _____
    Use of teacher-pupil planning activities _____
3. Teaching skills:
    Ability to plan with children_____
    Knowledge and use of games, etc. _____
    Knowledge and use of materials _____
    Provision for individual differences _____

Staff Relations and the Principal 369

      Stimulation of interest_____
      Motivation of group _____
      Classroom management and discipline_____
      Ability to evaluate progress _____
      Use of pupil-evaluation processes_____
      Use of significant counseling data _____
      Ability to work out behavior problems _____
  4. Organization and leadership of others:
      Delegation of work to others _____
      Obtaining efficiency through suggestion rather than force _____

      Looking ahead and planning an even flow of activity _____

      Keeping attention on major school issues _____
Comments: _____
_____
_____

Reviewed by _____ (Signed)_____
                                                                (Analyst)

Note: a separate form might be devised for non-teaching personnel who require certain physical characteristics and less so-called mental characteristics. If only one form is used the example here should be considered primarily for teaching personnel.

    The information to be collected on the Identification Form is concerned largely with identifying the job and describing the teaching or other work performed. The personnel concerned may experience some difficulty in listing how they spend their time; teachers in particular may feel unable to describe the teaching day in terms of specific activities, with an allotted time expressed in percentage terms for each experience. It should be emphasized that only general estimates are requested.

    The Personnel Form is so named because the data refer specifically to information needed for particular understandings of the position. The data called for under the item *level-of-position difficulties* is related to the Personnel Characteristics Form and is designed to point up any difficulties which may be encountered in the position.

    The Physical Demands Form is designed for securing particular data regarding the physical demands of a given position. Generally speaking, this form will be brief except when it is adapted for certain custodial or service jobs in maintenance, cafeteria work, and the like.

    The Personnel Characteristics Form covers the personnel characteristics required of the position. The amount of a certain characteristic required for satisfactory performance can be expressed in symbols suggesting the degree to which that characteristic is necessary for best performance. The principal will find that physical characteristics required for most teaching positions need not be broken down into specific items, as would be necessary for non-teaching jobs. However, the *teaching characteristics* item should be thought through very carefully. The characteristics suggested in this form may furnish clues for additional items. It should be obvious that the kindergarten teacher's position requires certain teaching characteristics different from those of the fifth-grade team organized horizontally. Some traits are common to all good elementary teachers, but the principal should design the form to show the degree to which each of these characteristics may be required for satisfactory performance in a particular teaching position. Careful consultation by the principal with each team leader and teacher will insure accurate wording of the form and emphasize the required characteristics. The actual wording of Part B in the Personnel Characteristics Form covers the *common characteristics* required by elementary teachers, and is intended as a guide for further rewording to bring out the characteristics required for various grade levels.

The four forms illustrated can be used more efficiently when a guide manual has first been prepared. The principal should ask the cooperation of all involved, both in preparing the guide manual and in constructing the forms to be used. It will be noted that there are spaces on each form for the signature of the analyst and others who review the data. The reviewers should be consulted before the data are collected. The school executive will find a more receptive and willing staff if he uses their abilities, acquaints them with purposes and philosophy, and receives their comments and suggestions in preparing the manual and forms as the work progresses. Of course, full responsibility for the job analysis must rest on one person who will give considerable time and effort to planning and organization. If the principal assigns this responsibility, the person he selects should be one who gets along well with the staff. He should be skilled in writing and be allowed sufficient time to carry out the work.

A Checklist for Action

It has already been suggested that the completed forms should be inspected by every individual concerned. This cooperative approach will eliminate mistakes and add to the usefulness of the information. If failures and confusion result, the analyst should not give up in discouragement. It is recommended that the principal make several trial runs, as it were, to get the feel of the job-analysis procedure. The following suggestions should be useful to the principal beginning his first job analysis:

1. Make sure the staff knows what is going to be done and why. Use each staff member wherever possible.
2. Do not select only the best performers as subjects for the job analysis write-up.
3. Help the staff see the advantages of the job analysis procedure.

4. Discuss each item freely with the staff.
5. Do not give the impression that the principal is trying to tell a staff member how to do his job.
6. Be sure to analyze the job and not the person who is doing it.
7. Be sure to cover all possible points. Ask for suggestions, criticisms, and help at every opportunity. Try to be thorough and accurate.
8. Avoid the injection of personal opinions. Write down the facts as they are revealed in the analysis.
9. Make available the job analysis results in some sort of handbook or other form. Perhaps a special meeting can be called for the purpose of bringing out the highlights of the job analysis.
10. Study the information to see what can be done to improve the school's educational program.

In order to show how these job analysis procedures can be employed in an actual situation, the following illustration is presented as it really happened:

> During the spring semester, Mr. Williams, the principal of a ten-room rural elementary school, learned that the seventh-grade teacher was planning to move into a high-school teaching position. Although no definite commitments had been made, and it was not even certain that the move would materialize, the principal felt he needed to get ready to meet the situation if it did develop. There were other complications that would arise, making the problem more complex than just hiring a new seventh-grade teacher. In reviewing the whole picture, the administrator came to the conclusion that he ought to have a written job analysis for his school. For one thing, it would help in placing his teachers in more suitable teaching stations.
>
> The principal spent the early part of the semester getting his staff to think in terms of a job analysis. After such preparation, they agreed with him that there were advantages to be realized from this project. Each form to be used for collecting the data was reviewed by a separate committee, and many useful comments and suggestions were offered. The teachers were especially helpful in wording the form with items that called for grade-level teaching characteristics. These were worded in such a way that the analyst would get specific data that would best describe the teaching characteristics particularly needed at each grade level.
>
> After thorough screening of the forms to be used for collecting data, the principal made his analysis. He was careful not to give the impression that he wanted to tell any teacher how to conduct his work. The items were filled in carefully in light of his observations, together with the teachers' own statements. It was done systematically and objectively, with facts rather than mere opinions being recorded. Upon completion of the analysis, and after additional comments and suggestions had been received from all participants, the principal summarized the data in a loose-leaf notebook according to grade levels and non-teaching personnel. He then

believed that he had achieved several objectives: (1) he knew more about each teaching position in his school; (2) the staff profited from the analysis in getting a new perspective of the total job; and (3) the principal felt more secure in matters of new-teacher selection and transfer of present staff members from one grade to another.

When school opened in the fall, the seventh-grade teacher had been appointed to his regular position. Apparently there had been no hurry or need for making a job analysis. However, a vacancy in a nearby high school faculty occurred rather suddenly. The aspiring high school teacher was soon to realize his wish. The fifth-grade teacher wanted to move to the seventh grade, a prospective teacher candidate felt she could handle the fourth grade, and the juggling of positions began. Actually, the hiring of a new teacher and the changes of assignment for the present staff could have been made without any job analysis data. Yet the principal used the write-ups frequently in his conferences with each teacher. There were no doubts in his mind or in the other person about the specific job. He found the data especially valuable in achieving common understandings about the respective positions. The new teacher particularly could see that the principal knew what was expected of her, and seeing that the job description was in writing had a good effect upon her. The principal felt that during this transition stage he handled placement problems more readily and efficiently, while the teachers felt that they too were clearer as to what was expected of them, and felt more secure about entering the new teaching positions. Thus the job-analysis program proved its worth in one instance by creating better understanding for the administration and the faculty.

If the principal of the elementary school plans and organizes the job-analysis program properly, he will be in a better position to contribute to educational progress. The task of the personnel-directed principal is not a simple one, but the use of this technique is one step toward achieving better relationships with school personnel, clearer understanding of duties, and more intelligent matching of the person with the right job. These benefits are possible with adequate job-analysis information.

SUMMARY

The emphasis in this chapter has been on factors which affect principal-teacher relationships. Teacher militancy in recent years is a new problem confronting the principal. His need to understand the background of this movement may help him acquire new strategies for working with his staff.

His role in teacher negotiations is still undefined, but it appears that he is caught in the middle regardless of which direction he leans. Perhaps his role is to lend his expertise as a consultant to either the board of education or the teachers on negotiable factors which affect school operation.

The job-analysis approach to the principalship, uses of a job-analysis program, and methods of conducting a job analysis are described. When principal and staff member have the same concept of various issues and problems in terms of duties, requirements, and skills of the school job, these common understandings will lead to more effective educational practices and improved teacher-principal relations.

SUGGESTED READINGS

American Federation of Teachers. *How Collective Bargaining Works.* Washington, D.C.: American Federation of Teachers, 1969.

Asnard, Robert R. "Directions in Negotiation." *The National Elementary Principal* 48 (September 1968): 21–23.

Carr, William H. "The Principals in Professional Negotiations." *The Bulletin of the National Association of Secondary School Principals* 50 (April 1966): 45–52.

Cronin, J. H. "School Boards and Principals; Before and After Negotiations." *Phi Delta Kappan* 49 (November 1967): 62–65.

Department of Elementary School Principals, National Education Association. "Report of the National Conference on Professional Negotiation." Washington, D.C.: National Education Association, June 1968, mimeographed.

Gross, Neal and Robert E. Herricott. *The Professional Leadership of Elementary School Principals.* Washington, D.C.: The Cooperative Research Branch Project No. 853, U.S. Office of Education, 1964.

Hart, Jerry. *Collective Negotiations: A New Outlook in 1966.* Athens, Ohio: The Center for Educational Research and Service, College of Education, Ohio University, 1966.

Herman, J. J. "Job Analysis for the Curriculum Coordinator." *School Management* 1, no. 6 (June 1962): 63.

Lieberman, Myron and Michael H. Moskow. *Collective Negotiations for Teachers.* Chicago: Rand McNally, 1966.

Minney, Ronzel D. "An Analysis of the Functions of Public School Principals in Collective Negotiation Procedures." Doctoral dissertation, Ohio University, 1970.

Redfern, George B. "Negotiation Changes Principal-Teacher Relationships." *The National Elementary Principal* 47 (April 1968): 20–25.

Shuster, Albert H. "Modified Job Analysis and In-service Education." *American School Board Journal* 150 (February 1965): 15–17.

Stinnett, T. M. *Turmoil in Teaching.* New York: Macmillan, 1968.

Notes

1. T. M. Stinnett, *Turmoil in Teaching* (New York: Macmillan, 1968), p. 34.

2. Ronzel D. Minney, "An Analysis of the Functions of Public School Principals in Collective Negotiation Procedures" (Doctoral dissertation, Ohio University, 1970), pp. 23-29.

3. William Carr, "The Principal's Role in Professional Negotiations," *The Bulletin of the National Association of Secondary Schools,* April 1966, p. 48.

4. Francis S. Chase, "Factors for Satisfaction in Teaching," *Phi Delta Kappan* 33 (November 1951): 128.

5. Minney, "Analysis of Functions," p. 26.

6. National Education Association, "Professional Preparation," *NEA Research Bulletin* 45 (October 1967): 88.

7. Jack Barbash, *Union Philosophy and the Professional* (Washington, D.C.: American Federation of Teachers, 1968), p. 2.

8. Minney, "Analysis of Functions," p. 63.

9. Office of Professional Development and Welfare, National Education Association, *Guidelines for Professional Negotiation* (Washington, D.C.: National Education Association, 1965), p. 14.

10. The American Federation of Teachers, *Constitution of the AFT* (Washington, D.C.: The American Federation of Teachers, AFL-CIO, 1968), p. 4.

11. Department of Elementary School Principals, National Education Association, Report of the National Conference on Professional Negotiation, June 1968, p. 22.

12. George B. Redfern, "Negotiation Changes Principal-Teacher Relationships," *The National Elementary Principal* 47 (April 1968): 22.

13. Minney, "Analysis of Functions," p. 150, 151.

14. James C. King, "New Directions for Collective Negotiations," *The National Elementary Principal* 47 (September 1967): 32.

15. Roger M. Bellows, *Psychology of Personnel in Business and Industry* (Englewood Cliffs, N. J.: Prentice-Hall, 1949), p. 61.

16. Albert H. Shuster, "Modified Job Analysis and In-service Education," *The American School Board Journal* 44, no. 7 (March 1965): 15.

17. See Commission on Teacher Education and Professional Standards, *Recommended Guidelines for the Selection, Placement, Supervision and Continuous Progress Evaluation of Educational Aides* (Columbus, Ohio: Ohio Education Association, 1970), 24 pages.

18. James Miller, "Teacher Expectations of the Administrative Role in Comparison to Actual Practices of Administrators" (Master's seminar paper, Ohio University, Athens, Ohio, 1961), p. 45.

19. Bellows, *Psychology of Personnel,* p. 63.

20. Wilson F. Wetzler, "Use of Job Analysis Towards More Effective Educational Administrative Practices," *Educational Administration and Supervision* 40 (February 1954): 114.

21. Ibid.

22. Carroll L. Shartle, *Occupational Information* (Englewood Cliffs, N. J.: Prentice-Hall, 1946), pp. 18-22.

23. Wetzler, "Use of Job Analysis," p. 115.

15

Evaluation

The term accountability is used here to mean that the principal is answerable to his superiors and the public for the results of the educational program. To assess the extent to which goals have been achieved, related to his own actions or those of others, the principal must become skillful in evaluation. It is through this process that he seeks the answers about the effectiveness of the educational process. Citizens and influential groups are now demanding appraisals which furnish them with "hard" data. The following statement by the Research and Policy Committee of the Committee for Economic Development is a case in point:

> Innovation in education whether it involves the use of new curriculum materials or new educational technology, has become essential if the schools are to be genuinely effective in achieving their aims and goals. Continuing assessment of the product of the schools also is necessary. This means the development of principles and techniques for critically judging the worth of whatever the schools teach and the effectiveness and efficiency of their methods of instruction.[1]

Evaluation is an inherent part of the administrative process. The principal endeavors to improve his behavior and that of his staff through practicing proper procedures and making provisional trials in solving administrative and educational problems. Before, during, and after each particular activity, the principal should demonstrate leadership ability and initiative in evaluation. His experience and knowledge guide his value judgments in deciding upon the correct and desirable aspects to be retained, and giving direction to future actions. He is primarily concerned with using evaluative techniques that will lead to overall improvement of the educational enterprise.

To be effective in any evaluation, the principal must first have a clear conception of his goals as an administrator, because it is in terms of these goals that he should constantly evaluate responses. The superior executive uses every available means to give all school personnel a clear conception of these goals before initiating leadership through evaluation. He will discuss, demonstrate, or explain in his endeavor to direct group thinking toward the most desirable features of educational behavior, until these aspects become agreed-upon bases or criteria for staff evaluation.

It is important for the principal to help the staff learn what kind of behavior leads to the best possible instruction. Then he must follow through by carefully observing staff performance so he can help them evaluate it. As suggested, until there is complete understanding of common goals, with constant striving to reach these goals by continuous evaluation of progress, administrative and educational improvement cannot take place. The principal exerts definite leadership by working with his staff, by studying with them objective evidence of their successes and failures, planning with them, and organizing for future experiences.

The broad role of the administrator in evaluation may be more specifically defined in the light of these functions: (1) He is accountable for appraising the general educational program of the whole school. Such factors as school plant, equipment, supplies, etc., are areas calling for appraisal, because they contribute to the primary task of assisting in the growth and development of children. (2) The administrator is concerned with devices and materials which aid him in appraising the competence of individual teachers. The difficult task of rating effective teacher behavior calls for insight and instruments for revealing strengths and weaknesses. (3) He uses materials or devices designed to provide criteria for evaluating the school. Several instruments of this nature are available to all school personnel, providing a base for directing improvement of the elementary school. (4) He uses evaluative devices and materials for appraising the status of or changes in human behavior in the classroom. A wide variety of prepared tests can further understanding of individual and group problems, interests, abilities, relationships, etc. (5) The administrator leads in evaluation of the curriculum. As an instructional leader he helps teachers evaluate the things children do in the classroom. (6) He helps parents and the community to view the total school program.

These six functions of evaluation by the principal suggest a wide and varied role, requiring understandings and leadership skills that must be developed to insure improvement of administrative and staff behavior. Since the problems of evaluation, testing, and measurement are so vast and complex, the practical emphasis then centers on the role of the principal as an instructional leader who uses certain evaluative approaches in administering the educational program. An understanding of the following problems can contribute to development of leadership through evaluation: (1) What does the principal need to know about evaluation in terms of its nature, philosophy, and changing concepts? (2) How can the principal assist the teacher in strengthening her role in evaluation? (3) How can the principal encourage the self-evaluation activities of pupils in the classroom? (4) How can the principal attain status as an instructional leader through evaluation of the curriculum and assessment of the results of the educational program?

AN APPROACH TO EVALUATION

The principal may find it necessary to obtain staff agreement on a definition of the term *evaluation*. A poll of teachers may reveal a variety of meanings which could contribute to confusion and misunderstanding when certain processes of an evaluative nature are applied. Some teachers may reveal negative attitudes toward the whole process of evaluation. Therefore, the staff should conduct research and group discussions under the guidance of the principal. The nature of evaluation, its philosophy, and its objectives should then emerge from the combined thinking of school personnel. Some comments are offered here to aid the principal in formulating concepts of his own.

The Nature of Evaluation

Tyler points out that in the past two decades, educational assessment, evaluation, and appraisal have undergone profound changes. Evaluation as a comprehensive term to include measurement has been used for many purposes which require appraisal. Development of new knowledge and technology in a rapidly changing social situation has resulted in the need for new instruments and new procedures for evaluation.[2] The nature of human occupations has changed from physical strength and manual dexterity to the various components related to intellectual activity, social sensitivity and skills.[3]

New directions in education have led to many innovations that require careful assessment to determine their value for general use, and to changes in the nature of evaluation procedures. In conceptualizing evaluation, Stufflebeam emphasizes the importance of decision making and the need for associated information to make and support decisions. He points out, however, that there is no adequate knowledge about relevant decision processes to aid evaluators charged with designing evaluations of educational programs.[4] Certainly, if the decision-making process is as crucial as Stufflebeam considers it, then the quality of the decisions becomes extremely critical. Decision making must be based on the best available data and a thorough examination of all alternatives. Educational decisions related to program evaluation have often been made on a judgmental basis, without reference to hard data. Such evaluations generally relate to the feelings of the evaluator as well as to those of others who have participated in the evaluation process. On the other hand, to evaluate on an on-going educational program or an innovation, it is not possible to use tight experimental design. As stated by Guba, the experimental design evaluation is well suited to the antiseptic conditions of the laboratory, but not the septic conditions of the classroom.[5] Stufflebeam's definition of evaluation states, "the provision of information through formal means, such as criteria, measurement, and statistics, to provide rational bases for making judgments which are inherent in decision situations."[6] His definition reveals his concern for hard data upon which decisions can be made. But the extent to which the practitioner can develop a theory for good evaluation practices for local school use is questionable when looking at the works of the theorists. Provus points out that although "there is new work going on in evaluation theory . . . there appears to be very little linkage between program evaluation going on in the public schools today and the kind of theory discussed by university theorists."[7] Here we are talking about measurement, or any form of information which can be qualified. Wrightstone[8] pointed out many years ago, however, that evaluation is broader than measurement, and deals with such areas as personality changes, attitudes, interests, ideals, ways of thinking, working habits and personal and social adaptability. Progress has been made in recent years to measure certain of these aspects of human growth, but much needs to be done before we have precise and reliable instruments which are valid for general usage. We will consequently confine our discussion to the use of measurement and the broader techniques of evaluation.

It is the responsibility of the principal to help his staff recognize the distinction between measurement and evaluation, and to lead them in practicing the evaluative processes. As the principal helps furnish these wider concepts and encourages more evaluative activities, the faculty may achieve improved classroom procedures for realizing goals. Certainly, classroom methods will be modified for attainment of desirable educational objectives whenever Wrightstone's views on evaluation are incorporated. Of course, teachers will not generally change classroom behavior simply because they have learned new evaluation techniques. The first step in getting teachers to accept this concept of evaluation is to show that the concept is feasible and consistent with the educational objectives of the elementary school. It is at this point that the principal must demonstrate skill in leadership. He must not only help teachers understand and appreciate broader concepts of evaluation, but must lead them to accept newer and changed ways of behavior. They will discover that different approaches to and methods of evaluation are realistic and efficient; in fact, to obtain practical results, there must be improvements over the older procedures of evaluation.

It can be seen that evaluation goes beyond measurement. For example, to discover the individual's standards in the classroom or the standards of a given school, evaluation becomes important. Although evaluation requires measurement, it is concerned more with the worth of the thing that is measured. To state it briefly, measurement tells "how much," while evaluation tells

Evaluation 379

"how good." The following illustration points up the roles of evaluation and measurement in actual practice in an elementary school:

Mr. Wright and his faculty established, by means of an achievement testing program for all grades, the mean achievement in reading, arithmetic, language arts, etc. It was found to be well above national norms. In personal and group living skills (courteousness, responsiveness, etc.) there was a high rating. The staff believed that these good results were indicative of their own professional competence. Then they began to *evaluate* their findings. They learned the socioeconomic backgrounds of their groups. A great number of children were from favored homes. Their investigations led them to look at the results of a similar testing program in a neighboring school whose children had less favorable home conditions. Although their norms were of course lower, a new perspective in evaluation gave the faculty of the "better" school some concern as to whether they were really doing as well as they could.

This illustration reveals how a faculty group can use evaluation to arrive at more valid conclusions. Until the principal or some other leader is willing to go beyond the usual acceptance of test scores, for example, and search them for evaluative meanings and more significant perspectives, no school can achieve a true picture of its contribution to a child's progress. If it is important to know the mean gain of a class on an achievement test that has been made in one school year, other factors must also be interpreted before we make decisions. When we look at comparisons of the mean gain between one group and another, we might not have the whole story. We need to determine, for example, if the gain at the top range of test scores is equal to the gain at the bottom range. This presents all kinds of problems in providing data for accountability. Noah[9] points out that there is no way of assigning weights to equal absolute gains in achievement scores occurring at different levels of overall achievement. We do not know if a gain of five points at the top of the scale is equal to a five-point gain at the bottom of the range. We must find an answer to this problem in using achievement tests in decision making. Are we to assume that equal gains at the top and bottom of the range are equally valuable? When we are faced with making decisions, it is apparent that we would not have enough data to decide to allocate more resources to improve the top or the bottom of the range of scores. Perhaps we need additional information from emperical data before reaching our decision. For example, are we apt to increase an achievement score but at the same time develop an undesirable attitude on the part of the learner? Certainly the principal needs to help his staff look at all the alternatives.

A Philosophy of Evaluation

School personnel should formulate a written philosophy of evaluation before attempting to establish a set of objectives. Consistent with the concept of administration set forth in this book, the principal invites faculty, staff, and interested laymen to participate in this philosophizing about evaluation.

First, the all-embracing goal is the fullest self-realization of each child. The task of all school personnel is to furnish leadership in helping determine those goals that are in agreement with our way of life. Second, a philosophy of democratic administration characterized by group action in solving common problems should undergird all educational activities. Out of this a philosophy of evaluation emerges to guide the principal, staff, and pupils—a philosophy which not only helps individuals decide what they really want and puts those wants into effect, but which also creates a climate favorable both to cooperative participation in establishing a program of evaluation and to suggestions for continuous improvement. The central question of where the school wants to go is vital, but only recognition and acceptance of the importance of the role of evaluation on a group basis will enable elementary education to continue to make progress. The principal is charged with giving leadership in this significant area of appraisal. A clearly-defined philosophy worked out and accepted by the school's educational leader and all others concerned will insure more opportunities for practicing these devices and techniques.

Objectives of Evaluation

Having developed a philosophy for an evaluation program, the principal can next furnish leadership by encouraging cooperative development of evaluation objectives to meet the needs of the school and community. The administrator will insure greater teacher security and a better sense of direction when the staff members understand the objectives of evaluation procedures in their school. The principal may derive cooperatively with his staff the following suggested objectives for the school:

1. *To focus attention on one or more problems.* One objective of evaluation is to encourage the teacher to identify a given problem needing further study and evaluation. For example, it may be necessary to give attention to children's growth patterns so the teacher can understand and appreciate a particular problem. This emphasis will require evaluation devices of measurement, in terms of such factors as age, physical development, etc.

2. *To examine value concepts related to the problem and to clarify them for mutual acceptance.* This objective implies that values define goals, and thus calls for mutual clarification and acceptance. From these value concepts may also emerge suggestions for ways of attaining goals.

3. *To set up some basis for judging the problem.* If the problem is how to observe children's growth in terms of social, mental, physical, and emotional aspects, evaluation obviously calls for some basis upon which to make the observations. Further study of some problems may also require a set of criteria for making decisions on procedure, and the like.

4. *To express the criteria in specific terms.* This objective of an evaluation

program is the real task of educators. Having established methods for observing certain aspects of growth, what kinds of behavior are to be considered ideal? For example, when both teachers and students understand what is expected in behavioral terms upon completion of certain chapters in the geography book, there are then specific goals to achieve and definite patterns of behavior to be evaluated. To approach it somewhat differently, the teacher may expect some behavioral changes to result from a study of the Suez Canal. These changes are, in effect, goals to reach, but they must first be clearly expressed and defined to determine the extent of change.

5. *To promote situation-analysis experiences.* A significant objective of evaluation should be promotion of situation-analysis activities. For example, the faculty may wish to observe and study classroom conditions to see how well certain educational objectives are being met. The evaluative activities call for use of different tools and techniques in order to discover difficulties in the classroom and ascertain their significance. Perhaps the evaluation will show advantageous modifications or changes. To lead to significant behavioral change, the process of evaluation must have a starting point in the form of a situation-analysis experience.

6. *To evaluate significant changes in behavior in light of value concepts.* When value concepts are defined and understood in the classroom or in staff relations, a further objective of evaluation is to appraise significant behavior changes in light of these concepts. If teacher and pupil perform this evaluation together, both may come to see more clearly the student's special needs. From the administrative viewpoint, the principal may consider staff behavior in terms of its compatibility with values sought by the school and staff personnel.

7. *To modify or to implement decisions.* New evidence gained through evaluation often suggests that decisions must be modified or implemented by school personnel. This objective of evaluation means that something constructive should follow from the findings. Unless some definite action takes place as a result of evaluation activities, there is little value or significance in such procedures.

These seven objectives of an evaluation program should be thoroughly discussed and agreed upon by school personnel. Any changes, additions, or modifications of objectives should be reviewed by the whole staff. These objectives should serve also to guide the teacher in classroom work. Furthermore, the principal may find them suitable as goals for an administrative program of evaluation which seeks to examine behavior from this viewpoint.

THE PRINCIPAL AND ACCOUNTABILITY

A new term, "accountability," has found its way into education jargon, and has caused considerable controversy among educational leaders. Although many educators agree on the meaning of accountability as it refers to public education, they have not been able to agree on the means to the desired ends. That is, many questions must be answered before the issues can be adequately resolved. Educators cannot escape responsibility for educational outcomes, but their efforts in the past have been little more than an account of people's "feelings" regarding the success of their programs.

We are being asked by federal and state governments, school officials, and parents to account for the results of the educational programs we have developed.[10] This includes the individual elementary school as well as the whole school district. We are being asked to produce actual gains in student achievement based on desired objectives specified in advance.[11]

There is little doubt that educators must do a more acceptable job of managing the vast sums of money turned over to them each year for the operation of the educational enterprise. But now we are being asked to account for this financial outlay in measurable relationships between dollars and program results. It is not the purpose of this chapter to deal with accountability in relation to funds, however, but to examine some basic concerns of our constitunencies and suggest ways of evaluating not only the educational program, but the outcomes of this program.

There is no school system that does not believe in some form of evaluation; but, at the same time, many educators have constantly balked against attempting to measure the results of their product, on the basis that they cannot follow patterns established by industry, which deals with an inanimate product on an assembly-line basis. The authors take the position that this is not an "either/or" issue, but one about which the principal and his staff can do something as they are accountable to the public for the results of their educational program. It is hoped that this chapter will provide background for the principal on issues and challenges to be met in dealing with accountability, as well as identify some characteristics of a broad, comprehensive program of evaluation to meet the growing demand of the public to know what is being accomplished in the public schools.

HISTORY OF ACCOUNTABILITY

In the mid 1800s in England, soon after the amalgamation of the Education Department at Whitehall with the Science and Art Department at South Kensington, the vice president of the Privy Council on Education became responsible for the new department. J. F. D. Donnelly, who assisted the secretary of the whole department, promoted a scheme for paying teachers based on the results of their pupils' success in examinations set by the Department each May.[12]

In 1858, The New Castle Commission surveyed elementary schools in Great Britain and abroad, and after three years, recommended that an examination be given to every child in every school to which grants were paid to ascertain whether indispensable elements of knowledge were being thoroughly acquired. The teacher's position depended to a large extent upon the results of these examinations.[13]

These efforts were an attempt to improve the quality of teachers, since most teachers in elementary schools had no professional qualifications at all, but in fact, what happened was that those possessing them were recruited for other than professional reasons which appeared to have political overtones. "Stories of hardships and harshness were evoked by this practice of dispensing funds to schools and were alternately to shock and amuse members of Parliament for more than a quarter of a century." "One official, however, forecast that if it did not promote efficiency, it would at least be cheap, which, because of the economy of the times, was important to the lawmakers. But this practice of accountability was placed entirely on the teacher and led to many malpractices, such as deliberate teaching by rote memory to defeat the inspectors."[14] Such practices were also found in the early schools in America. Elementary principals in the early 1900s called attention to the unfairness of the New York Regents' examinations which were required of every student without consideration for the community and neighborhood differences where teachers taught. It was believed that some teachers used practices that were injurious to pupils to insure that pupils passed the examinations.[15] These accounts of practices in American schools, however, have had lasting effects on educator's attitudes toward accountability and its relationship to measuring outcomes.

Emergence of the scientific era in American public education brought great emphasis on tests of all kinds for measuring anything from I.Q. to achievement in subject areas. In fact, Judd stated in 1918:

> the superintendent who reports to his board on the basis of mere opinion is rapidly becoming a relic of an earlier unscientific age. There are indications that even the principals of elementary schools are beginning to study their schools by exact methods and are basing their supervision on the results of their measurements of what teachers accomplish.[16]

But for the most part, during the first half of the twentieth century educators rejected the use of standardized instruments for determining the extent to which schools were achieving their goals. Tyler, writing in the 68th Yearbook, points out that "new ideas, new procedures, and new instruments of evaluation in earlier periods came and went like fads in fashion because these innovations in evaluation were not deeply rooted in the needs and developments in other educational areas."[17] Tests were given and results compiled and compared with national norms or with other schools within the same district. But with few exceptions, these tests were not used to reveal the extent to which schools achieved certain educational goals.[18] Cunningham mentions that achievement-test scores become information sought after by the public and protected by administrators.[19] Obviously, test data without interpretation in layman's language can be misleading. For example, a mean gain of 1.5-grade level for an academic year might appear to indicate great progress. But we need to ask if a 5-point gain in the standard score at the top is as good or equal to a 5-point gain at the bottom of the range of scores. We believe that if the public wants achievement-test data, it should be made available, but it must be interpreted in laymen's language. Now the question before educators is not whether we are going to have accountability, but whether we are going to develop a workable plan that will serve children, community, and educators.

There is today a sustained effort to develop practical approaches to the problem of accountability. The following statement is evidence of a cooperative effort between the New York City Board of Education and the United Federation of Teachers to work out a solution to this problem:

> The Board of Education and the Union recognize that the major problem of our school system is the failure to educate all of our students and the massive academic retardation which exists especially among minority group students. The Board and the Union therefore agree to join in an effort, in cooperation with universities, community school boards, and parent organizations, to seek solutions to this major problem and to develop objective criteria of professional accountability.[20]

All in all, principals must not wait until public pressure forces them to take a stand. They must be prepared now to develop an acceptable approach which will relate input—the child—to the program, and thus be able to predict with some degree of reliability the output—the educational product—at the end of a given number of years of schooling. That is, we need to know what happens to a child who experiences a particular educational program for a major portion of his childhood.

Relationship of Accountability to the Individual School

We have stressed throughout this book that the local school must be free from the constraints of the central board of education to develop its educational program in relation to the needs of its immediate community. Although accountability can be focused at the national, state, or district level, it is the intention here to deal with it as it affects the individual elementary school. Dyer points out three general principles embracing accountability:

> 1. The professional staff is to be held collectively responsible for knowing as much as it can (a) about the intellectual and personal-social development of the pupils in its charge, and (b) about the conditions and educational services that may be facilitating or impeding the pupils' development.

Evaluation 385

2. The professional staff of a school is to be held collectively responsible for using knowledge as best it can to maximize the development of its pupils toward certain clearly-defined and agreed-upon pupil performance objectives.
3. The board of education has a corresponding responsibility to provide the means and technical assistance whereby the staff of each school can acquire, interpret, and use the information necessary for carrying out the two foregoing functions.[21]

It is interesting to note that Dyer holds the principal, teachers, and even the specialists such as school psychologists, guidance workers, etc., responsible for knowing children and understanding as much as possible about them and the teaching-learning process. The principal has the responsibility to assist teachers in understanding what is expected of them in terms of knowing and applying information about children to their instructional procedures. To maximize each pupil's development implies the use of specialists, new technology, and various services which will enhance learning. Maximization of development also requires teachers to know which teaching strategies are appropriate for each learner. Not only is it important in this concept to know what facilitates pupil development, but it is equally important to understand conditions that might impede pupil growth. In addition to accountability of the teaching staff, the board of education is also accountable for providing technical assistance and appropriate information and facilities to enable each teacher to carry out her program effectively. The principal must inform the board of teacher needs so it can meet its obligation.

There are certain conditions within the teaching-learning process which teachers cannot control and for which they should not be held accountable, conditions such as the socioeconomic level of pupils' parents. Neither can teachers change home conditions, but, through parent involvement in educational programs, parents' attitudes can be changed, and thus have a profound affect on their children. Teachers cannot change the size of their buildings or their classrooms, but they can have some influence in choosing the organization for pupil learning that would function best in their building. Certainly, teachers cannot change the nature of the community in which they are employed. That is, the ethnic make-up of the community, the number and availability of social agencies and the extent of poor housing, all are conditions surrounding the school on which the teacher can have very little influence toward producing rapid change.[22]

Groups Responsible for Accountability in the Schools

The public, and those administrators who do so, are not justified in holding teachers solely accountable. Accountability must become a basis for reconciling differences between groups. Administrators, teachers, parents, children, boards of education, and citizens in general, all have a responsibility in the accountability process. Each group will obviously differ in its expectations of schooling. But these groups must interact in order to bring about common understandings and agreed-upon expectations. It becomes the task of the principal to work with each of these groups to see that they respond to their particular roles and identify their responsibilities in the accountability process. That is, the child has to recognize his responsibility in the learning process. His social behavior, and a positive attitude toward learning, are tied in with his success and that of his teachers. When each group identifies its role in the accountability process, the system has a reasonable chance of succeeding because a basic ingredient has been added—that of communication. When communication takes place, modification of expectations and refinement of goals become possible, resulting in more effective educational programming.

The Principal's Role in Accountability

When the principal, with his staff, faces realistically the conditions in the school environment which they can control and those conditions which are beyond their control, attention can be given to defining objectives for the school as a whole and, more specifically, for each year or grade level. Teachers, after studying the profiles of the children assigned to them, should formulate behavioral objectives which will indicate the level of input and expected output *for each child*. That is, what does the child bring to this teacher in September, and what are some attainable expectations for him by June? (It can readily be seen that teachers should be employed for longer periods of time than nine months each year if the job is to be accomplished and if teachers are to have time to study children and properly plan their learning and living experiences.)

Teachers now become accountable for achieving the objectives they have established. It is not unreasonable to expect a teacher to teach children how to read or improve their reading at any given grade level. The principal must recognize the conditions under which the teacher is working, and know whether the teacher is using the best methods available to her.

We feel strongly that schools must be humanized. In fact, this book emphasizes a child-centered approach to education. But the point here is that it is equally inhuman for a child not to learn basic skills because of a poor teacher. His security may depend on his ability to learn the basic skills. Those of us who have been principals all know teachers who were not at all successful in teaching skills. If, year after year, these teachers fail to raise the level of achievement in reading, for instance, for a given percentage of the pupils in their classes, some action must be taken. In a nongraded school which emphasizes the individual, the system of accountability must be based on what is accomplished with individual children and results measured against the children's own progress. While schools which

Evaluation

are graded might use uniform education procedures, one may hope that even in this type of school concern will be for individual growth.[23] No system of accountability will function if failure is rewarded. That is, the teacher who is *not* successful at teaching reading might be required to follow a prescribed plan for teaching reading as designated by the principal or the supervisor. But when a teacher is successful—regardless of her methods—she should be free to innovate, or to following one or more of many teaching methods.

The Unsatisfactory Teacher

No system of accountability will work if the principal sanctions poor performance year after year. On the other hand, a system of accountability is predicated on the availability of tests for assessing pupil performance. While tests are available for measuring pupil progress in reading, we do not have instruments for assessing all the desired goals of the elementary school.[24] Educators will have to decide whether to begin programs of accountability in those areas where valid instruments are available and hope to improve on those which are not valid.

A teacher who is consistently unsuccessful in helping pupils achieve basic skills will need to be transferred to the level of teacher-assistant or, if the teacher does not have tenure, it may be necessary to remove her from the system. This will require some type of agreement with the union or teachers' association when such conditions exist. But unions or teacher associations must work out dismissal procedures for those who have been admitted to the profession but are unsuccessful in working with children. Unions or associations cannot condone poor teaching when children's futures are at stake. It becomes important to see that the procedures for taking such action are carefully spelled out and agreed upon by the union and to be certain such actions are not abused. If the union does not agree to developing a workable plan, accountability is not possible. Thus, for such a plan to work requires the cooperation of teachers, principals, parents, children, superintendents, the board of education,[25] and teachers' organizations (unions and associations).

Educators are caught between the "do gooders" and the "bad guys" in trying to work out plans and procedures for determining accountability. There are those who believe that because someone is a fine person and is in the classroom, he has a right to continue as a teacher even if the results of his teaching do not justify his retention. On the other hand, there are those who would, without valid evidence, dismiss people from teaching. The plea here is for the principal to provide leadership in bringing together the teachers and community representatives in cooperation with the board of education to work out a reasonable plan for what they expect of a teacher and a principal in terms of accountability.

There are, to be sure, a broad range of goals in elementary education, and for some of these goals we are unable, to date, to determine the extent of our success in achieving them. But one fundamental goal that devolved in the elementary school since its inception is the teaching of basic skills. We need to recognize each child's differences in readiness at each stage of growth. Principals must provide leadership to help teachers use appropriate diagnostic tests and techniques to determine these differences for each child. When working with teachers, we need to get away from class and group norms if we are going to be accountable for *each* child. Class or group norms may have a place, but too often they are misunderstood, or do not reveal necessary diagnostic data about individual performance for which the teacher is held accountable.

Most educators have given lip service to the philosophical position of accepting each child for himself and taking him as far as his potential will permit. This implies that we use certain measurements to determine where he stands at a given time and how much he has accomplished during a specified period of time. We cannot determine how much a child achieves in any of the basic skills during an academic year unless we know his level of achievement at the time the new teaching begins. It thus becomes the task of the educational leader to work closely with each teacher in analyzing test results as well as performance at the beginning of the year and during the learning periods throughout the year. The principal, then, working closely with the teacher, is better able to determine the teacher's success in helping each child achieve the school's objectives as related to the basic skills. This is not, of course, the whole teaching job, but we cannot wait until we have developed objective instruments to determine success in the affective domain, although much progress has been made in this area in the last decade.[26] We suggest that, after 75 years of development of the science of measurement, we begin to look at this area of the school's responsibility by using the instruments available for determining how successful we are and then doing something about the causes of our failure in certain areas. We cannot continue to condone practices which do not yield satisfactory pupil achievement.

Performance Contracting

As a result of the new technology available in education, industry has decided it can enter more directly into the educational process by contracting with school districts for certain educational programs. For example, Behavioral Research Laboratories of California has contracted with Gary, Indiana, Public Schools. BRL has guaranteed to raise the achievement of pupils from the inner city attending the Banneker Elementary School. In return, BRL will receive the average cost per pupils in the Gary schools, or over $2,000,000, during the four years of the contract. BRL will return the money for any pupil who fails.[27]

Such educational programming has resulted in an array of problems for the teaching profession, such as: Who do the teachers assigned to a building under a performance contract work for—the board of education or the contractor? What role does industry play in the hiring and firing of teachers? The authors, however, believe in the need for hard data collected from any innovative research efforts. If we can teach children the basic skills through a "systems approach" or any type of programming or technology more effectively than we have done through conventional means, and if the data support this, then we need to determine the teacher's new role in the education process. That is, we must not turn our backs on innovations if they prove successful simply because they change the process of education which we have heretofore held sacred. In a very real sense, performance contracting facilitates or is compatible with accountability. If the contractors succeed, they are paid for their success; if they fail, they are not paid.

We spend millions of dollars each day for education for which no one accepts accountability. Yet we know many of our efforts are inefficient and nonproductive. Principals must work to develop means by which the staff, including the principal, accepts accountability for pupils' progress. Recognizing that there are both affective and cognitive learnings to be acquired, we might look at the overall task to be accomplished from the point of view of what the new technology, with all of its "hardware," can do better for children than teachers have been doing, and what it is that teachers can do for children which technology cannot. We can thus differentiate the respective roles and build a program of accountability around these.

THE PRINCIPAL APPRAISES HIS STAFF

The public demand for accountability has precipitated the requirement of many school districts for teacher evaluations. It has been pointed out that the principal's leadership is essential to developing a sound program of accountability. The principal is the key person in providing leadership for developing an evaluation program that will satisfy teachers, community, and the board of education. Although the principal should provide leadership for this function, he should actively involve all who are immediately concerned.

There are several reasons for teacher evaluation or appraisal.[28] Some of these are: (1) to help the teacher to look at herself in terms of her strengths and weaknesses; (2) to assist the teacher in identifying certain teaching procedures which can be improved; (3) to improve the total instructional program; (4) to keep poor teachers from getting tenure; and (5) to reward outstanding teachers.

A variety of techniques will be needed to improve the total educational program. Information collected from objective sources to facilitate decision-making in teacher evaluation will have far-reaching implications; therefore the principal must guard against hasty action.

Principal's Role in Evaluating His Faculty

In most elementary schools, the principal is charged with the responsibility for appraising staff performance. That is, he is held accountable to the board of education and the community for the quality of the instructional staff. To evaluate his staff effectively, he needs a carefully-developed program acceptable to his faculty. If they are already involved in a satisfactory evaluation program, he will need only to spend time each year orienting new staff members to the procedures and listening to suggestions they may have for modifying the program. The principal must be able to answer questions about his staff, and these answers must be based on objective data. For example, he needs to know the competencies of each staff member, their strengths and their weaknesses, their personality differences, and their past teaching experiences.

Most principals, although they might agree that appraisal is a necessary part of the job, have not had experience in working with a sound appraisal system. They have spent time in classrooms checking a rating scale, but they have not dealt with a system which measures both quantitative and qualitative aspects of their staff. Experience in working with a program of teacher evaluation will build the principal's confidence and will give him the additional security he needs as he works with the system. As he uses the program, the principal will become better adept at carrying it out and will improve his own skills in using it.

Some Pitfalls to Avoid. Like all techniques and procedures the principal uses, there are always a number of "do's" and "don'ts" involved. We have stressed throughout that the principal is a democratic leader. Teachers are apprehensive about appraisal, but research investigations indicate that, if they are going to be appraised, they prefer that the principal be the one to do it. Some important points for the principal to keep in mind as he works with his staff are:

1. Help the teacher understand that appraisal is a way to help her improve her weaknesses.
2. Step lightly when dealing with a teacher who already shows evidence of a personality conflict with the principal.
3. Don't dominate the staff in any group or individual activities.
4. Develop a mutual climate of relationships.
5. Show a sincere interest in the teacher and her problems, regardless of their difficulty.
6. Develop a team relationship with the faculty in all activities, including appraisal.

Evaluation 391

   7. Do more than be a good listener; take action on teacher needs.
   8. Emphasize the positive—don't focus on faults and inadequacies.
   9. Allow the teacher to express her opinion without fear of reprisal, even if it differs from the principal's.

A Workable Appraisal Process

The appraisal process suggested here is a simple one, but the principal as well as his staff must grasp its significance in its entirety. The authors recommend the following procedures for carrying out a program of teacher evaluation:

1. Plan an initial conference with each teacher to be appraised.
2. Prepare thoroughly and thoughtfully for this conference.
3. Establish the right place and a mutually convenient time for the conference.
4. Have the teacher consider specific goals or objectives she wishes to achieve during the year.
5. Help each teacher evaluate herself.
6. Relate supervision to the appraisal process.
7. Arrange for a final appraisal conference.
8. Be well prepared for the end-of-the-year conference.
9. Plan action for the new year.

Planning the Initial Conference. The success of this initial appraisal conference might well determine the success of the process. During this conference, the principal should be a good listener, learning as much as he can from and about the teacher. At this conference the principal seeks to encourage the teacher to think about herself in terms of a few goals or objectives she has for improving some teaching function. It is not necessary for the teacher to state these specifically at this time, but a mutually acceptable date should be set at which time the teacher will turn into the principal her written goals for the year. If these do not seem acceptable to the principal, a second conference may be necessary, but it may be equally effective to respond in writing with suggestions for rewording the goals for easier evaluation. Regardless of the acceptance or rejection of the teacher's goals, the principal should send his response in writing so it may become part of the record.

Relating Supervision to the Appraisal Process

The reader is referred to chapter 6 for a review of conference details, since they will not be treated here. The importance of the principal's role following the initial conference cannot be overemphasized. The principal has an important function in respect to teacher's goals. It is his responsibility to help make each teacher the best teacher possible. To accomplish this he will have to analyze each teacher's goals to determine his responsibility in the process. That is, does the teacher want specific suggestions for diagnosing differences in certain pupils' performances in mathematics? Does she want to learn effective techniques for using the overhead projector? Does she want to improve her skill in individualizing a given curriculum area? These are but a few of the goals for which the principal has a definite responsibility in helping the teacher. If he fails to carry out his supervisory function here, he is neglecting his responsibility. This process will involve the principal in different activities than those in which the routine office administrator finds himself involved. But *the principal is an instructional leader.* This appraisal procedure will require a determined effort on his part to *earn* the role as an educational leader.

Helping Teachers Follow a Plan of Self-Evaluation

As the year moves on, the teacher should begin to make her own records of her feelings and objective evidence of her success in achieving her goals. It should be made clear, however, that such notes are not for the principal, and in no way should they be used to incriminate the teacher. But this information becomes the basis for the teacher to plan her next step in the goal-achieving process. The information also might be used by the teacher in planning her final appraisal conference with the principal. She needs to learn to keep her self-evaluation as objective as possible. She may ask herself, have children who were at the bottom of the reading test in September improved their scores significantly by the end of May? Does the teacher have additional evidence that these children read better and more than they did in previous years? This kind of data provides a basis for the teacher to determine whether she has achieved her yearly goals.

Final Appraisal Conference

At the end of the year the principal is ready to meet with teachers in the final appraisal conference. He must be well prepared for this conference. He must have worked enough with each teacher to have accurate data about her progress toward achieving her goals. This final conference is critical, particularly if the teacher is up for tenure. Some far-reaching decisions may now have to be made. But the quality of the conference and the agreements reached by the principal and teacher concerning her success are the most important aspects. It might be that the teacher and the principal will agree on the next steps to be taken and what additional assistance the teacher will need. Out of this conference, then, may come the goals to be achieved during the next year. If evaluation is continuous, this conference, regardless of its level of success, is only the beginning of an ongoing process. The final report of the conference should be agreed upon and signed and dated by both teacher and principal.

Whether or not this can be an annual activity for each teacher depends

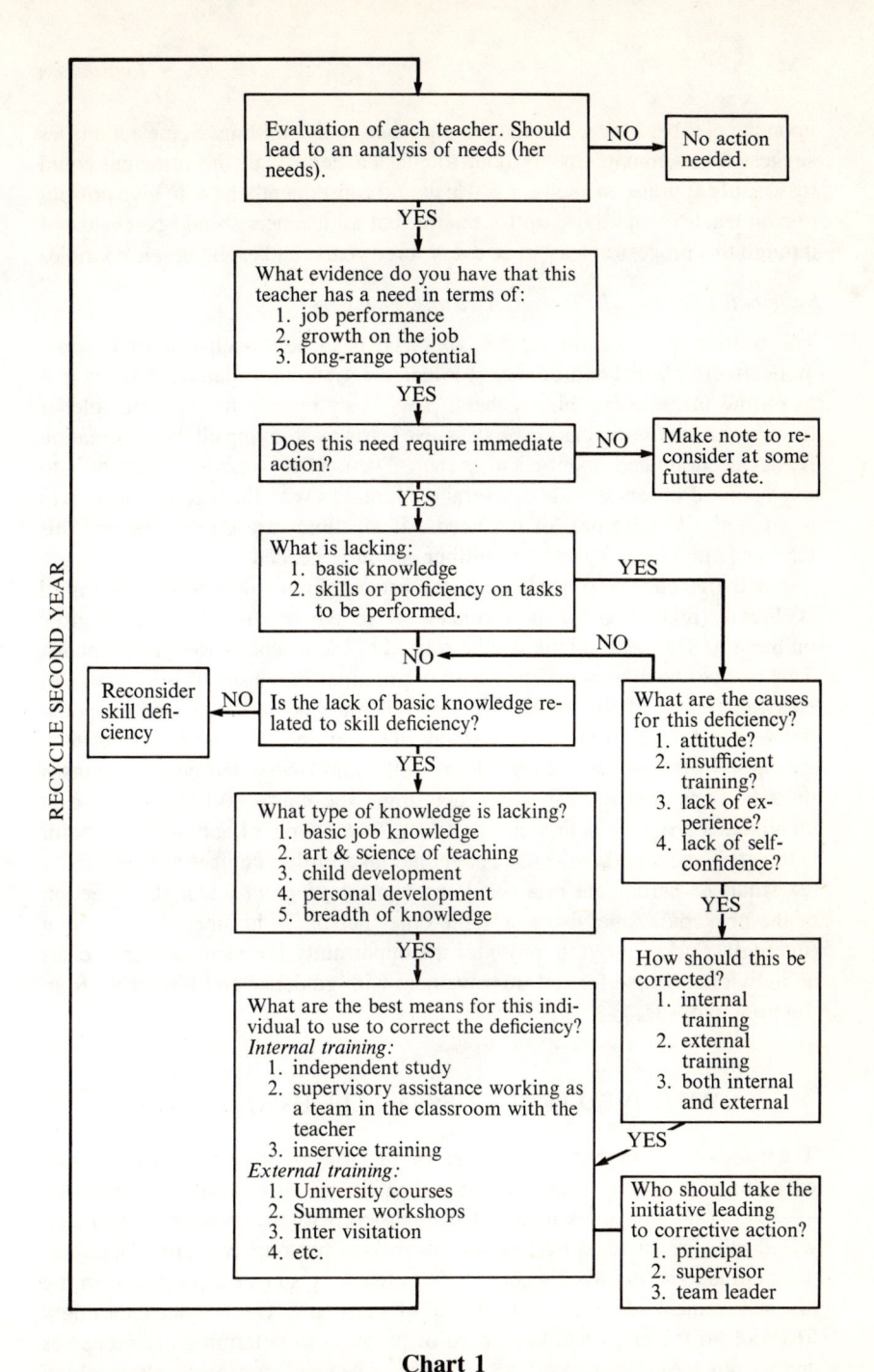

```
                    ┌──────────────────────────┐
                    │ Evaluation of each teacher. Should │  NO   ┌──────────┐
                    │ lead to an analysis of needs (her  │──────▶│ No action│
                    │ needs).                            │       │ needed.  │
                    └──────────────────────────┘       └──────────┘
                              │ YES
                              ▼
                    ┌──────────────────────────┐
                    │ What evidence do you have that this│
                    │ teacher has a need in terms of:    │
                    │   1. job performance               │
                    │   2. growth on the job             │
                    │   3. long-range potential          │
                    └──────────────────────────┘
                              │ YES
                              ▼
                    ┌──────────────────────────┐  NO   ┌──────────────┐
                    │ Does this need require immediate  │──────▶│ Make note to re- │
                    │ action?                           │       │ consider at some │
                    └──────────────────────────┘       │ future date.     │
                              │ YES                    └──────────────┘
                              ▼
```

What is lacking:
1. basic knowledge
2. skills or proficiency on tasks to be performed.

— YES → What are the causes for this deficiency?
1. attitude?
2. insufficient training?
3. lack of experience?
4. lack of self-confidence?

Is the lack of basic knowledge related to skill deficiency? — NO → Reconsider skill deficiency

What type of knowledge is lacking?
1. basic job knowledge
2. art & science of teaching
3. child development
4. personal development
5. breadth of knowledge

How should this be corrected?
1. internal training
2. external training
3. both internal and external

What are the best means for this individual to use to correct the deficiency?
Internal training:
1. independent study
2. supervisory assistance working as a team in the classroom with the teacher
3. inservice training

External training:
1. University courses
2. Summer workshops
3. Inter visitation
4. etc.

Who should take the initiative leading to corrective action?
1. principal
2. supervisor
3. team leader

RECYCLE SECOND YEAR

Chart 1

Appraisal Action Flow Chart

upon the number of teachers the principal has in his building. Some authorities suggest that a maximum of about fifteen teachers is all the principal could reasonably appraise in one year.[29] He would consequently have to give priority to new teachers and those up for tenure, but all teachers should be evaluated through this process at least once every three years, and each year, if possible.

Systematic Appraisal Plan for Assisting Teachers

The primary purpose for teacher appraisal is to help each teacher become more effective with children. Chart 1 depicts a systematic plan for the principal to follow in assessing his teachers. This chart reveals the specific role of the principal in the evaluation process. He starts by studying all the information he has accumulated about each teacher. Then, after a minimum of three to five hours of observation and several conferences with the teacher, he arrives at an analysis, with her, of her needs. If all things are going well and this teacher is making progress, no further action is needed.

For the teacher who needs help, the principal must determine if the need is directly related to job performance or to the teacher's failure to grow on the job. The need might also be related to the teacher's long-range plans. That is, does he plan to seek an assistant principalship, a supervisory position, etc. Regardless of the need, the principal must decide what action should be taken and when. If immediate action is needed, then the task is to determine the cause of the job deficiency. Here, skills, knowledge and performed tasks must be separated or isolated to determine the cause. When the cause is identified, corrective action can be taken. The course of action at this point is to determine whether the teacher should take further courses at a university (external) or participate in a self-improvement program under the direction of the principal, supervisor, or some other person within the school system (internal). Such a program provides the opportunity for each teacher to chart an individual course for self improvement with guidance and leadership from the principal.

IMPROVED PRACTICES IN SELF-EVALUATION

Teachers are becoming more aware of the role of the child in evaluating educational progress. This growing realization of self-evaluation is grounded in sound principles of learning and is consistent with the democratic approach which calls for active participation in all areas of personal concern. Therefore, the child is to be involved whenever he is reaching some decision concerning his achievement of certain educational objectives.[30] The teacher then might first look to the child and his record of progress to determine her successes and weaknesses. She can often find clues to ways of improving her teaching through involving pupils.

Self-evaluation for Improvement

Vital to any efforts of a teacher to improve in her profession is her ability to identify areas of weakness. The teacher must be willing to try to see herself as her pupils and colleagues see her if real improvement is to be gained. The following experience focuses on this process:

> A teacher once told her principal that she wanted to begin the year as a "different" teacher; that she wanted her pupils to learn out of an inward desire rather than from a feeling of fear. This teacher had a reputation of whipping nearly every pupil in the room before the end of the year. While the teacher had identified her needs for improvement, she was perplexed with the "know-how" of teaching. The principal helped this teacher organize a new plan for teaching. The problem was not one of an inexperienced teacher, as this teacher had been teaching eighteen years. But through good school leadership exhibited by the principal, the teacher for the first time sought information concerning self-improvement. The teacher was unaware of the many avenues which were open to her in releasing children for creative learning. After a most successful year, the teacher was requested by some parents to have her class present their year's learning to the P. T. A. at its last meeting. At the conclusion of the presentation of the learnings experienced by the pupils, the teacher concluded with what she termed "a confession." She stated that this was her most successful year of teaching and said, "What's more, I have enjoyed it because I didn't have to whip a single child." This in itself was quite an innovation for the teacher.

Self-evaluation for Improvement through Personal Growth

The principal who has established a warm, friendly rapport with his staff members is in an excellent position to assist teachers in the self-analysis process. His leadership in helping teachers recognize the need for self-evaluation must be in the nature of developing cooperatively agreed-upon criteria for evaluation. One group of teachers developed and used the following procedure to note improvement in their teaching:

> Keeping accurate records of comments made by various people, being more observant of their own participation in social activities, observing changes in the behavior of pupils themselves and in other adults, and listing new procedures used and types of enrichment provided in work.[31]

Many self-evaluation checklists could be introduced here which would enumerate the various aspects of growth under the above procedures. However, the most effective instrument is that which is developed by the principal and his staff. Such a procedure builds understanding among the staff members of the meaning of the items in the list.

The principal may work with his staff in the following ways to design an instrument for teacher self-evaluation: (1) assist staff members to identify the present stage of growth, and (2) help individual faculty members recognize which level of growth each has achieved, as reflected by classroom practices.

As an illustration, an instrument may be designed to reflect certain levels of growth in "classroom procedures" as follows:

CLASSROOM PROCEDURES[32]

LEVEL I	LEVEL II	LEVEL III	Level IV
a. *Planning*	a. *Planning*	a. *Planning*	a. *Planning*
The teacher has little understanding of cooperative planning.	The pupils are given little opportunity to participate in planning. The teacher plans the selection and use of materials as they are related to topics.	The suggestions of children are recorded by the teacher and used as they seem helpful.	Teachers and pupils work together with each accepting the contributions of all members as worthy of consideration by the group.

These levels of growth are guides for the teacher to determine his own immediate attainment, but they may also serve as goals to be achieved. The important concept here is that if teachers develop procedures similar to those listed previously, they will have a better understanding of self-evaluation and will be more willing to use it, since the procedures will not have been forced upon them by the administration.

Ostensibly, any instrument for evaluating teacher growth should include:

1. Teacher-pupil relations,
2. Organization and instruction,
3. Curriculum planning,
4. Participation in school-wide activities,
5. Teacher-staff relations, (including teams), and
6. Teacher-parent-community relations.

Development of the four-level scale in these six areas should be done in such a way that use of the instrument will contribute to a secure feeling and build confidence on the part of teachers, as well as encourage them to identify their progress through their own efforts and abilities.

Organization of a Pupil Self-evaluation Program

The principal is now offered suggestions for giving faculty leadership that should encourage self-evaluative activities and explain how self-evaluation may be conducted at any school or grade level. The discussion is developed in stages, or phases, any of which may serve as a point of departure for the principal in dealing with his own situation.

Stage One. The principal develops cooperatively with staff and interested school patrons a philosophy for a self-evaluation program by the child. No formal or elaborate procedures are necessary. Acceptance of the process itself must be gained, since better results will be obtained when individuals know what they are striving for and understand the reasoning behind the activity. The principal has many techniques at his disposal, such as planned faculty study meetings, panels, P.T.A. meetings, written communication, consultants in workshops, etc. These approaches may bring about better cooperation when the need for self-evaluation activities for the child is revealed, and when objectives are defined.

Stage Two. The principal encourages each teacher to work out in each class some overall procedures. Guided by the maturity level of the pupils, the teacher will utilize class time to introduce an unfamiliar technique to the class members. The process may be slow and gradual, and will probably call for much direction and help to acquaint the children with techniques of self-evaluation. At this stage it will be helpful for the teacher to develop with the group a flexible list of standards of performance for the classroom. Some instructors find that performance standards can be worked out in a very general way. For example, the group will decide on some things they believe they should accomplish in the fifth grade, such as being able to use the library more efficiently, learning how to read more quickly, etc. The definition of standards for arithmetic, reading, writing, and so forth are also important. Although everyone is not able to reach the same standard-level, the children have some definite notion of the mark at which they are aiming.

One teacher working with third-grade children developed through teacher-pupil planning a graph which showed the norm for her pupils in spelling during the previous three years. Each child made a copy of the graph and placed his score on the graph following his spelling test. The children worked in groups and took their spelling tests when they believed they were ready for them. By observing the graph, they were able to determine the extent of their own improvement or regression, as well as to make a comparison with the established norm. Notable improvement was observed in spelling, but even more important was the fact that the final mark received each six weeks did not come as a surprise to the child. Thus the learner was aware of the progress he was achieving while the learning was taking place.

Stage Three. Growing out of performance-standard setting will be the development of specific criteria by which the children can gauge themselves. Young children cannot be expected to give exact meanings in properly-stated terms. Even teachers may need help in phrasing the criteria. Yet there can and should be active participation as the group decides on a standard for each specific learning experience. A brief and simple list of criteria may be all that is necessary, and of course at the primary level the teacher will have to direct the process carefully.

The class should quickly recognize two patterns in using self-evaluation. They will have an overall set of standards for the group, and specific criteria for individual skill development. There will be occasions when the class will want to evaluate itself as a group. Three questions may be asked: (1) What are we doing well as a group? (2) What do we need to do differently to improve? (3) How should we go about doing it? Depending on the learning situation, the teacher may wish to keep these three questions before a class for evaluation purposes.

The second pattern of self-evaluation emerges from the emphasis given to individual progress. The three questions above are restated in personal terms. These questions lead the pupil to focus attention on himself and call for development of self-aids, which lead to the next stage.

Stage Four. Teachers and pupils should develop checklists or forms to aid in group or individual self-evaluation. In the primary grades such forms must be handled by the teacher, although children should have some voice in their preparation and know something about them. The teacher will have to work out a form with the class for each basic skill or type of behavior to be evaluated. Provision should be made for self-evaluation in basic skills. Space should be provided on the form for checking such qualities as individual participation, contributions, strengths, weaknesses, and success in achievement of objectives. Even a "final" grade may be asked for from the child. The child should find space on the evaluation form to indicate progress in other traits—for example, work and study habits, thinking, social objectives, etc. Having discussed and listed such characteristics, he will be acquainted with meanings. It will be difficult for any child to be objective and accurate in self-evaluation, yet it is his responsibility to perform this evaluation and improve his skills of self-appraisal.

Administration of a Self-Evaluation Program

No self-evaluation procedures are successful unless school personnel accept those conditions that have been discussed up to this point. The principal and teachers face the responsibility of administering their program according to requirements similar to the following:

1. The success of self-evaluation depends upon getting the child to accept goals, providing experiences which enable him to reach them, and keeping records of progress. The pupil keeps folders of his work containing plans, samples, comparisons, activities, individual and group and other necessary materials.

Evaluation

2. The principal recognizes the values of self-evaluation and attempts to provide time in his school day to encourage teacher use. He may suggest ways for teachers to find time for the teacher-pupil conference by helping them see, for example, that they can organize the learning experience so that non-conferring students will be more or less self-directed while a conference is taking place.

3. The teacher knows the conference with the pupil is the heart of self-evaluation. Assuming that the principal supports the idea, it is important to use follow-up procedures. Planning is a necessary function and requirement, since the teacher must know many things about the child *before* the conference takes place. Activities must be organized efficiently so that when the conference is held, the teacher and pupil will have the necessary forms completed and autobiographies written, which will constitute focal points for the discussion.

4. Teachers and pupils must follow through on the results of the self-evaluation. To list some statements is valuable, but unless the teacher keeps her own records in order, plans new experiences in light of the evaluation, and then tries to find newer insights, the process of self-evaluation becomes merely a crutch for the insecure teacher who is not sure what mark or score is to be given and collects data to back her up in case pressure is placed upon her.

The Self-evaluation Record

We have noted that the success of pupil appraisal depends upon keeping records of individual and class progress. The principal will find some commercial forms useful, but each teacher should consider compiling a folder with appropriate forms for each child. The process of assembling the material and forms can be valuable both to students and teachers. The following nine recommendations may be helpful in providing guidance to teachers who are setting up self-evaluation programs in the classroom and who need help in devising forms and keeping records.

1. *The scholastic record form.* The pupil should have a folder that contains either his entire scholastic record or at least some indication of how well he has achieved up to his present grade level. Central files will contain this information, and the school staff should decide to what extent and in what form the information should be made available for the child's folder. Some idea of the pupil's strengths and weaknesses must be kept current so that a continuing scholastic record will become more significant and adequate as time goes on.

2. *The autobiography form.* An organized and directed plan formulated by the teacher should center on getting the child to write an autobiography, or to tell the teacher answers to specific questions. This information is

more likely to aid the teacher in giving guidance than help the pupil in a self-evaluation program. However, if the autobiographical account is organized properly with the objective of assisting in self-appraisal activities, the child in the upper elementary grades should certainly profit from thinking in terms of his interests, friends, group contacts and memberships, and home life. The alert teacher keeps in mind the full development of all aspects of the child and aids him in gaining personal understandings which may prove useful in self-evaluation during the school year.

3. *The work-attitude form*. Although general tests of intelligence and aptitude are given for guidance purposes, some attention should be given to the ways in which children attack their work and adjust to the class. The child should realize through self-evaluation and teacher-help that he is, for example, working hard and faithfully, and is achieving at a given level of expectation. Careful help is needed from the teacher to bring about a realistic understanding of the child's capacity to learn without revealing actual test scores or implanting pessimistic or optimistic ceilings of individual achievement.

4. *Samples of work*. The pupil will certainly want to include a variety of work and activity samples in his folder. Such concrete evidence is particularly valuable in noting progress or lack of it.

5. *The conference or interview form*. The pupil will want to keep a record of any conferences or interviews with school personnel. The teacher may work out some kind of conference form which will facilitate note-keeping by the child or the teacher.

6. *The self-rating form*. The child approaches self-appraisal by either writing or talking about his own behavior. His own comments about his behavior are the most significant and valid things to be recorded. Behavior criteria appropriate to the grade level should be worked out in advance by the class and should include such items as playing fair, self-direction, consideration of others, cooperation, persistence, ability to face criticism and failure, responsibility, open-mindedness, and so on.

7. *The physical development form*. The pupil may want to keep in his folder some records of his physical growth and development. There are many possibilities in this area which can be worked out by teacher and pupils that will not duplicate any formal program conducted by the health and physical education teacher.

8. *The test-scores progress form*. One of the records most important to the child is that of the test scores and progress being made. Probably individual subjects will suggest or determine the type of form for this record. In the primary grades, the form should be used and interpreted largely by the teacher.

9. *The goal-seeking form*. In addition to learning their strengths and weaknesses, test scores, etc., pupils need to consider desirable goals for achieve-

ment. The steps necessary to achieve them should also be included in self-evaluation. In fact, the emphasis on teacher-pupil identification and selection of purposeful goals is one of the highlights of learning in the modern elementary school. This goal-seeking form may have several uses. One use is for teacher and pupil to decide together the particular goals for a certain subject-matter area. For example, there may be a decision to make understanding of the process of long division a definite goal. Each child may indicate this on his form, just as a matter of record and systematic training. Another use is made of this type of form when teacher-pupil conferences are held and again a decision is reached as the child realizes the need to attain a particular goal, such as more work in long division.

The pupil's folder should include these nine areas of information, with appropriate forms developed by administrator, teachers, and pupils. Each grade level must work out suitable forms and self-evaluation techniques at the level of understanding and experience of the group. Teachers should not find the use of these devices an overwhelming task. They need only recognize the full possibilities of employing these nine approaches where suitable, or including other techniques better adapted to their needs; the skills that result when children are allowed to enter into a self-appraisal program will more than compensate for the additional class time needed to follow through.

SUMMARY

The elementary principal practices skills in evaluation for improving education in the elementary school. His task is primarily to improve instruction, but he is also responsible for evaluating all services that contribute to the general welfare of the child, including the teacher.

The principal and his teachers are held accountable for the school's educational program. Through his leadership, a program of accountability must be worked out which is acceptable to the board of education, the community, and the teaching staff. Teachers and principals must learn evaluation techniques which will yield objective data useful in the decision-making process about school innovations, the ongoing program, and teacher accountability. Modern evaluation techniques, however, do not always yield objective data. Teachers should work to improve their techniques for determining pupil progress as one means of humanizing the elementary school.

The principal is responsible for appraising teacher performance. To be effective in this role the principal must become skillful in the appraisal process and use it as a means of improving the overall educational program.

SUGGESTED READINGS

Beatty, Walcott H., ed. *Improving Educational Assessment and an Inventory of Measures of Affective Behavior.* Washington, D.C.: The Association for Supervision and Curriculum Development, National Education Association, 1969.

Bloom, Benjamin S. "Learning for Mastery." *Evaluation Comment 1*, no. 2. Los Angeles: Center for the Study of Evaluation of Instructional Programs, University of California at Los Angeles, May 1968.

Bloom, Benjamin S., J. Thomas Hastings, and George F. Madaus. *Handbook on Formative and Summative Evaluation of Student Learning.* New York: McGraw-Hill, 1971, Sections 1, 3, 4.

Browder, Lesley H., Jr. *Emerging Patterns of Administrative Accountability.* Berkeley: McCutchen, 1971.

Coleman, James E. *Equality of Educational Opportunity.* FS 5-238:38001. Washington, D.C.: U.S. Department of Health, Education and Welfare, Office of Education, 1966.

Goodlad, John I. and Frances Klein. *Behind the Classroom Door.* Worthington, Ohio: Charles Jones, 1970.

Liberman, Myron, Guest Editor. "Eight Articles on Accountability." *Phi Delta Kappan* 52, no. 4 (December 1970): 193–255.

Martin, Reed and Charles Blaschke. "Contracting for Educational Reform," *Phi Delta Kappan* 52, no. 7 (March 1971) 406–10.

Pfeiffer, John. *New Look at Education: Systems Analysis in Our Schools and Colleges.* New York: Odyssey, 1968.

Redfern, George. *How to Appraise Teacher Performance.* Columbus, Ohio: School Management Institute, 1963.

Notes

1. *Innovation in Education: New Directions for the American School* (New York: Committee for Economic Development, 1968), p. 13.
2. Ralph W. Tyler, ed., *Educational Evaluation: New Roles, New Means. The Sixty-Eighth Yearbook of the National Society for the Study of Education,* Part II (Chicago: University of Chicago Press, 1969), pp. 2, 3.
3. Ibid.
4. Daniel L. Stufflebeam, "Evaluation as Enlightenment for Decision Making," in *Improving Educational Assessment: An Inventory of Measures of Affective Behavior,* ed. W. H. Beatty (Washington: The Association for Supervision and Curriculum Development, National Education Association, 1969), p. 42.
5. Egan G. Guba, "Methological Strategies for Educational Change" (Paper presented to the Conference on Strategies for Educational Change, Washington, D.C., November 8–10, 1965).
6. Stufflebeam, "Evaluation," p. 53.
7. Malcolm Provus, "Evaluation of On-Going Programs in the Public Schools," *The Sixty-eighth Yearbook of the National Society for the Study of Education,* Part II (Chicago: University of Chicago Press, 1969), p. 244.
8. J. W. Wrightstone, "Evaluation," *Encyclopedia of Educational Research* (New York: Macmillan, 1950), p. 403.

Evaluation

9. Harold J. Noah, "Educational Needs Rational Decision Making," *Teachers College Record* 72 (December 1970): 188–200.

10. Stephen P. Klein, "The Uses and Limitations of Standardized Tests in Meeting the Demands for Accountability," *Evaluation Comment,* Center for the Study of Evaluation, U.C.L.A., 2, no. 4 (January 1971): 1.

11. Leon M. Lessinger, "Accountability for Results: A Basic Challenge for America's Schools," *American Education* 5 (June 1969): 2.

12. W. H. G. Arytage, *Four Hundred Years of English Education* (Cambridge: The University Press, 1965), p. 120.

13. Ibid., p. 124.

14. Ibid., p. 125.

15. Paul Revere Pierce, *The Origin and Development of the Public School Principalship* (Chicago: University of Chicago Press, 1935), p. 16.

16. Charles H. Judd, "A Look Forward," *The Measurement of Educational Products, Seventeenth Yearbook of the National Society for the Study of Education,* Part II (Bloomington, Ill.: Public School Publishing Co., 1918), pp. 159–60.

17. Ralph W. Tyler, *Educational Evaluation,* p. 391.

18. D. E. K. Feaster, *A Survey of the Educational Programs of the West Virginia Public Schools* (Charleston: Legislative Interim Committee, State of West Virginia, 1957).

19. Luvern L. Cunningham, "Our Accountability Problems," in *Emerging Patterns of Administrative Accountability,* ed. Lesley H. Browder, Jr. (Berkeley: McCutchen, 1971), p. 47.

20. Myron Lieberman, "An Overview of Accountability," *Phi Delta Kappan* 52 (December 1970): 195.

21. Henry S. Dyer, "Toward Objective Criteria of Professional Accountability in the Schools of New York City," *Phi Delta Kappan* 52, no. 4 (December 1970): 206.

22. Ibid., p. 207.

23. See John I. Goodlad and M. Frances Klein, *Behind the Classroom Door* (Worthington, Ohio: Charles A. Jones, 1970), pp. 85–87.

24. Klein, "Use and Limitations of Standardized Tests," p. 2.

25. Aaron Wildavsky, "A Program of Accountability for Elementary Schools," *Phi Delta Kappan* 52 (December 1970): 215.

26. See Donald J. Dowd and Sarah C. West, comps., "An Inventory of Measures of Affective Behavior," *Improving Educational Assessment and An Inventory of Measures of Affective Behavior,* Section II (Washington: Association for Supervision and Curriculum Development, N.E.A., 1969), pp. 90–158.

27. James A. Mecklenburger and John A. Wilson, "The Performance Contract," *Phi Delta Kappan* 52 (March 1971): 406.

28. This section on appraisal has been adapted here from a School Management Seminar on Teacher Appraisal, directed by George Redfern for School Management Institute, Worthington, Ohio, 1965, (mimeographed).

29. Ibid.

30. Developed by the authors with the help of Lydia Purser Meeks, fifth-grade teacher, Harrisonburg, Va.

31. *The Characteristics of a Good Elementary School* (Richmond: Virginia State Board of Education, 1949), p. 35.

32. Adapted from "A Guide to Teacher Growth Through Self-Evaluation," with permission of the Norfolk City Public Schools, Norfolk, Virginia.

Name Index

Anderson, Robert, 72, 97, 125

Bair, Medill, 212
Bass, Bernard M., 24, 25, 65
Bay, Christian, 107, 126
Beggs, David W., III, 98
Beliske, E. L., 25
Bellows, Roger M., 374
Benne, Kenneth D., 24, 157
Bennis, Warren G., 24
Berman, Louise B., 159, 179
Berson, Minnie, 180
Bowman, Garda W., 322, 324, 325, 332
Burr, James B., 51
Burton, William, 160

Campbell, Roald F., 51, 65
Carlson, Stanley C., 77, 98
Caswell, Hollis, 159, 166
Chase, Francis, 356, 375
Chin, Robert, 24
Coch, Lester, 20, 25
Coffield, William H., 51
Coppersmith, Stanley, 98
Cory, N. Durward, 155
Culbertson, Jack A., 51
Cunningham, Luvern L., 51, 383, 403

Davis, Harold S., 299
Davis, Ralph C., 5, 25

Dean, Stuart E., 97
Dewey, John, 107, 126
DeYoung, Chris A., 281, 291
Dowd, Donald J., 403
Drummond, T. Darrel, 300, 302, 331
Dyer, Henry S., 384, 385, 403

Enochs, James B., 52

Fantini, Mario, 125
Feaster, D. E. K., 403
Ferguson, Donald G., 220, 246
Forester, J. J., 57
Foster, Walter S., 206, 212
Frazier, Alexander, 179
French, J. R., 20, 25
French, Will, 291
Frost, James A., 247
Frymier, Jack, 70, 97

Gans, Roma, 126
Giles, H. H., 10, 25
Goldman, Harvey, 24
Good, Carter, 128, 155
Goodlad, John, 67, 83, 93, 97, 134, 265, 403
Gordon, Ira J., 246
Gouldner, Alvin, 4, 25
Gregg, Russell T., 51
Griffiths, Daniel E., 24, 25, 65

405

Grooms, Ann, 82, 98
Gross, Neal, 7, 25, 52, 281
Guba, Egon G., 155, 378

Halpin, Andrew W., 24
Hamilton, Robert R., 291
Hatch, R. N., 219, 246
Hathaway, Genevieve E., 152, 155
Heathers, Glenn, 69, 77, 97
Heidenreich, R. H., 24, 25
Hemphill, 4, 65
Hencley, Stephen P., 51
Herrick, V. E., 255, 265
Herriott, R. E., 7, 25, 52, 281
Hill, George E., 241, 247
Hillson, Maurie, 97
Holmans, George C., 24
Howard, Alvin, 97
Hummel, Dean L., 247
Hunter, Madeline, 125

Jacobs, Leland B., 301, 331
Jacobson, Paul B., 52
Jenson, T. J., 51
Judd, Charles H., 403

Kaplan, Louis, 247
Kepler, Mabel B., 313
Keynes, Edward, 24, 109, 126
King, James C., 358, 374
Kirk, Samuel A., 250
Klausmeier, Herbert, 79, 97, 125
Klein, Stephen P., 403
Klopf, Gordon J., 321, 324, 325, 332
Kopp, Ozzie, 77, 92, 97

Lessinger, Leon M., 403
Levine, Daniel U., 125
Lewis, Arthur J., 25
Lewis, Ervin E., 25
Leiberman, Myron, 403
Lippmann, Walter, 107, 126
Lodgsdon, James O., 52

McIntyre, Kenneth E., 51
Mager, Robert F., 85, 86, 98
Maier, Norman, 25
Meade, Edward J., 155

Mecklenburger, James A., 403
Meil, Alice, 180
Miller, James, 374
Minney, Ronzel D., 355, 358
Morrison, J. C., 51, 52
Muntyan, Bozidar, 157, 179
Murphy, Judith, 98

Naylor, Douglas H., 291
Neagley, Ross, 51
Nerborig, Marcella H., 126
Newell, C. A., 51
Noah, Harold J., 379, 403
Noffsinger, Carl, 212
Norton, J. K., 51

Otto, Henry J., 160, 169, 179

Parsons, T., 24
Pharis, William L., 51
Pierce, Paul R., 51, 52, 403
Pierce, Truman M., 126
Ploghoft, Milton E., 25, 51, 121, 126
Prince, T. C., 169, 180
Provus, Malcolm, 378, 402

Reavis, William C., 160, 179
Redfern, George B., 358, 374
Rehage, Kenneth, 83, 98
Reutters, E. E., Jr., 291
Ricci, D. M., 24
Rothney, John W., 265
Rubin, Louis J., 155

Sargent, Cyril, 25
Schumpter, Joseph, 108, 126
Shane, Harold, 75, 115
Shannon, Robert, 212
Shartle, Carroll L., 374
Sheehan, Pete, 125
Shuster, Albert H., 25, 51, 121, 126, 212, 374
Sinclair, Robert L., 25, 65, 86, 87, 98
Singer, Ira, 84
Smallenburg, Harry, 288, 291
Smith, Bertrand, 52
Smith, Glenn E., 247
Spears, H., 83

Index

Stennett, T. M., 355, 356, 374
Stufflebeam, Daniel L., 377, 378, 402
Stulken, E. H., 52

Thayer, Virginia E., 313
Thelen, Herbert A., 25
Traughber, James V., 291
Tyler, Ralph W., 377, 383, 402

Valett, Robert E., 331

Wayson, William, 4, 25, 52
Weber, C. A., 4, 25
Weber, Mary E., 4, 25
West, Sarah C., 403

Wetzler, Wilson F., 25, 374
Wilcox, Preston, 24
Wildavsky, Aaron, 403
Wilds, Elmer H., 52
Wiles, Kimball, 155
Williams, Oscar H., 25
Wilson, John A., 403
Witmer, J. Melvin, 225, 247
Woodward, Richard G., 212
Wrightstone, J. W., 378, 402

Yarmolinsky, Adam, 328, 332
Young, David B., 132, 155
Young, Whitney, M., Jr., 125

Subject Index

Accountability
  groups responsible for, 385
  history of, 382
  performance contracting, 388, 389
  and the principal, 381
  principal's role in, 386
  programs of, 11
  relationship to individual school, 384
Administration
  autocratic, 15
  compared with business practices, 19, 20
  democratic, 14
    check list for, 43
  human relations in, 22
  job analysis approach, 359
  of large school, 334, 335
  planning for, 333
  psychological approach to, 14, 16, 17, 19
  of small school, 334, 335
  using psychological procedures in, 21
Administrative behavior
  areas of, 53
  goal seeking, 55
  goal setting, 54
  tasks, 3
Administrative coordination
  of educational activities, 59
Administrative roles
  determining, 57

Administrative tasks, 3
  involving people in, 61
Aides, teacher. *See* Paraprofessionals
Appraisal, teacher, 389
  final conference, 392
  initial conference, 391
  pitfalls in, 390
  principal's role, 390
  reasons for, 389
  staff performance, 60
  in relation to supervision, 391
  systematic plan for, 394
  as a workable process, 391
Association for Supervision and Curriculum Development, 64
Audio-visual aids
  administration, 310
  location, 300
  purchase, 275
  used in in-service, 204
Autonomous school, 6
  advisory councils, 112, 113
  budget making, 282
  curriculum, 161
  decentralization, 111
  definition, 6
  early recognition of, 29
  need for guidelines, 36
  neighborhood, 111
  personnel functions, 56
  selecting principals for, 112

408

Index

Auxiliary services, 292
  categories, 293
  counselor, 294
  health, 311
  lunch, 314
  other personnel agencies, 328, 329
  psychologists, 294
  reading specialists, 298
  school social worker, 297
  speech therapist, 296

Beginning teachers, 141, 188, 189
Behavioral objectives
  aids to writing, 85
  essential for change, 85
Bilingual education, 173
  Spanish speaking, 173
Budgeting
  components of, 282
  disbursements, 286
  principal's role in, 280, 283
  school receipts, 284

Calandar, school
  annual (*figure*), 346
  daily (*figure*), 347
  weekly (*figure*), 338
Certification
  basic to the principalship, 38, 39
Change
  building bridges for, 91
  community support for, 90
  failure to, 110
  hierarchy for, 88
  information disseminated for, 91
  pattern for instituting, 89
  role of assessment, 89
  role of principal, 84–88
Children. *See also* Pupils
  caring for ill and injured, 271
  value conflicts, 110
Citizens
  concepts held by, 105
  role in controlling discipline problems, 123
  sharing in decision making, 108
  understandings of, 105

Classroom
  characteristics of modern, 162
  control of, 119–123
  departmentalized, 169
  self-contained, 170
Classroom libraries, 302
Closing of school, 349
Collective negotiations, 357
  effect of on principal, 357
  principal's role in, 359
  Rhode Island law on, 357
Common School Teachers' Association, 28
Communication
  administrative, 62
  dissemination, form of, 91
  existing lines of, 105
  flow of, 16, 17
  function of school office in, 269
Community
  characteristics of, 104, 105
  components of life in, 102, 103, 104
  discipline, problems of, 118
  guideposts for behavior, 100
  integrating all segments in, 108
  issues, problems, 117
  leadership in, 101
  nature of, 102
  physical and economic security, 114
  prime responsibilities in, 100
  principal's role in, 18, 113
  securing support from, 116
  unity in, 114
  utilizing, 11
Community power structure, 10
  guides for studying, 109
  identifying, 109
  principal's role in, 107, 108
Conference method, 145, 147
  case, 237
  duties of leader, 148
  final appraisal plan, 392
  parent, 258
  personal conference, 204
  planning, 391
  skills for, 147
Consultation with staff (administrative), 59

Cooperative teaching, 83. *See also* Team teaching
Cooperative program in educational administration, 31, 35
Counselor, 237
  services to administrators, 239
  services to teachers, 238
Curriculum
  administering, 160
  beginning revision in, 175
  bilingual, 173
  committee, 200
  controlled by principal, 161
  effect of materials on, 163
  interpreting to community, 177
  meaning, 157
  outcomes of, 177
  planning, 175
  principal's role in, 176
  scope, 158
  sequence, 159
Custodial staff, 320
  facilitating work of, 321

Dalton Plan, 75
Decision making, 6, 7
  by citizens, 108
  group, 19
  local school advisory council, 112
  principal's role in, 17, 18
  sharing in, 135
Department of Elementary School Principals, 26, 30, 31, 35, 38, 274
  development of, 30, 31
  growth in membership, 31
  professional organizations, 36
Department of Elementary and Secondary School Principals, 30
Departmentalization, 168
Detroit Study, 9, 52
Discipline
  as a community problem, 118
  helping beginning teachers in, 120
  philosophy of, 119

Early childhood education
  Headstart, 172
  pre-school, 173
  values of, 173
Educational activities
  coordination of, 59
Educational administration
  cooperative program in, 31, 35
Educational media center. *See* Multimedia center
Elementary school
  autonomous, 6
  Dalton Plan, 75
  demand for conformity, 69
  Gary Plan, 73
  graded, 72
  humanizing, 7
  nongraded, 73–75, 166
  organizational patterns, 66
  problem in financing, 68
  racism in, 9
  special service personnel, 231
  ungraded, 73–75, 166
  Winnetka Plan, 75
  written philosophy for, 190
Emergency services, 313
Evaluation
  definitions, 377, 378
  nature of, 377
  objectives, 380
  philosophy, 380
  role of principal in, 376

Faculty meetings, 198
Far West Laboratory for Educational Research, 205
Field trips, 164
Financing
  lunch program, 317
  school activities, 283, 284

Gary Plan, 73
Goal setting
  administrative behavior in, 55
  imperatives for the principal, 93
Grading system, 167–69, 254–58. *See also* Marking system
Grouping
  activities, 74
  dual progress plan, 77
  individual progress plans, 74

Index

methods, 76
subject, 74
Groups
  broaden base for decision making, 108
  minority, 110
  power, 107, 108
  racial, 108
  working with, 111
Guidance program, 225
  counseling, defined, 244
  counselor, 237, 294
  educational services, 241
  information service, 240
  initiation of, 218
  for large schools, 223
  occupational, 241
  organizing of, 221
  orientation service, 241, 242
  philosophy of, 216
  principal's role in, 217
  pupil inventory, 227
  for small schools, 222
  testing program, 253
Guidance services
  to administration, 239
  to teachers, 238

Health appraisal, 313
Health environment, 311
Health services, 312
  basic aspects, 313
  principal's role, 312
  school nurse, 312
Humanizing practices, 7, 8

Individual progress plan, 74
Individually Guided Education (IGE), 79–81
Inner-city schools
  failure to meet children's needs, 111
  meeting black needs, 113
  racism in, 110, 111
  shifting populations, 113
In-service education
  beginning teacher's needs, 188, 189
  conferences, 183
  defined, 181
  devices for, 195, 196

faculty meetings, 198
helping older teachers, 193
instructional council for, 184
interest groups, 200
for married teachers, 194
need for, 186
principal's contribution to, 182
professional associations' role, 49
professional days, 197
workshops, 183
Instructional council, 184
  organizational pattern for system-wide, 185
  schematic of, 185
Instructional media center. *See* Multi-media center
Internship
  nature and purpose of, 47
  for principal's preparation, 40, 47–49
Intervisitation, 152

Job analysis, 359
  forms for, 365–69
  methods of making, 362–65
  uses of, 361–62

Kellogg, W. K., Foundation, 31

Leadership
  acquired, 3
  approaches, 4
  in the community, 102, 116
  defined, 2
  effective, 12
  factors of, 5
  responsibilities, 14
  situation theory, 4
  trait theory, 4
Legal problems
  emergency services, 311
  Rhode Island law, 357
  in supervision, 132
  teachers' lunch hour, 315
  Virginia laws, 126
Librarian
  qualifications for, 310
Library
  classroom, 302

services of, 300
Local school advisory councils, 112
 relationship to central board of education, 112
 working with, 111, 112
Lunch program, 314
 administering, 316
 financing, 317
 for indigent children, 315
 legal requirements for teachers, 315
 mobile service centers, 315
 National School Lunch Act, 317
 relationship to educational program, 317

Marking system
 defining terms, 255
 formal written reports, 257
 improvement of, 254
 modern concepts, 255
 organizing, 256
 parent conferences, 258
 practices, 167–69
Media center. *See* Multi-media center
Middle school, 70, 77, 78, 81, 82
 characteristics of pupils, 82
 most common pattern, 81
Militant teachers, 135, 225
"Minimum Standards for Ohio Elementary Schools, 1970"
 pupil services, 245
Minority groups
 failure in meeting needs of, 111
 major groups in U.S., 111
 Spanish-speaking, 173
 used as paraprofessionals, 326
 working with, 110
Multi-media center, 299
 administering, 310
 equipment for, 306
 patterns of internal organization, 300
 physical requirements, 302–10
 pupil expenditures, 303
 services of, 300
 staff, 303
 use of volunteers in, 301
Multiunit school, 79–81
 advantages of, 81

committee for, 79–81
organizational chart, 80
unit meetings, 79

National Association of Elementary School Principals. *See* Department of Elementary School Principals
National School Lunch Act, 317
Negotiations, 357. *See also* Collective negotiations
New York Regents Examinations, 383
Nongraded schools, 73–75, 166

Objectives, 192
Ohio State Department of Education, 40, 133
Ohio University, Center for Educational Research and Service, 145
Opening day of school, 348
Organization of schools, 65
 basis of, 67
 combined grades, 74
 court mandates, 68
 Dalton Plan, 75, 166
 defined, 70
 departmentalized, 73
 Gary Plan, 73
 graded, 72
 for guidance services, 221–23
 individual progress plans, 74
 legal aspects, 68
 multiple track, 73
 nongraded, 73, 74, 75
 pattern for, 70
 patterns tried, 72
 recent developments, 77
 role of principal in change, 83–88
 of school population, 249
 social maturity grouping, 73
 structure to eliminate inequalities, 72
 team teaching, 78
 Winnetka Plan, 75, 166

Paraprofessionals, 90
 aid in understanding children's problems, 113
 benefits of, 323

Index

essential areas for concern, 323
introduction to school system, 325
number of, 322
tasks performed in library, 301
teacher aides, 322
volunteer aides, 327
Parents
checklist for conference with, 123
conferences with, 258
responsibility in discipline problems, 123
working with, 123
Performance contracting, 388, 389
Physical education, 297
Planning, administrative, 333–54
annual calendar, 346
closing school, 349
daily calendar, 347
developing skills in, 342
guide to, 343
long-range, 344
for opening day, 348
pre-school opening, checklist, 347
school year, 345
short-range, 344
weekly calendar, 338
Policy making, administrative, 56
Politics and educators, 110
Power groups, 10, 319
Preparation programs for principals
apprenticeship, 46
graduate, 40
internship, 40, 47
Pre-school conference, 196
Pre-school education, 172, 173
Principal
administering curriculum, 160
assistant, 339
and beginning teachers, 141
budget making, 280
certification, 38, 39
classroom visitation, 145
community understandings, 102
decision making, 17, 18
and community issues, 117
criteria for selection, 30, 40
early duties of, 28, 29
emerging professional leader, 30

goal seeking behavior, 55
major problems faced by, 6
and management, 130
planning time, 336
as resource person, 18
role in guidance, 217
role in initiating change, 84–88
role in power structure, 107
source of authority, 21
using resource persons, 142
work day, 13
Principal, assistant, 339
functions of, 340
selecting, 339
Principal's calendar. *See* Calendar, school
Principalship
development of, 26, 27
duties of, 13
effects of social, economic, political factors on, 34, 35
full-time, 26
history of, 27–35
new directions for, 11
professionalization of, 35–37
scope of, 13
standards for, 41
Professional days, 197, 198
Professional growth
imperatives for the principal, 94
individual activities, 152
need for in changing age, 149
setting stage for, 150
use of incentives, 150–51
Professional organizations
contributions of, 36
principal's need for, 37
provide leadership for inservice education, 49
of teachers, 208
Progressive Educational Association, 34
Promotion, pupil
appraisal for, 261
corrective or remedial function, 261, 262
improved practices, 259
policy, 260
Public relations, 287

Pupil personnel policies
  classification for learning, 250
  gifted, 251
  marking system, 254
  mentally retarded, 250
  physically handicapped, 251
  promotion, 259–61
  testing program, 253
Pupil progress. *See also* Marking system
  marking and reporting, 167–69
Pupil self-evaluation, 396
  administration of, 398
  record of, 399
Pupils
  caring for ill and injured, 271
  classification for learning, 250
  classification of, 165
  educational placement, 248
  gifted, 251
  health records, 231, 352
  inventory service, 227
  orientation, 241, 242
  personnel policies, 248
  records of, 228, 235
  registration form, 350
  retarded, 250
  self-evaluation, 396–99
  value conflicts, 110

Racial imbalance, 68
Racism, 9, 10, 111
Reading specialists, 298
Records
  anecdotal, 235
  case conference, 237
  cumulative, 229
  financial, 283, 284
  health, 231
  parent conferences, 235, 236
  pupil progress, 232–35
  teacher conferences, 235
Report cards. *See* Marking system
Role playing, 209

Schedule, daily, 161
School calendar. *See* Calendar, school
School Management Institute, 184
School office

  communications center, 269
  functions of, 266
  keeping records, 277
  and use of instructional supplies, 274
  responsibility for emergency drills, 273
  using parent volunteers, 286
School psychologist, 294
School secretary
  functions of, 269, 270, 288
  need for, 288
  of teachers, 289
School social worker, 297
Schools. *See* Elementary school
Secretary. *See* School secretary
Self-evaluation, pupil, 396
  administration of program, 398
  records, 399
Self-evaluation, teachers
  for personal growth, 395
  improved practices in, 394
Sex education
  early programs, 174
  position of U. S. Office of Education, 175
  principal leadership, 174–75
Special teachers
  art, 296
  music, 296
  physical education, 296
Speech therapist, 296
"Standards (Minimum) for Ohio Elementary Schools, 1970," 245
Student teaching, 203
Substitute teachers, 278
Supervision
  changing patterns of, 127
  characteristics of, 129
  classroom visitations, 145
  conference method, 146
  defined, 128
  democratic, 133
  giving assistance in, 137
  help for teachers, 141
  legal responsibility, 132
  of paraprofessionals, 324
  principal's emerging role in, 129–33
  psychological principles of, 136

shared authority, 135
staff agreement on goals of, 134
utilizing resource persons, 142

Teacher aides. *See* Paraprofessionals
Teacher militancy
causes of, 355–57
Teachers
autonomous, 130
beginning, 143, 188, 189
demands for autonomy, 131
male, 194
married, 194
militant, 135, 355–57
need for supervision, 138
older, 193
professional growth, 149
professional organizations, 208
shared responsibility, 134, 135
substitute, 278
unsatisfactory, 287
Team teaching, 78, 82–84, 207, 208. *See also* Cooperative teaching
advantages of, 83
defined, 83, 84
Testing, planning program for, 253
Transportation
bus supervision, 319
related to instruction, 318, 319

Ungraded schools, 73–75, 166
University Council for Educational Administration, 35
University interns, 203, 204
Urban education
dominated by whites, 111
inner-city schools, 110, 111
problems of, 110

Virginia school laws, 126
Visitors, classroom, 145
Volunteer aides. *See* Paraprofessionals

Winnetka Plan, 75
Wisconsin Research and Development Center for Cognitive Learning, 79

R00111 55070

CHICAGO PUBLIC LIBRARY
HAROLD WASHINGTON LIBRARY CENTER
R0011155070

THE CHICAGO PUBLIC LIBRARY
EDUCATION DEPARTMENT

FORM 19